A FIRESIDE BOOK PUBLISHED BY SIMON & SCHUSTER INC.
NEW YORK   LONDON   TORONTO   SYDNEY   TOKYO

THE
POWER
OF THE
FAMILY

*Mastering
the Hidden
Dance of
Family
Relationships*

MICHAEL P. NICHOLS

Fireside
Simon & Schuster Building
Rockefeller Center
1230 Avenue of the Americas
New York, New York 10020

FIRESIDE, SIMON AND SCHUSTER and colophons are registered
trademarks of Simon & Schuster Inc.

Designed by Barbara Marks Graphic Design
Manufactured in the United States of America

10 9 8 7 6 5 4 3 2 1
10 9 8 7 6 5 4 3 2 1 pbk.

Library of Congress Cataloging in Publication Data

Nichols, Michael P.
  The power of the family : mastering the hidden dance of family
relationships / Michael P. Nichols.
     p.   cm.
  Bibliography: p.
  Includes index.
  1. Family—United States—Psychological aspects. I. Title.
HQ536.N53 1988
306.8'5'0973—dc19   88-21246
                                                                CIP

ISBN 0-671-67189-8
     0-671-64408-4 pbk.

To Goldye and Bill Sher
and Fred Sher,
for expanding my
family and
enriching my life

CONTENTS

more interesting. Unfortunately, pumping iron works only on muscles other than the heart.

If only we could banish the anxiety of being dependent on those around us, of needing and being needed by other people, surely then we would be free. But there is a paradox. As long as we refuse to acknowledge our connection to others, we can never be fully reconciled to ourselves.

The truth is we are not free and independent agents. Many people wear themselves out struggling against this reality, because accepting family bonds, like accepting the limits of one's character, feels like an act of surrender. Life in the family *does* define and limit our freedom, but family life also offers untapped potential for personal happiness and fulfillment.

Families have rules and an irresistible power. Living in the real world, trying to cope with family and relentless work and economic pressures, is like being caught in the rapids. The current is strong, and we often feel helpless in its grip. If we struggle and fight against nature, we feel controlled and helpless. Swimming against the flood only leads to exhaustion and defeat. The secret is to let go, adapt to the flow of the current. The instant that happens we are free to maneuver. As we allow the current to move us along, we discover amazing freedom of movement.

The enormous potential for satisfaction and emotional refueling present in family life is often neglected, taken for granted, or pursued in self-defeating ways. Some people turn away and bury themselves in work or after-hours distractions. They drink too much, eat too much, and soothe themselves with shopping expeditions they know to be meaningless. Those who do try to create meaning and satisfaction in family life often find their efforts defeated by their ignorance of the invisible rules by which family systems function. This book is written to help readers understand how family systems work and how to apply that understanding to mastering the familiar challenges of family life.

———◆———

Do we really need another book on family life, especially one not devoted to some specific issue—divorce, say, or difficult children—but rather covering the whole span of a family's life? Although there are many fine books on family problems, few address the full scope of ordinary family life and virtually none get at the hidden dance of family dynamics. I decided to write this book because I believe that family life can be much richer and more rewarding when people learn something about family dynamics—how families work, how they get stuck, and how to get them unstuck.

Therapists sometimes doubt that ordinary men and women can change their lives without professional help. We see people caught up in the blind, dominating power of habit, and it is easy to think they need us. Therapists often develop a jaundiced view of human nature. We see people at their worst. Our clients come to us in crisis, when reason and compromise are often swamped by anxiety. These people may have difficulty profiting from explanations. They are generally stuck in their own point of view, not open to understanding what others in the family want or to seeing their own role in perpetuating problems.

One of the reasons family therapists abandoned psychology in favor of systems thinking is that individuals often seem powerless to control what happens in their families. I do not happen to believe that people cannot understand and control the forces acting on their lives. The trick is to recognize the ways in which our lives are interconnected with those of our families, and then instead of ignoring or fighting against these patterns, to discover the nature of that interconnectedness and turn it into creative living.

In order to bring the ideas of family dynamics to life, I have described the story of one family's therapy. The family I have chosen is an ordinary middle-class family, one I hope will strike chords of recognition in the reader's experience. Family therapists often treat dramatic cases of severe pathology—anorexia nervosa, schizophrenia, physical and sexual abuse. These cases of extreme human unhappiness hold a fascination for most people—the fascination of the bizarre and the terrible. They also show family dynamics in bold relief. I have chosen a different kind of drama: the drama of ordinary people trying their best to muddle through life's everyday trials. I have tried to describe what is typical, making no pretense of sublime universalism and no claim to perfect objectivity. At various points in this book, some readers may ask, "What about childless couples?" or "How does this apply to gay couples?" To these questions, my answer is that I have concentrated on the most typical family developments, sacrificing the breadth that is often possible in textbooks for the depth that is easier to achieve by limiting the focus. This book is not meant to be all things to all people.

In order to protect the anonymity of my patients and to provide the richest possible portrait of family experience, I have drawn a composite picture from two families I treated. This is not a fictional family but an amalgam of real details. The story of the family's progress through therapy will emphasize themes common to family life in the eighties: a couple who spend all their energies at work and raising children, leaving little time for their marriage or for fun; a woman who compensates for disappointment in her relationship with her husband by becoming overinvolved with her children, pushing her husband even further to the periphery of the family; and a man, uneasy with intimacy, who turns his aspirations for recognition to the world of work.

When I first met the Simpsons (as I shall call them), they were a couple at their wits' end, futilely remonstrating with their son, Jason, who alternated between ignoring and defying them. Beginning with the the initial phone call for help, I will trace the family's treatment from beginning to end, providing detailed accounts of actual clinical sessions and enriching these accounts with the personal experiences of all the participants. I will open the door of the consulting room to explain the mechanics of family therapy and demonstrate how this exciting new approach works. I will also delve into the family's experience of therapy and of their lives, before and after treatment. The Simpsons—and, I hope, readers—will discover that they are part of each other; they do not lose their separate identities, but their recognition of interactional patterns gives them new power over their lives.

Each chapter deals with a new challenge in the seasons of a family's life, opening with a dramatic account of how the family faces a problem and how they attempt to resolve it. Then follows an exposition of the principles of family dynamics, which help explain the dilemma and point to its solution. Finally, each chapter offers detailed strategies for optimal resolution of the challenge in question. Every chapter introduces a few new concepts, but I do not believe that every situation requires a special set of explanations or that life well-lived is a highly technical enterprise. Instead, readers will discover that a few basic concepts from family systems theory, once understood, can be applied to help make family life richer and more satisfying.

Not every problem is solvable, at least not in the sense of an examination that is either passed or failed. Some problems don't go away. Indeed, we will see that some attempted solutions to everyday human problems only make things worse. We will also see how the pursuit of problem-free relationships keeps some people from ever finding satisfaction. Many problems, however, even some of the most vexing—I am happy to say—can be resolved. Finding solutions may take courage and willpower, but even they are not enough. Courage and willpower only take us as far as the limits of our imagination. The result may be ineffective "more-of-the-same" strategies. Finding solutions may take an understanding of how family systems work. This requires a shift, a new way of seeing things—like stepping back from a Van Gogh painting to see the patches of color blend into a coherent picture. This book will illuminate patterns of interactional psychology that govern our lives. By the time readers finish the book they will be equipped to see themselves as members of an interacting unit, controlled and defined in some ways, but they will also be aware that one person is capable of changing an entire system.

I have included a list of recommended readings for those who wish to read further about various aspects of family dynamics and change. These are not just texts of academic reference, but pragmatic and useful books to help readers expand their understanding of family dynamics and apply that understanding to the specific phases of family life. In writing this book I have done my best to translate the jargon of my profession into language that is clear and direct. Where I have retained some technical concepts, I have tried to make their meaning clear. For convenience, I have also included a glossary at the end of the book to help clarify terms used to describe family dynamics.

Writing this book was exhilarating and exhausting. Exhilarating because I have written about what I believe in—the rich possibilities of family life, and family therapy's special powers to liberate those possibilities. Exhausting because I had to fit the writing into an already full life. Seeing patients, teaching, and spending time with my family keeps my pretty busy. Adding in time to write this book made me a little busier. I tried not to allow the writing to interfere too much with other commitments, but inevitably there were times when it did. For understanding that and supporting my writing, I would like to thank my boss, Bill Grosch, who has always believed in and encouraged me.

My wife, Melody, has some mystical power that enables her to know when I need long hours alone to work and when I need to do something special with the family. That she knows me so well is her special knack. That she gives so generously is why I love her so so much.

My children, Sandy and Paul, have always been very considerate of my fussiness about noise when I'm writing. Thanks, kids. More than that, thanks for being so much fun to be with that I was rarely even tempted to give up my weekend afternoon outings with you.

As anyone who has tried it knows, writing is tough work. Sometimes it flows and is a great joy, other times it drags and is— a drag. I owe thanks to my friends who read and commented on various sections of the manuscript, especially Susan Schwartz and Elsa Efran. I would also like to thank my agent, Jay Acton, without whom this project would never have been started—I would not have believed in myself enough to attempt it. Finally, thanks to Tim McGinnis, who possesses two happy talents as an editor: He is unfailingly supportive and he is a wizard at shaping unpolished writing into the best that it can be.

1

DISTURBING THE PEACE

"CAN YOU HELP US?"

I was just leaving my office at the medical center when the phone rang. *Let it ring,* I thought, *I want to get home.* But have you ever noticed how loud and insistent a phone gets when you try not to answer it?

"Hello, this is Doctor Nichols."

The voice on the other end sounded distraught, near tears. Most callers are polite and a little hesitant; I could tell this woman was upset, she just launched right into her story. "This is Sharon Simpson, Doctor. I'm calling about my son, Jason. He's been giving us more and more trouble; lately he's become totally unmanageable. He's defiant and rude. He does what he wants, when he wants, with no respect for his father or me. He used to be an excellent student, but this year his grades are slipping badly. He's barely passing any of his subjects. Last Saturday night he came home at two o'clock in the morning and he smelled like a brewery. So we grounded him. No more going out for a month. He went crazy and screamed obscenities at us, and then he ran out the door. He stayed out all night. We know where he went, to his friend Kevin's house. But we just don't know what to do anymore. Can you help us?"

"It sounds like you're having a pretty rough time," I said, and then added, "How is this affecting other members of the family?" This was my opening gambit in an attempt to broaden the definition of the problem. When families are having difficulties with "unmanageable" children, they want someone to step in and take over. As a family therapist, I wanted to find out why they hadn't been able to take charge themselves.

"The problems with Jason have created quite a strain between me and my husband. He pulls us apart. Stewart's not home much, and when he is, he wants things peaceful and quiet. So, sometimes he ignores Jason and sometimes he cracks down on him too hard. It was his idea to ground Jason for a month. I thought that was too much. And once or twice he's hit him. Not too hard, but it scares me anyway. My husband's a big man, and Jason is only sixteen. He could hurt the boy. Our little girl, Heather—well, she's not so little anymore, she's in the ninth grade—she's the opposite of her brother. She doesn't misbehave at all, but I don't want her getting ideas from Jason."

"It seems like a good idea that you called," I said. "What I'd like to do is set up a meeting with the family and find out more about what's going on, so I can see if I can help."

"You want to see all four of us?"

"Yes. It sounds like Jason's problems are affecting the whole family, so I'll need to see everybody to get as much information as possible."

"Well, I don't know. I doubt if my husband can come. He's a professor at the university and his job keeps him pretty busy."

"I understand, but it's essential that I hear from everyone, to get as many points of view as possible. I'll tell you what. I have an opening next Saturday at nine. Why don't you tell your husband that I said I have to see everybody, at least for an evaluation, and then call me back to confirm that you'll be able to make it."

"Okay," she said, but she didn't sound very happy about it.

I went home wondering if I would hear from her.

The next afternoon I returned to my office from a contentious faculty meeting with just enough time for a cup of coffee before driving downtown to meet with a group of therapists I supervise at a low-cost clinic. By habit, I checked my messages and found one from Mrs. Simpson. She'd called to say they'd be at my office Saturday morning at nine. I suppose I should have been pleased, but I'm never easy about seeing families with teenagers. Whatever problems there are have usually gotten pretty bad. Even though this is how I make my living, Mrs. Simpson's note stirred up a lot of uneasy feeling—about the family's pain, the inevitable struggle over the conditions of treatment, and the pressure on me to deliver. It's so much easier with younger children.

LOOKING FOR LEVERAGE

When I walked into the waiting room at nine o'clock on Saturday, the Simpsons were sitting there waiting. I consider that a good sign. People who come late or don't bring the whole family always have reasons ("The parking was terrible," "Ginger has a cold"), but the ones who have trouble organizing themselves to get there on time often seem to have trouble making a success of therapy.

I introduced myself, and Mr. Simpson stood up. He was tall and slender. His long graying blond hair was slicked back and he wore wire-rimmed glasses. "Hi, I'm Stewart Simpson. This is my wife, Sharon; this is Heather; and that's Jason." Sharon Simpson shook my hand but didn't smile. This was serious and she looked it. Her face was tight, set in an angry look; her dark hair, streaked with white, made her look all the more severe. Heather stood up and nodded. Like her father she was slender, and she had his coloring. Her hair, worn long and loose, was the reddish blond of a golden retriever. She was kind of pretty but she didn't seem to know it yet. Jason remained slouched in a chair in the corner. It was easy to see who the bad guy was.

"Please come in," I said, and watched them file out of the waiting room and into my office. Jason was the last one in. Shoulders hunched over, hands thrust in the pockets of his torn blue jeans, head down, hair in his eyes—that adolescent walk.

My consulting room is furnished with plain, functional furniture. At one end, near the window, is a large oak desk; along one wall is a small brown sofa, along the other wall are four tired-looking green easy chairs. One of the chairs wobbles unsteadily on its legs. I keep planning to get it fixed or get a new one, but most of the people who sit on it are too preoccupied with other things to notice.

This morning I had the chairs and sofa arranged in a semicircle, with a chair for myself slightly outside the semicircle, facing them. That way I could address the family—with them but not quite part of them.

As the Simpsons arranged themselves around the room, they began to drop the guarded formality of the waiting room and settle into more familiar roles. The change was most noticeable in the case of Mr. Simpson. The man who greeted me in the waiting room was direct, businesslike. Even though it was a weekend, he had dressed up: light gray herringbone sports jacket and dark gray slacks. He looked directly at me and spoke with assurance, one professional to another. But the man who sat down with his family was transformed. No longer was he Mr. Simpson, a person of authority, used to dealing with professionals on an equal footing; now he was a husband and father, and the difference in his demeanor was striking. He looked older, worried, and not at all sure of his authority.

Heather sat on the sofa with her mother, and Jason sat in the corner, as far away from the others as he could manage.

"So," I said gently, "who would like to begin?"

Mr. Simpson looked at his wife and said, "Why don't you start?"

"Okay," she said, and then she launched into a litany of complaints. "Like I told you on the phone, it's Jason. He's become totally disrespectful. He thinks he can do whatever he wants, whenever he wants, and he pays very little attention to anything we tell him. He's *constantly* getting into trouble. I didn't want to tell you this over the phone, but the latest thing is he's gotten into pornography. A few weeks ago I found some of those filthy magazines under his mattress. I was disgusted! I threw them out, but this week I found more in his closet."

Her tone was hard, mean. I was surprised: this old-fashioned intolerance from a well-educated woman? My first instinct was to challenge her—"What's so unusual about a teenaged boy looking at pictures of naked women?" But her angry determination warned me that to make this point would only disqualify me as an expert and relegate me to the status of yet another person who was against her.

I glanced at Jason to see how much this was embarrassing him, but all I could see was a sneer. Bravado? I could prod him to answer his mother, but this was not the time. Now I needed to hear from each one of them, to build an alliance of understanding, before getting into the battles to come. I turned to Mr. Simpson and asked, "What do you think?"

"Sharon is right. Jason has always been a problem. He's been willful and stubborn since he was little, and now that he's getting older he thinks he can do whatever he wants. I agree with Sharon, only . . . maybe sometimes she worries too much. This business with the magazines, I don't know if that's abnormal for a boy his age."

"What! I suppose you think it's all right for him to fill up our house with that trash. *You* don't care what happens to the boy. Suppose he becomes addicted to pornography?"

I interrupted, saying, "Okay, hold on. Let's come back to this point. But first I want to hear from everybody."

First interviews are so difficult. At some point it's important to allow or even provoke family members to have their usual fights so I can see what happens: who attacks, who withdraws, who takes sides with whom. But to them it may feel like the same old thing—the hateful, frustrating conflict they came here to put an end to. I want them to have their fights, but later—and with a difference. I'll want to see how the argument between two people fits into the whole pattern of the family, and I'll want to have enough leverage to push the participants past the usual unproductive wrangling that leads nowhere.

＊

What's going on so far? First we hear about an "uncontrollable adolescent." Then, Mrs. Simpson's complaints become a harangue and an attack, first on the boy, then on his father. Maybe she's an "overcontrolling mother," a "shrewish woman." Blaming the mother is an easy trap to fall into. One of the hardest members of a family for most people to empathize with is an angry mother. But maybe the problem is Mr. Simpson: he doesn't support his wife. However, nothing is gained by shifting the blame from one family member to another. It's hard, very hard, to get away from blaming, *and* very difficult to get beyond the view of people as separate selves in conflict. But the secret of family therapy is to discover how disparate problems and private quarrels fit into the overall structure of the family.

＊

Next I turned to Jason. "What do you think about your parents' complaints?" (I said "your *parents'* " rather than "your mother's" because I didn't want to expose the split between the parents prematurely. That might turn out to be a significant problem, but that's not what they had come here for, and whatever else I did, I wanted them to come back next week.)

"She's always on my case. Nothing I do makes her happy. So what's the use of trying? I don't see how coming here is going to do any good."

Although the parents, as architects of the family, have the most power to decide whether or not to return and give therapy a chance, it is nevertheless important to try to develop rapport with every member of the family. The trouble was, in this family it was going to be hard to sympathize with one person without alienating someone else. I did my best. "I see. You think your parents are too hard on you, and you don't really feel like being here. Maybe it seems like you have nothing to gain by changing the way things go on at home. . . ." And then, without waiting for an answer: "So, Heather, where are you when all this arguing takes place around the house?"

"I don't know." Period. Heather took her lower lip between her teeth and stared down at the rug, used to not being asked, or not answering. Maybe I was too direct.

"What grade are you in, Heather?"

"Ninth," she said, eyes on the floor halfway between us.

"Do you go to the same school that Jason does?"

"Yes. Only I don't see him much at school; he hangs around with the older kids."

"Heather, does it bother you, all the arguing between Jason and your parents?" This not-so-innocent question was my attempt to find out whose side Heather was on.

"Yes. He's always getting into some kind of trouble. I don't see why he doesn't do what he's supposed to." So, here was my answer: Mrs. Simpson was in control and Heather was still in line. "Only . . ."

Mrs. Simpson finished for her daughter: "Heather doesn't like all the noise. She's quiet. She likes to read."

"Only, what?" I insisted, trying to meet Heather's eyes.

"What?" her mother tried to coax her.

Heather shook her head. As I was to discover, she could go stubborn like that. Silence was her power, her only power.

Now I had heard from each of them. I could see that Mrs. Simpson was in charge, an angry, domineering woman, and I could see that Jason was the only one who fought openly with her. Mr. Simpson claimed to be on his wife's side, but he wasn't very convincing. If he supported her at all, it was only grudgingly. And Heather seemed the picture of the good girl, only . . . only, I didn't know what. What I couldn't yet be certain of was how accurate these impressions were, and how they all fit together.

DIALOGUE: SETTING THE SYSTEM IN MOTION

Now I was ready to let them talk, to see how the family functioned to air grievances and solve problems. I was interested less in what they said, though, than in who said what to whom, and how. And I was interested to see if certain dialogues would be allowed to go very far before a third person stepped in. One thing I was not interested in, however, was getting into endless, fruitless debates, the kind I felt sure Jason and his mother were expert at. My assumption was that these two could go at it all day like cats and dogs, without really getting anywhere. Besides, I wanted to probe the flexibility of the family's organization by trying to activate the two less central figures, Heather and Mr. Simpson.

"Tell me, Mr. Simpson, what does Jason do that bothers *you* the most?"

Mr. Simpson glanced at his wife and then back at me. "I don't know. I guess it's his arrogance. I work very hard to support this family. We have a nice house, they have everything they want, but they take it all for granted. These kids don't know how lucky they are."

Jason muttered under his breath, "Sure, Dad, tell us about the good old days."

"What did you say?" I asked.

"Nothing," Jason replied.

"See? That's what I mean. He's so damned snotty; you just can't talk to him."

"That seems like a shame. If a man can't talk to his son, there's no way for the two of them to understand each other. You don't feel like he respects you; and he, well, I'm not sure what he feels. Why don't you ask him? Try to talk with him now."

"You heard the doctor, Jason. You've got to learn to respect me; I *am* your father, you know. Why don't you ever—"

"Don't be so critical, Stewart," Mrs. Simpson interrupted. "The doctor said *you* should try to understand how *Jason* feels."

"That's interesting," I said. "You don't think your husband can do it by himself, so you come in. That's interesting. Is that the way it happens at home?"

"Ha! That's a laugh," Mrs. Simpson answered. "He *never* talks to the boy; it's always up to me."

It was striking the way she called her son "the boy." She didn't use his name, as though he was not "Jason," not a separate person, only her son. It was a peculiar distancing mechanism.

Mr. Simpson tried to answer his wife's complaint. "You never give me a chance. You're always criticizing me for not paying enough attention to him, yet whenever I do say anything, you take *his* side. What's the use?"

I interrupted. "You said over the phone that Jason is pulling you apart. Kids can be awfully difficult and they sure know how to divide and conquer. It seems that you and your husband have slightly different ideas about how to handle your son, and that can be a problem. Perhaps the two of you could talk about that."

———◆———

This would be a turning point in the interview. This kind of invasion can be very threatening. Mr. and Mrs. Simpson had not come to me to air their disagreements; they came hoping I would do something about Jason. Unfortunately, the something I was doing was looking into the conflict between the two of them, which might be part of the reason Jason was getting into trouble. Nine times out of ten, when a child misbehaves and continues to misbehave, the parents are pulling in different directions. Otherwise, they would form a united front and crack down effectively.

———◆———

Mrs. Simpson felt vulnerable, exposed. She had expected therapy to be a dialogue, but hoped the dialogue would be with an outsider, an expert, someone who would take her side, someone who would help, not push her to do what she did not know how to do. She paid careful attention to my suggestion, just like my cat does when I tell her not to chase birds. Instead of talking to her husband, she turned to Jason. "You never do anything I ask you. And you lie!"

"I never—" But he didn't get to finish. Most families are more reserved, but these two were on each other like a shot. She reviled him with a pent-up rage, and although he tried to fight back, in the end he was no match for her—at least not verbally.

Their acid tones should not obscure the fact that these two were intensely preoccupied with each other. The connection might be conflictual, but it was as strong as Krazy Glue. Regardless of who else was speaking, these two addressed themselves to each other. When I asked a question, they responded in a deliberately provocative manner, with barbed comments and rhetorical questions, expertly baiting one another. They fought, but it was a little like the play-fighting of puppies: snarling and growling and nipping, but no real biting. Perhaps the conflict between Jason and his mother served to diffuse a more virulent conflict between the parents, and at the same time was made worse by the parents' inability to form a united front. I wanted to see the pattern *and* test its elasticity.

Once again I interrupted. "I don't think you're going to get anywhere with Jason unless you two parents talk over your differences and come up with an agreed-upon strategy for dealing with him. And I don't think you can do that without preventing Jason from interrupting you. Talk to your husband. What do you want him to do? Talk to your wife. You two need to work together."

This time they complied.

Mr. Simpson crossed his left leg over his right, clasped his hands together around his knee, and held on. I looked where he looked. I noticed the puffiness under Sharon Simpson's eyes. Tired eyes. It was a pretty face—large brown eyes; a full mouth; thick, wavy, dark hair—a face in that long transition between young and middle-aged. The signs of strain and complaint showed around the eyes and mouth, and some isolated strands of gray— white, really—appeared in her hair. She was, I realized, more than pretty. She was a beauty. And yet she seemed to take pains to downplay her looks. She wore no makeup except for a little dull red on her lips. I guessed she had a good, somewhat generous, figure, but it was hard to tell because of the baggy yellow sweatsuit she wore. It was a nice face, but she tightened it when she turned to glare at her husband.

"You don't care about us. All you care about is that precious career of yours. For years I've tried to get you to be more involved with this family, but you're always too busy. Even when you are around, you're so grouchy you make the rest of us nervous. All these years you've left everything to me. Who drives the children everywhere? Who waits till all hours when Jason's out late? Not you. You have to get your precious sleep. Do you know what Jason's midterm report card looks like? No, you haven't even looked at it."

"No, I didn't see the report card. Where was it?"

"I put it in your hand last Sunday night. 'Not now,' you said." Her tone was a nasal, mocking caricature. "It's always 'later' with you. With you, later never comes."

Mr. Simpson's cheeks got red. He looked away, bitter, and lapsed into silence.

I wasn't ready to let it end this way. Sometimes my job is no more complicated (and no easier) than refereeing a boxing match. I just have to keep the spectators from entering the fray and prevent either of the combatants from leaving the ring before they finish the fight. "Can't you answer her?"

"No," he said, looking at me. "She doesn't want my opinion, she just wants everything done her way. It's the same thing with Jason. She still treats him like a baby, telling him what to wear, snooping around in his room. No wonder he's angry."

"Tell her," I urged.

"What's the use? She complains that I'm not more involved. Maybe that's true. But maybe it's not just because I'm some kind of selfish monster. Maybe I'm just sick and tired of her constant criticism. If you want to know what I think, I think that when the children upset her she takes it out on me."

"That's not fair," she said, starting to cry. "Nothing's ever your fault. You're always *so* innocent. Poor you. It's got to be me. I'm always wrong." Now she was sobbing.

"I'm sorry, honey. I don't mean I'm all right and you're all wrong. You know that. It's just . . . I mean, sometimes I can't take all the criticism. I get upset." He leaned forward and reached for her hand, but she pushed him away.

IT MUST BE A MARITAL PROBLEM

The second false conclusion we might draw is that the real difficulty in the Simpson family is a marital problem: The parents don't get along and the boy's misbehavior is a product of that conflict. It wouldn't be the first time a disobedient child exacted a father's revenge on a wife he secretly hates but fears. Unsettled conflict between husband and wife, frozen in place by emotional distance, affects how each of them relates to their child's struggle for independence. Mrs. Simpson hangs on too tight, too long, while Mr. Simpson subtly undermines his wife's discipline as a way of getting even. And, as is often the case, the boy's symptoms mask the very conflict of which they are a product.

This is true, but it's only a partial truth. Jason's rebelliousness is due in part to his mother's overinvolvement with him, which is to a certain extent a product of her underinvolvement with her husband. When family members sense these, or similar, connections, they think in terms of simple cause-and-effect, and look for someone to blame. This type of thinking mistakenly casts each of them in inflexible roles—the rebellious teenager, the shrewish mother, the cold and distant father—and obscures the rich interconnections among all the members of the family.

LINEAR VERSUS CIRCULAR CAUSALITY

The idea of *linear causality* is that event A causes result B. This is the way we are used to thinking and it works fine for some things. If your favorite geranium turns yellow (effect), go ahead and look for a simple cause. Not enough sunlight or too much water may turn out to be the direct determinant of your plant's unhappiness.

Human unhappinenss is a bit more complicated. From the perspective of *circular causality*, behavior is seen as a series of moves and countermoves in a repeating cycle. The illusion of unilateral influence tempts each member of the Simpson family to believe that there is one cause (A) for every effect (B). Jason believes that his mother's excessive demands make him disobey ("If only she were more reasonable, I would do what she wants"). She, on the other hand, thinks that if he would just do what she asks, she wouldn't have to be on his case all the time. Thus are they trapped in the linear perspective. Each of them is convinced that if only the other would change, things would be better, and therefore each keeps trying to put the pressure on. But once things become stuck in a recurring cycle like this, change rarely occurs, because instead of changing the dysfunctional pattern, they simply act it out more forcefully. Some families only break the cycle by giving up on each other. Even in those rare cases when blaming is replaced by recognition of one's own role ("Maybe I've been too hard on the boy"), the illusion of linear casuality is maintained.

Replacing the usual habit of thinking linearly and beginning to think in terms of recurring cycles helps us approach everyday relationship problems with a new and more productive outlook. You don't get along with your boss? Instead of worrying about whose fault it is, or who started what, try to consider the relationship as a series of moves and countermoves that go around in a circle. When he calls you into his office to discuss a new project, he lectures you about cost efficiency and proper procedure. You listen respectfully but with growing annoyance that he cares more about bureaucratic forms than he does about quality results. You agree with him, sort of, but put in a word or two about doing the job right. He gets irritated and tells you to do it his way. The meeting ends with both of you unhappy, and each of you knowing why.

Circular thinking means figuring out that when he does X, you do Y, and he does X, and you do Y, and so on. Remember, if Y is what you do, Y is all you can change. This does not mean that he is right and you are wrong, or even that you have to give in to him. For example, one possible change in the cycle is to agree with him, and then do what you wanted to do in the first place. This may or may not solve the problem. It probably will if his real agenda is wanting to tell you what to do and have you agree with him; it probably won't if he really wants to monitor exactly what you do (most bosses don't). In any case, circular thinking will help you discover solutions in situations where linear thinking leads to a dead end.

To understand the circular process in the Simpson family it is necessary to recognize that the cycle is *triangular*, not bilateral. This is true of most family problems, as we shall see. Because Jason's relationship to Sharon is related to her relationship with Stewart (and his relationship to Jason is related to Jason's relation-

ship with Sharon), change in any one of these links will reverber-
ate to the others. In plain English, getting Sharon to back off from
Jason—and stay backed off—requires getting her more involved
with Stewart (or with friends, or some other adult outlet). You
don't change one side of a triangle without affecting the others. In
the triangle involving Jason and his parents there were three
places I wanted to see change: (1) Jason and his mother more
separate, (2) Stewart and Sharon closer, and (3) Stewart more
involved with Jason. Remember: All three changes are interrelated.

The easiest place to start is often the most dormant relationship, the one not entrenched in conflict. So, I decided to see if I
could get Mr. Simpson more connected with his son. Later, I
would tackle the more difficult jobs of getting him more involved
with his wife and of pulling her away from Jason. Unless I found
a way to accomplish this, Mrs. Simpson's attempts to dominate
her son might very well drive a more-or-less normal adolescent
into ever more extreme acts of rebellion.

———◆———

"Mrs. Simpson, you said you were worn out by all this
bickering. I think you may feel even worse than you let on. You
seem pretty discouraged. Do you sometimes feel like nothing you
do or say matters, and that things just never seem to improve?"

"Yes," she said quietly.

"Would you be willing to pull back a little and let your
husband take a more active role in disciplining Jason?"

"*Willing*? Yes, of course, that's what I've been trying to tell
you."

"So, Mr. Simpson, would you agree to take a bit more of an
active role with Jason?"

"Sure, I guess so," he said without conviction.

"Which is it, 'sure' or 'I guess so'?"

"I said I would."

"Okay, fine. Why don't you begin by talking with Jason about
one area where you'd like him to improve this week. Just pick one
thing and try to come to a clear understanding about that."

"Alright, Jason, you heard the doctor, what about starting
with your homework? No going out or watching TV until you
finish your homework."

Jason looked at his father absently, looked at me absently, spotted his mother's look and said to her: "What business is it of you guys *when* I do my homework? As long as I get decent grades, I think it should be up to me when I do it. Besides, I can do half of it in homeroom and the rest in study hall."

Mrs. Simpson lit into him with a fury. "You lie! That's the worst thing about you. You say that you do your homework and you don't. It's gotten so that we can't trust a thing you say. You've become a rotten, spoiled brat!"

All the cockiness went out of Jason's face. She blistered him. But when she was done, both father and son just looked at me. Their eyes said, *See what I have to put up with?*

The ensuing silence lasted several tense minutes.

———◆———

Transactions routinely occur in families within familiar limits, defined by habit, that maintain *homeostasis*—a balanced steady state of predictable routine. My job is to increase the intensity to force them to go beyond that threshold. This is the difference between success and failure with families—bumping hard against stalemated interactions, but then using intensity to push past the point of impasse. I must speak loud enough to be heard, but not so loud as to make them back off.

———◆———

"Mrs. Simpson, do you really want Jason to grow up? Are you sure? Because what you are doing is not helpful."

Jason broke in: "*She* doesn't control me. *I'm* an individual."

"Sure you are, but your individuality is affected by the way you feel you have to rebel against your parents' authority. It's as though you think that you can only be a man by defying them."

Then I turned again to Mr. Simpson. "Your staying outside keeps your wife overburdened. Why do you do that? You must have a very good reason."

Mrs. Simpson blurted out, "It's that precious job of his. He thinks that's the only thing in the world that matters."

I tried to goad him into fighting back. "There you are again! She's on your back again. How do you do it?"

"I didn't say a word!"

"Exactly."

"You said that I should try to talk to Jason. Well, I tried, but you saw what happened. She won't let me."

"What I see, Mr. Simpson, is that every time you pull back, your wife takes over. And, Mrs. Simpson, every time you take control or criticize his way of handling Jason, he pulls back. Is there some way you can help your wife feel that she doesn't need to take over? Is there some way you can let your husband get involved other than by nagging him?"

"I guess I could pull back, take a rest as you say, and give Stewart more of a chance to take over."

"That's good, but Jason won't let you. He's hooked on dragging you in. He knows he can get around you. He's not so sure about his father. How are you going to respond when Jason baits you by behaving like a stubborn thirteen-year-old? Are you always going to take the bait?"

———◆———

I thought, *If Jason could learn to talk to his father, he would be less tied to his mother.* I said, "If a mother interferes, a son will not get to know his father and the father will not know his son. And that's sad. Jason, I doubt this will make any sense to you, but if you don't learn to relate to your father you may always have trouble relating to men. Mr. Simpson, your son is growing up without you two knowing each other. Get to know him. Why don't you talk to him now, explain your point of view. After all, shouldn't a father and son understand each other?"

"I don't think he wants to hear it," Mr. Simpson answered. "He doesn't care what I think." (They exchanged looks.)

"Go ahead, give it a try," I said.

Cheek muscles tense, frowning with the unaccustomed effort of instructing his son about life, Mr. Simpson told Jason that a man has to learn to do what he's supposed to do. It starts in the home, but it extends into your career. There are important things to do. Much to accomplish. It was a ponderous lecture, filled with words like "respect" and "self-discipline." I winced listening to this. Stewart Simpson didn't have much practice talking to his son and he wasn't very good at it. I could see how much trouble he had understanding how Jason was feeling. I wanted to teach him how to get through to his son. But I held back from commenting on his pontificating manner because I wanted to deal with transactional patterns rather than with individual family members' particular characteristics. Besides, what I needed to do now was get Mr. Simpson more involved, not add to the weight of criticism in this family. Nagging is nagging.

I took my cue from Jason's monosyllabic responses. "Jason has taught you to ask what's on his mind in such a way that he only has to give short answers. Can you change in such a way that he can talk more like an adult—so that he can begin to grow up."

My goal was not just discipline—or distance—but to establish a hierarchy, which means putting the parents in charge. To do so I would have to break down the pattern where one parent did all the childrearing while the other remained on the periphery. They wanted to throw me the problem of Jason's behavior, like a hot potato; instead I threw it back to them. Therapists can't save children, even though some try; the parents have to.

These two parents have probably been distant for years. Why? She attacks and he withdraws—and, or, when he withdraws, she attacks. Who started it? *It doesn't matter.* Either one of them could stop it. But their distance has left a void in their lives. Mr. Simpson fills the empty space with work; his wife fills it with an overly close attachment to the children. This worked when the children were small; now it doesn't work so well. Jason has grown to a point where his mother's tight control provokes him to rebel to struggle free. The more he struggles, the more she tightens her grip. Now Jason is trained to rebel—not only to maintain autonomy in the face of his mother's control, but also to fill a missing role in the family: to be the man in his mother's life.

Jason thinks his problems will be over once he gets out of his parents' house. (Don't we all?) He's wrong. The pattern slowly becomes etched in his character. He'll rebel to a certain extent at school, and if he continues to define his autonomy as opposition, he'll do so later into manhood. Who knows, maybe twenty years from now he'll be on some therapist's couch trying to resolve a "problem with authority." If so, life will provide him with a series of trials. Dealing with his mother would be the final exam. He can put it off indefinitely, or, with my help, learn to pass it now.

To complicate things further, Jason's mother's relentless attacks have devastated his self-esteem. The pornography and masturbation are one way of dealing with his hurt pride. These things may seem like an expectable part of adolescent sexual experimentation, but Jason overdoes it. He retreats into his room and soothes his wounded ego with teenage fantasies. Unless he curtails this habit soon, it may have a detrimental effect on his social life, and it may perpetuate the age-old male tendency to think of women as either domineering mothers or sexual playthings.

———◆———

Although I had broadened the focus of problems in the Simpson family to include his parents, I had neglected Heather. It was easy to do. She was so quiet. But if there's one thing I've learned, it is that trying to do family therapy without drawing in all members of the family can be a big mistake. Besides, I worried that in subduing her own nature to conform to her mother's rule, she had become inward, a shy girl with a good reputation but few friends. I made another effort with Heather.

"Heather, are you always this quiet?"

"I don't know. I don't really have anything to say."

"What effect does the tension at home have on your social life? Do you try to get out of the house more? Do you hesitate to invite friends over?"

"No."

I felt challenged by Heather's timid truculence, but I wasn't about to cajole her to open up to me. Failure would make me appear impotent, and allow Heather to continue to lose by winning. Success, unlikely as it was, might show up her parents—timid daughter opens up to sensitive, compassionate therapist. No, better to get them to talk to their daughter.

"I don't seem to be getting anywhere. You two are the parents; can you get Heather to talk about how she feels about all of this?"

Mrs. Simpson asserted that she knew exactly what Heather felt and Heather agreed. I said, "That sensitivity and closeness is very important when children are young; it's what makes you such a good mother. But now they are beginning to grow up." And then, to Heather, "Does it sometimes bother you that Mother speaks for you?" Finally, to Mr. Simpson, "Can you help Heather speak to your wife about this, because your wife is too strong for Heather."

Just then I happened to notice the clock on the wall above Mrs. Simpson's head. Five after ten—we were well over the hour.

"Well, I'm afraid we're out of time. There's a lot more to talk about, and I'd like to see you again next Saturday at this time." I did not make it sound like a question.

Mrs. Simpson looked at her husband. He said, "Okay, we'll be here."

They didn't talk on the way out. Each one was absorbed in private thought. I could imagine what was going on in their minds. Jason was probably thinking, *I'm outta here! This therapy business is going to be just like I thought it was—a lot of pointless arguing, all designed to get me to be a goody-goody wimp, like precious Heather.*

Heather most likely didn't want to come back either. Only she wished Jason would quit causing trouble. Sometimes she hated him.

Mrs. Simpson had a mixed reaction. She seemed to like me; though she thought I was somewhat detached, she apparently felt that I knew what I was doing. What I was doing, she sensed, was putting pressure on the family to handle a problem they had already tried in vain to solve. She had hoped that I would take a more active role. Why must everything fall to her?

Mr. Simpson doubtlessly resented being there. One thing he was sure of, he did not want to open up old feelings about the marriage. But maybe coming here would be enough to make Sharon stop worrying so much and always picking on Jason. If she backed off, maybe Jason would stop being so damned defiant. Why couldn't this psychologist just tell her that? Why did he have to stir up the whole family, disturbing the peace?

———◆———

This consultation with the Simpsons was the beginning of a new approach to their problems with Jason. Instead of focusing on the individual in isolation, I focused on the person within the family. My framework is family therapy, a body of concepts and methods that approaches the individual in his interpersonal context. Therapy based on this framework is directed toward changing the organization of the family. When the organizational pattern of the family group is transformed, the lives of every family member are altered accordingly.

To say that people are products of their families is certainly not a new idea. Surprisingly, however, treating whole families together as a method of resolving family problems is relatively new. What's more, seeing that families have an overall organizational structure that shapes the lives of their members is newer still. As we shall see, discovering these patterns in a family is like turning on a light in a dark room.

2

FAMILY THERAPY

O_{ne} thing we rarely doubt is our selfhood. Even if we spend much of our energy focused outward, toward making our way and getting along with others, we do so with a sense of being separate and distinct self-contained personalities. This is what gives continuity to our lives: There is a coherent unity, "myself," as an organizing center of our existence. Always a little self-conscious, we may measure ourselves against others and see ourselves through others' eyes, yet we retain a sense of singularity. I am me, they are them.

Under duress, we retreat even further into selfhood. Some beleaguered individuals withdraw to lick their wounds, others strike back, and some reach out for help. When people seek professional help, they tend to go alone. What do they seek? Healing? Yes, but also sanctuary, refuge from troubled and troubling relationships. Buffeted about in love and work, and unable to find comfort and solace at home, adults come to therapy looking to find lost satisfaction and meaning. Parents, worried about misbehavior, reticence, or lack of achievement, send their children for guidance and direction. Ironically, though, parents who send their children for therapy may be less interested in the child—the child's personal discontents—than in wanting to "cure" the child of misbehavior. In many ways psychotherapy has displaced the family's function of resolving the difficulties of everyday life. Once we hid inside our family shells from the harshness of the outside world; now psychotherapy is likely to provide our haven in a heartless world.

Today, however, there is a new approach to understanding and treating human problems. In this new approach, family therapy, people are no longer isolated from emotional sources of conflict; instead, problems are addressed at their source. Family therapy emerged in the mid-fifties when therapists noticed some puzzling relationships between a patient's progress and the family's response. Often, improvement met not with relief and gratitude, but with criticism, anxiety, and frequently the eruption of symptoms in another family member. The patient got better but the family got worse.

Don Jackson, one of the founding parents of family therapy, observed some very strange reactions among the relatives of his individual patients.[1] In one case, Jackson was treating a woman for depression; when she began to improve, her husband called to complain that her emotional condition was getting worse. When she continued to improve, the husband lost his job. Eventually he killed himself. Apparently this man's sense of security was predicated on having a sick wife.

In another case, a husband urged his wife to seek psychotherapy for frigidity. When after several months of treatment she became less inhibited and more sexually responsive, he became impotent. A more familiar example of a relationship that maintains its balance only so long as one partner remains symptomatic is a marriage in which one spouse is an alcoholic and the other spouse subtly encourages the drinking. Evidently, some people are better able to accept a needy, dependent partner than one who is a competent and capable adult. Others, despite what they may say, may be more comfortable with an emotionally distant spouse than one who makes active claims on the relationship.

One of the most striking examples of the power of the family is the impact that families have on young adult schizophrenics. Time after time, clinicians like Jackson noticed that patients would improve in the hospital only to deteriorate dramatically as soon as they went home. Moreover, even brief visits from their families often caused stable patients to become acutely unbalanced and irrational. These observations led Jackson to conclude that families act as units and that their most powerful motive is to preserve the status quo. This discovery prepared the way for family therapy, but the movement did not actually begin until therapists took the significant step from interviewing individual patients in their offices to observing them in their natural context—interacting with their families.

Unlike many innovations, family therapy was discovered more or less simultaneously by several clinicians. In the following sections I will describe how some of the originators of family therapy developed their ideas and how they put these ideas into practice.

Lyman Wynne

The bizarre thinking of schizophrenics has long fascinated and baffled mental healers. The severity of schizophrenic madness, making the sufferers appear possessed or enchanted, made them seem beyond the realm of human experience. Before the pioneers of family therapy began to look at pathological patterns of communication, schizophrenia was regarded as something inside the patient. The patient was sick, and the hallmark of that sickness was disordered thinking.

What family therapy researchers discovered was that schizophrenics are not mad in some illogical and incomprehensible way, but that their madness was an understandable consequence of growing up in chaotic and confused—maddening—families. Lyman Wynne's particular contribution was demonstrating that thought disorder was transmitted from parents to children by deviant patterns of communication. Among the features of communication found to have a disorganizing effect on children's thinking were: unintelligible remarks, inconsistent and ambiguous referents, disqualifications (not disagreeing with opinions but discounting the person), continually changing the subject, and extraneous, contradictory, and illogical comments. Today, we know that schizophrenia is not *caused* by family interactions (there is an innate biological component), but the course of schizophrenia is directly affected by what goes on in the family.

Wynne and his colleagues discovered two patterns that were characteristic of disturbed and disturbing families: *pseudomutuality* and the *rubber fence.*[2]

Pseudomutuality is a facade of harmony that some families cling to like a life raft in a stormy sea. Many of the parents in these families suffered from painful early separations which left them with an unnatural dread of separateness. Pseudomutual families are obsessed with fitting together so closely that there is no room for the differentiation of separate identities, no room for recognition and appreciation of any divergence or self-interest. The family cannot tolerate either deeper, more intimate, relationships or independence. This forced and phony togetherness masks splits and conflicts as well as deep affectionate and sexual feelings, and prevents both conflict and greater intimacy from emerging. The strangely unreal quality of emotion in these families distorts communication and impairs realistic perception and rational thinking. The emotional chaos in these families breeds mental chaos in their children.

One pseudomutual family that I treated masqueraded as a democracy. Although the family had six children and therefore a need for order, there was an aching absence of any structure or idea of leadership in this family. Whoever spoke used the pronoun "we"; although they were talking about themselves, themselves seemed to encompass the whole group. After a couple of sessions, the myth of this perfectly happy family began to crumble and I realized that the mother was as powerful an autocrat as I've ever known. Her absolute control was maintained in part by her steadfast avoidance of showing it. Only one child ever seemed to oppose her. That child, a girl of thirteen, opposed her mother only by failing to eat. She was anorectic. In a desperate attempt to control something in her life, she was destroying it.

The pseudomutuality in this family was almost impossible to break through. They had an engulfing manner which gave the impression of sharing each other's feelings and motivations, rather than gaining any mutual recognition and acceptance of differences and conflicts. They had chosen (if that's the right word) to forego the satisfaction of spontaneous individuality in favor of the security of togetherness. They were always "We"—in agreement about everything. The family was like an arthritic piano player: They could strike only chords of agreement; they were too glued together to play individual notes. There was only one disharmony, and that was a tragic one.

———◆———

Few of us grow up with real psychosis, and yet there is a little bit of craziness in most families. One way we correct that is through outside contact with the larger world. Children learn from their friends and teachers that not everyone shares their own family's quirks and peculiarities. The families that Wynne studied, however, had a way of quelling any signs of separateness, inside or outside the family. The *rubber fence* was his evocative term for an invisible barrier that stretches to allow unavoidable contact outside the family, such as attending school, but snaps back to restrain the children from having too much to do with any outside influence. A similar kind of protective clannishness is practiced by some orthodox religious families and those who deliberately insulate their children to preserve their ethnic heritage. These families have rational reasons for preserving something they consider worthwhile. Disturbed families, on the other hand, are simply terrified to see any signs of individuality in their children. The family role structure thus remains all-encompassing, and participation in the larger culture is severely curtailed. The most damaging feature of the rubber fence is that precisely those who most need contact outside the family to correct family distortions of reality are the ones who are allowed it least. Instead of being a unit of a larger society, transmitting its norms and values, the pathological family becomes a complete society, closed off and stifling.

———◆———

I once treated a family in which the children were taught to believe in spirits. The children weren't crazy, but they accepted as fact what their parents told them and they had little contact outside the family to convince them otherwise. The parents of this family were committed to the extreme of parochial narrowness. Mistrust of the world at large sealed them inside their apartness. The children had enormous difficulty adjusting to school, but the parents blamed the school and retreated further within their own fortress of denial.

In a context where togetherness is everything and no significant outside relationships are tolerated, recognition of personal
differences may be impossible, short of the blatantly bizarre
behavior seen in schizophrenic reactions. A disturbed adolescent
may thus finally achieve the status of separateness, but is then
labeled schizophrenic and expelled from the family. Acute disturbance in one of these young people may be considered a desperate
attempt at individuation, which not only fails but also costs the
person membership in the family. If an acute disturbance becomes
chronic, the now defeated patient may later be reaccepted into the
family—crippled, but no longer protesting.

Gregory Bateson, Don Jackson, and Jay Haley

One of the most creative and influential groups in the history
of modern psychiatry was Gregory Bateson's schizophrenia
project in Palo Alto, California, in the 1950s. Bateson, the brilliant
English anthropologist whose wide-ranging ideas continue to
influence family therapy years after his death, assembled a group
of eclectic talents with catholic interests, including Jay Haley, John
Weakland, William Fry, and Don Jackson. Although they studied
subjects as diverse as otters at play, a ventriloquist and his
dummy, the training of guide dogs, the meaning and uses of
humor, the social and psychological significance of popular movies, and the utterances of schizophrenic patients, the organizing
theme of all their research was the nature of communication.

All communications, Bateson observed, have two different
levels or functions: *report* and *command*. The report (or content) of
a message is the information conveyed by the words. In addition,
though, every message carries a second meaning, a command,
which is a comment on how the report is to be taken and a
statement of the nature of the relationship. For example, the
message "I love you" contains a report of information and an
attempt to define the nature of the relationship. Depending on the
context, the speaker may mean "I love you (You were such a good
boy to clean your room)," or "I love you (You can trust me, take
off your clothes)." There are no simple messages.

This second level of communication, *metacommunication*, is at a
higher level of abstraction and, though sometimes hard to notice,

a very powerful factor in human relationships. Although we may not use the term, metacommunication is absolutely essential to the way we regulate our relationships.

Metacommunication is especially noticeable when we come in contact with strangers. A person sitting next to you on the plane says, "Nice day," an opening wedge in what might become an extended conversation. In response you may stare harder at your book or magazine and grunt, "Yes," or put the book down, look up with a smile, and say, "Yes." In attempting to define the nature of our relationships, we qualify our messages by posture, facial expression, and tone of voice. When we say that different cultures "have a language all their own," we mean that their reports need translating. Raymond Chandler, the hard-boiled detective novelist who wrote *The Big Sleep* and *Farewell My Lovely*, once described a certain form of refined British snobbery, listing the following expressions and their American translations: "I simply adore her" means "I'd stick a knife in her back if she had a back." "I rather care for that" means "Give it to me quick." And "I'm simply impossibly in love with him" means "He has enough money to pay for the drinks."[3]

Even animals metacommunicate. Notice, for example, how two dogs play at fighting. One leaps at the other, they tussle, they nip each other, but neither one fights seriously or inflicts any real damage. How do they know they are playing? Clearly they must have some means of metacommunicating, or indicating that the attack is only playful. When it comes to schizophrenia, the paradoxes of communication are not so amusing.

From their interviews of hospitalized patients, Bateson and his colleagues concluded that the bizarre speech of schizophrenics was not crazy in some meaningless way, but made sense in the context of pathological family communication. The most famous expression of this idea was the *double bind hypothesis* (first described by Bateson, Jackson, Haley, and Weakland in a 1956 paper entitled "Toward a Theory of Schizophrenia").[4]

Here's how the double bind works. Suppose a mother is uncomfortable with closeness and affection. When her child approaches her, she instinctively recoils. But she cannot tolerate the idea of herself as a cold, rejecting parent, so when the child responds to her discomfort by pulling back himself, she contradicts the first message of anxious withdrawal with a new one of feigned affection. "What's the matter, don't you love me?" This again puts the child in the wrong. Notice, by the way, that this is more than mere contradiction; the two conflicting messages occur *on different levels of abstraction:* the mother's words are loving; her posture speaks a different truth. The child is caught in a double bind. No matter which message he tries to obey, he will disobey the other.

The child is in a similar situation to the man whose wife shouts at him, "You should be more self-confident!" or, as in an example from the paper, to the Zen pupil whose master holds a stick over his head and says fiercely, "If you say this stick is real, I will hit you with it; if you say the stick is not real, I will hit you with it; and if you say nothing, I will hit you with it." What can you do? A wise Zen pupil will see alternatives beyond those posed by the master— such as grabbing the stick or running away. But the child, caught in the grip of the double bind, can neither run away nor comment on the impossibility of his situation. What he *can* do, pitifully, is become confused, and speak in a confusion of real and unreal utterances. In this situation, being crazy makes sense.

From their interest in patterns of communication in schizo-phrenic families, the Bateson group stumbled into family therapy. Once they began to meet with schizophrenic families to observe their bizarre ways of dealing with each other, they were moved by the families' evident suffering and tried to cure the schizophrenic patients by talking the families out of their confused ways of speaking. Coming in as protectors of the patient against his relatives, they ended up as critics of how everyone in the family behaved—including the patient. The original view of the patient as victim ("family scapegoat") of a conspiracy to keep him sick yielded gradually to the notion that the family itself was sick.

While Bateson was the undisputed scientific leader of the group, Don Jackson and Jay Haley were the most active in developing family treatment. Jackson wrote many influential papers in which he emphasized above all else the homeostatic qualities of families. The conservative nature of families derives from their need to maintain cohesion and stability in the face of the internal stresses of development as well as the external threats to the family's equilibrium. In healthy families there is a balance between stability (the family must maintain integrity in the face of environmental vagaries) and change (the family must adapt to the developmental needs of its members). Unhealthy families, on the other hand, tend toward a rigid homeostasis. Their interactions may seem odd and they may be unsatisfying, yet they are powerfully self-reinforcing. These families cling tenaciously to their rigid and inflexible structures, preferring the devil they know to the unknown. Change is regarded not as an opportunity for growth, but as a threat and a signal to change back.

In moving away from mentalistic inferences to observations of the way families function as groups, Jackson found that he needed a new language. Many of the terms he used described the arrangements between husbands and wives: *family rules* (and rules about how to negotiate the rules), *quid pro quos*, and the dichotomy between relationships that are *complementary* and those that are *symmetrical*.[5] This distinction had been observed earlier by Gregory Bateson during an anthropological expedition to New Guinea with his then wife, Margaret Mead. *Complementary* relationships are those in which people play different roles that fit together. If one is dominant, the other is submissive; if one is weak, the other is strong; if one is logical, the other is emotional. *Symmetrical* relationships are based on equality and similarity, as between peers, and the resulting interactions are matching, mutual, or competitive. Readers will notice that the traditional marriage based on sex-role stereotypes is complementary, and the new-model, two-paycheck family is (supposed to be) symmetrical.

According to Jay Haley, every message is part of a struggle for control in relationships.[6] Will the relationship be symmetrical or complementary? Each party maneuvers to be the author of that definition. Here is an example from my practice.

———◆———

Donna and Alan were a busy young urban professional couple, whose marriage was mired in constant conflict. Their pattern was a familiar one. She was a compulsive perfectionist who nagged at him to help out more around the house. He was a laid-back noncombatant who resented his wife's constant pressure and responded with sulky agreement to her demands, but then dragged his heels about carrying them out. Watching their conversations was like watching a nun scolding a petulant little boy. The more she scolded, the more petulant he became—and the more petulant he became, the more she scolded. After a few months of therapy, they had broken this cycle and were feeling better. He was volunteering to help out more (and saying an honest "No" to requests he did not agree to), and she was asking less of him and refraining from criticizing the way he did things.

Fine. But I was concerned that the improvement might not last, because the change seemed negative—she was *not* complaining, and he was *not* shirking. So I said, now that they had broken this cycle, perhaps it was time to create some other, more positive changes. I told Alan that I thought he should negotiate to get more of what he wanted for himself, and I said to Donna that she should help him, so that he would be less bitter and resentful. Donna, who understood that she was paying a price for Alan's resentment, complied. "What do you want?" she asked him. "You've always said you wanted more time for yourself; would you like to pick one day a week to do something by yourself?"

Alan talked about maybe playing basketball on Monday nights, but he seemed about as comfortable as a cat tiptoeing around the rim of a bathtub. I asked him if he was reluctant to have this discussion for some reason. Was he guilty about asking for more? He replied by saying that *she* should have some time off, she was the one who worked so hard. This seemed very important to him, so I pointed out to her that she could do something for him by doing something for herself. "It will make him feel better about the relationship."

What's gong on here? Was Alan trying to balance the ledger, so that Donna would feel less resentful and therefore have less to complain about? Perhaps, but he was also trying to reverse the complementarity in the relationship. Changing from her nagging him about housework to her coaxing him to do something for himself was a small change; she'd still be one-up. Alan wanted to alter the pattern of the relationship from complementary to symmetrical—*that* would make him feel better than having (being given) a night out with the boys.

◆

According to Haley, this kind of jockeying for control goes on in every relationship. Normal families work out patterns that more or less suit them. Disturbed families, on the other hand, may generate psychiatric symptoms in a perversion of this struggle for control. One person's symptom controls the relationship, while at the same time obscuring the fact that any control exists. Haley uses the example of a woman who has anxiety attacks when she is left alone. The woman's husband cannot complain that she is controlling his behavior, because *she* is not requiring him to be at home—the anxiety is. Her behavior is involuntary. The nonverbal message of the symptomatic family member is: *It is not I who wants (or does not want) to do this, it is something outside my control—my nerves, my illness, my anxiety, my bad eyes, alcohol, my upbringing, the Communists, or my spouse.*[7]

Haley's ideas about treatment were influenced by his association with Milton Erickson, a brilliant hypnotherapist whose dramatic and unconventional cures made him a cult figure in family therapy. Thus the therapy that emerged from the Palo Alto group was a blend of two very different kinds of influence. Bateson, the anthropologist, showed the way to understanding families with careful, detached observation; Erickson, the alienist, contributed a host of clever interventions designed to reverse destructive patterns in families by provoking change—with or without the family's understanding.

Bateson and Erickson, the anthropologist and the alienist, epitomize two different traditions that have coexisted in family therapy from its inception. One tradition, inspired by the strategic magic of hypnosis, emphasizes pragmatic problem-solving and takes a dim view of insight. The other tradition emphasizes careful study of family patterns, and holds out hope that family members themselves can learn to understand and change these patterns. If Jay Haley has been the most eloquent spokesman for the strategic position, Murray Bowen is the doyen of understanding and self-directed change.

Murray Bowen

At the same time that Gregory Bateson and his colleagues were studying schizophrenic communication, researchers from a clinical rather than communications background were studying the same population. Chief among these was Murray Bowen, one of the towering figures in the history of family therapy.

While at the Menninger Clinic in the 1950s, Bowen was working on the premise that schizophrenia was the result of a symbiotic tie with the mother. His clinical studies, however, led him to the conclusion that schizophrenia was a sign of pathology in the entire family, and he took the momentous step of hospital-izing whole families for study and treatment. This step had enormous political as well as scientific implications. From a scientific point of view, readers will notice that the important breakthroughs in understanding how families work came only after people began observing whole families interacting together. Politically, hospitalizing the entire family is a way of countering our cultural reflex to step in and take over when families have severe problems. When we put one family member in a psychiatric hospital, it is a well-intentioned way of assuming the family's function. Many families, products of a culture of interventionism, are ready, willing, and able to expel their problem members when things get rough. Bowen's philosophy was to support the family in their need, rather than to take over for them.

Bowen's observations of family functioning were the source of inspiration of some of the most thoughtful and influential ideas in family therapy.[8] Here I will summarize three major themes of what is known as "Bowen Theory": the role of the *extended family; triangulation;* and *differentiation of the self.*

The first expression of Bowen's understanding of the role of the extended family in the development of emotional problems was the *three-generational hypothesis* of schizophrenia. According to this theory, the grandparents of the schizophrenic child are relatively normal people, but the mother was overly attached to one of the children, who as a result remains emotionally stunted. This child grows up and marries an equally immature spouse. The issue of this marriage is one child who is so symbiotically tied to the mother that he becomes schizophrenic. Although we now know that family pressures alone do not cause schizophrenia, Bowen's observations have demonstrated how emotional prob-lems are passed down through the generations.

While no one doubts the formative influence of family on shaping our personalities, many people imagine that once they leave home they are grown-up, independent adults, free at last of their parents' influence. Some of us prize our individuality and take it as a sign of growth to separate from our parents, and measure our maturity by how independent we are of family ties. Others wish they could be closer to their parents, but find family visits too painful, and so gradually learn to stay away to protect themselves from continuing disappointment and hurt. (If your nose gets bloodied a few times, you grow less willing to stick it out.) Once out of range of the family's *mishegoss,* most people forget and deny the discord. But as Bowen discovered, the family remains within us. Wherever we go, we carry unresolved emotional reactivity to our parents in the form of a vulnerability to repeat the same old patterns in intense relationships.

If your father nags *and* you can't stand it, you may be forever overreacting to nagging from other people. Likely you will respond in the same adolescent way you responded to your father—with avoidance, flying into a rage, or choking on unexpressed fury.

Bowen's notion of unfinished emotional business with our parents is similar to psychoanalytic object-relations theory, according to which early interactions with parents form lasting mental images through which we filter and distort all future relationships. The crucial difference between Bowen's theory and psychoanalysis is Bowen's conviction that the best way to overcome childish emotional reactions is to resolve them at the source. Since our relations with parents are the source of all other relationships, the best way to make ourselves better able to cope with any relationship, according to Bowen, is to establish mature, one-to-one connections with our parents. We can and should go home again.

To map out patterns in the larger family, Bowen developed the *genogram,* a visual diagram of the family tree going back in time and extending laterally to our spouse's family, graphically illustrating the continuity of family patterns. These diagrams reveal, often with a shock, how certain problems, such as alcoholism or emotional alienation, are spun out through the generations. Once we see the larger picture, the family begins to seem like a huge interconnected web. And like a spider's web, anything that touches one spot will ripple throughout the whole system. The genogram helps to show all this, and serves as a road map for revisiting our emotional past as it lives on in our families.[9]

Returning home to work out better relationships with our families has a double-barreled benefit. Not only do we increase the network of emotional support in our lives, we also increase our understanding of how emotional systems operate and improve our ability to relate to all kinds of people. In the Bowenian scheme, therapeutic visits back home are a kind of *in vivo* psychoanalysis. We will see how this process works in later chapters, especially Chapter 6, "In-Laws."

Another central theme in Bowen's work is the ubiquity of triangles in human relationships. Though we are all familiar with the idea of triangles, few people realize how important—and destructive—they are in our lives. According to Bowen, the triangle is the smallest stable unit of relationship. This seems to contradict our usual understanding of relationships as between two parties.

Think of the most important current relationship in your life. Got it?

You may have thought of your spouse, or boyfriend or girlfriend, or perhaps even a professional colleague. When this relationship was forming, it was just between the two of you. But relationships between two persons are unstable; when tension develops in the relationship, you begin by doing your best to resolve it, but before long one of you will triangle in a third party. When things get sticky with your boss, for example, you start to complain to someone else. This seems harmless enough, but although this innocent triangulation allows you to blow off steam, it tends to freeze the relationship problems in place. The classic instance of triangulation occurs, as we shall see in the Simpson family, when conflict between a husband and wife is defused— though not resolved—by focusing on the children.

Important as is the idea of triangles, the cornerstone of Bowen's theory is the concept of *differentiation*. According to Bowen, human nature contains two sets of opposing forces: those that bind personalities together and those that fight to break free toward individuality. He called these predilections *fusion* and *differentiation*. Fusion is a form of emotional stuck-togetherness, similar to Lyman Wynne's concept of *pseudomutuality* and, as we shall see later on, Minuchin's concept of *enmeshment*. But what makes fusion even more interesting is that it is both an intrapsychic and interpersonal concept—it exists both in the inner space of the personality and the outer space between persons. Within the mind, fusion refers to a blurring between thinking and feeling. Fused, or *undifferentiated*, people hardly distinguish thoughts from feelings; their intellects are so flooded by feeling that they confuse objective thinking with emotional reaction.

Lack of differentiation between thinking and feeling occurs in context with lack of differentiation between oneself and others. Because they are less able to think clearly, undifferentiated people have little autonomous identity. They react emotionally to the dictates of family members, arguing or agreeing by ingrained instinct rather than thoughtful reflection. Asked what they think, they say what they feel; asked what they believe, they repeat what they've heard. They either conform or pretend not to, as though doing the opposite of what's expected were a true sign of independence.

Differentiated people, on the other hand, are able to take definite stands on issues because they are able to think things through, decide what they believe, and act on those beliefs. This enables them to be in intimate contact with other people without losing their sense of self—who they are and what they believe. Differentiation should not be confused with *emotional cutoff*, the reactive flight that sometimes masquerades as independence. Emotional cutoff is only a disguised form of lack of true differentiation.

One further point about differentiation and fusion is that we should not fall into the either/or habit that characterizes so much thinking about human nature. These polar forces are part of all people and all relationships. We shift back and forth from differentiation to fusion whenever we become sufficiently anxious. As there is no need for despair, there is no room for complacency. We are all vulnerable to fusion in ourselves and in our families. *And*, as you will see, we are all capable of breaking free.

Salvador Minuchin

In the early days of family therapy, the movement was dominated by a few charismatic personalities, among them Nathan Ackerman, Virginia Satir, and Carl Whitaker. These dazzling clinical performers (there's no other word for it) were also gifted teachers who inspired thousands of therapists lucky enough to see them at work. Their impact on the field has been less lasting because they were not systematizers; they left behind no body of theory nor any large group of disciples. One notable exception, however, is Salvador Minuchin, a therapeutic wizard whose dramatic and compelling therapy sessions set a standard against which other family therapists judge their best work.

Born and raised in Argentina, Salvador Minuchin began his career as a family therapist in the early 1960s when he suggested to his colleagues at the Wiltwyck School for delinquent boys that they begin treating the boys together with their families.[10] Minu-

chin and his associates, including Braulio Montalvo, E.H. Auerswald, Bernice Rosman, and Richard Rabkin, discovered two
patterns common to troubled families. Some families are *enmeshed*,
chaotic and tightly interconnected, while others are *disengaged*,
isolated and seemingly unrelated. Both types lack clear lines of
authority. Enmeshed parents are too overly involved with their
children to maintain a position of leadership and exercise control,
while disengaged parents are too distant from their children (and
each other) to provide effective support and guidance.

Minuchin's work at Wiltwyck was so successful that in 1965 he
was invited to become director of the Philadelphia Child Guidance
Clinic. The Clinic, located in the heart of Philadelphia's black
ghetto, then consisted of less than a dozen staff members. From
this modest beginning Minuchin created one of the largest and
most prestigious child guidance clinics in the world. During much
of the 1970s, the Philadelphia Child Guidance Clinic was the
Mecca of family therapy. This preeminence was due in part to
Minuchin's renown as an incomparable therapist, in part to the
excellence of a training program that attracted clinicians from all
over the world, and in part to the elegant simplicity of structural
family theory.

A functional family structure requires clearly marked boundaries. The boundary separating the parents from the children
should be strong enough to maintain the parents' position of
authority, but not so rigid as to limit the children's access to
parental guidance and support. Therapy, in this "structural
model," is adjusted to fit the needs of a particular family.
Enmeshed families are encouraged to develop an effective hierarchy, in which the parents are in charge, and both parents and
children are helped to become more independent and autonomous. In disengaged families, the goal is to break down isolation
by increasing interaction and helping family members become
more involved in positive ways.

In the hands of a trained professional, structural family therapy
is an enormously powerful tool.[11] The most effective way to
change symptoms is to change the family patterns that maintain
them, and therefore therapy is directed at helping the family
modify their functioning so that family members can solve their
own problems. Changing the family is a two-step operation. First,
the therapist joins with the family in order to help them discover

what is problematic in their structure. Then, by readjusting boundaries and patterns of interaction, the therapist changes the behavior and experience of each of the family members.

———————◆———————

The diversity of family therapy's origins was perpetuated in a proliferation of rival approaches.[12] In the 1950s, family therapists were bold pioneers, busy opening up new territory and staking their claims against unfriendly elements in the mental health establishment. While they were struggling for legitimacy, family clinicians tended to emphasize their common beliefs and down-play their differences. Troubles, they agreed, come in families. Moreover, families are not simply groups of individuals; they are complex social units organized to maintain the balance and equilibrium of the collective entity—even, in some unhappy cases, at the expense of the individual. The founding parents of family therapy were not interested in personalities, in what goes on inside people; they were interested in what happens *between* people, the way families are organized and the way their members communicate.

But even then there were great differences, which became clearer as one moved from ideas about how families work to methods for treating them when things go wrong. This raises an important point. Although it is easy to think of family therapy as just another of many techniques for treating psychiatric symp-toms, it is more than that. Family therapy is a radically different way of viewing human relationships. The family is more than a collection of separate individuals; it is a system, an organic whole whose parts function in a way that transcends their separate characteristics.

In retrospect, progress often seems logical, even inevitable. Today, when people hear about the discovery that families act like units, governed by a single purpose, the response is often, "What took them so long?" The answer is that therapists—like the rest of us—are trapped in an individualistic perspective. The idea that we are part of a system larger than ourselves challenges the view that an individual's life is a personally authored story. For this reason it is difficult to grasp and even more difficult to accept.

Individual therapists have always had a compelling logic for treating patients one by one. At least since Freud, psychotherapists have recognized the profound influence of the family on an individual's emotional problems. Even the best of parents may pass on their own harsh superegos, with the result being children who grow up a little bit neurotic—afraid of their own natural drive for pleasure and afraid of their own anger. A loving, involved mother may be too involved, smothering her children with love, choking off their autonomy and initiative, and leaving them ill-equipped to set off into the wide world. A concerned father, who only wants the best for his children, may drive them too hard, pushing them to excel in school and at sports, making a contest out of life itself—especially where he himself sought success but did not quite make it.

Considering all the possible unhealthy influences that our families can have on our lives, what could be more natural than to separate the patient from the family in order to conduct treatment within the safe confines of a private therapeutic relationship? Freud, convinced that neurotic conflicts were spawned in early interactions between children and their parents, sought to isolate the family from treatment, as though the family were an infectious agent to be kept out of the psychoanalytic operating room.

It is tempting to describe this deliberate exclusion of relatives as naïve and wrongheaded—part of a fossilized view of emotional disorder, namely that problems are hardened remains of the past, firmly embedded inside the patient's head. Actually, this view is not entirely wrong. Our personalities are shaped by earliest experience. But this is only half the story. Both the memory of past experience and the current reality of family relationships affect our lives. There are, however, two very practical reasons for starting with the outer part of the equation, the contemporary family context.

For one thing, the present-day family has an immediate impact and a continuing influence. Unlike the family of the past, they can be included in therapy. Thus, the existing family offers more leverage for change than the remembered one. Another reason why family therapy is often so immediately effective is that the dynamics of family relationships are less familiar to most people than are their own personalities. Therefore, by learning about how families work, we can most readily expand our ability to resolve our own dilemmas. The older we get, the fewer the startling insights about our personalities. Oh, a man may discover in midlife that his pursuit of career success is a means of compensating for insecurity, or a woman may realize that she's afraid to get angry lest no one love her, but for the most part we know ourselves pretty well. The same cannot be said, however, about family relationships. There are, as we shall see, a number of essential facts about the ways families function and influence our lives that most people are unaware of.

Family therapy may sound like a good idea, but many parents are averse to being treated as part of their child's problem. This resistance stems in part from thinking that interdependence implies responsibility implies fault. Sharon's question "Why *can't* Jason behave?" attributes the problem to the boy. In a society that deals with lack of energy by taking vitamin pills, parents are tempted to find mechanical solutions for human problems. "Sick" in the medical model may be an advance from "bad," but it still locates the problem inside the individual—where there may be least leverage for change.

3

THE MAKING
OF A
FAMILY
THERAPIST

W_{hen}
I first started seeing families I was fascinated. Here, right in front of me, were played out all the passions and conflicts I had only heard about secondhand when I treated people individually. Some things became very clear very fast.

———◆———

One of the first patients I saw in my early training was Luke Clagett, a five-year-old boy brought to the child psychiatry clinic after he set a fire in the closet of the apartment where he lived with his mother and sister. The note I received from the intake interviewer said little other than this, except that his mother said, "He acts kinda strange and don't play much with other kids."

Fire-setting, along with running away and cruelty to animals, is considered an ominous symptom in a small child, so I wondered if this little boy might be psychotic. I saw him, as was the custom then, individually, in a room equipped with toys designed to let him express his feelings in play. Naturally, his mother was excluded from these sessions, lest her presence inhibit him.

For three weeks Luke played quietly while I watched and made encouraging comments. The only thing remarkable about his play was that he was rather listless. He liked to play with stuffed animals and look at pictures in old copies of *The Ladies' Home Journal*. Unlike other boys his age, he never reached for the dart gun or water pistol, and although he was interested in the large, stuffed Bozo doll, he never punched it or wrestled with it. Luke was quiet but he didn't seem particularly strange, certainly not psychotic.

When I decided to invite his family in, it was more out of confusion than conviction. What I saw cleared up the confusion. Mrs. Clagett, Darlene, was twenty going on fifteen. She was pretty—a strawberry blond with a nice figure—but *so* young. Dressed in a striped tank top and a short skirt, she looked more like a teenager ready for a date than like a mother coming to the doctor's office. She seemed totally out of her element as a parent. Tanya, the little three-year-old, was a handful. No quiet toys for her! She ran around the room, grabbing one toy then another. She banged, yelled, threw things, and generally did a pretty good imitation of a roomful of kindergartners when the teacher steps out. (The teacher was out.) I waited for Mrs. Clagett to quiet her daughter down. I had a long wait.

Luke seemed utterly lost; instead of becoming more adventurous with his mother present, he seemed even more shy. He sat next to her, hanging on to her arm, and once or twice he tried to climb up onto her lap. His mother ignored him. She also ignored Tanya, as though Tanya's wild behavior were nothing out of the ordinary. All she wanted to talk about was her boyfriend, Norbert, and all the troubles they were having. Things started to fall into place. Luke, the little fire-setter, was not a seriously disturbed youngster; he was a lonely little boy, poorly supervised and starved for attention. Nor was his mother some kind of cruel or neurotic parent. She was a not-quite-grown-up young woman, too preoccupied with her own problems to pay much attention to her children. It only took a minute to see.

Although I had no special knowledge of family dynamics, I did have enough common sense to realize that the number-one priority in Darlene Clagett's life was working things out with her boyfriend. Once she did that, and had some security and a little love in her life, she was able to turn her attention to her children. That and a little counseling from me was really all it took to make a big improvement in Luke—in all of them.

I was elated. A whole new world of possibilities opened up. Instead of seeing separate individuals acting and reacting to each other, I began to see consistent patterns that tied families together. Misbehaving children, for example, usually turned out to have a couple of parents pulling in different directions. After I saw that a few times, of course it made sense. How is some six- or five- or eight-year-old going to get away with leaving dirty dishes around the house, biting her baby brother, or sassing her parents unless they let her? But why? Parents aren't stupid. The problem usually turned out to be that they undercut each other's authority, either because one was strict and the other lenient, or because they were angry and fought through the children. I was amazed at how many times a parent would complain about something in a child that was similar to what the other parent did.

Gradually I became more attuned to the fact that what my patients presented as one person's problem often turned out to involve other members of the family. Moreover, this interconnectedness was not usually apparent until I brought in the entire family for a consultation. "Johnny is misbehaving" usually meant that the parents weren't pulling together; "I'm depressed" often meant that a woman was emotionally abandoned by her husband; and "Pam is lying and stealing" often meant that Pam wasn't getting enough attention from busy parents.

Still, something was missing. I could see certain patterns and I began to see the family acting as a group, but nothing that I had learned prepared me to understand the family's underlying organization. Many of the concepts that we studied in graduate school were *dyadic*,—that is, they referred to something going on between only two people. As I was to learn later, what goes on between two people is partly a function of what goes on between them and a third (a woman who is overinvolved with her mother cannot be fully engaged with her husband) or other activities (a workaholic husband will not be close to his wife, while a man who is merely putting in time at a boring job may require more togetherness than his busy wife can tolerate). I was learning about discreet processes—marital schism and skew, conflict-avoidance, scapegoating—rather than how to understand a family's overall organization.

I learned all the lingo—pseudomutuality, splits and alignments, identified patient, and so on. But even though I got A's on my exams, I was just doing C work with my patient families. About a third of the people who come to a therapist are in a crisis that will soon resolve itself unless the therapist does something really stupid (like prescribe antidepressant medication for someone who is mourning a loss). Another third will get better in family therapy merely through the process of talking things over with the whole family. That leaves one more third, those people whose complaints are due to ingrained problems in the family. These problems will not pass away of their own accord or clear up quickly just by talking things out. These problems require some basic changes in the way a family is structured—changes that the average person does not understand how to bring about, and that I, as a young family therapist, didn't have a clue about. That is, not until I studied with some of the great masters of family therapy (including Salvador Minuchin, Jay Haley, and Murray Bowen)—not just masters of technique, but masters of making the whole business fall into place.

BEHIND THE ONE-WAY MIRROR

After completing my Ph.D. studies, and three years of practical training, I took a job as an assistant professor in a university to pass on my wisdom to the next generation of students. I was a certified expert in psychotherapy and family therapy. My diploma declared it and my license confirmed it. For a while, I even believed it.

I knew enough to keep most of my students awake in class most of the time, and I continued my two-out-of-three success rate with patients. It wasn't long, however, before that other third really started to bother me. It wasn't just that I couldn't cure everyone, but that I was keenly aware I simply did not comprehend, much less know how to reorganize, the basic structure of families. I began to seek out as much advanced training from as many experts as my time and budget allowed. I read everything I could get my hands on, I attended as many workshops as I could find, and I spent extended periods of time at several of the leading family therapy training centers. One of the products of all this study was my comprehensive textbook, *Family Therapy: Concepts and Methods.*[1] But much more important to me was learning to understand how families work, why they get stuck, and how to help them get unstuck.

In the course of all this advanced study, I encountered many vehicles for learning—books, lectures, co-therapy with experts, videotapes, seminars, et cetera and so on— but nothing had as powerful an impact on my understanding as observing and being observed behind the one-way mirror.

What the telescope is to astronomy, the one-way mirror is to family therapy. It is a tool that opens up whole new realms of observation and understanding. When a patient is interviewed alone in a consulting room, it's natural to conceive of him or her as the locus of problems. But when patients are observed interacting with their families, it is impossible to see only one person as the problem. Bringing symptomatic families together for observation was the beginning of family therapy. Equally important was the innovation of the one-way mirror, which enhanced observation and therapy alike. From their vantage behind the glass, researchers and clinicians have been able to study the processes of family interaction, and help the therapist in the room organize observations and plan interventions.

Sitting quietly in a darkened observation room watching a family session unfold in the next room enables observers to do more than eavesdrop on what is happening. It is a unique vantage point that permits them to see patterns emerging. What makes it so unique is that it is not once, but twice removed from the subjective distortions of family members. Family members, whether at home or in a therapy session, are usually too busy framing their own responses to hear—really hear—each other's complaints and entreaties. Much less are they able to see the interlocking pattern of their communications. The family therapist is in a better position not only to hear what family members are saying, but also to see how their behavior follows recurring sequences. Yet even the therapist in the consulting room is subject to a disadvantage, a disadvantage that is hard to describe: he or she is flooded by swirling undercurrents of emotion that stir up anxiety and blur the focus on underlying patterns of interaction.

Families come to therapy full of anxiety, full of pain. It isn't easy to apply for psychiatric treatment. Therapy is expensive, time-consuming, trying, and—like it or not—still stigmatized. By the time they ask for help, many people have given up on themselves and are ready for an expert to take over. Even the most resolute self-reliance gives way in prolonged periods of personal stress. Families worn out by their problems, and discouraged by their inability to solve them, turn to experts, full of hope not only for solutions, but also for someone to lean on—an all-powerful authority, someone to borrow strength from. Facing the complex and shifting demands of troubled families clamoring for help, therapists feel a tremendous pressure. A family's unhappy frustration invites therapists to move in where they do not belong, into the client family, and forget their place, which is outside.

Experienced therapists learn to resist this pressure to intrude, learn to understand that the impulse to take over—to soothe a frightened child, for example—is a response to a missing function in the family. If a child needs soothing, why aren't the parents providing it? But this is easier to preach than to practice. That's one reason the one-way mirror is such an advantage. The same mirror that lets sight and sound pass through, screens out much of the emotional pressure in the consulting room. Sitting behind the radiant shield, out of range of the heat of passion, it is much easier to observe patterns of interaction.

———◆———

Trying to discern the underlying rhythms of a family while interviewing them in the consulting room is like trying to catch the drift of a new dance while one is caught up in the noise and excitement of a crowded nightclub. Remember the session with the Simpson family described in the first chapter? Once they dropped their polite formality, they started arguing and interrupting whenever a hot subject came up. I'd ask Mr. Simpson a question; he'd say something, innocently undercutting his wife; she'd feel the unspoken hostility and snap at him; he'd shut up and sulk; and then Jason would say something provocative. When things heated up, the session got pretty chaotic. That the chaos in a family is patterned chaos is something that takes a little practice to see. Reading my description, which was not innocent of organization, is analogous to sitting behind the mirror. The reader, like the observing student or supervisor, less distracted by the passions and personalities in the room, can observe in relative tranquility the steps of the family dance.

When I first met the Simpsons in the waiting room, I saw no family, only four people. Even after years of studying family patterns, even though my intention was to figure out how they interacted, I still responded automatically to them as individuals. I was struck by the two faces of Mr. Simpson—the self-confident professional and the self-effacing husband. I had a little trouble seeing past Mrs. Simpson's shrill anger to the hurt and disappointment underneath. I thought Jason's adolescent bravado was less well-practiced than many I've seen. And I wondered about Heather. Was she merely quiet and shy, or was she lonely and depressed? It takes deliberate effort to get past this preoccupation with persons.

The human personality is so compelling, so endlessly fascinating, that we automatically respond to people as unconnected individuals. We are repelled by one, drawn to another. And we know so much about people. We know that parents should be firm but talk nice to their children. When we see a woman shrieking at her kids, we know she is wrong and should be taught to be firm but calm. In fact, there is so much that we already "know" that it's hard to see something new. Behind the mirror we are less burdened by common sense.

The great French neurologist Jean Martin Charcot once advised Freud to look at things again and again, until they themselves begin to speak. In the messy world of reality there is often too much going on to hear. If we can observe from behind the one-way mirror—or in some other way removed from the pressures of interaction and response—things do begin to speak for themselves. With a little emotional distance, we can observe family life and concentrate not on personalities and facts, but on patterns: who says what to whom, and how; and then what? If we are freed of the necessity to respond and if we direct our attention to the recurring sequences in the family's muddled whirl, we can simplify and abstract the confusing welter of data. We can discover a patterned dance, where family members, the dancers, see only private struggles and occasional collisions.

Sitting behind the mirror week after week, session after session, and case after case, therapists began to see the same patterns repeated over and over again. The muddles of life are endlessly diverse, but the number of basic stories of family life are relatively few. Let me illustrate.

———◆———

I was recently asked to consult with a therapist who was treating "an extremely complex situation." The family consisted of two deaf-and-dumb parents and two girls, a thirteen-year-old deaf child, also mute, and an eleven-year-old hearing child who could speak. The parents wanted the therapist to explain to the girls the importance of obeying parental instructions and the need for the young women to learn to take on more responsibility for household chores. The reason the parents felt they needed professional help was that their deafness made it difficult for them to explain all this adequately to the children. What made the sessions so confusing were all the complications introduced by the various combinations of deafness and hearing. The therapist could speak directly to the younger daughter but had to address the parents and older daughter through an interpreter. So, in order to ask the older daughter to explain her feelings to her parents it was necessary to ask the interpreter to translate the request to the daughter and then wait for the explanation and the answer to be translated. But when all is said and done, the story of this family was simple. This was a family in which the parents did not claim and exert their authority over two spirited and precocious daughters on the verge of adolescence. Sitting in the room, having to cope with all the complications, this was much harder for the therapist to see than it was for the consultant sitting safely behind the one-way mirror.

———◆———

Having firmly established its utility, the one-way mirror has become so popular that many family therapists who don't have one feel handicapped. So, where does all this leave the average reader? This emphasis on technology may unfortunately reinforce the idea that family therapy is a highly technical enterprise. It can be, and in the hands of professionals it often is. But it needn't be.

The essential benefit of psychological therapy is that it adds something new—novel advice, perhaps, or a new way of looking at things. The fresh perspective that family therapy offers is that our live are coordinated within our families such that what "they" do is a function of what we do. It is an enormous insight, and one that puts us in charge of our own lives. The woman who complains that her husband never spends any time with her and the children can stop complaining and start analyzing the pattern that maintains this state of affairs. She may discover that as long as she tries to coax her husband to join her in children's activities, he says no. She could reverse this pattern by asking him to invite them to do something he likes. This particular solution may or may not work. The point is that it attempts to alter the usual problem-maintaining sequence.

The essence of family therapy is to discover the pattern surrounding a problem and change it. For people interested in solving problems in their own families, this means more than simply "trying something different." It means discovering how the system is going and reversing it—or, to put it more accurately, expanding the available pathways of family functioning. For example, parents who try various ways to solve problems for their difficult adolescents may be doing so at the expense of their own relationship *and* at the expense of the adolescents' learning to solve problems for themselves.

To "get it" in family therapy is to realize that while we are inescapably bound together, we are ultimately free—free to get what we want and need out of family life. Unfortunately, this is not likely to happen as long as we remain ignorant of family dynamics or assume they are so complex that only an expert can modify them.

THE PROVINCE OF EXPERTS

Our lives are built around so many complex instruments and agencies that we cannot hope to understand them all. Besides, so much of our own energy is spent in trying to get by or get ahead that we have little left over to attend to our own households. Who has time to learn how to fix a toaster or master the new tax laws? When the toaster breaks, we buy a new one or consult an electrician; and even those who cannot afford the services of an accountant now take their taxes to H & R Block.

The same specialization that fractionates our material world also affects things more human. Life in the 1980s has grown so complex that we now have specialists in every aspect of health and well-being. No matter what ails us, somewhere there is a specialist to turn to. Nowhere is this more true than with problems in living.

Troubled and uncertain, struggling family members redouble their dependence on experts, fastening on them longings for peace of mind. As our faith in the family gets weaker, our trust in technology gets stronger. In this climate of specialization, when we suffer from personal problems we turn to psychiatric (and pop psychology) experts for explanations and solutions. What makes psychological explanations so attractive is that they tend to absolve the individual of responsibility. To say that people cannot face painful feelings or that they neglect their families because of fragile egos is to imply that they cannot help it. If we cannot help what we are, it seems to follow that we cannot change. By extension this logic leads to a vastly inflated estimation of the need for experts to solve our problems.

Unfortunately, family therapists have contributed more than their share to this overestimation of the need for expert intervention. Their doing so is a by-product of an emphasis on the homeostatic and nonrational features of family life.

Communications theorists describe families as rule-governed, cybernetic systems with a tendency toward stability, or homeostasis. If a member of the family deviates from the family's rules, this triggers negative feedback; the family reacts to force that person to change back. Thus families, like other living systems, maintain their interactions within a relatively fixed range in order to remain stable in the face of normal environmental stresses. In the early days of family therapy, practitioners were struck not only by the fact that families tenaciously resist change, but also that they do so like mechanical systems: Their homeostasis is not deliberate or thought-out; it is instinctive.

This metaphor of the mechanical system, which captured so many aspects of the ways families function, unfortunately implied that the family was a machine—a "rule-governed, cybernetic system"—with no heart and no mind. One of the implications of this model is that if the family is a mechanical unit, the therapist must be a mechanic. That is, if family members act blindly to preserve a status quo that may have outlived its usefulness, it is up to the therapist to recalibrate the system—indeed "tune-up" is one of the favored metaphors among the family therapists. Not all family therapists, of course, adhere to this mechanical model, but many (especially adherents of "the strategic school") deny that insight or understanding is necessary or even useful to change family systems. The majority of family therapy techniques are not designed to get people to gain insight into what motivates their behavior, but simply to get them to change it.

Are family therapists a callous lot that they treat the family as a machine with no heart and no mind? No, of course not. But in the practice of a profession notorious for its burnout rate, there has always been an overemphasis on the power of technique and an underemphasis on the power of the family. The counterpart of the sage and powerful therapist is the blind and powerless family. Indeed, individuals often do seem powerless to control what happens in their families. Family life, conceived in romance and born of the urge to procreate, often becomes a school of suffering. We learn to live with heartache and disappointment because we do not learn to see the latent but untested possibilities in our families. We narrow down the world to make our way in it, but over the years we get stuck, bogged down in a limited range of behavior that takes us so far and no farther.

Family therapy seeks to mitigate our suffering by unfreezing automatic patterns of interaction and expanding the family's range of action. "Automatic patterns of interaction" are not involuntary—mindless perhaps, but mindless in the sense of unstudied and compulsive habit rather than in the sense of a machine that has no mind.

One way to stop reacting automatically is to do simply that: pause; check impulsive, reflexive responses; learn to see options; avoid unthinking reactivity; and understand how families work. Families become mature and flexible the same way individuals do, by deliberating between impulse and action, substituting thought for thoughtlessness. To say that the family is a system means that human nature is a product of interaction; behavior is constructed in the reciprocal give-and-take of interdependent social beings. Our lives are bound together such that what we do is, to a large extent, a product of what others in our families do. But—get this— what *they* do is to an equally large extent a product of what *we* do. One person can make a difference. *One person can change the system*. But first it is necessary to learn how the system works.

———◆———

How do we learn to see the self-defeating patterns in our own family lives? Some lessons can be drawn from the one-way mirror. One lesson is that we see better that which we are not actively participating in. To begin with, it may be easier to discover self-defeating patterns of interaction between your spouse and the children. Remember to concentrate more on process than content—blur your attention to the specifics in favor of concentrating on who says what to whom, and how.

Suppose your wife complains about how hard it is to get your kindergartner off to school in the morning. Both you and she have some idea of what the problem is and what form the solution should take, but remember the lesson of the mirror: Try to remove the filter of biased consciousness; focus on what you *see*, not what you know or assume. Here's what you might see. At 6:30, she wakes him up and says blah-blah. Then she goes downstairs and cooks breakfast. Half an hour later, she goes up again and says blah-blah, blah-blah. Both of them get upset. He comes downstairs, half dressed, and eats his breakfast. She says blah-blah and goes upstairs to fetch his shoes and socks. Then she says blah-blah-blah while she finishes dressing him. Finally, with more upset, she gets him to the corner and onto the school bus. Once a week, there's more blah-blah and more upset, and he misses the bus. On these occasions, she drives him to school.

Not only have I picked a simple (though, believe me, common) example, I have also described it in such a way as to make the process obvious: The mother takes too much responsibility for the child; she says blah-blah, instead of making him do what she expects. Above all, the example is inadequate because it includes only one segment of the family. "But, but . . . " a husband may be thinking, "it has nothing to do with me; it's my wife's problem." Wrong. The family is a system, one whole entity. Even when you are not actively participating, you are involved. In the example above, a complete description of how the system works is: The mother nags the boy to get ready, and when he dawdles she nags more, and if he misses the bus she drives him to school, *and* her husband looks on critically.

This description, simple as it is, is a description of how the system works. (The best way to see how the system works is to keep it simple. Don't leave anyone out, but keep it simple.) The most effective way to introduce change is to alter the basic pattern. Create a new pattern, not by tinkering with the old one—the wife nagging harder, or the husband telling her that she's doing it all wrong—but by trying something novel, something discontinuous with the old pattern. What can you come up with? Almost any change in the basic pattern will work. The real secret is not finding specific solutions for individual problems, but discovering the direction the system is going in, and then changing it.

————◆————

Once we discover self-defeating patterns of interaction in our families, we still have to change them. Self-help books often suggest that change is easy. Why not? This satisfies the human urge to discover simple solutions to hard problems—and it sells books. But let's face it, even where the need for change is self-evident, we often seem unable to manage it. Why else do we find it so maddeningly difficult to stick to healthy diets and exercise regularly?

In the remainder of this book you will discover a variety of concepts for understanding how family systems work. Some of them may be so strikingly applicable to your own situation that things will suddenly fall into place and change will occur almost easily. Almost. You will have to overcome two stumbling blocks. The first is the temptation to wait for, hope for, or cajole other family members into changing. Don't. They won't change. They are who they are. Get used to that.

But—this will sound like a contradiction—*you* can change them. Two people occupy a certain space in a relationship; if one of them changes, the relationship changes. Period. The other person may resist changing temporarily, or put pressure on you to change back, but if you stand fast, the change will stick.

Once you take personal responsibility for changing your own role in relationship patterns, you may have to break some old habits. Admittedly, it is never easy to break longstanding habits. It takes work, but the rewards are enormous. From personal experience and from treating hundreds of unhappy families, I know that to change relationship patterns you must go through certain stages. First you have to discover the pattern. See how all the members of your family play a part, but concentrate on your own role. Second comes the initial attempt to change. Then comes the pressure of others who naturally resist most changes. Then comes the hard part: holding firm to your resolve. Habits are comfortable. Even destructive habits usually induce no obvious or immediate pain. Changing habits requires thought, deliberate action, and often temporary discomfort. But once they are adopted, you can feel just as comfortable with new habits as with old ones.

Many people approach change with uncertainty about their ability to succeed. Look around you. You will see countless people falling short of their goals because they attack them without confidence or determination. Let me tell you a quick story. A friend of mine was an expert in behavior therapy. He was conversant with all the latest technologies for changing behavior—reinforcement, behavior-charting, contingency-contracting, and so on. A few years ago, he moved out of town and several months went by when we didn't see each other. When I finally saw him again, he had lost thirty pounds. He looked great. Naturally, I was curious to know what scientific methods he had used to lose the weight. When I asked him, he said he simply made up his mind. "Goddammit, I was tired of being fat!" Just like that? Yes.

If in the following pages you discover patterns of family interaction that apply to your situation, my advice is this: Get very clear about what you want to change. Don't fool yourself. Half-assed resolutions are worse than no resolutions at all. Wanting to change and planning to change won't accomplish anything. Only changing will. I will try to help by making some things about family life clear, but only you can put what you learn into practice. Now, before going on, let me summarize the basic lesson of family therapy.

There are two leaps forward in understanding that family therapy makes possible. The first is that our lives are interconnected and that everything we do is affected by family relationships. In practice, this insight yields a number of concepts describing interactions between pairs of individuals—dominant-submissive, pursuer-distancer, and overfunctioning-underfunctioning. Many of these polarizing patterns of control are extremely useful, and I will explain and demonstrate how they work in subsequent chapters. These concepts enable us to get past thinking of ourselves in isolation, and give us the power to transform difficult relationships we once felt victimized by.

But there is another, even more important, leap of understanding—that of seeing the whole family as a structured group, a whole within which these separate processes of interaction are organized. Perhaps a brief example may help to make this important point.

A mother who is concerned about her daughter not having enough friends tries everything she can think of to encourage the daughter to socialize. She criticizes the girl for reading by herself when other children are around; she urges the daughter to invite friends over after school; and she takes the girl to swimming and tennis lessons, in the hope she will meet other children. The mother tries everything, but her everything is only one thing. All these well-intentioned efforts occur within a pattern. The *process* is that the mother tries to use her relationship with her daughter to help the girl develop relationships with other children. Up to a point this may help. But when the mother repeatedly criticizes and coaxes, it becomes counterproductive. The mother is inadvertently perpetuating an overdeveloped mother-daughter relationship. It doesn't matter what she *says* ("Go play with other children"). What she *does* is spend too much time—and too much criticism—on a relationship inside the family, smothering the daughter with her worry and robbing her of the freedom of movement to make friends on her own terms and in her own time. The mother is overinvolved.

But why? Most people look for the answer to this kind of question in habit (that's what mothers do), character (this mother is overprotective), or child-rearing philosophy (she believes that parents should do everything they can for their children). A family therapist looks for the answer in patterns of relationship—not reasons or philosophies, or motives, or shoulds or shouldn'ts, just actions. A woman who is overinvolved with her daughter is probably underinvolved with her husband. Whose fault is that? *It doesn't matter.* What matters is seeing that the daughter's shyness is now—paradoxically—perpetuated by the mother's "helpfulness," which in turn is a product of her distance from her husband. The whole family is involved in the problem. Always? Always.

———◆———

Before going on, I'd like to clear up some possible confusion about the basic concepts of family therapy. For one thing, I've said several times that the family is a "system"; does that really mean anything other than that family members are intimately involved with one another?

Yes, it does. A system is more than the sum of its parts; it is the parts *plus* the lawful (ordered) ways they function together. Because everything that anyone in a family does affects the whole system, almost any change will affect all members of the family and the way they function together.

Another question that some people ask is, "With all of your emphasis on current family interactions are you saying that the past doesn't matter?"

Not at all. Both the past (all the lessons of childhood) and the present (what's going on in the family now) have profound effects on our behavior. I'm just saying that it's easier to change what's happening in the present than to reorganize the influence of the past.

When I say that psychology—the point of view of the individual—and systems thinking are both valid, some people wonder if I really mean that the family systems point of view is better. The answer is, no, not necessarily. Behavior can be thought of as a personal and a family product. In both the person and the family there are hidden forces at work. Understanding more in either dimension—inner or outer space—can help us get on with our lives more effectively. The reason that learning about family patterns is so useful is that most of us know more about ourselves than we do about our role in systematic patterns in our families. Moreover, asking what's wrong with the person is less productive than asking what's going on in the system, because personalities are harder to change than interactions.

Many people wonder, When is the right time to seek professional advice? When you have exhausted your own coping strategies. Some people seek professional help at the drop of a hat, others hold off until things have gotten out of hand. My advice is to consult a mental health professional when a family member has a pronounced problem that does not seem to respond to the person's or the family's attempts to resolve it. Your own attempts should include: facing problems squarely, talking over your concerns and complaints with other members of the family, taking a look at your own role in the family process, and confiding in one or two good friends.

Once you decide that you need a professional, how do you find the right therapist? Talk to two or three people in a position to give you a good recommendation, people who have had a successful course of therapy or faculty members of a local department of psychiatry or psychology. Look for therapists who are recommended by more than one source. Then arrange for a consultation. See what you think. Don't expect therapy to be fun or easy, or the therapist to be your friend. But if you really dislike the therapist, or if after a couple of sessions you have no confidence in that person, go elsewhere.

Once they realize they have the option of choosing diametrically different types of therapy, people wonder when a family therapist would be more appropriate than an individual therapist. The truth is that there is plenty of overlap. Individual therapy works best when a person's life is stable, nothing in the family or environment has changed in quite some time, and the distress seems to be clearly in the self. If you (or someone else in the family) are aware of certain troubling personal reactions but can't seem to change them, then perhaps an individual therapist can help.

The clearest indications for family therapy are those problems that concern children or a couple's relationship. If you are unhappy about someone else in the family, definitely consider family therapy—a professional secret is that the person who is most unhappy is the one with the most leverage to change the family. I wish I could suggest talking over with a professional the decision of what kind of therapy to choose. Unfortunately, most are partisan.

Many readers are skeptical about being able to discover the family dynamics in their own families. First I say that our behavior is patterned in ways we do not suspect; then I say we can discover these patterns. It's just a little hard to accept both points.

Let me try another way of putting it. All human behavior is subject to habituation. Any action that is repeated frequently becomes cast into a pattern, which can then be reproduced with an economy of effort and eventually becomes the taken-for-granted way of things. "Here we go again" becomes "This is how things are done." This predictability ensures stability and security, *but* may persist when the pattern is no longer functional.

We can discover family patterns best when we most need to, at points of transition.

The family is a social unit that faces a series of developmental tasks. Each new stage of development requires a shift in the family's organization. One of the keys to successful living is recognizing the need to reorganize and having the flexibility to do so. Flexibility enables a family to adapt to changing circumstances. In the following chapters I will describe some of the tasks involved in normal family development, and we will see how the relative successes and failures of the Simpsons led them to the point where we met them—in a therapist's office.

4

LOVE'S YOUNG DREAM

*I*n love's young dream, everything is possible. Real marriages, un-happily, often turn out to be quite painful. For many people marriage turns out to be a tragedy of lost illusions. No wonder, when you consider the combined effect of naïve expectations, passivity, and unforeseen social and economic pressures that can unravel even the best accommodations. There is a way out of this predicament, but it does not begin with denial or avoidance.

◆

Sharon and Stewart didn't talk much after the first family session. She liked the therapist. He seemed to know what he was doing, but she thought it best not to say much to Stewart about it. Stewart wasn't sure what to think. It would be nice to have an ally, to not always be the bad guy, but he didn't really want to get too involved right now. He had too many other things on his mind.

The following Monday night Stewart was driving home from work. The snow was sloppy brown slush. He still remembered how lovely it had been in the morning. Pure and white, soft and lovely.

When he did get home the driveway wasn't plowed, so he had to park on the street and trudge through the snow to get to the front door. By the time he got into the house his feet were cold and wet and he was ready for an argument.

"Did you have any trouble getting home?" Sharon wanted to know.

"No, the streets are pretty clear," Stewart said on the way to getting himself a glass of sherry.

"Dinner's almost ready, honey, come and sit down."

"Where are the kids?" he asked.

"Jason's out, I'm not sure where, and Heather's up in her room. Please come to the table."

"Can't you wait five minutes until I've had a drink and a chance to relax?"

Now Sharon was mad. She hadn't said a word about his being so late, and here he was snapping at her. "Do you have to have a drink every night? Can't you just sit down and be with me, without having something to drink first?"

Shit! Why don't you leave me alone for one minute? Just because your father doesn't drink doesn't mean the rest of us can't. This is what Stewart thought but didn't say. Instead, he just got quiet. They ate dinner in silence. It wasn't pleasant. Afterwards, to make up, he started clearing the dishes. Sharon shrieked at him, "Don't do me any favors! You never help me with anything, and you won't talk. You still haven't said a word about our meeting with Dr. Nichols, and I'm afraid to even bring it up. Anything I say you just tune me out. The least little thing, and boom! up goes that wall you hide behind." Then she ran into the bedroom and slammed the door.

His annoyance was drowned in fear. If she was this hot over his silence, what would she do if he said what he really felt? It never dawned on him that he could walk away. Or that he could shout just as loud as she could. She had him afraid, and that only made him more ashamed, fanning his secret anger. In the house he was paying for, she had him afraid.

If the marriage lasted another twenty years there would be graduations; vacations, many of them happy; a father who cried at weddings; grandchildren; and more. But now there was only this awful fight. He hated her.

A faint sound of sobbing came from the bedroom. Many nights this, her surrender, had been for him the final weapon of defeat. Not tonight. He'd be damned if he was going to go in there and make up. Let her apologize. *Just once* let her say , "I'm sorry." Fat chance.

Later, after the eleven o'clock news, tiredness overcame him and he tiptoed quietly into the bedroom. He slipped off his clothes and dropped them on the floor, then climbed into bed, making as little noise as possible. It was too dark to see anything, but he knew she was awake. This knowledge banished sleep.

They both lay still in the darkness, straining to be silent, invisible to each other. It was as though if there were no noise, they weren't there together. Some nights she seemed to make noise just to irritate him, to punish him for not paying attention. Not tonight. Tonight she was like a wild creature, still and noiseless, not wanting to be discovered. *She must really be mad*, he thought, and his stomach gurgled.

After a long while, Sharon's breathing became more regular and then took on the rhythm of sleep. But for Stewart sleep didn't come. He went over their argument, all the reasons he was right and all the reasons she was wrong. *What did I do? She's such a spoiled bitch.*

As he lay there thinking, or rather brooding, he was distracted by the slight swish of Sharon's nightgown when she rolled over. Memory ambushed him. He remembered, only for a moment, a rather different occasion when his heart had been slaughtered by just the rustle of her dress.

"WE'LL SING IN THE SUNSHINE"

Sharon and Stewart met in Nantucket. He was working as a busboy at the Snooty Fox in the summer between his junior and senior years in college. One night about ten o'clock Sharon walked in with her parents. She looked familiar, like someone he'd seen at college, but he couldn't be sure. Girls didn't dress like that in college. She was wearing a red silk dress and a double strand of pearls around her neck. He guessed they were real. She sat with her parents in the corner across from where he was clearing up. Long dark hair, a full mouth, and large dark eyes—she certainly looked familiar, but more like Sophia Loren than the girl he'd seen on campus.

To his surprise, she came over to him. His heart thumped hard. "Don't you go to Hartwick?" she asked.

"Yes, I do, and you're . . ."

"Sharon, Sharon Nathan."

"Have you been here before?" he heard himself saying, but he was flustered. She looked so sophisticated, so sexy. Her perfume drifted over him. He didn't know what kind, but he wouldn't forget that fragrance.

Then he heard her say, "Well, I guess I'd better be getting back to my parents. We're taking the ferry back in the morning, but maybe I'll see you on campus."

"Yes," he said. *Yes!* he thought. As she walked away he watched the pleated skirt of her dress sway back and forth, swishing softly against her stockings.

Back at school Stewart was on the lookout for her. He had to see her again. She was so gorgeous, he didn't have the nerve to ask her out. Instead, he asked about her. Sharon Nathan, he found out, was from New York—that explained why she had seemed so at home in the Snooty Fox—and she had been going with a senior who broke up with her last spring when he graduated.

The first time Stewart ran into Sharon he was too nervous to do much of anything but make small talk. How was your summer? What classes are you taking? and so on. What surprised him was that she seemed so friendly. She must just be a nice person, he thought.

He kept finding excuses to talk to her. Nothing they talked about was very profound—Stewart was embarrassed by his inability to speak a single interesting word to her, and Sharon was disconcerted by her inability to draw him out. He saw her beauty as exotic and somehow mysterious. She was "the other," someone strange, different—someone who stood for all the things he felt were missing from his life. He couldn't have told you what these things were, and in fact, Sharon's "otherness" was something he only barely apprehended.

Feminists argue that "otherness" implies difference, implies inferiority—women as "the second sex." But to Stewart, Sharon's differentness exerted a magnetic pull. She found him different too. He was more serious than most of the other boys she'd known.

And he seemed to give her enough room to relax and be herself. She was so used to boys crowding her, pressing in on her. Stewart was different, and funny too. It was refreshing.

Unsure of himself, Stewart fell back on his sense of humor. He was so good at wisecracking and imitating certain professors' mannerisms that not too many people saw his compulsive jesting as a distancing mechanism. When a person makes jokes and puns in a social situation—no matter how clever the joke and its author—the joker has momentarily drawn back, making connections that he would not think of if he were fully involved in the social moment. But Sharon didn't seem to mind. Not yet, anyway. And the fact that she laughed at his corny jokes made him feel that she liked him.

Stewart's heart was no longer his own, but the step from chatting to asking her out was too big. Like the gulf between the poor and the rich—it just seemed unbridgeable.

Finally, in the middle of the fall, he got up the nerve to ask her out. To him it was a momentous occasion; to her it was a date to the movies. Later, on the steps of her dorm, he asked if he could kiss her. She said no, and walked in. He was crushed. Later she told him, "You should have just done it. Why don't you have more self-confidence?"

Stewart was hurt. It had taken nerve to ask Sharon for a kiss, and her "No" hurt. In his mind it was more than "No, I don't want to kiss you; it was "No, I don't really like you; no, there's no chance we can have a relationship; no, you aren't in my class." So he did what would become a pattern in their relationship. He withdrew to lick his wounds in self-pity. He avoided her. And he rehearsed in his mind how he would never give anyone a chance to hurt him again. He daydreamed of becoming a monk—he'd be alone and pure and safe. It was only a daydream, but he spent the next few days living out an imitation of it. He avoided people; he got up early, studied hard, and went on long, solitary walks.

Stewart found a certain solace in this monk's pose. He didn't need anyone, he told himself. Sometimes, however, he found himself imagining that he was an object of great interest to the people he was avoiding. His friends would see him as brave, mysterious, lonely. And Sharon, Sharon might guess how hurt he was. Maybe she'd be sorry for what she'd done. Maybe . . . oh, forget it. He wasn't going to let himself think about it.

Sharon did notice. Not that she thought of him as a mysterious monk, though—more as a boy whose feelings are too easily hurt. At first she was annoyed that he was so sensitive, but then she thought it was rather sweet. One night she saw him in the library and waited to talk to him. It was ten-thirty when he finally left. Sharon caught up to him on the steps outside, and walked beside him in the darkness. "Hi!" she said and tried to take his hand.

Stewart jerked his hand away and said, "What do you want?"

"Don't be mad. I missed you."

Stewart was confused. This was what he wanted to hear, but he wasn't sure he was finished punishing her.

Sharon cleared up the confusion. "Come here," she said, and she put her hands on his face, drawing his mouth down to hers. As their lips met, her mouth opened, all warm and wet. Her tongue snaked into his mouth, darting across the inside of his lips and against his tongue. Oh, it was thrilling! Now he didn't ask a thing. He slid his hands underneath her sweater and started to caress her breasts beneath the silky material of her bra. Sharon arched her back slightly and made a soft moaning sound. Her breasts tingled and her nipples got hard; the soft brush of his fingers felt so good. But then she thought about where they were, and gently took his hands in her own and put them around her back. Still plastered up against him, she said, "We can't do this here. Can I see you tomorrow?"

"Yes."

Stewart met Sharon the following night outside her dorm at seven-thirty. She took him inside, into the big sitting room off the front lobby. There weren't any lights on, but Stewart could hear rustling noises from one or two other couples. Sharon led him over to a big leather couch in the corner and immediately started kissing him again. It was like before, only better. Her mouth was so hot and wet, he never wanted to stop kissing her. And she didn't stop him either. He kissed her back hard and pushed his tongue deep into her mouth. They kissed until their mouths ached.

Sharon's heart was racing, her breath was fast and shallow. She felt Stewart's hand slide over her blouse and rest on her breast. As gently as she could, she put his hand on the top button of her blouse. His hands trembled as he unbuttoned her blouse. Then he started cupping and squeezing her breast underneath her bra. Didn't this boy know what to do? She reached behind her back and unhooked the snaps. Without bothering to remove the bra, his hands greedily sought her breasts, stroking, rubbing, moving. He couldn't seem to keep still. Still, it felt good, and Sharon leaned back with dreamy eyes, hoping to absorb all the pleasure she could.

They started seeing each other almost every day. They went to meals together. He walked her to class. They studied together. Sharon watched him at soccer practice and she came to all the home games. They were a couple. After supper they went into town to the movies or drank beer and listened to music at the Chicken Shack. At the end of the evening they usually ended up on the couch in her dorm. Sometimes they even went there right after supper.

They didn't go all the way, but Stewart didn't care. He'd never known so much passion. He was crazy for her. This must be love.

Sharon was in like with Stewart. He had brains and ambition. He cared about serious things, not like her family. Someday he'll be somebody. If only he had more self-confidence, she thought. Given time, she could fix that. He really did have a lot of potential.

The rest of the year went by in a hurry. The leaves changed color and fell, the snow came and went, and then it was spring, time for Stewart to decide what to do in the fall. He'd planned to go to graduate school in English. Iowa, maybe, or Berkeley. But now he didn't want to be so far from Sharon. So he applied to and was accepted at Cornell. Ithaca wasn't far from Hartwick, or from New York for that matter.

They talked about marriage as if it were a game. Sharon said they should live in Switzerland, in a big chalet on the side of a mountain. Stewart said they should have four children, all looking like little Sharons. But Sharon had made it clear that she couldn't marry someone who wasn't Jewish. And Stewart wasn't at all sure he was ready to get married anyway. As a token of this understanding, Sharon said that the then popular "We'll Sing in the Sunshine" was "our song."

The following year, Sharon's senior year, she saw Stewart almost every other weekend. Once or twice she drove to Ithaca, but mostly he came back to Hartwick. Then there were weekends in New York. Sharon went home a lot, and Stewart loved to visit her in the big city. It was nice to go back to Oneonta and Hartwick, but those weekends in the city were magic. Sharon always seemed eager to see him and she always had something planned. Off-Broadway plays, concerts, trips to Chinatown and Greenwich Village, romantic dinners, watching the stars come out from a rooftop bar—Stewart loved it all. His romance with the city was all tied up with his romance with Sharon.

Their time together was when he truly came out of himself. The rest of the time he was a watcher. He watched people on the street and even in classes when he got bored. Of some he approved. He admired most of his professors, and people who seemed at ease and self-sufficient. But of many more he disapproved. So many people were frivolous, crude, loud, gum-chewing slobs. Not Sharon. With her, he talked about all the things he cared about—how the great writers knew so much more than psychologists about the human condition, and how people waste their lives getting and spending money. Here was someone to whom he could say anything, all the serious ideas and opinions he'd been storing up for years. Sharon took it all in.

Their weekends were compact high-energy periods with no letdown. Sunday afternoons ended in the Greyhound Bus station. They'd sit talking, waiting for the bus, ill-at-ease in those awkward predeparture moments. It was hard to talk in the bus station and hard not to. They'd kiss hard and then he'd climb aboard. She always waited and watched him pull away. He never loved her more.

Once he was in his seat and the bus was moving, all the tension that relationship brings was relieved. It was time to go back. He usually read for a while and then looked out the window, watching the trees and houses roll by. Later, the loneliness hit. There was nothing to look forward to. It was a gentle loneliness. He almost enjoyed it.

Sharon finished up her senior year without enthusiasm. She had no plans for the future, and with Stewart away she felt that her present was just going through the motions.

After Christmas, Stewart bought a car, a faded green Volvo 122–S with forty thousand miles clearly showing on its exterior. Not too pretty, but only six hundred dollars, and it ran just fine. The fact that having a Volvo made Stewart feel a little special didn't hurt either.

Things were falling into place for Stewart. He was settling into graduate school, doing a lot better than he thought he would. But by late winter he got real lonely. He realized he didn't want to be without Sharon. Suddenly the idea of marrying her seemed like the best idea in the world. Thinking about having her there with him all the time, in his apartment, in his bed at night, he forgot his earlier doubts.

It was 4:00 A.M. when the telephone in Sharon's bedroom rang. "What's wrong!" she said when she heard Stewart's voice.

"Nothing. I'm lonely. I want to see you."

"Okay, come this weekend."

"I will. I'll be at your place around noon."

"I'll be waiting," she said.

"Good night. I love you."

"Me too."

He wasn't going to hit her with it right away. They would have the whole weekend, then if everything was okay he would ask her on Sunday. He drove down on Saturday and they had dinner with her parents. Family style. Sharon's mother just put all the food on the table and everybody helped themselves. It was very different from what he was used to. At his house things were more formal. Sunday, Stewart and Sharon went out for brunch. Afterwards, walking in Central Park, he asked her.

"I love you. I want to spend my life with you. Will you marry me?"

She was shocked. He had asked her before, sort of kidding. She had smiled and said, "Let's wait. See what happens." They dropped it. But this is what happened. Sharon's eyes filled with tears. She put her face in his sweater. Trembling, she said yes.

It was late when Stewart finally got into his car for the long drive back. Out on the highway the snow was beginning to stick, and the right lane was filling up with cars slowing down. On the radio, Frankie Lyman was singing, "Why Do Fools Fall in Love?" Stewart didn't pay any attention to the words; he just kept driving and listening to the beat. He didn't care about the snow; he sped along in the fast lane, drunk on happiness.

WHY DO FOOLS FALL IN LOVE?

It's no secret that getting married is among the most important and least rational decisions a person ever makes. The point is not that people really are fools, or that getting married itself is irrational, but that the decision is usually too clouded over with a romantic haze for us to see clearly who we are marrying or what marriage is all about.

Often, love comes first; friendship comes later, if at all. Too bad it isn't the other way around. With friends we are easy. The great thing about friendship is that we can be ourselves and talk about almost anything. Friendship is based not on need, but on enjoyment and trust. Our friends just like us. In love, need is great, and we put our best foot forward.

Sharon and Stewart were very much in love and they shared a great deal. He revealed to her secret hopes and ambitions that he would never trust to anyone else. She let down her guard and showed him her little-girl side. He loved it when she talked baby talk. It made her seem so sweet and vulnerable—and made him feel securely protective. She was like a kitten who curled up on his lap. How could he not love her?

Still, there was plenty they didn't know about each other. Some aspects of their personalities they deliberately held back, other traits simply would not surface until later, after they were married. Most of us suppress the most childish parts of ourselves when we leave home. Teachers and bosses and friends and lovers won't put up with the same crap our parents did. But later, after we marry and are once again in a family situation, most of us regress and begin to react to stress and frustration like adolescents. That's one reason the first few months of marriage can be so trying.

The question *Why do people fall in love and get married?* interests no one less than young couples in love. That's what makes going into the reasons—unconscious wishes, idealized fantasies, life histories, relationships with parents, values, aspirations, and so on—seem a little superfluous. Most people aren't interested when it counts.

Requests for premarital counseling used to be one of my favorite professional duties. What could be more rewarding than helping two people on the road to Happily Ever After by giving them a few well-chosen words of wisdom. Ha! Most of the couples who sought me out for premarital counseling were people who had serious problems getting along together. I often recommended that they postpone the decision to marry until they found out if they could work out their difficulties. After all, there's no sense marrying someone you can't get along with, right? Wrong. In my experience, it didn't matter how poorly matched these couples were, or how successful they were at resolving their problems. Their minds were already made up: What will happen can't be stopped. Aim for acceptance.

◆

Sharon and Stewart had well-thought-out reasons for getting married. They thought they knew each other pretty well and the little they didn't like they thought would improve with time. Beneath the surface of conscious considerations, they were propelled by a powerful yearning to escape loneliness, and pulled together by a deep, instinctive urgency.

As a child, Sharon had been obedient but indulged. She was admired for being pretty, but because she was a girl she was not quite taken seriously. Her future, it was assumed, was family. Just that. Sharon had ambitions but she was programmed for domesticity. Petted at home and allowed to get by on promise at school, she lacked the self-discipline and driving need for personal achievement that propels some people into professions. By the time she met Stewart she had already accepted defeat in the realm of personal ambition. Twenty years ago this was not unusual.

Stewart was a young man, deeply insecure, driven to achievement, and uneasy with intimacy. Sharon was equally insecure, but rather than exercising independent initiative, she was driven toward merging herself with someone stronger. Stewart's proposal made everything right, for that moment canceling every trace of unhappiness in her life. She had wanted to end the confusion of emotions that had made her adolescence so miserable. When Stewart spoke the magic words "I love you," he conjured up all the fantasies of falling in love. Notice "falling" in love—a passive drop into happiness. It sounds automatic, like presents on your birthday or that last-day-of-school feeling in June. Living is hard—alone or together—but there seems no limit to the human hope for happiness served up on a plate.

Stewart's fear of his own weakness masqueraded as strength. He avoided casual small talk, and the eyes in Sharon's heart saw supreme strength of character. Sharon was a girl afraid of being on her own who took on the guise of a perfect companion. Naturally they fell in love—with each other's projected image.

"I DO"

Sharon never imagined how much there was to be done to arrange a wedding. There were caterers, flowers, a band to pick, what music to play, who to invite, choosing the invitations, who should sit where ("You can't put Aunt Adele at *that* table!" her mother said), and on and on. Weddings were supposed to be romantic. This was turning into a chore.

The night before the real thing, after the rehearsal, Sharon's father staged a big family dinner at the Empire Room. While everyone was eating and drinking and laughing and making toast after toast, Sharon watched Stewart. He was smiling and talking but he seemed out of place, uncomfortable with all these people— her family. *It's a mistake*, she thought. *I don't love him. He's just a boy.*

The day of the wedding Sharon woke up at 6:00 A.M. She was nervous, sick to her stomach. She went with her mother to Vidal Sassoon's, where they both had their hair done. All that money and it still didn't turn out very well. And naturally, her face broke out. Today of all days. But she didn't let it get her down, besides which she was too caught up in the flow of all there was to do to spend much time thinking.

Stewart spent most of the day alone. He had breakfast with his friend Roger, who'd flown all the way from California for the wedding, and lunch with his parents. Mostly, though, he wanted to be alone. He did a lot of walking. Way up Broadway, over to Riverside Church, and then all the way down to a terraced garden he'd seen with Sharon on the east side of Central Park. Walking and thinking. He didn't think about the wedding, or the marriage, or even Sharon. He deliberately avoided these subjects, and concentrated instead on "bigger" things: what he wanted to do with his life, how fleeting everything is. And he worked hard at noticing things: the dark, swirling color of the Hudson, rushing toward the sea, the wide-eyed fascination on the faces of shoppers gazing at the glittering array of elegant objects in store windows. Material lust, he thought. Stewart was preparing for the wedding in the same way he prepared to take an exam or give a lecture: by keeping his anxiety at bay through walking and looking and thinking.

Sharon and her family were late getting to the temple. Her

father was nervous. He was quiet, tense, short with people. She had never seen him like this. As soon as she walked into the temple and saw Stewart, she felt fine, calm. He smiled. Everything was okay.

The bridal room was packed with people. Her dress was not quite what she wanted. But when she put it on, everyone oohed and aahed. It was fun. She was excited, a little bit out of it.

The wedding itself went by so fast that neither Sharon nor Stewart had time to focus on other than a few stray details. Despite her attempts to cover them with makeup, Sharon was painfully aware of the two red blotches on her chin. She noticed the tears that filled her father's eyes just as they were to walk down the aisle. She'd never seen him cry before. *He* really *loves me*, she thought. The ceremony was a blur. There was the rabbi, and Stewart, and behind her everyone who loved her; and then she heard herself say, "I do." And it was done.

Stewart was aggravated by all the picture-taking. Every time he tried to talk with somebody or have some champagne, the photographer was dragging him away. "Okay, let's have the bride and groom and the bride's parents." *Whose wedding is this?* Stewart thought. But then he knew the answer. It was Sharon's family's wedding. So he allowed himself to be pushed along like a leaf in the wind. He just kind of stood outside and watched. The photographer was not content to record what was really happening, she had to stage it. Everything was posed—this group, that group—and some of it much too precious for Stewart's taste. Pictures of him kissing Sharon, pictures of her feeding him cake. These things should be private.

Once Stewart stood next to Sharon under the canopy of flowers, everything stopped. All the noise, the pushing and pulling, and the loudness, all the foolishness. It was quiet. His heart was full. The rabbi's words sounded right. Sharon was beautiful. She looked like a woman and a little girl all at the same time. "Do you . . . ?" "Yes, I do!" he said with all his mind. Then the spell was broken, and the rest of the night was back to bedlam.

They went back to Nantucket for their honeymoon. It seemed fitting. The first day on the island Sharon had her period and she was constipated. That put a crimp in Stewart's fantasies of endless, unrestrained sex. He felt resentful, cheated, as though she were holding out on him. (*Now, of all times,* he thought.)

Sharon felt lousy. She hadn't planned on this either. She felt a little guilty, and a lot annoyed that Stewart wasn't more solicitous.

Still, they managed to have a good time. The summer season doesn't really get started until the Fourth of July, so they had the beauty of the island without the crowds of midsummer.

Walking along the beach, they met an older couple, Bill and Emily Robinson, who'd been coming to the island every summer for twenty years. They ended up spending a lot of time with Bill and Emily. It was fun being with them.

Bill knew someone with a yacht, and one night they went for a cruise in the moonlight. Sitting close on the deck chairs, sipping wine—this was what they had wanted. Sharon snuggled up to Stewart and slipped her hand inside his shirt. She whispered, "I love you." They were happy.

5

POSTMARITAL DISILLUSIONMENT

*T*he honeymoon didn't last long. They couldn't afford to stay in Nantucket for more than four days. Besides, Stewart had to get back to start work as a teaching assistant for the summer session.

The apartment he'd found for them to start married life in was inexpensive but cozy. The living room, bedroom, bathroom, and kitchen had seemed plenty big enough to Stewart. He couldn't wait to have her there with him. But when they filled it up with Sharon's furniture, driven up from New York by U-Haul, it seemed more than a little crowded. Sharon told him it was charming, but that same week he heard her tell her mother over the phone that the kitchen was the size of a phone booth. That was just like her, he thought, always exaggerating.

For the first few weeks they felt extraordinarily close. Their needs fit together like interlocking pieces of a puzzle. It was like dating, only without anyone watching over them and without having to part at the end of the night. This closeness made them open up even more, making it possible for each of them to relax into themselves—to be less on their best behavior and more open to their full natures, not just the sanitized versions they wore on the surface. The trappings of permanence awakened Stewart's strong needs for satisfaction and security. Being married made him feel more sure of himself. Now he was really an adult. He had a wife—a beautiful and intelligent woman—for everyone to see. It was a reassuring reflection of his own worth.

At home with Sharon he felt safe enough to let down his defenses and give in to his suppressed wishes for self-indulgence. It was nice to relax and let her take care of him. Sharon gave Stewart lessons in how to enjoy himself. She liked cooking for him and she got a kick out of buying things for him that he thought were indulgent—expensive shirts, an enormous blue bath towel. "You spoil me," he said.

"Yes, and you love it," was her knowing reply.

Sharon brought to marriage two conflicting sets of expectations. She earned approval by working hard, taking care of others and sacrificing her own needs to theirs. It made her happy when Stewart needed her. All she asked was a little appreciation. But the same heart that wanted to give also harbored a strong wish to be taken care of. In the newness of marriage, everything he did for her made her feel secure and loved. He showed his anxious desire to please by bringing her little presents—flowers one day, a Baby Ruth bar the next. And there was enough intimacy to make her aware of the depth of her craving for emotional connection. It wasn't candlelight and wine she wanted, but the ability to be open, about herself and himself, about their feelings and wants. He seemed to want the same thing, and together they basked in the warmth of each other's love.

Stewart drew Sharon into the circle of his friends in the English department. She loved it. They were so interesting. They started having frequent parties, and their little apartment became a kind of emotional headquarters for several single graduate students. It was at one of their parties that the Assistant Dean of Students told Sharon that she could use some part-time help advising freshmen. The job worked out fine. Sharon took pleasure in mothering the students, and the extra money helped too.

◆

In marriage, buried aspects of our personality are disinterred. We leave home, most of us, in the midst of growing up. Then we step out into the wide world, putting our best foot forward. Marriage recreates family, and family is the place where we become who we are. Marriage also involves a thrust toward completion and integration of the self. Mates are chosen not only on the basis of congruency in personalities, but also out of longing for completion and growth.

When courtship begins, we trot out our best selves. *Maybe she'll like this one.* Later, except for the most insecure, we show our partners a few more selves, testing for commitment. While they were dating, Sharon had gotten to know several Stewarts—the serious and thoughtful student, the worshipful suitor, the little boy who played soccer with such abandon. She thought she was marrying two or three of these guys: the one who made her laugh, the one who seemed so responsible, and the one who occasionally made her feel safe enough to let go. Secretly (even from herself) she hoped she was marrying a series of possible selves to complement the various selves in her own character. When she felt like being Grace Kelly, he would be Cary Grant; when she was scared, he would be brave; and when she needed to be held, he would be there.

Unfortunately, none of these compatible pairings last for long.

After her first day working at the Dean's office, Sharon walked into the living room where Stewart was sitting on the couch.

"How was your day?" he asked.

"Fine, thanks." But she couldn't relax in his embrace without him starting to grope. He couldn't just hold her; he had to feel her with his restless, insistent hands. He was never still, and she was never relaxed.

Where had all these other Stewarts come from, the one who was always pawing her, and the one who knew how to talk but not listen? It was a strain always having to listen to the intrigues of the English department. Some of it was interesting, but he hardly ever talked about anything else. Sharon had things on her mind, too. Didn't he care? Never mind. Maybe her role in life was to make others feel better. She had been the good daughter, now she would learn to be the good wife.

Sharon discovered it was nice to be needed. She enjoyed cooking for him and making him feel better. It gave her a kind of power. But often Stewart wouldn't let her be close to him. Sometimes he took her for granted; sometimes he shut her out. He got so annoyed when she blurted out whatever was on her mind, regardless of what he was doing. He always seemed to be preoccupied. Reading or watching television, his posture said, *Don't speak to me, I'm busy*. But she wanted in, so sometimes she started talking anyway. (*Couldn't she read body language?*) His version of talking was to interrogate her, asking her complicated questions about things *he* was interested in. He wouldn't let her just be herself.

Oh, well. You marry everything, like it or not. It took Sharon a few months to realize this, and a few more to accept it—well, accept the idea anyway.

"WHY ARE YOU SO MEAN TO ME?"

Yes, opposites attract, but they may have trouble living together. It's a little like visiting an exotic foreign city. Part of the fascination is the allure of a strange culture. People pay a lot of money to visit faraway places—the ancient, walled, rabbit-warren bazaars of Marakesh; the volcanic islands in the Pacific; the canals of Venice or Amsterdam. Living there, however, may prove difficult. That's why, prosaic as it may sound, similarity of background is one of the most powerful predictors of marital satisfaction.

◆

Sharon had been drawn to Stewart for many reasons, but perhaps none greater than that he seemed more serious and substantial than her family. Now she discovered that the other side of that seriousness was his morose manner and his inability to let her get too close too often. His favorite phrase seemed to be "I have to go." He was always trying to get somewhere. He couldn't just be.

The seriousness of purpose and self-discipline she had so admired in Stewart now seemed to make him rigid and compulsive. There was a tense deliberateness about everything he did. Even matters that normally require only brief consideration— whether to go to the movies, how to spend Sunday morning— became matters of serious deliberation. Most of the time he was preoccupied with himself and his career, following the imperative

"I should," as if determined to overcome some obstacle. Sharon admired him for being conscientious and hard-working; but he overdid it. He did not forget himself or lose himself. Hence it was difficult for him to give himself over to her, or their relationship. He was estranged from his own wants and desires and, as Sharon discovered, rarely aware of her needs and feelings.

Some of what had fascinated Stewart about Sharon when they were courting later got hard to take. With strangers she was shy. She certainly was no wallflower, but out to dinner with friends or at parties, she had little to say. More than once she whispered to Stewart, "Don't leave me alone; I have nothing to say to these people." He found this endearing in a girlfriend but confining in a wife.

At home she was transformed. He had seen it with her parents. Now, gradually, with him she became a chatterbox. Stewart was just the opposite. He saved up his talking for special occasions. At home, he wanted to be left alone. They were so different.

Although most people did not take her for an insecure person ("How could *she* be insecure?"), Sharon was always alert for signs of rejection. She never minded taking the initiative—inviting people out, throwing parties—but once she took it into her head that someone was neglecting her, nothing Stewart said could dislodge the thought. Although neither of them realized it, these discussions could have been about their own relationship. His attempts to soothe her only made her angry. "You're on *her* side!" Eventually, he stopped trying. Another subject for silence.

———◆———

When it came to loving, they both did it in ways that were familiar. The trouble was they each tried to give what they wanted for themselves. As a result, the marriage became suffused with misunderstanding and conflict.

At a conscious level Stewart had done everything he could to avoid recreating the drabness of his own family. Sharon was *not* drab. But unconsciously Stewart expected that Sharon would duplicate the things he liked about his home. So did Sharon. They each attempted to recreate the relational world with which they were familiar. Family therapist Carl Whitaker once put it this way: "There is no such thing as a marriage, only two scapegoats sent out by their families to perpetuate themselves." The vehemence with which some people deny this truth attests to the force of this motive and our reluctance to be controlled by it.

There were a few things his parents did that annoyed Stewart. His mother constantly criticized his father's overinvolvement with his career, and his father was helpless in the kitchen. He noted these things, and a few others, and decided that his marriage would be different. (Later, he would learn much more about his parents by observing how they treated his own kids.) But for the most part it never occurred to Stewart that there were other kinds of marriages.

So many things about the way his parents lived together Stewart just took for granted as "the way things are." His mother, for example, was both competent and independent. She took care of most of the household chores and she liked being by herself. Stewart's dad frequently went out for the evening with his friends and was away for weeks at a time on business. The family did some things together, like going on picnics in the nearby mountains, but more often they went off separately. Sometimes Stewart went fishing with his father for the weekend; sometimes he and his mother sat around reading, while his father was off with his cronies. His parents were more independent than most, but Stewart didn't know that. They were . . . well, just parents.

Sharon was more aware of her family, and there were a number of ways she had definitely decided her marriage would be different. She did not want to be tied down to family obligation and tradition. She wanted to travel and meet interesting people. Stewart was more than different, he was going places. Sharon liked this in him, but like most of us, she never suspected that the attraction of opposites reflects a measure of unconscious self-hate. So much of what appealed to her about Stewart had to do with disappointments in herself and in her family.

It infuriated Sharon that her parents never said directly what they wanted. Instead they implied and hinted—it was all so vague. They always gave noncommital answers, reserving their options, trying to get what they wanted but without saying so. And she hated how bossy her father was.

Notice that these attributes—bossiness, lack of candor—are personality characteristics, not patterns of relationship. Like Stewart, Sharon took much of her parents' way of relating for granted. In her case, moreover, the example was reinforced by seeing the same patterns acted out by a large network of uncles and aunts and cousins. Sharon didn't mind that Stewart put so much energy into his career because her own father had always worked hard. She was used to it. But after work, she expected the same kind of togetherness her parents shared.

Stewart, with extremely independent parents, expected things to be different. Differences like these are easier to manage in courtship. In marriage two things happen: We loosen up some of our careful consideration, becoming more the people we are, *and* whatever differences exist begin to polarize each other.

The idea of a "family unit" suggests happy harmony. Actually, the family unit is an organism in conflict, an organism in unstable balance. Two people come to marriage with different perspectives and different dispositions. Thus conflict is inherent in the nature of the organism. Conflict is neither good nor bad; it is inevitable. Some conflicts are resolved by compromise, but others are exaggerated by the inevitable polarizing effect of two people living together, both of whom feel pressure to change—the other one.

Stewart loved sports. For every season, he had equipment and a regular routine of disciplining his muscles into shape. Even as an adult he played so hard that Sharon couldn't tell where play left off and work began. Sharon was a robust person, with strong, womanly muscles and absolutely no interest in sport or exercise. Stewart tried to encourage her. "Why don't you get in shape?" But he expected her to do it on her own, and she wasn't interested. When she asked him to go bicycle riding with her, he said, "You're too slow." Remarkably, he hadn't a clue as to how unkind he sounded.

So, instead of coming together, at least on these things, they moved further apart. As a result of polarization, conflicts within each of them became conflicts *between* them. An ambivalent inner balance between pairs of conflicting impulses (short-tempered/long-suffering; dependent/independent) is resolved by projecting one's own motivation onto the spouse. Mates begin to fight, in each other, denied and repudiated aspects of their own personalities. One partner becomes weak, the other strong; one is victim, the other victimizer; one is hysterical, the other obsessive. What appear to be personality differences may be partly based on character, but small differences are exaggerated. This projection

and polarization impedes each one from integrating latent posi-
tives in the self, because these are played out by the other. The
tough man is unable to integrate his softer side to the extent that
his wife acts emotional and helpless. A nice model is the couple
who can take turns being the kid, or being sick. Unfortunately,
Sharon and Stewart were better at splitting roles than taking
turns.

———◆———

One of the forms that polarization took with Sharon and
Stewart was an escalating series of arguments, terrible arguments.
It usually started with Sharon feeling neglected. He'd walk away
from her at parties, and stay after school drinking with his friends
while she was waiting supper for him. He never seemed to care
what she was feeling. She tried not to say anything, so as not to
injure that bundle of sensitivities she had married. (Was anyone
ever as sensitive to criticism as Stewart?) But after a while she'd
get fed up. It wasn't fair.

"You don't care about anyone but yourself!" These complaints
were totally unanticipated by Stewart. For no good reason (that he
could see) she'd start in on him, speaking in that special voice of
hers: shrill, cruel, mean. He was defenseless before it. There was
no way to prepare for these outbursts; they just arrived, like sleet
storms. She yelled at him and he cringed.

How could a man so brave in thought be so timid in confrontation? He used to think he was good at fighting, but that was with
his fists. He had no defense against this. When a relationship
required sustained verbal expression of that inner life and the full
range of feelings that accompany it, then it became impossible for
him. The louder she shouted, the less he heard. "Yes, yes," he'd
say, meaning, *Please stop, I can't stand it*. But she knew he didn't
hear her, and she kept at him. Eventually, he'd walk out and slam
the door, leaving her alone, crying.

After a fight, they both went over and over it in their minds,
nursing their resentments. He felt cheated, bitter, disappointed.
Marriage was bringing out a meanness in her. She was like a big
baby, yet her ferocity scared him. He could think of no way out
except escape. He had to leave her, he couldn't live with this.
Later, when he realized that he wouldn't leave, *couldn't* leave, he
felt like a coward. The real cowardice was not being able to listen

or fight back. Maybe he couldn't listen until he first learned to fight back.

After she cried herself out, Sharon was ready to forgive him, but that wasn't enough. Forgiveness is never enough. It means that one accepts something as done and excuses it, but assumes that with forgiveness comes the assurance that it will never happen again. It will happen. All those things we hate in our mates, the awful, annoying, and inconsiderate things they do, they will do again. Acceptance means accepting the person as she is or as he is, warts and all.

Sharon was always ready to make up before Stewart was. He'd still be sulking and she'd be trying to be nice. After a day or so he'd break down. He'd be sitting alone somewhere and start to think of her with fond detachment, loving her and pitying her, and feeling bitter regret for all the cold space that grew up between them. Moments of affection and reconciliation were such a relief that he purchased them by giving in, by falsifying the truth of his feelings. It was easy, and it became a habit. He'd bring her a present with a note enclosed expressing what he had trouble saying out loud: *I'm sorry.* She was generous with forgiveness.

◆

When needs clash, it feels like the other person is being cruel and selfish. More than once, after a fight, Sharon broke down in tears and sobbed, *"Why are you so mean to me?"* Stewart only thought it, and never more than ten times a week.

In Stewart's opinion, Sharon was addicted to attachment, in constant need of affectionate attention. What used to drive him crazy was that she always wanted to talk. If they sat in the living room reading, she'd interrupt every few minutes to read some boring tidbit from her magazine. It broke his concentration and made him furious. But he didn't know how to say anything. Instead, he just turned on the television.

Stewart had rarely dated before he met Sharon because he feared rejection. Now he adopted a submissive attitude toward his wife. His own dependency needs and aggressive tendencies were so strongly suppressed that he was hardly aware of their existence. All anger was banished. She saw his attempts to withstand her emotional onslaughts as aloof, nonfeeling. "Don't just stand there like a stone!" she'd scream at him when he wouldn't fight back.

Inside, he was appalled by the vicious, exaggerated things she said. The worst was, "You don't give a damn about anybody—all you care about is yourself!" His reaction was to withdraw even further. She'd pursue him, still on the attack, feeling lonely, deserted, but showing only her fury. They seem trapped in this pattern.

What made it all so painful was that they had both expected marriage to be relatively conflict-free. The way it was at home. The way they remembered it, anyway.

We evaluate events not only in comparison to past experience but also in comparison to imagined possibilities. Most of us grow up with an image of a happy marriage and family life. Not that our own families were necessarily happy, but even if our parents were at war, hot or cold, we hoped things would be different for us.

The experience of marital arguments is quite different when linked to the possible scenario "Marriage will be wonderful" than when linked to "Marriage will have a certain number of fights." Sharon was used to arguments. In her family people said what they felt. As a result there was plenty of conflict but also a sense of being able to air gripes and work things out. Stewart's family was just the opposite. He was not prepared for Sharon's outbursts of temper. She had never expected to marry someone who would punish her with aggrieved silence just for expressing her feelings.

We should know better, still the myth of placid normality endures, supported by two-dimensional images on television comedies. This picture of people living in harmony, coping cheerfully with the few and amusing problems that crop up, crumbles whenever anyone looks at a real family with its normal problems. Unfortunately, this model is still fixed in our heads as a standard against which we judge our own families.

A family that works is not one without conflict; it is one in which the partners know how to settle conflicts when they arise.

Sharon was willing to try to work things out. Unfortunately, Stewart was unprepared to tolerate her way of working things out. He felt devastated and withdrew into a den of self-pity. He came out once in a while to look around, but the slightest chill sent him scurrying right back. It was a pattern that would last for years.

—◆—

So. What's going on here? The story is familiar enough. Two decent people doing the best they can, still they make things very difficult for each other. They meet and fall in love, and each finds the other by turns different, fascinating, and finally frustrating. Nobody gets beat up, nobody becomes an alcoholic or bulimic or addicted to cocaine, and so the story lacks some of the drama we are accustomed to seeing on television and in the movies. And yet the quiet tragedy of two ordinary people who make each other unhappy is every bit as sad as those other, more dramatic, problems. Unhappy is unhappy.

Sharon and Stewart each had their own point of view, at best sporadically sympathetic to the other one. You, the reader, may have a wider view. Sitting back, outside the range of hurt and blaming, perhaps you can see the unfortunate misunderstandings, the poor choices, and the inability to compromise—two young people with too great a disparity in their backgrounds to fit together easily, and too little experience to know how to work at it. Accurate as this assessment may be, it stays well within our familiar way of thinking about families: as collections of individual personalities. When they married, Sharon and Stewart also created something new, a system, a unit, a whole entity. And this new entity has certain laws of it own.

No, the individual personalities of Sharon and Stewart don't disappear, or even merge; nor do traits like courage, compassion, and unselfishness cease to be important. Nothing is destroyed, but something is created. Family systems function according to patterns that incorporate but also transcend the characteristics of their individual members. Caught up as we are in the everyday flow of family life, it is hard for us to see these patterns, harder still to navigate them without experience or guidelines. (One of my patients recently told me, "You've seen situations like ours hundreds of times. This is the first time for us.") In the sections that follow I shall introduce a series of concepts to help you better understand married life, and how to make it work.

IDEALIZATION

In our culture, love is put forward as the *summum bonum* of human relationships. Love is sanctified and regarded as sacred. Objectivity is inhibited. To analyze love implies a certain amount of sacrilege, a desecration of what should be cherished rather than understood. In twenty years of asking married couples what attracted them to each other, I have yet to hear a really thoughtful or interesting answer. Intelligent, good-hearted people can tell you a lot about many things, but very few can say much about why they fell in love.

Most of us marry a dream. Marriage is going to be a safe haven in which we get all the nurturance and care and tenderness and understanding that we didn't quite get in our own families. What's more, we expect this cozy nest will be a place where we can unlock our passion. Marriage will do away with loneliness and frustration, it will make us stronger and safer—and it will make us feel better about ourselves. It usually does. For a while.

Romantic love always promises more than it can deliver. The vivacious and passionate woman Stewart thought he married turned out to be dependent and demanding, or so it seemed to him. Sharon's attentive lover metamorphosed into a selfish and thoughtless husband. When her idealized fantasies were disappointed, Sharon started to criticize Stewart. He felt wounded and withdrew. Some of her criticism was, of course, valid. But little or none was heard. Sharon didn't even have a chance to respond to Stewart's complaints; he never voiced them out loud.

At this point it may seem that I am painting a relentlessly negative picture of married life. I don't mean to. Most people are happy when they marry; that's why they marry. Even Sharon and Stewart, despite all their problems, were content much of the time. The idea I wish to emphasize is that the inevitable disappointments that come into our lives can be faced and understood, and can serve as the basis for constructive action. The alternative is that even in a basically sound relationship, disappointments fester and, in some instances, slowly poison the relationship.

Couples can and do struggle through their dark moments and unhappy times to build a relationship with affection, happiness, and love. To do so, however, they must get past their early disappointments without falling into the trap of feeling victimized and blaming their partners for all their dissatisfaction. Disappointment (and blame) are magnified the more the relationship is based on fantasy and wishes. Sadly, most couples discover this only after they are already married. For a time, "for better or worse" feels like for worse.

Fantasies seem to break down in the face of experience. In fact, they never die, but live on in subterranean secret hopes.

Men and women react to frustrated expectations in various ways. Some become grievance collectors, hoarding slights and affronts as though they were coupons in a game that eventually entitled the bearer to a prize. Sharon was a little like this. Some run away. Stewart had several ways of doing this: retreating behind a book or the television, having "to go somewhere important," walking out when things got hot, and (his secret preoccupation) daydreaming of escape. Others actually grow up. This is, of course, the most difficult task of all.

Stewart kept his eyes wide open, fixed squarely on what Sharon "should" be and how unfair it was that she wasn't. He was cursed, he thought, with imaginative powers which conjured up dreams his bride couldn't live up to. For one thing, she did not turn out to be the sex goddess of his daydreams. (Like many young married people, Stewart thought that her response to him was entirely her doing.) For another thing, she didn't seem capable of living her own life. The eager, affectionate woman he fell in love with was turning out to be a wife-child who made *him* responsible for making her happy. Why couldn't she live her own life? Marriage, he thought, was a tragedy of lost illusions.

◆

Perhaps this all seems to add up to something that everyone knows: "Love is blind." (Well, everyone but lovers know.) Like most familiar aphorisms, this one carries a good deal of truth. Another adage cautions, "Keep your eyes open before marriage and half-shut afterwards." Lovers are often blinded by their feelings and so do not clearly see the beloved. But the metaphor of blindness is not quite right; it is strictly negative—*not* seeing. Love also works a positive distortion on our vision—we aren't so much blind as we see what we want to see.

Sharon wanted to find someone kind and serious, strong enough to know what he wanted and attentive enough to love her well. And she found him—or rather, half found, half imagined him. Stewart yearned for someone who would love him completely. She would look up to and admire him, and she would always be there for him when he needed her.

The name for this mechanism of illusion is *idealization*. In this case putting a name to a familiar human experience does more than call it to our attention. Idealization is a complex, motivated, psychological phenomenon, which, once we understand it, tells us a great deal about the progress of love—and disenchantment.

According to Freud, idealization is based on a dual process of projecting our best hopes for ourselves onto the loved one, while vigorously suppressing negative feelings.[1] Lovers project their "ego ideal"—their own concept of a perfect personality—onto the loved one. What the lover wishes to be, he or she fantasizes the beloved as being. The second part of the process is *reaction-formation*. Idealizing someone is also a way to defend oneself against recognizing dangerous aggressive feelings. Men or women who always make a point of saying how "wonderful" their spouses are may be protecting themselves from facing their own anger and resentment. In Freud's view, falling in love is an irrational, immature, and unrealistic response based on reawakening romantic yearnings of childhood. This is one reason why part of what we long for in a spouse is the perfect parent we wished we had.

An alternative, complementary, and equally useful explanation for idealization comes from Heinz Kohut's psychology of the self.[2] Kohut believed that we develop a healthy and secure sense of self when our parents fulfill two essential needs. The first is for what Kohut calls *mirroring*, the admiring praise that most parents give automatically to nurture their child's sense of worth. Mirroring, a form of empathy, is so important to the development of self-esteem that I shall have a good deal more to say about it in later chapters.

The second way that parents help strengthen the growing child's personality is by providing a model for *identification*. Children look up to their parents, not only as people strong enough to take care of them, but also as images of what they themselves will become when they grow up. Little children idealize their parents as a way of enhancing their own sense of self-worth. The child draws strength from imagining that the parents are extraordinarily powerful because the parents are perceived as part of the self (Kohut's term for this blurring of identities is *selfobject*) and models for what the child will become.

Thus, parental admiration and inspiration are the building blocks of the child's inner resources. Chronic or traumatic failures in either empathy or idealization weaken the child's self-esteem and leave him or her forever hungry for compensation. The child who longed in vain for praise grows to adulthood alternately suppressing the craving for attention, then letting it break through in relation to anyone who seems a likely source of admiration. Similarly, people who were painfully disillusioned about their parents' worth may always be searching for someone to lean on, to look up to, to borrow strength from. In some individuals, like Sharon, this longing is manifest and takes the form of open dependency. Others, like Stewart, mask their longings with a show of independence and strength, yet nevertheless secretly yearn for a mentor (someone to lean on) and worshipful attention (mirroring).

As you see, idealization and disillusion are not merely part of an inevitable and unvarying process. The degree and nature of the idealization tells us a great deal about the person. The more insecure—deep-down insecure—we are, the more we look for, and find, people to idealize. We meet someone special and we fall in love with a blurry blend of that person's real qualities and our own projected longings.

An interesting sidelight about people with a strong need to idealize is that these same people typically have highly ambivalent relationships with their parents, especially their fathers. Although they may feel very strongly about their fathers, they have usually been disillusioned, disappointed in them. The strong and continuing need to idealize is partly a product of this disappointment.

Of what practical value is understanding the dynamics of idealization? Psychotherapists use it as a thread to unravel core deficits in self-esteem. In therapy, idealization is likely to be manifest tangibly as the patient transfers unsatisfied longings for someone to look up to onto the therapist. Good therapists understand the function idealization serves in the psychic economy and they use this information to help patients understand and modify their tendency to first idealize and then devalue others. But you don't have to be in therapy to study your character and improve your marriage.

Remember this: Idealization is a method we use to compensate for our own feelings of inferiority. The object of idealization may be flattered by being put on a pedestal—that is, until the inevitable disillusion sets in. Then the person is punished for being what they always were: a flesh and blood human being. People marry in order to make up for something missing and to protect themselves from unhappy feelings. Since it is asking too much of any relationship to sustain all these needs, disappointment inevitably sets in. It isn't so much the disappointment that is the problem, rather it is the person's blindness to the process of idealizing and devaluation. Instead of reflecting on why we needed to exaggerate our partners' virtues, we blame them for letting us down, and sometimes look elsewhere for the missing satisfaction.

Try this. Make two lists, the first a list of all your spouse's faults and failings; the second, a list of your inflated expectations of marriage and your mate. Search your memory in order to recall what you felt in the early days of your relationship. Working on one list will prod your memory of the other.

The first list might include such things as: All he seems to want to talk about is himself; she isn't interested in serious conversation, she's always changing the subject; he doesn't express his feelings, he's always hiding behind a wall; she's not as interested in sex as I thought she was; he's so selfish; and so on.

The second list, which takes a little more thinking and a little more honesty, might have such things as: I was hoping my partner would always be interested in me, what I was thinking and feeling, what happened to me during the day, and what my plans for the future would be—in other words, he (or she) would be completely interested and perfectly understanding; I thought my partner and I would always be able to show our emotions openly, that there would be no barriers of feeling between us; I expected my spouse to be there when I wanted to be intimate, but also to respect my need for privacy and to leave me alone much of the time; I thought sex would be glorious, and that he (or she) would intuitively respond to my needs.

Recognize the dream for what a dream is—a fantasy. Try to own your fantasies as what *you* want, what's missing in your life. Instead of blaming your spouse, own up to what you have and haven't done with your own life. You may have married your spouse partly to fill in missing spaces in yourself, but that's not really the way relationships work. "Getting it" in this exercise means understanding—really accepting—that he or she is exactly the person he or she is. Come to terms with that.

Discover who the person you married really is. Let this person be who he (or she) is. You might as well, he or she will be anyway. This is also the beginning of allowing yourself to be who you are—not someone who needs to be what your mate needs *or* someone half-finished who needs a "better half." The missing parts of yourself? Accept some deficiencies, change others.

Sometimes allowing yourself to be who you are can be straight-forward, as when you calmly carry through your plans to do certain things even though your spouse questions the need. On other issues you may have to fight for what you believe. Better to fight, though, than cheat yourself and blame your partner. Better for both of you.

ACCOMMODATION

Young people often think of marriage as a state—the state of matrimony. But marriage is not something you enter, like the state of Texas; it is something you create. When two people in love decide to share their days and nights and futures, they must go through a period of often difficult adjustment before they complete the transition from courtship to a functional marriage. They must learn to *accommodate* to each other's expectations and ways of doing things. If marriage is the union between a man who can't sleep with the window closed and a woman who can't sleep with it open, accommodation is the process of working out a compromise.

With or without the term *accommodation*, the idea that marriage begins with a period of adjustment is familiar to everyone—especially everyone who's married. Usually, however, we think of this process as involving two separate persons working out a pattern of compromise. Marriage is more than a partnership between two separate persons; it is the formation of a new unit, a spouse subsytem. In the mathematics of marriage, one plus one equals one.

The two separate personalities don't disappear, of course. Nor is the systems explanation "right" and the psychology of sepa-rateness "wrong." It's not either/or. Psychological and systems explanations are different levels of discourse on the same theme, human behavior and relationships. Sometimes it is useful to think in terms of one level of description, sometimes the other.

Because we see relationships from a perspective that does not, can not, encompass ourselves, we are accustomed to thinking of separate personalities. They do this, we do that. Sometimes, rarely, the other way around. We work hard at life, doing the best we can to get by or get ahead. And we work hard at relationships. When the usual way of looking at relationships—us and them—takes us as far as it can, it is particularly useful to switch to a new perspective. The effort to understand families as systems is well rewarded by an expanded ability to make relationships work. So, while family systems explanations are not better or worse than psychological ones, the average person will learn more about family life by studying the new and less familiar perspective.

The family as system, the less familiar viewpoint, is not some meaningless abstraction. A family system is a real entity whose functioning is partly a product of separate personalities and partly a product of superordinate laws of the group. Take accommodation, for example. We are most familiar with this word in its verb form: *To accommodate* means to adjust oneself to circumstances. Even more familiar is the form *to be accommodating*, which means to please others, to get along by going along. But accommodation is also a process of mutual adjustment, some of which goes on outside of awareness.

A considerate person who visits a strange household will adjust to the hosts' way of doing things. But when two people join together to form a family, they must learn to accommodate to each other's needs and preferred styles of interaction. To the extent that they recognize this and conscientiously cooperate, the process will go more smoothly. But even if one or both partners does not accept the need for compromise, they are automatically subject to the systematic process of accommodation. So, why not make it easier by being deliberate?

A number of tasks face a newly wed couple but none more pressing than the need to accommodate to each other in large and small routines. Some of these routines are little things that one or both spouses may not care much about (what color dishes to buy) and some they have already explored during courtship (what movies they prefer, what restaurants they like). But some things are new—new to the couple, not to the individuals. Each partner expects transactions to take forms that are familiar. Both of them try to organize each other in patterns that are familiar or preferred, and press the other one to accommodate. Some things are easy. He learns to accommodate to her wish to be kissed hello and good-bye. She learns to leave him alone with his paper and morning coffee.

These little arrangements, part of the process of accommodation that cements the couple into a unit, may be accomplished easily or only after intense struggle. Each spouse will have areas in which he or she cannot permit flexibility. Sharon and Stewart, like many newly married couples, were each more or less blind to their own rigidities. Stewart was so well aware of giving in to Sharon on some big issues that he overlooked his lack of easy adaptability to the little occasions of life. He changed religions for her but he couldn't let her pick which direction to walk in, and although he always asked her which restaurant she wanted to eat in, nine times out of ten he responded by saying, "Why don't we go somewhere else tonight?"

Sharon left her home, her family, and friends for him. She cooked for him, and she put up with people she didn't like in order to please him. And yet she hardly realized how jealous she was of anything he did without her—his spending time with his friends or even just sitting quietly with a book. She pressured him into togetherness, but to her it didn't seem like a pressure or an imposition; it only seemed natural.

———◆———

Considering the emphasis I've put on the need to accommodate, some people might wonder what happens when couples don't learn to accommodate to each other. Does that mean the marriage will end in divorce? Not at all. Being happy isn't the only reason people stay together; a lot of people live together unhappily ever after.

There are two common alternatives to successful accommodation: fighting and mutual indifference. Enmeshed couples who fail to accommodate often resemble tired boxers in the late rounds. They're worn out but keep punching anyway. Disengaged couples who don't learn to accommodate develop a pattern of mutual coexistence without cooperation. It's a domestic version of the cold war.

Another objection I hear frequently is that when I talk about accommodation, I seem to suggest that the way to a happy marriage is to give in all the time. When they hear me say that letting the other person be right will resolve a lot of difficulties, many people protest, "That's what I do all the time—give in."

Yes, a lot of people do give in much of the time, and yes, successful accommodation does require a good deal of compromise. But the main thing I want to get across is that once you see your relationship as a unit, you will realize that you can change the other person by changing yourself—not who you are, but what you do in relation to that person. Not fair? Maybe not, but it puts you in charge of getting what you want.

———◆———

The other side of accommodating to each other is reorganizing the couple's involvements with the extrafamilial world—work or school, friends and family. The commitment to the marriage is made at the expense of other relationships. The degree of investment in the new relationship may depend upon how much is given up in old relationships. Stewart kept the same apartment and the same career. Sharon gave up her job and her friends and her family to move away with Stewart. Naturally, she demanded more of the relationship.

BOUNDARIES

One sweltering afternoon in July Sharon came home from work, took a cold shower, and sat outside in the shade to wait for Stewart. When he finally got home, he looked frazzled. "Hi," he said, panting like someone who had just returned from forty days in the desert. Sharon watched him go inside. She waited for him to come back and talk to her. She had a long wait.

Stewart was halfway through his second gin and tonic when it hit him. Now the alcohol took effect. His head was light. He became self-conscious. He wanted to be high but not out of it. The line between mellow and muddled was very thin, and he'd crossed it.

Sharon came in and started talking. He put on a look of exaggerated attentiveness, hoping to dispel any hint of the dizzy confusion he really felt. It seemed to work. Sharon talked on. It took so little to keep her talking.

"You look beat," she said.

"I am."

She told him that going to the community pool for a swim would be more refreshing than sitting around under the air conditioning.

"Okay," he said. "Just give me a few minutes."

At the pool, he plunged into the cool water and took a long, slow swim. All the heat and tension went out of him. Finally, he hoisted himself up the side (no ladder for him) and stretched out on one of the long lawn chairs, letting the sun and air dry him. His eyes found the blue spaces in the trees where the sky shone through. It was the first time he felt relaxed in days. He just wanted to sit quietly for a few moments, feeling refreshed, cleansed. But then Sharon came over and started talking. She wanted to know if he could take some time off so they could visit her parents. He felt the gloom settling in again. Couldn't she leave him alone for a few minutes?

◆

Stewart and Sharon were dealing with one of the most pervasive of marital problems, the drawing of personal boundaries. Boundaries exist on two levels: behavioral and emotional. Behavioral boundaries refer to the preferred amount of separateness or togetherness in relationships. The second, emotional, level had to do with distinguishing which thoughts and feelings and wishes are within the self and which are within the intimate partner.

As readers may remember, these two levels of boundaries were described by family therapists Murray Bowen and Salvador Minuchin. According to Bowen, there are two major human needs: the need to be a separate self and the need to be connected to others. Although it is possible to satisfy both these needs, there is a tension between them, and most people lean either in the direction of being close or of being independent. Obviously this *inner* tension between autonomy and intimacy is related to the *outer* pattern of togetherness and separateness that Minuchin referred to as *enmeshment* and *disengagement*.

Bowen's *fusion* and Minuchin's *enmeshment* both deal with the consequences of blurred boundaries, but they are not alternate terms for the same thing. Fusion, like the psychoanalytic term *individuation*, is a quality of individuals—it is a personality variable existing *within* the person. Enmeshment is strictly a social systems concept—it occurs *between* individuals or groups. In explaining different aspects of family life, I shall have occasion to use both these ways of describing relationship boundaries, but before returning to the Simpsons I'd like to make one important point. As everyone knows, how we behave is related to how we feel. Those who find intimacy difficult and become anxious if they are too close too long naturally tend to seek their privacy. Likewise those who are uncomfortable with independence automatically prefer togetherness. *But*—and here's the point—we do not always have to act in accordance with our feelings.

To behave more flexibly in a relationship system, you sometimes have to act counter to what your feelings dictate. A lot of people remain stuck in unhappy patterns of relationship because they assume that overcoming troublesome feelings is a precondition for changing their behavior. They think, for example, that in order to move closer to someone they have to overcome their anxiety about intimacy, or that in order to give their spouse more space they have to be comfortable by themselves. In this way, many people let their feelings run their lives. As we will see, it is possible to transform family relationship patterns by changing your habitual mode of response, *whether you feel like it or not*. This does not, however, mean that it is necessary to fight with your feelings—*I* shouldn't *get upset*. Feel what you feel, but decide how you will act. Often, by the way, new patterns of interaction will help you feel differently.

———————◆———————

Understanding emotional boundaries, past and present, does much to clarify the difficult early months of Sharon and Stewart's marriage. By now you have already figured out the general patterns of enmeshment and disengagement in their respective families of origin.

Sharon's family was enmeshed, Stewart's was disengaged. Remember that when Stewart and Sharon first met she was a college student spending her summer vacation with her parents. Then too there were her frequent trips home for the weekend during her years at college. If we knew them better, we'd have seen additional signs of enmeshment. Bedroom doors in Sharon's family were always open, people in her family felt free to interrupt one another, and it was rare that her parents did anything separately.

So far we've heard less about Stewart's family. Perhaps that's one indication of their disengagement. Few of them came to the wedding; that's another example of separateness. And I described how Stewart's father often went off by himself fishing or with friends, and that his wife never seemed to mind.

Reading even these brief descriptions, you may be having a personal reaction. "What's wrong with taking a vacation with your parents?" or "So, what's so unusual about a man going off fishing?" Talk of boundaries stirs strong feelings, and most people react personally. We are prone to take our own built-in preferences for emotional closeness or distance as the standard. Just like Stewart and Sharon, our families' truths are embedded in us.

Remember the relief Stewart felt at the end of weekends with Sharon in New York, when he climbed aboard the bus? Even under the influence of infatuation, he could only stand so much closeness. Sharon, on the other hand, felt no relief at the end of the weekend, only longing. In fact, it gave her an uneasy feeling when she sensed that Stewart was in a hurry to board the bus.

Looking at the relationship from Stewart's point of view, it might seem unfortunate that he didn't get to know Sharon better before marriage. Perhaps if they'd spent more time together Stewart would have decided that they were just too different to get along. Her clingy dependence was hard to live with. Or if they had spent more time together before they got married, Stewart and Sharon might have learned to work out more compromises. He might have learned to argue with her, before being married to her made him afraid to try. But it was not accidental that Stewart proposed while they were living apart.

Stewart is the sort of person who loves best from a distance. It was his ability to get away that made intimacy possible. If they had been closer longer, there would have been a better test of his love. He might not have passed.

Because of the long-distance courtship, Sharon did not have to learn to become a separate self. When Stewart wasn't there she still had her family. This, of course, used to be the common pattern in women's lives. There are songs about it: leaving one home for another.

Stewart and Sharon entered matrimony each looking for a different kind of bliss. He sought a relationship with intense moments of coming together, spaced out (well spaced out) by periods of time alone. While they were courting he thought only of being close to Sharon, but that's because he took his privacy for granted.

People like Stewart who are concerned about having space, experience requests for intimacy as invasions of the inner self. Now when she crowded him, he couldn't go home. He was home. Telling lies is one way of protecting your autonomy. It would be years before he told her deliberate falsehoods, but he learned quickly that a man can be angry about something but avoid exposing himself to conflict by not discussing it. Pressed by her demands for emotional closeness and unable to fight back openly, he started holding in his feelings, shutting her out of his inner reality.

Sharon expected something quite different. One of the things she loved about Stewart was his ardent, openhearted warmth. He was so eager to be with her when they were apart. She assumed that after they were married they'd share the same closeness, only more naturally. There would be fewer separations and less pressure to be on guard. Married, she'd be free to be herself. Why not? He loved her, didn't he? She thought they'd always be together.

What caused them so much pain was not the assumption on both their parts that things would be what they were at home; it was the feeling that their way was the right way, the natural way, and the other person was unreasonable, inconsiderate, and cruel not to understand. How could he go off and leave her alone so often? How could she crowd him so much? Did she want to smother him?

At this point some people might question whether or not bringing in the concept of systems and explaining how they are formed and regulated might be overcomplicating matters. Take boundaries, for example; isn't it really just a matter of personality? Men tend to be more distant and women want to be more intimate; isn't that just the way things are?

There is some truth to this, but not much. The element of truth comes from the fact that, at least in our culture, men used to be brought up to be primarily achievement-oriented, and women more oriented toward relationships. But the need to be close and the need to be distant is not just male and female psychology. In plenty of couples it is the man who wants to be together all the time and the woman who cherishes her privacy. It's a matter of how you were brought up, not your genitalia.

Futhermore, even within the same couple, patterns of closeness/distance often change over the years. The reason for this is that the boundary between the couple is a function of the boundaries between them and the rest of the world. A young husband may be so attached to his job that he doesn't get very close to his wife—it's not only time, but also a matter of limited emotional energy. Later, he may want to move closer to her, but perhaps she has now learned to accommodate to his distance and has filled the empty space with other interests—friends, her own career, or children.

No task is more crucial to marital satisfaction than working out boundaries. And nothing is more important to accommodate. Not only the boundary between them, but also, as we shall see in the chapter on in-laws, the boundary separating the new couple from the outside world.

HOW TO SUCCEED IN MARRIAGE BY REALLY TRYING

I thought of titling this section "Happily Ever After." It sounds so much more positive, and anyway, who wants to have to "really try"? Life is tough enough without having to work at relationships. Besides, didn't we always believe that it isn't necessary to learn anything about marriage and family life? We expected it would come naturally. Although I don't want to convey the impression that good relationships require endless effort, the truth is most of us have to work hard to overcome certain habits in order to make relationships work.

Many people find it difficult to accept the significance of idealization in the early years of marriage. They are so painfully disappointed that they think more about how their spouses let them down than about their own idealized fantasies—and what that says about them. People are ready enough to accept the fact that they approached marriage with certain romantic illusions, but idealization is more than that. It is more than a matter of naïve, false expectations; it is an active, specific, personal creation of our own needs, based on something missing in the self. The more complete and whole we are, the less we need to idealize our mates—and the less frustrating we find the early years of marriage.

Unfortunately, most of us react badly—in predictably human but self-defeating ways—to painful disappointment in marriage. Some people turn to fantasies of escape when they feel trapped. Stewart was like this. After a fight with Sharon, he'd withdraw to lick his wounds, and think how awful she was, how unfair life was turning out, and what a terrible mistake he'd made in marrying her. If only he hadn't married her, just think of all the freedom he'd have.

When couples come to see me for marital therapy, very often one spouse engages in this kind of passive wishful thinking. With some people this takes the form of obsessive rumination. They think endlessly about all the reasons to leave *and* all the reasons they can't. Like most obsessions, this one traps the person in the illusion of limited alternatives—in this case, either leave or stay. And like most obsessions, it draws attention away from more active solutions.

The adolescent girl who obsesses about binge eating and strict dieting is distracted from other things that might be more important but more scary—like fighting openly with controlling parents, say, or making friends and dating. People who are preoccupied with thoughts of leaving often avoid doing anything active and constructive about their relationships. When unhappily married clients consult me, not knowing whether to go or stay, I often suggest they try to make it work. I call this a "trial nonseparation." If they try hard and things don't improve, that may help them decide. Besides, it only takes a minute to leave.

Another trap is the reassuring hope that fulfillment merely waits on the next step—a new love, more money, a child, or six children. We live, most of us, aiming toward the future. Things may not be so hot now, but they will be when . . .

One of those "whens" is when the other person changes. Sharon kept hoping that Stewart would change. *Maybe when he finishes graduate school and gets a job he'll spend more time with me,* she thought.

Actually, there are two traps here. The first is projecting blame for a couple's problems onto one of them—the other one. The second trap is slipping into the habit of thinking of a relationship in terms of two separate persons, forgetting that in the interaction a new entity, the couple, is born. I'll take the first one—projecting blame—first.

The watchword of unhappy people is *"They* have to change for me to feel better." A related axiom is "No matter what, I have to be right." An awful lot of family quarrels are maintained by two people each trying to be right. The problem is that most of us assume that in order for us to be right, the person we are in conflict with must be wrong. The truth is, we are always right. At least about important things. We always remember what we remember, feel what we feel, think what we think, and for the most part, we always do the best we can. So does the other person.

The instant you let the other person be right, a great many disputes will automatically clear up, or at least lose their toxicity. Moreover, you don't have to falsify your feelings in a faked-up show of acceptance. With a little practice you can learn to see that the other person has a legitimate position, and acknowledge it. Now, all this may sound relatively obvious. It is. The reason, one reason anyway, why married partners have such a proclivity for projecting blame and assigning fault is that they are still smarting from disillusioned idealization.

When our mates fail to live up to our fantasies we feel let down, bitter, angry, and disappointed. Do we think, *I distorted who that person was because I needed to make up for certain lacks in myself?* No. We're too busy being bitter. They didn't measure up. They fooled us.

How we idealize is partly a product of the culture we grew up in. Men grow up expecting women to fill in certain missing parts of their lives. A man could be (act) strong and dominant, work hard and play hard, knowing that there would be a woman in the background, someone soft and selfless, taking care of him and later the children. Women, especially those over thirty, married expecting that their husbands would take care of them. Oh, not necessarily in any obvious way, but nevertheless the economic reality was that a woman thought she could count on a man for financial support. So, the more successful the man, the better the catch.

Today's children are growing up in a world not bound by such stereotyped conceptions. But most of the rest of us were caught in transition, learning to understand new rules with our heads but still carrying the old models in our hearts. Men and women need to develop new standards by which to judge mates. Women must learn to focus more on emotional availability than productivity, more on trustworthiness than appearance, and more on goodwill than achievement. Men must learn to think of prospective wives as separate persons, not beautiful partners whose glamour will reflect their own potency in public and take care of all their wants in private.

If you're not married but thinking about it, ask yourself, *Is this a person I can really talk to? Does this person like me? including my big nose, my love of the outdoors, my enjoyment of socializing?* Many people assume that something about them needs fixing and if they can change that or disguise it, they'll be irresistible.

Unfortunately, by the time most people think about why they chose a particular mate, they have already done so. In matters of the heart, hindsight is usually much clearer than foresight. What to do?

We can begin to put our marriages on a firmer footing by letting go of the dream of perfect love and harmony. What makes family life so painful is not conflict and discord, but inadequate ways of resolving problems—negotiating around some of them and arguing out others. Marital conflicts are like rainy days, inevitable. You can give them extraordinary power over your life by working yourself into a state when they develop: *Oh, this is awful, dreadful; it's so unfair!* You probably know people who react this way when it rains.

When it rains you get wet. When you and your spouse quarrel, you'll get upset. But if you get it straight in your mind that periodic quarrels are inevitable and get over feeling that you can avoid or prevent them, then you can begin to concentrate on strategies for resolving these stormy upsets.

Next, reassess your image of the perfect partner you wished for. Get to know the real person you married. Accept that the other person is just the way he is, or she is. This may be the single most important secret of successful relationships, and I will return to it again and again.

Once you start learning to accept that the person you married is the person you married, you can turn your attention to working out accommodations. When we think of accommodation as a transaction between two people, the two most important things to keep in mind are compromise and negotiation.

Compromise is easier to talk about than to bring about. Young married couples have a difficult task. While they are willing to learn to relate intimately, they don't want to be controlled or taken for granted. Naturally they resist giving in on certain issues; still, they also have to give up some things and give in to each other. It is possible to give in without a feeling of surrender.

We are most generous when our own needs are met, or we are confident that they will be. A sense of personal power helps, as does faith in the goodwill of your spouse. But you don't have to limit yourself to blind faith in your partner's goodwill; you can create it by being as generous as possible, giving in on those things that are more important to your partner than to yourself. Much of the compromising that takes place in the early period of a relationship does not require much discussion. Each of you will accommodate to some of the other person's wishes without need for negotiation. Some things, however, do require negotiation.

Making demands may seem the opposite of giving in; one is selfish, the other generous. Not really. Both contribute to enlightened self-interest; successful accommodation maximizes satisfaction in a relationship. Some people are better at giving in than making demands. They make an effort to accommodate to some of their partner's wishes (usually less than they think) and then assume that the partner will automatically sense what they want in return. If they don't get what they want, they brood on how unfair it all is, and then turn sour.

Part of accommodation is speaking up for what's important to you. It's not quite either/or—either you win or you lose. Expressing your wants and having them acknowledged is itself a significant victory. At the very least the two of you understand each other. This may sound mawkish. But it really is so important to give and receive understanding, that even unresolvable conflicts are bearable if each of you can acknowledge and tolerate your differences.

◆

There were also many things that Sharon and Stewart didn't talk about. He didn't say much about her family. He wished they were less intrusive but was afraid that if he said so, Sharon would never forgive him. She didn't say much about his work. She thought he used it as an excuse to avoid her, but instead of speaking up she just felt hurt. And for sure neither one of them talked about sex. Too bad, because sex was one of their biggest problems.

Sex is a problem with a lot of couples, most of whom imagine others have it pretty good. The sad thing is that so many husbands and wives can't even talk to each other about conflicting wants and needs. Talking about differences won't necessarily resolve them—life is more complicated than that—but it certainly is a shame that men and women feel so guilty and angry that they can't at least acknowledge each other's feelings.

———◆———

We usually think of accommodation as a process that takes place between two separate persons. It is that, of course, but it is also something else. It is part of the development of a new unit. Creating a working marriage means developing a sophisticated system of mutual aid between two parts of a single system, an organism, that minimizes the demands made on each one and avoids as much as possible the internal friction of competitiveness that exists between unjoined individuals.

I have mentioned this idea now several times—the family as a system, marriage as a unit, 1 + 1 = 1. It is a slippery concept, hard to grasp in dry abstraction, and even harder to see in flesh and blood marriages. At least, hard to see without a little practice. Perhaps a visual illustration will help. Remember the Chinese symbol for yin and yang, the male and female forces in the universe?

Notice how together they are complementary and occupy one space. Relationships are like that. Together two people occupy one space, the space of the relationship. Because of this, if one of you changes, that changes the relationship, and *the other person will automatically change*. If a woman wants to change her husband—and they are part of a unity—the only way to change him is to change herself. If she becomes less competent around the house, he will become more competent.

Many people intuit this principle but underestimate its force. Fear holds us back. We're afraid that if we change, the other person won't; things may not get done, or worse, our partners may leave us or stop loving us. Suppose you both work and yet you get stuck with all the shopping and cooking. Talking it over, asking the other to help or, better, share the chores, may result in some change. But don't count on it; talking is overrated. If you stop doing some chores, the other person will start to—eventually.

That's another thing that holds people back. Change takes time, and often we give up before giving accommodation a chance to work. If you stop picking up the mail, or making the morning coffee, or getting the paper, the other person will likely take over rather soon. If on the other hand you're tired of sitting around watching television on Friday night and you start buying tickets to go out or inviting people over, it may take some time before your partner accommodates to the change. He or she may grumble and complain. Remember, it isn't talking that changes things—only changing things does that. Be sympathetic, look for areas where it is easier for your mate to be flexible (maybe movies instead of concerts). But don't change back. Hang in there.

The examples I've chosen are deliberately prosaic. Other changes may be even more intimidating, but the same principle applies. For example, suppose your husband doesn't share his feelings with you. You've tried asking him to, you've tried criticizing him for not doing so, and you've tried giving up. These are only my examples. You have to consider what you've tried; this means starting to think about patterns of interaction instead of personalities. Try something different. Try accepting and acknowledging whatever feeling he *does* show. If he says, "I don't feel like talking about it," say, "Okay, you'd probably like some peace and quiet." If he says, "My boss is an asshole," let him tell you about it, don't argue or give him advice. Feelings aren't problems to be solved, and they aren't quarry to be caught—hot pursuit only chases emotion away.

If you change from a person who pulls for feeling and pushes for disclosure to one who is receptive and responsive, your mate will gradually start sharing more feeling. *Nota bene*, this may take time. Changing your part of any relationship pattern creates space for new behavior and pressure on the other person to move into it. Can you change everything this way? No, but you can change plenty. Moreover, once you recognize the power of the relationship *and* your power to affect it, you will begin to feel more in charge of your life and your family, and less like a victim.

6

IN-LAWS

A familiar psychological cliché has it that men marry women like their mothers, women marry men like their fathers. If anything, Sharon and Stewart seemed to have chosen mates who were the opposite of their parents. Stewart loved and admired his mother. She was highly intelligent, extremely competent, and full of energy. But she was also a very private person, a woman not given much to conversation or outward signs of affection. She often seemed to prefer her own company to that of anyone else. Unlike Stewart's mother, Sharon was warm, outgoing, openly affectionate—and she loved to make a fuss over him, something his mother never did.

Sharon's memories of her father were happy memories. Mostly she remembered him doing things for her. Once, when they were staying at a motel by the beach, Sharon thought the tap water tasted funny, so her father went to the store to buy her a quart of bottled water. He was always doing things like that. Only as she got older did she begin to see that the other side of this solicitousness was control. There was never any doubt of his love, but he was so domineering. Nothing could be less true of Stewart. He was never outwardly demanding, and—unlike her father—he seemed to respect her as an independent person.

Another interesting parallel was that Sharon's father, like Stewart's mother, was clearly the dominant partner in the family. Thus, both Sharon and Stewart grew up in households in which the parent of the opposite sex made most of the visible decisions and demonstrated the most energy and competence around the house. The effect on their expectations should be obvious: Sharon expected her man to repair faucets, empty the garbage, and deal with car salesmen, landlords, and bill collectors; Stewart expected Sharon to do these things. In short, they both wanted mates who made up for lacks felt in their parents, but who at the same time possessed all the virtues of those parents—different, yet the same.

Relationships with the past continue to exert a powerful and abiding influence on our lives. Stewart and Sharon both showed a desire to leave the past behind them, to begin afresh. The difference was that Stewart thought he already had, while Sharon doubted that she could. Sharon felt tied to her family by loyalty and tradition. And it was this tie that set up some of the most painful conflicts in the early years of her marriage to Stewart. Her relatives were a sensitive issue, part of a murky and complex past, the network of all that still had a hold on her. Stewart was suspicious. He was jealous. He couldn't accept anyone else's claim on her.

Stewart fooled himself the way many of us do. He thought distance made him independent. He had no wish to be the cringing sort of person he took his father for, nor did he care to be as lonely as his mother. But—not to worry—he had moved out and moved on. He would write his own story.

————◆————

Stewart had gotten to know Sharon's parents during his visits to New York. On his first visit, they'd invited him to stay for dinner, letting him know that as a friend of Sharon's he was welcome.

Dinner was served family-style on a long, formal dining room table. Mrs. Nathan shuttled back and forth from the kitchen to the table, bringing platters of gefilte fish, challah, sweet and sour meatballs, oven-browned potatoes, and noodle pudding. Mr. Nathan wanted to know what Stewart was studying, and did he like the college, and what was he planning to do with his future. Stewart tried to answer all his questions, but there didn't seem much to say. The questions seemed perfunctory, and so were Stewart's answers. Besides, Sharon and her mother kept interrupting, Sharon to elaborate on what Stewart was saying, her mother to urge more food on him.

It was a genial, hectic meal. As Sharon and Stewart were preparing to go out for the evening and Mrs. Nathan was still trying to get him to have another portion of noodle pudding, Stewart would not have guessed that this would be his last supper at the Nathans' for quite a while.

As soon as it became clear that Stewart was more than a college friend of Sharon's, that they were dating, her parents became noticeably cool toward him, a coolness he found difficult to comprehend. Sharon told him they didn't like the idea of her dating a non-Jewish boy, but Stewart could hardly believe it. Not being Jewish, it just did not make sense to him.

For a while, this stupid prejudice—that's how he thought of it—puzzled more than angered him. It wasn't until much later, after he and Sharon were married, that he allowed himself to feel the full weight of his anger. In the early stage of his relationship to Sharon, deep down in his heart he didn't feel fully worthy to be accepted, though not for anything having to do with religion—or race, or culture, or whatever the hell it was. He was insecure and not at all sure that he deserved Sharon. And as we have already seen, he held such a tight rein on his anger that he didn't always feel it.

Stewart saw so little of Sharon's parents that he learned of the next switch in their attitude from her. When they started to realize that Sharon was serious about Stewart and might actually marry him, their resistance stiffened briefly—there were one or two shouting matches between Sharon and her father—then melted. Not only did they give in to the inevitable, they seemed to forget their earlier reservations and became, once again, very warm toward Stewart. He learned from Sharon that the night he proposed, her parents called up all the relatives to tell them the good news.

◆

When Stewart took Sharon home to meet his parents during Christmas vacation, he had no thought about their getting married, he just wanted to show her off to them, and them to her.

Sharon was a little apprehensive. Stewart had painted such a glowing picture of his parents that she expected them to be highly intellectual, sophisticated, and reserved. Actually, they were quite nice and down-to-earth. Mr. Simpson was friendly, just short of effusive (Stewart was embarrassed), and he seemed genuinely glad to meet her, Stewart's friend. He was, after all, much more like her family than Stewart had led her to expect.

Mrs. Simpson, accepting Sharon on approval, showed every courtesy. She asked about New York. Where did Sharon like to shop? and what were her favorite restaurants? She was perfectly friendly, but hard to read. With her, there was always something held back, a little something in reserve. Sharon wondered how much Stewart's mother really liked her. Mrs. Simpson was polite but never really engaging in conversation, and she said next to nothing about herself. Much of the time she was off in the kitchen or working on one of her many projects. It would be some time before Sharon realized that the reserve was just Mrs. Simpson's way.

Mr. and Mrs. Simpson—or "Earl" and "Nancy," as they insisted she call them—accepted Sharon right away and made her feel part of the family group celebrating Christmas. This was not her first contact with Christmas festivities, but this was a little closer, more special. She went with Stewart and Mr. Simpson—"Earl" (it was hard to get used to)—to pick out the tree, and then the four of them hung decorations taken from an old wooden box in the attic: shiny, fragile ornaments; yellowed strings of popcorn; tinsel; and plastic icicles. It was fun. Christmas morning, she went with them to church and then back to the house for a big breakfast before they opened the presents. Everything seemed to follow tradition—they all knew exactly what to expect, including Earl Simpson's mock-pompous way of passing out all the presents.

If the visit was a test, everybody passed. Sharon could tell that Mr. Simpson liked her. He was not one to hold back his feelings. As for Mrs. Simpson, it was a little harder to tell what she thought. Why, for instance, did she make it a point to say what a fine people the Jews were? Sharon decided that the condescension didn't mean anything. She like the Simpsons. They were good, interesting people. There was nothing about them to create reservations in her mind about Stewart.

After he proposed, Stewart took Sharon to visit his folks again.

He wanted to tell them in person. His father was thrilled. His mother was pleasant, but Sharon thought she had reservations. Nancy showed so little emotion that it was difficult to know what she thought. With Sharon's own parents, there was never any doubt. In fact, though, she thought very little about Stewart's family; they were okay and that was enough. She was marrying Stewart, not his family. She didn't think much about her own family either. As she saw it, she and Stewart were leaving their families to marry each other.

"ALONE AT LAST"

One of the many reasons people marry is to break away from their families. For Sharon, this was a very deliberate motive. She was escaping their suffocating influence, her mother's narrow, mean view of the world, and her father's always telling everybody what to do. Stewart was less concerned about his family; he thought of himself as long ago emancipated from his parents. The consciousness of being still embedded in his family did not yet fit in that rather dense group of ideas he had about himself. Now that he and Sharon were getting married, there would be no one else to interfere; they'd be alone at last.

Remember Carl Whitaker's quip, "There's no such thing as marriage, only two scapegoats sent out by their families to perpetuate themselves"? Once in history this was clearly the case. Family ties counted for a lot: lineage, political power, the control of kingdoms. Then the nuclear family evolved. Now we have marriage by love. Our parents don't select our mates, we do. And since we select partners in love, not their families, we tend to underestimate the importance of the family. This is especially true in this country, where the mobility of the American worker puts hundreds of miles between different units of most families. Middle-class America in particular has dismissed the extended family. A corollary of the myth of the hero—that is, that we are self-determining masters of our own destiny—is the myth of the impermeable boundary around the nuclear family.

The first thing to realize about extended families is that they do exist. They don't go away. They exist as *introjects*, internalized images of the way family life should be, and they also exist as real networks of relationship, which have the potential for complicating and enriching the new couple's marriage. In the early years of marriage, the complications often seem more apparent than the potential for enrichment. Complications take the form of conflict with in-laws and unfinished emotional business with one's own parents.

Every marriage exists within a multigenerational system, which is the source of the biological and psychological endowment of the spouses. Relationships with in-laws are only the most visible tip of that enormous system. In the case of the Simpsons and the Nathans, two families who would never have pursued a social relationship were being joined by a permanent bond that neither side ever sought. Whether or not the two extended families in fact ever had much to do with each other after the wedding, they were still joined by their influence on Sharon and Stewart.

The two families of a couple will have both a direct and an indirect impact on their marriage. (Most people are amazed to discover the complex and powerful connections between events in one generation and effects in another.) To begin to see this influence it is necessary to look at ongoing relationships with the extended family, especially at points of transition, which consist of any addition to the family system, subtraction from it, or change in the status of a family member. The most important of these transitions are marriage, birth, adolescence, midlife, retirement, and death. An elderly parent dies and a forty-year-old father tightens his grip on his teenage son just as the boy is trying to break away. His father's father's death may not have seemed very important to the teenager, yet its effect of making his father more insecure and demanding may have a profound impact on the boy.

People who speak of the "joining together of two families" conjure up images of a happy union of two cultures, of increasing their membership and bringing new ideas and new blood to enrich a large network of kin. The reality is more often like the old science-fiction movie, *When Worlds Collide*.

INVADERS FROM ANOTHER PLANET

Stewart's parents came to New York two days before the wedding, and the night before the rehearsal, Stewart's father took the two families out to dinner. Sharon felt a little strange. She couldn't quite figure out if there were two families (the Simpsons and the Nathans) or three (her parents, his parents, and Stewart and her).

Mr. Simpson, who wanted to play the gracious host, insisted

on taking them all to Little Italy, to a *wonderful* restaurant he had eaten at many years ago. He didn't remember the name, but he knew where it was. "You'll love it," he assured the Nathans. He hailed a cab, and after they all squeezed in, Mr. Simpson told the driver to take them to Little Italy. They would walk around a little and then find the restaurant.

At first the walk was pleasant. The two fathers strolled ahead, each one enjoying the chance to talk to the other. From behind, it looked to Sharon as though her father was doing most of the talking and Mr. Simpson was doing most of the listening. Stewart was more interested in observing the women. What would his mother think of Mrs. Nathan?

They went down one block and up another. Mr. Simpson couldn't seem to find the restaurant. Maybe it had gone out of business. He didn't mind, or at least he didn't show it. No problem, they could walk around and pick another place to eat. After all, it was a warm evening, everyone was having a good time. Why worry? Mrs. Nathan leaned over and told Mrs. Simpson that it wasn't a good idea to walk around this neighborhood at night. Sharon overheard and told her mother that she worried too much. They were all getting a little edgy.

Two blocks and six menus later, Mr. Simpson found a place he liked. "Ah, what atmosphere," he said, looking around at the candlelit room with murals depicting scenes of Italy on the walls. Mrs. Nathan thought it was a little dark. Sharon was hungry. Mr. Simpson told the headwaiter that they were celebrating a wedding, and asked him if the food was good. Mrs. Simpson gave Stewart the kind of look conspiratorial students exchange when the teacher makes a fool of himself.

So, Sharon thought, Stewart and his mother found Mr. Simpson's open show of emotion annoying, but instead of saying anything they just got aggravated. In the years to come, Sharon would have reason to remember that look of cold disdain.

Mr. Nathan ordered champagne and they all drank quite a bit. Stewart could tell that his parents were nervous. They acted like themselves, only a little more so. His mother got quiet and his father got sentimental. He rose to make a toast to the young couple and to the joining of the families. It was a nice toast, but maybe a little long, Stewart thought. Glancing in his mother's direction, he saw her sitting stiff, her fixed smile betraying nothing of what she felt. Was she embarrassed? he wondered. No one else seemed to mind.

Stewart hated his father's sentimentality. Other people saw his father as polite and genial; Stewart saw a relentless seeker of approbation. He didn't like it in his father and he refused to see it in himself. His father reminded him of Peter Lorre sucking up to Humphrey Bogart in *Casablanca.* The Lorre character didn't really like the Bogart character, he was just a weak person currying favor. Stewart sometimes felt the same emotions; he just wouldn't let them show. He tried so hard to be different from his father that he was sometimes brusque, even rude.

After a while, Stewart relaxed his anxiety about his father and began to pay more attention to Sharon's parents. He saw them more clearly now, through his mother's eyes. Sharon's father was warm and open but—as usual—a little bossy. He insisted they order red wine with their food even though Sharon wanted white, and at one point he told Stewart's mother she should order veal instead of fish because they were in an Italian restaurant. Stewart could see his mother freeze up. He thought she was pleasant, trying to like them, but he could see they weren't really her kind of people.

Sharon's mother told a couple of jokes that Stewart thought were a little crude. He was surprised. But he was not surprised when she made a few pronouncements about the big event. A wedding, she told him solemnly, was a "watermark" in a person's life. And later, she said that marriage was a "sacred institute." He thought of a seminary. Stewart, in the arrogance of youth, mocked her silently. He would be making similar slips of the tongue before he was forty-five. As we shall see, one of the more painful things about growing up is discovering in ourselves flaws we thought the exclusive province of others.

It was quite late when they finally finished dinner and found a taxi to take them back uptown. Sharon was tired and nervous about the rehearsal tomorrow. Stewart was remembering who said what at dinner. He was still very proud of Sharon, but about his in-laws he was not so sure.

Sharon thought the wedding itself went fine. Everybody seemed to have a good time, and the families got along okay. Stewart said his mother was nervous, but Sharon didn't think so. What she did think, but didn't say, was that Stewart was a little stiff toward her family. He was civil, but he was not enthusiastic. It did not occur to her that he would someday turn this chilly correctness on her.

At the reception, Stewart again became very aware of how different the two families were. Sharon's parents were okay, but some of her aunts and uncles were pretty loud. The aunt with the cast-iron permanent showed up wearing the kind of overelaborate dress he'd only seen before in technicolor movies. It was purplish-red, and she wore a long feathered boa that didn't quite match. She was not a woman to let colors scare her.

All the kissing and handshakes would have tired out a politician. Stewart decided that this was Sharon's family's affair and so he just let himself go along with the flow of events. The first quiet moment came when he went to the bathroom. He stayed a little longer than necessary, trying to collect his thoughts. When he returned and stood in the doorway, watching all of Sharon's people drinking and dancing and chattering away, he thought he belonged in this family like a scoop of ice cream in a glass of beer. But the thought passed quickly, and he went back in just in time for some more family pictures.

Sharon was exhausted when she and Stewart finally got ready to leave. On their way out, she overheard her mother say to her father, "At last, they're settled." It's a familiar sentiment—as though a wedding resolved something rather than coming in the middle of a complex process of changing family status.

ACCOMMODATION AND BOUNDARY-MAKING WITH THE IN-LAWS

The process of accommodation and making boundaries that goes on between newly married partners also includes their families. When they marry, the couple faces the task of separating from each family of origin and changing the nature of their relationships with parents and siblings, and in-laws. Loyalties must shift. For the newly married couple to function effectively as a unit, the spouses' primary commitment must be to the marriage. For their part, the families must support and accept the break.

Most people understand—in principle—this need for separation. In practice, misunderstandings often complicate the process. In almost every couple one partner is more involved with his or her family. The best thing the spouse can do is try to understand and accept this tie, and the best thing the more family-centered partner can do is reassure his or her mate of the primary commitment to the marriage.

———◆———

A couple in their mid-thirties once came to see me, saying they were having terrible fights and she was threatening to move out. Everything was fine in their marriage, they said, except for one thing. Royce felt Angie was too attached to her parents, spent far too much time with them, and worried about them excessively. Angie, trying to be reasonable, said yes, maybe she was very attached to them, but what was wrong with calling on the phone once a week or so, and visiting them every two or three months? The couple had gone round and round, and were at an impasse.

Though dissensions over in-laws are not unusual, this one was unusually intense. Instead of compromising their differences, both spouses kept pulling harder in opposite directions. The more contact Angie sought with her family, the more Royce resisted. Conflicts like this one don't go away, but I helped them reduce it to manageable proportions by breaking it into three constituent elements. The first was clarifying the boundary around the couple. Did she really want to leave? I asked Angie. No, she loved him. I helped her see that she needed to convince Royce of that— that her primary emotional attachment was to him, not to her parents. How could he doubt that? Angie wondered.

The second problem was how they communicated with each other. Contrary to popular belief, human problems rarely clear up when people learn to "communicate" better. Clear communication doesn't dissolve conflict the way New Improved Tide destroys stains, but it does clarify the nature of the conflict. With a little help from me, Angie and Royce were able to understand how the other one felt about their one big problem. He could see that she didn't want to be disloyal or unfaithful, or anything of the kind, she just wanted to see her parents. She could see that he felt they didn't have enough time alone together, and he didn't want to share her. A little empathy can prevent differences from growing into major aggravations.

Once the boundary issue was clarified and the two of them were communicating better—saying what they felt, not attacking each other, *and* showing that they understood what the other was feeling—the hard part, working out compromises about what to do, got easier. The actual mechanics of deciding how often to visit, and whether both of them would go or only Angie, never got simple, but they were no longer freighted with all the extra emotional baggage of bitterness and misunderstanding.

Incidentally, one thing that helped immensely was that Angie agreed in advance to leave her parents' when Royce wanted to go. Once he felt some control, he was much more willing to stay. *And*—what Angie really appreciated—he stopped saying disparaging things about her family's traditions.

———◆———

When two people marry, from two separate emotional cultures comes a new one. As we have seen, the spouses have to decide which rituals and traditions to retain from each family, and which ones to develop for themselves. The couple's parents can help avoid conflict in this process by scrupulously avoiding criticism of their son-in-law or daughter-in-law, and their family traditions. If a parent makes the mistake of criticizing, the son or daughter can gently but firmly defend the spouse. This has nothing to do with what's right or wrong; it has to do with demonstrating loyalty. This much may be obvious. What may be less obvious is that this same primary loyalty to the spouse needs to be demonstrated in all conflicts, no matter what the issue. It's certainly okay to argue or disagree with your spouse, but it's not okay to openly take sides with someone else on an emotional issue, or to be "neutral." In matters of the heart, if you're not with me, you're against me. Stewart Simpson had to learn this the hard way.

———◆———

After Stewart and Sharon were married, she got into regular fights with her father on almost every visit. Sharon wanted to be treated like a woman and a wife. Her father paid lip service to her new status—even playfully calling her "Mrs. Simpson"—but by the second day of any given visit he started treating her as though she were still a child, his daughter.

He was always inspecting her house, finding something to complain about. "This drawer shouldn't stick like this." "Why don't you get that screen replaced?" Another thing that annoyed her was that whenever she tried to tell him something she or Stewart had done, he'd change the subject around to someone he met five years ago or a second cousin who had done the same thing, or something vaguely similar. But the worst thing, the thing that really drove her crazy, was the way he baited her with ethnic jokes ("Did you hear the one about . . . ?") and conservative political remarks that even he probably didn't take seriously. If Sharon tried to challenge him, he dismissed her opinion as though she were still a college student. His favorite expression was, "When you've lived a little longer, you'll understand these things."

Half the time she tried to ignore him, and sometimes they could find a subject to discuss without arguing. Eventually Sharon, who loved him and wanted to be close, would let down her guard and open up to him. Invariably, he'd then say something mean or dismissive. When this happened the fights were terrible.

One particularly bad fight occurred when Sharon and Stewart drove her parents to the airport, and then had to wait two hours because the flight was delayed. Stewart could see that Sharon was tense, her patience worn thin by her father's constant fault-finding. "These goddamned airlines never run on time." "Why don't they have a decent place to eat in the airport?" "If only you'd called ahead to find out if the plane was on time, we wouldn't have had to spend all day in here."

By this time she'd had enough. She snapped, "Why don't you just shut up!" He flushed and said, "Don't you *dare* speak to me that way, young lady!" Sharon lost it. She flared up and started screaming at him, by now totally hysterical.

Stewart stood there, frozen, as Sharon and her father shouted at each other. Before Stewart could think of anything to say, Sharon ran off down the hall, sobbing. He was rooted, unable to move, still shocked at the fury of her outburst. She wanted him to follow her, he knew that as surely as he knew anything. But she was wrong. He stood there awkwardly, not wanting to be with her parents, but unwilling to support her temper tantrum. Lamely he commented, "She sure gets upset sometimes."

After several minutes he went to find her. Too late. She was wounded and furious that he hadn't followed her. She'd needed him, and felt deserted.

———◆———

When two people get married they often handle conflicts with each other by using their families. Wise families honor the sanctity of the new union, offering their support but keeping their distance. Ah, but how much distance? We all have our own standards for what constitutes the "right" amount of distance. Most spouses vary in their judgments about how much continuing involvement to have with their families. As if this weren't hard enough to resolve, their parents are likely to further complicate the process of separation and boundary-making by projecting their own standards onto the new couple.

Stewart wanted Sharon to move away from her family—but not too close to him. Her parents wanted her and Stewart to be close—to each other, maybe; to them, definitely. Caught between competing demands for her affection, Sharon could not get far in either direction without a crippling sense of disloyalty. So, she did what most of us do: shifted back and forth in response to her feelings.

When she felt ignored by Stewart, Sharon moved closer to her mother—shifting from one side of the triangle to the other. She looked forward eagerly to visits home, where she could once again bathe in the warm love of her family. When she and Stewart arrived, her family enveloped them. Sharon loved it—for about twenty-four hours. Then she began to feel smothered. Her parents would begin to get on her nerves, and in response to her exasperation, she'd move toward Stewart. She'd get fed up with her mother's gossip and her father's not listening to her, and suggest that she and Stewart go off alone together—something her parents found intolerable. They didn't say much, but they blamed Stewart for refusing to fit in, and for taking Sharon away from them.

Sharon's binding obligation to her family had a positive and a negative pole. The togetherness ethic was so strong among her people that whenever she ventured too far from them, physically or emotionally, guilt feelings arose within her and pulled her back, every bit as effectively as a dog's leash. It was not obligation alone that kept her tied to them. She also felt a positive, loving bond.

Stewart sensed, though probably could not have described, both of these pulls, and resented them equally. Obligation, he thought, was stupid. As for the still-strong bond of love, Stewart thought of it as dependency.

◆

In addition to honoring the new couple's independence, there is also stress on the families to open themselves up to an outsider who is now an official member of the inner circle. Once they reconciled themselves to Stewart, Sharon's parents were glad to have a new member of the family. They thought of it as an addition, like adding a spare room onto the house. Stewart had other ideas. He was marrying Sharon, not her family. He loved her. But his version of love was like a hunter's love of deer, not something the herd would take kindly to. Sharon's people were prepared to respect the new couple's rights, but they never anticipated how distant Stewart would choose to be.

Sharon was caught in the middle. She knew that her parents would like to see more of her and Stewart, and she knew that he would like to see less of them. Consequently, there were arguments about how often to visit, and the visits themselves were always tense.

At first, Stewart and Sharon's parents, aware of their conflicting claims on Sharon, made extra efforts to be polite. Stewart tried to get close to Sharon's dad. He prided himself on his ability to tolerate Mr. Nathan's brusqueness, and he tried to ignore the unbelievable bossiness. There was only one way to fry an egg, mix concentrated orange juice, or get from one part of town to another. All Stewart could do in the circumstances was what he knew how to do. He went along—he was good at that—but he did so at a cost. It hurt his pride, and because he was humoring Mr. Nathan, he couldn't really like him. As Stewart began to feel more sure of himself, he began to speak up. He told them he didn't want to call them "Mom" and "Dad," and he frequently refused to go along when Mr. Nathan proposed little excursions.

Once the barriers of politeness were dropped between Stewart and his in-laws, it didn't take them long to find each other out. And what is it that they so quickly found out? It was not a rounded picture, or even the essential character of the others; it was that which made them different. Stewart found out that Mrs. Nathan was loud and superficial. She was one of those emotional types—not with the exuberance of high energy, but with the caprice of easy emotion. With her, everything was a florid show of feeling. She was easily agitated, needy, greedy. For her part, she thought her son-in-law was a cold fish. She greeted him effusively, though he knew she didn't mean it. Stewart aimed his kiss to one side of her mouth but she turned slightly so that their lips met. It seemed natural to her. To him it wasn't. And her laughter was jarring, like music turned up too loud. She was all the things his mother wasn't.

◆

Unlike Stewart, Sharon was drawn to her in-laws. She especially admired Nancy, whose independence and competence was such a contrast to her own mother's boisterous emotionalism. Nancy was a good listener, too. She always wanted to know what Sharon was doing, how things were going—and she did not interrupt or change the subject to talk about herself. In fact, it was hard to get her to say anything about herself. Sharon's questions about how things were going provoked discussions mainly of a meteorological nature. "How's everything down your way, Nancy?" "Oh, fine. We're having a lovely spell of warm, sunny weather."

Time only confirmed Sharon's earlier impression that her mother-in-law was friendly but reserved. She was easy to talk to but impossible to get to know. Nancy seemed genuinely fond of Sharon, but she never called—it was always up to Sharon or Stewart—and she always had some excuse for not visiting.

One Christmas when Sharon and Stewart were visiting his parents, Sharon suggested that Stewart go with his father to get the tree, so that she'd have a chance to talk with Nancy. "Good idea," Stewart said. He liked the fact that Sharon wanted to be close to his mother. Maybe she'd have more success than he did. His mother, he knew, judged women by their qualities, notably patience and loving, only men by their deeds. Surely Sharon got high marks.

As soon as the men left, Sharon sat down by Nancy in the living room and started talking. Not more than five minutes went by before Nancy excused herself to start working on dinner. Sharon, who felt uncomfortable in other people's kitchens, picked up the paper and waited for Nancy to return. Half an hour went by, and things got quiet in the kitchen. Sharon got up and went to see what was happening.

There was Nancy, sitting and smoking, smoking and coughing. A half-inch-long ash hung, poised at the end of her cigarette. Sharon was watching it, waiting for it to fall, when Nancy happened to look up and see her standing there. "Oh, hi, I was just about to stuff the turkey."

Sharon was a little hurt that Nancy left her sitting alone, but she didn't think it was personal. Nancy just liked to be by herself. She seemed to prefer her conversations brief, then she withdrew from company like a visitor going home. Uneasily, Sharon reflected that this was the woman who taught her husband how a person should be.

How different these Simpsons were from her family! In her family nobody did anything alone.

Many newly married spouses go through a period of wishing to be adopted by their in-laws. Here, too, opposites attract. But in most cases this attraction passes. Just as Stewart found Sharon's parents intrusive, smothering, and chaotic, she gradually concluded that his parents were too reserved, isolated, and cool for her. They, especially Nancy, didn't seem to want to get involved. Her parents wouldn't let go.

Every move Sharon made to close the circle around Stewart and her represented an implicit threat of disloyalty toward her family. They resisted exclusion and fence-making, and Sharon herself was conflicted as well because—no matter how committed she was to Stewart—her heart had unshakable allegiances of its own.

INVISIBLE LOYALTIES

Stewart could tell from Sharon's voice that the person she was talking to on the telephone was her mother. There was that animated eagerness in her voice, a readiness to share some bit of news, or grow annoyed. "*Mother*, he's already an assistant professor. Most people start out as an instructor." She talked about him, defended him. It made him feel good. The nicest things he heard from her were often things he overheard. He kept his eyes pointed at the television set and turned down the volume. Low enough to listen to Sharon on the phone but not, he hoped, low enough to be noticed.

Sharon didn't talk about him for long. She was already onto the subject that interested her most, the thing that kept her connected to her parents and separated from him: her family. Aunts and uncles and cousins and husbands and wives and children. Everything they did, everything they said, was still vitally important to her. Aunt Zelda was in the hospital and cousin Fredda didn't even visit! Cousin Ralph's wife, Suzi, was having her whole house painted. *Where* did she get all that money?

Stewart was annoyed. If Sharon loved him, she would forget about all that nonsense.

Stewart never put it (even to himself) in so many words, nevertheless he had expected to replace Sharon's parents. Two human beings, bound together in love and kindness—they shouldn't need anyone else. This seemed to Stewart a natural culmination of their love, a just and romantic ambition which shouldn't be so hard to accomplish. Like so many expectations, this one was not thought out, and so never examined. Too bad, because this false hope would prove a great disappointment to him and a source of even greater conflict for Sharon.

To Sharon, it seemed that he wanted to keep her hermetically sealed off from her family. But—and this is what made it so unfair—he did not in return give himself over to her freely. He wanted all of her but did not give all of himself. Instead, he kept himself private, self-contained, in a cocoon within a cocoon.

One of the great mistakes we make in marriage—in any relationship—is wanting to change the other person. When you marry, you marry the whole person, not just the parts you like, the whole package. Part of that package is your spouse's relationship with his or her parents. Stewart didn't anticipate this and couldn't accept it. But whether he liked it or not, once or twice a week he got a reminder.

Stewart saw his wife as being overly attached to her mother. Why all these calls? What he didn't see was that Sharon had wanted to leave her family for the marriage, but finding Stewart less emotionally available than she expected, she had turned back to her family to satisfy her need for intimate connection. Stewart had a way of expressing contempt that only fortified her loyalty to her family. When they fought and Stewart got really mad, he hissed at her, "Just like your mother." Sharon was infuriated. But what she hated even more was that when she dared to say something nice about her father, Stewart would snap, "Then why didn't you marry your father?"

Sharon and Stewart and her parents formed a triangle, with sides of interchangeable length; the more distant he was from her, the closer she moved to them. Instead of accepting her ties to her family, or recognizing his role in the triangle, Stewart tried, though not very directly, to pull her away from them.

———◆———

In-laws can be part of conflict resolution or nonresolution. The outcome depends upon two factors. First, we must accept our spouses' loyalty to their parents; second, we must not displace unresolved conflict from one relationship to another.

In my experience, the people who most jealously oppose their spouses' bond to their parents are insecure—about themselves and about their marriages. They don't have strong ties to their own families, and usually don't have many friends. My advice is to allow your spouse as much freedom as possible to relate to his or her parents, otherwise your resistance, spoken or not, will set up a constant tension and remain a source of irritation. In a functional marriage, each spouse takes responsibility for the relationship with his or her family and works toward getting along with them. The best thing you can do is to join your spouse.

Stewart, unfortunately, couldn't understand this. As Sharon tried to remain connected to her parents, he increased his demands that she should accept his truth more than her family's. As a result, she began to feel like a victim of his jealousy. Before they married, she would not have believed that the man she loved could turn out to be so stubborn and possessive. But she had seen only half his nature then, as one sees the crescent moon when it is partly masked by the shadow of the earth. She saw the full moon now, the full man.

The more hostile Stewart grew toward her family, the more she felt threatened and the more she resurrected her mother as her protector. Consequently, the issues to be resolved were not kept between Stewart and Sharon, but were shifted to between him and her plus her mother. When Stewart criticized her mother, Sharon felt herself attacked. Not only did his criticisms set up a loyalty conflict for her, but she also realized that his attack on her mother was a displaced attack on herself. He felt free to call her mother shallow, dependent, and unimaginative. Weren't these the things he secretly thought about her?

The in-laws play two roles in loyalty conflicts. They make demands, implicit as well as explicit, and they serve as convenient targets for displaced tensions.

The formation of a marital bond requires each partner to shift his or her primary emotional attachment from the parents to the spouse. As couples attempt this shift, a variety of problems can develop. Some parents continue to struggle for primacy in their children's lives.

Even though Sharon's parents accepted Stewart and supported the marriage, their implicit message was that if she moved too far away, Sharon was ungrateful, unappreciative—a deserter. "How can you leave us when you owe us so much?" This feeling is magnified when a child knows that her parents' whole lives are focused on their children. Jealousy or resentment of the chosen mate may be disguised, but it is still there. That's why some children remain forever fixed in loyal, guilt-ridden obligation to their parents.

Loyalty implies you owe something to someone. Interpersonal loyalty, on the other hand, refers to the existence of structured group expectations to which all members are committed. Even though Sharon changed her name to Simpson, she did not thereby cease to be a Nathan.

Aside from whatever demands they actually make, in-laws are easy scapegoats for family tensions. Some mothers cannot accept the fact that their sons want to put distance between them. They prefer to hold their daughters-in-law responsible for alienation of affection. It is easier to begrudge your daughter-in-law for keeping your son to herself than to admit that your son is not as responsive as you wish. It is easier for a wife to resent her mother-in-law's intrusiveness than to confront her husband directly for not keeping his mother from interfering.

Ultimately, what makes in-laws difficult is our ambivalence about our own parents. Sharon and Stewart both expected their partners to handle their families for them. Sharon expected Stewart to pull her away, which to some extent he did. And Stewart often handed the phone to Sharon when his mother called. He wanted the connection but didn't know how to make it.

In-laws are notoriously difficult, but they are not the most feared species in the family jungle. Sharon may have had confused and conflicted feelings about Stewart's parents, but she had less at stake than he did. After all, in-laws are only in-laws. Her in-laws were his parents.

PAST TENSE AND IMPERFECT FUTURE

By the time we grow up and get married, each of us has two relationships with our own parents. One is based on the past. It consists of the memories we have of growing up, of how our parents treated us and how we felt about them. This is the repository of fond memories, frustrated longings, assumptions about relationships, and expectations for life. The second relationship is the real, ongoing relationship we have (or don't have) with the flesh-and-blood parents who exist in the present.

Ironically, the first relationship, the one in our minds, is more alive for many people than the second one, the real, contemporary relationship. The real relationship is often frozen in place by the one in memory.

The family is made of strange glue—it stretches but doesn't let go. Even in families like Stewart's, where contact is cordial but distant, the family adheres to the next generation in the form of unfinished emotional business.

This unfinished business is known as *fusion*—the blurring of psychological boundaries between the self and others that is so ubiquitous in families. The opposite of fusion is emotional maturity and independence—*differentiation*. An easy mistake is to confuse the pseudo-independence of the person who avoids his or her family with genuine differentiation. Differentiation means achieving an autonomous identity, not putting distance between yourself and your family. When it comes to family, you can run but you can't hide.

Sharon and Stewart were both still emotionally fused with their families, though they demonstrated it in opposite ways. Lack of differentiation may take the form of continued intense involvement, as in Sharon's case, or, as in Stewart's case, *emotional cutoff*. In the process of differentiation, "I" becomes increasingly differentiated from "we." But Sharon was leaving one "we" (her family) for another (her and Stewart, as a tightly bonded unit). Part of her plan had been to create a new family, an improved version of the old one, in which she would take care of Stewart and he would reciprocate. But the old family did not disappear, nor did its claim on her, and she faced a struggle to balance the old relationship with the new.

Unfortunately for her, the man Sharon was trying to become

fused with was allergic to intimacy. Stewart was leaving a family where he denied and avoided connection to form a marriage where he instinctively tried to do the same. For a poorly differentiated man like Stewart, sustained intimacy is threatening, as though it might negate his separateness entirely. Getting close feels like losing control. Stewart wanted to be close, but he was afraid of being absorbed. In the face of this anxiety, his natural reaction was to keep his distance.

◆

Although the past is gone, we can't seem to let go. When we think about our parents and when we visit them, there's that tension. Slow to accept that they are who they are, and that whatever happened happened, we go on wanting something from them. We long for that someday when they will make up for what we missed; when they will change; when they will apologize; when they will finally treat us the way we want them to. We want everything from them—everything but the real love that is available.

Some people, like Sharon, long actively for their parents to start respecting them, and work to bring this about; others, like Stewart, avoid thinking about it but secretly yearn for missing shows of love and attention. Somewhere, lost in the heart, is a strong part of us that never really grows up until we stop needing our parents to make things right.

Some people invest their whole lives in a struggle with their parents. I've met men and women of fifty who are still furious with their parents' lack of attention, or because their mothers don't come to visit them as often as they visit other members of the family. Such bondage!

Attempting to alter the script of the past, many people create needless tension with their parents by trying to get them to change. Many more, bitter about past injustices and convinced that their parents will never change, avoid them altogether, meanwhile keeping the past alive in the form of bitter memories. In reality, of course, the only thing that can be changed in the present is the present itself. Once you quit struggling to make your parents into the people you wish they'd been, you can begin to form a relationship with them as they are.

And what about the past? Your mother's harsh treatment,

your father's neglect, all the ways they let you down? Does all this go away, or cease to matter? No, but it's over. The best thing you can do about the past is to remember it, and try to understand what happened, what effect it had on you, and how you can avoid acting out the same scenarios with your own children. As for the parents you remember, forgive them. Perhaps you can understand why they did what they did. Perhaps not. But believe this: They did the best they could. We all do.

———◆———

One of my patients, a young man of thirty-five, had a very rough childhood. His mother alternated between angry tirades and periods of depression. When she was depressed, she neglected her six children; when she was angry, she beat them. His father was a heavy drinker and rarely at home. Growing up in this atmosphere, my patient learned to be wily and resourceful, but unfortunately he also learned to keep his feelings to himself and not to trust anybody. This may have helped him in business; it did not help him as a husband and father. Exploring this past and its impact helped my patient understand himself better, and once he could see how he had become so closed off, he was able to start opening up more with his wife and children. However, when it came to reestablishing a relationship with his parents, he balked.

"Okay, so the past is over," he said. "But they still haven't changed. They still ignore me. Last week was my birthday and they didn't even send me a birthday card."

Like a lot of us, this man was still collecting grievances. Maybe that isn't quite fair. Perhaps I should say that his parents were still disappointing him. What he complained about was absolutely true, and he was perfectly justified in complaining. What he missed, though, was understanding that relationships are circular. What they do is a function of what we do, and what we do is a function of what they do, et cetera. True, my patient's parents didn't send him a birthday card. But that isn't too surprising since he hadn't called, written, or visited them in years. Am I saying it's his fault? No, I don't care whose fault it is. The point is this: Relationship problems are kept going by both parties, *and* either party can break the cycle. This truth is easier for most people to accept with regard to relationships where they feel more powerful—with their children, or young friends, or junior colleagues at work. With big people we often feel one-down and don't see as easily our ability to turn things around. Nowhere is this more true than with our parents.

———◆———

Why bother? If your relationship with your parents isn't all that it should be, so what? Sure it would be nice if things were better, but there are too many other things to worry about— earning a living, paying the bills, trying to find a little time to relax. In a life crowded with imperatives, it's easy to put off anything optional, like working on the relationship with your parents.

Why bother? Because there are two benefits of almost incalculable worth. The first is mastering unresolved emotional sensitivity to the things your parents do that drive you crazy. The second is increasing the active network of your relationships.

The best clue to the nature of the unfinished business with your parents may be the triggers that set off emotional reactivity in you. Those who are cut off from their families, like Stewart, may be a little unclear about what their parents do that stirs up adolescent overreaction in them. Stewart thought that the link of dependency which united him and his parents had completely severed, but little by little he was reminded that it still had a palpable existence. It was as thin as a hair, but there were moments when he seemed to hear it vibrate.

———◆———

Stewart still called his mother when he achieved some professional success, and she still responded with that cool lack of enthusiasm that punctured his pride like an icepick in a tire. Sharon saw it. Stewart's mother was the one audience who would never give him a standing ovation.

Stewart was a person who wanted to be admired but was afraid he wouldn't be. That's what made him reign in his excitement over his accomplishments. "Don't play games," she'd tell him when he'd try to be coy about something he'd done at work. His game was to minimize his success in hopes that it would provoke her to praise him lavishly. But how could she praise him when he was so indirect?

The emotion we're talking about is shame—the painful feeling of being unworthy, which lies at the heart of many people's basic sense of self. Stewart held so much back because he was afraid of not being responded to—or worse, of being disapproved of or mocked. Fearing that his craving for admiration and praise might lead to disappointment, Stewart kept a lot inside. Sharon used to chide him for always being a pessimist. The reason for Stewart's pessimism was that he didn't allow himself to get his hopes up; he was that afraid of disappointment.

Stewart carried a different legacy from his father. Mr. Simpson was a man who exercised iron control with a velvet glove. As a boy, Stewart was allowed so much freedom that he never learned to rebel. At eight he was permitted to go anywhere he wanted on the bus, and by the time he was ten he often took long train trips to visit his relatives. It wasn't until Stewart was seventeen that his idea of what he should be allowed to do exceeded his father's tolerance.

One Friday night as Stewart was about to go off to the movies with his friends, his father asked what picture they were going to see. It was a Brigitte Bardot movie. "Absolutely not!" his father said. Stewart was stunned. His father had never told him what movies he could or couldn't see. How could he start now? Out of politeness, Stewart agreed. He wouldn't have known how to frame a disagreement. You don't argue with your father.

That's when he started doing things on the sly. Previously, he had never felt the need. But he was too old to start taking orders, and it didn't make sense to get into a hassle. Why bother?

Stewart brought this same sneaky streak into his marriage. It was not that he did anything wrong; his own conscience was too strong for that. But sometimes, in little matters (like spending extra money or staying after work to have a drink with somebody), he found it easier not to say anything than to risk the possibility of an argument.

———◆———

Those who are still actively embroiled in their families, like Sharon, usually know exactly what their parents do that drives them crazy. They loved her but treated her as extensions of themselves. This meant that, on the one hand, they placed a lot of expectations on her; on the other hand, they did not take her seriously.

Parents can help children differentiate when they stress the child's responsibilities within the family—dressing and washing without help, putting away toys—while at the same time making it clear that this is done in preparation for assuming later responsibilities outside the family. Sharon's parents gave her very few responsibilities, and never talked about "when you grow up" or "when you get married." It was as though they couldn't accept the idea.

Conversely, anything that attaches rigid priorities to the child's service to the family will usually be restrictive—functioning within a narrow range defined by the family's needs. Sharon's family needed someone to play the role of "good daughter," and she was it. Roles, like this one, may not describe the reality of the person as much as that person's place in the family system. In Sharon's family, where the collective sense of "family" was more important than the individuality of its members, such roles were extremely powerful.

When she got married, Sharon imagined that her parents would take her more seriously. She had so many hopes for their visits. They would see her grown up, happily and comfortably married. At last, they'd give her what she wanted: attention *and* respect. These bright hopes were what made her so anxious— eager and tense—about her parents' visits. Stewart couldn't help but be affected. He did not look forward to his in-laws' visits. He didn't like seeing Sharon get so frantic about how the house looked, and what she would cook to please her father, and where they could go to entertain her mother. Worse, he felt smothered when they showed up. When he saw this rigid family system closing in around him, Stewart thought he might suffocate. It was as if their presence were a blight—everything withered before it.

Stewart didn't like it when Sharon got so frustrated with her parents (Why did she let them bother her so much?), but he didn't mind when she turned to him for support. He could sympathize with her when she said how awful they were—and he didn't have to risk saying the same thing himself. This was, however, only the immediate result of Sharon's stormy relationship with her parents. In the long run, she transferred her thwarted needs onto Stewart.

Frustrated longings for love, appreciation, and approval can have a great impact on a person's marriage. These longings may be denied or minimized; they may be projected onto others; or they may be covered over by feelings of anger, resentment, rejection, or even numbness.

The idealized in-love phase of early marriage renews the hope for the perfect parent who will make up for old disappointments. The more impossible the expectations and longings, the more certain it is that the marital partner will become a source of disappointment and frustration. No wonder Stewart couldn't understand Sharon's anger at him; it carried so much extra weight.

———◆———

The degree to which the personhood of each partner remains connected to and defined by his or her family of origin shapes how flexible and accommodating the marital pair will be. This is really just another way of saying that unfinished business with our parents gets in the way of our working on new relationships. Once we begin to resolve how we feel about our parents—the minute that happens—we can get on to the business of relating to our spouses as real people, not as shadows of the past.

The best way to improve relationships with your parents is to build a personal connection with each one of them, and then to discover—and change—your part in destructive patterns of inter-action. Sharon, for example, might have tried to spend some time alone with each of her parents. In her case, this wouldn't have been easy; her parents came as a matched pair. A surprising number of people who think they have a decent relationship with their parents almost never spend time alone with one of them (especially the parent of the opposite sex). Sharon was occasionally alone with her mother. But the intimacy of this contact was limited because they always talked about other people. Sharon's mother was especially fond of complaining about her husband. Sharon, interested and sympathetic, listened, but she would have done better to try to make the conversation more personal—to talk about her mother and herself.

To spend a little time alone with her father, Sharon might have offered to take him out to lunch. With her mother, the goal would have been to make the conversation more intimate, more personal. With her father, her goal would be to notice what he did that got her so upset and learn to control her reaction—not necessarily to suppress her feelings, but to respond in a less volatile way. Her old pattern with her father was to initiate conversations, telling him what Stewart was doing at the university, or about someone interesting she had met, or some plans she had. He listened, but not for long. When he changed the subject, she felt totally discounted. If tensions were low enough, she'd just withdraw; if anxiety was running high, she'd explode.

To break this cycle there are a number of things Sharon could have done. She might have begun by asking her father about himself. Perhaps by showing some interest in him she could have relieved him of some of his urge to interrupt when it was her turn. Or she could have told him directly that she felt bad when he cut her off or otherwise didn't take her seriously.

Once you see what the old unsatisfactory pattern is, you can make improvements with almost any change. The trick is to remain calm, and not respond automatically. By the way, this is easier to do on a planned outing than in the heat of the moment of hectic family get-togethers.

◆

In order for Stewart to improve relationships with his parents he'd have had to find a way to get a little closer to his mother, and to be more honest with his father. Getting closer to his mother would not have been easy. Pressing shy persons for intimacy only drives them away. Telling her directly that he wanted to be closer, asking her personal questions, or even fishing for her approval of his career would have had the opposite effect from the one he intended.

It helps to remember that there are degrees of intimacy, from friendly superficial conversation, to expressing things personal but not revealing, to sharing more intimate thoughts and feelings, and finally to talking about the relationship itself. To become more intimate with someone, take one step at a time. Don't exceed the other person's comfort level. You can gauge this by noting what subjects seem to make the other person anxious. Jimmy Carter's revelation that he lusted after women in his heart shocked some people because he made public what is usually kept private; he was more intimate with the American public than they cared for him to be. Stewart's mother, who after all was fairly sophisticated, thought Jimmy Carter's announcement silly. She would not have had the same reaction to a similar confession from her son.

Stewart was closer to his father. In fact, they got along pretty well. The one thing Stewart might have done differently was to disagree more openly and let his father know when he was annoyed at him. Stewart was already an expert at ignoring what offended him and going along when he didn't feel like it. He needed to practice arguing, speaking up, and fighting back. In fact, he and Sharon would have been good coaches for each other.

———◆———

Sharon and Stewart might have made these changes but they didn't. The pressing demands of young adulthood—forming families and building careers—make most people defer working things out with their parents. If contact is painful, we protect ourselves with distance the way Stewart did, or, like Sharon, endure it as inevitable. Most people see what their parents do that they don't like, but make the mistake of thinking that nothing will change unless they can get through to their parents—or maybe lightning will strike and transform them into the better people we think they should be.

Instead of dwelling on the awful things your parents do, think of their behavior as a link in a chain. Dig out the patterns of relationship, even those which are not apparent. Then change your part; the system will shift. Remember the two benefits: The more we resolve conflicts with our parents, the less we will be caught up in acting out similar defensive and reactive patterns with our husbands and wives; *and* we will have the positive pleasure of getting along with our parents. The closer and better our relationships with our parents (and siblings and friends) the less likely we are to make our marriages into protective cocoons. Trying to meet all of your needs in one relationship is putting too much emotional pressure on that relationship. It can lead to an explosion.

Incidentally, the same two benefits accrue to developing better relationships with your in-laws. Getting to know and accept your in-laws will help you to better understand and come to terms with your spouse, as well as adding to the size of your family.

Developing healthy relationships with your in-laws is a way of contacting the partner's past, and a way to come to terms with parts of your spouse that you have trouble accepting and knowing how to relate to.

The more Stewart could have learned to tolerate Mr. Nathan's bossiness, the better able he would have been to deal with Sharon's bossiness. Ignoring Mr. Nathan and humoring him was a false solution, because it reinforced distance and dishonesty. A better solution would have been for Stewart to speak up, even if he found it necessary to use a kidding tone. As for Sharon, if she could have found a way to get closer to Mrs. Simpson, she'd not only have been making a friend, but also learning how to break through the Simpson wall of solitude.

———◆———

Most couples have a relatively short interval between marriage and the birth of the first child. (This is changing but not as much as people think.) Therefore, most young people have only a short time to adjust to this phase of life before moving on. It's hard to take on new tasks while still carrying the burden of what's left unfinished.

Loyalty commitments to parents are especially pertinent to the raising and training of children. So even though Sharon only shrugged when her parents asked their favorite rhetorical question, "So, when are we going to be grandparents?" she felt some responsibility not to disappoint them. Consciously, she was a long way from being ready to become a mother; unconsciously, she felt an undischarged obligation to give her parents what they wanted.

7

THE DEPRESSED YOUNG MOTHER

*O*ne soft summer night when they were driving home from a party, Stewart said, "Let's have a baby. I want a little Sharon." They'd been married four years. Stewart was teaching at the state university in Albany, and Sharon was working in the department of admissions. She didn't know what to say. She assumed they would have a baby someday, but she hadn't really thought about when. Was this "someday," already? All she said was, "Okay."

They didn't have long to wait. Sharon's doctor said it might take at least six months to conceive (something about the pill causing a hormone imbalance), but it was less than two months after she said okay that the gynecologist confirmed she was pregnant.

She was just about to call Stewart when the phone rang. It was Stewart. "Well, what did the doctor say?" "I'm definitely pregnant, we're going to have a baby," she answered. Stewart shouted something into the phone; it sounded like "Yahoo!" For once, there was no mistaking his feelings.

That night he came home with flowers and took her out to dinner at the little French place she liked so much. He really made a fuss over her. It felt good.

The first three months of the pregnancy were awful. Sharon was sick to her stomach every afternoon. The first two or three days of nausea were bad enough. What made it worse was that it just continued, day after day. Finally, she went to the doctor, who gave her some antinausea medicine. She wasn't crazy about the idea of taking medication while she was pregnant, but on the other hand, she wasn't crazy about vomiting every afternoon.

As her body swelled to adapt to the growing fetus, Sharon's mind slowly adapted to the idea of becoming a mother. Nature, she guessed, was resolving her ambivalence. When she first felt the baby turning inside her, it became a definite reality. Stewart was less interested. He got excited the first time he felt the baby moving, but after that he wasn't particularly curious about what was going on inside Sharon's belly. He was a bystander. He was concerned when she said the baby was kicking ("Does it hurt?"), but his concern was limited to her. The new life growing inside her seemed beyond the reach of his imagination. *Maybe all men are like that*, Sharon thought. Stewart thought she was too preoccupied with herself.

As slowly as the first few weeks of the pregnancy dragged on, the last few raced by. Labor came on fast—three weeks early. Sharon woke Stewart and said she was having contractions. "You couldn't be," he said. "It must be a false alarm." After that the contractions stopped, and Stewart went off to work. "Call me if anything develops."

At two that afternoon Sharon called to say that the contractions were coming regularly and the doctor said it was time to go to the hospital.

Labor was hard and long. Lamaze helped. At least Sharon knew what to expect. Stewart was good, too. He was always calm in emergencies. When the pain made her lose concentration, Stewart was right there. He helped her get control of her breathing. Still, the night dragged on. It was well after midnight when they finally wheeled her into the delivery room. Sharon was groggy now, but she knew it was almost over. For the rest of her life, she would remember lying there in that theater of bright lights, with the doctor and nurse urging her, "Push, push, push!" God, it hurt.

Sharon saw the baby when his head and shoulders were out. *"There's a baby coming out of me!"* She had known it all along, but suddenly there he was. The next thing she saw was Stewart holding the baby, crying and smiling at the same time. Maybe there would be a rainbow, Sharon thought dreamily. Then they handed her the tiny bundle. She loved him. She had loved him in her belly, but this was different.

When Stewart came back the next morning, Sharon was sleeping; the baby was in the nursery. He stood in front of the glass watching all the little babies, full of feeling. But he didn't stay long, he wanted to see Sharon. He sat down as quietly as he could in the chair next to her bed. Sharon looked exhausted now, and frail, and very beautiful.

Sharon opened her eyes and smiled when she saw Stewart. "Did you see him?" she asked.

"Yes, he looks just like you."

Just then the nurse knocked softly. "Anybody in here want to see a baby?" Then she brought Jason in on a little cart and handed him to Sharon. Sharon couldn't stop looking at him: his fat little cheeks, his curly dark hair, his perfect body. She was taken by surprise by the wave of love she felt for her baby. *Her baby!*

While Sharon looked at the baby, Stewart looked at Sharon. She had never looked so angelic as she did then, lying propped up on her pillows with her dark hair cascading over her shoulders and the tiny infant in her arms.

For the rest of her days, there were many moments from that day Sharon would always remember. Most of all she loved looking at Jason. God, she thought, made babies that helpless and adorable so everyone would want one, and want to take care of it. In sleep, Jason looked like a little doll or an angel, defraying the suggestion of all the effort to come.

◆

Riding home with a new baby was one of those emotionally supercharged experiences that takes only a few minutes and lasts forever. Sharon's heart was full and everything was vivid. The sunshine was bright on the lawns and flowers, and the air was warm but not hot—perfect. Sharon felt the same kind of intense awareness of things that she felt coming out into the open air after being in a museum or a movie. Only this time she was very tired. She kept looking down at the baby. It still didn't seem real. Her feelings were all jumbled up. It was a little like coming home from a shopping trip with some wonderful new purchase. She remembered the feeling of satisfaction she'd felt when they brought home the big air conditioner for their bedroom. Once they wrestled the big box up the stairs and finally got it installed, it was great: instant relief. But a baby—what were they going to do with a baby?

The house was more or less ready. Stewart had talked her into putting the baby in a separate bedroom ("You want to get some sleep, don't you?"). Some friends had lent them a cradle, and they had gone to Babyland to buy a changing table with a padded top and lots of little compartments to put things in. What else did they need, really, except a few little sleeper suits and diapers? Since it was Stewart's idea to use disposable diapers instead of the cloth ones, he'd gone to the store to buy a supply. He showed Sharon the four boxes of infant-size Pampers and said, "This ought to last us a while."

———◆———

At first, Sharon worried about the baby. He looked so tiny and helpless. How would she know when he needed something? She found out.

Nature, it seemed, had designed things so that parents *had to* take care of their infants. At least that's the way it was with Jason. He hollered to be fed and wailed when he was wet—he seemed so sensitive to having a wet diaper—and sometimes he cried just to be held. Jason's demands were so intense and unrelenting that the first month was a blur of pervasive fatigue and frustration. Nothing had prepared them for this.

That first day home from the hospital, it was quite late when Sharon finally fell exhausted into a deadening sleep. She was still exhausted when she woke, thick and groggy with dreams. She was on a train, speeding through the night, its whistle shrieking. When she tried to focus on where the train was going, she became aware of a baby's cry. A baby? Then she remembered. She glanced at the clock. It was 2:00 A.M.—oh, she was tired! She kept her eyes shut, hoping Stewart would get the baby so she could drift off again. She waited. Nothing broke the sound of the baby's persistent cry. After another minute she said, "Stewart, do you want to bring me the baby?"

"Aw, come on, Sharon! I have to be up early for work; why don't you get him? You're the one who's going to have to feed him anyway."

Sharon didn't say anything. As she went to get the baby she thought, *So this is the way it's going to be.*

Over the next few weeks the weight of the baby's demands slowly sapped Sharon's strength to the point where she felt she was always in a fog. In those unbroken days and nights, it was like having the flu, but one that doesn't go away—and nobody sends you to bed and brings you ice cream. You're the mother now.

Sharon hadn't really recuperated from childbirth. She still had pain and soreness from the episiotomy, and engorged breasts. Her back ached, and she could feel it getting worse every time she bent over to pick up Jason. And she still had vaginal bleeding with clots and cramps. Add to this her anxiety about the baby and her disappointment in Stewart for leaving everything to her and you have a recipe for postpartum depression.

According to a recent authoritative study by Eugene Paykel and his associates, 20 percent of new mothers experience a mild to moderate form of depression during the postpartum period.[1] Among the main contributing factors are worry, fatigue, and lack of any personal time. Sharon did not actually become clinically depressed, but she was among the two-thirds of new mothers who, according to Ramona Mercer, are blue and cry easily.[2] Sadly, many of these women are ashamed of themselves for being unhappy. It isn't supposed to be this way, is it?

THE IMPOSSIBLE JOB

Being a parent is the ultimate training in humility. Nobody expects having an infant to be as much stress as it turns out to be, and few remember afterwards how hard it was. The human mind softens the hard edges of reality. Besides, there are plenty of incentives. When the children are babies, we can—and do—provide almost everything they need. And we exert such a profound control over them. They're ours. It's a good feeling.

The most famous plague for parents is their children's adolescence, but nothing quite matches the physical strain most parents go through during the first few months of infancy. A lot of people forget how hard it was. Time blurs the memory of all the effort and anxiety, and of course there are compensations. Wonderful compensations.

◆

While she was still in the maternity ward, Sharon was surprised to learn that it would be a couple of days before real milk began to flow through her breasts. (Before that, a small amount of fluid known as colostrum is all that comes out.) It took a little while to get the hang of nursing, but when she did, it was an indescribable source of satisfaction. She held the baby in her arms, and when he felt the nipple near his mouth, he rooted around trying to get hold of it. He'd make a little O with his tiny mouth—Sharon called this his "foody face"—and search eagerly until he found what he wanted. He looked so blissful while he suckled. After a while, when Sharon's milk began to flow automatically at nursing time, she had the sensation of letting go and feeding the baby as though straight from her own heart.

Sharon wanted Jason to have a pleasant, stimulating environment, and so she bought a collection of artistic greeting cards, sealed them in plastic, and hung them around the inside of his cradle. She chose ones with bright, pleasing colors. Mondrian, Klee, and Rousseau were her favorites. When she made mobiles to hang over the cradle, she took pains to turn the shapes—little boats and animals—sideways, so he could see them when he looked up. She even read to him in French, so that he would get used to the sounds. But it was two or three months before the baby noticed much of what was going on around him.

Jason proved to be an extremely demanding and fussy baby. From the start, he slept little and ate a lot. Not until he was eight months old did he regularly sleep through the night. He was a greedy eater, but it was hard to tell when he was going to want a big feeding or a small one. His unpredictable eating and sleeping patterns were exhausting. Sharon never knew what to expect when she put him down for a nap or to sleep for the night. He was full of stubborn purpose. Sometimes he would lie quietly and give himself up to sleep. At other times outrage twisted his face into an angry red mask. Then the wailing started. When Jason cried, Sharon felt sad and helpless. Should she pick him up, like she wanted to, or should she let him cry himself out, as Stewart and the pediatrician suggested? She was never sure. Meanwhile, she felt guilty and frightened.

Sometimes after a late-night feeding, Jason would shriek on and on, while Sharon lay there, hoping he would drop off to sleep. The wailing would stop the way it started—all of a sudden there would be silence, and Sharon felt like a hostage released.

At two months Jason began to suck on his fingers and smile. At four months he enjoyed being pulled up to a standing position. He was so full of life! His favorite thing was splashing in his bath, but there never seemed to be a time when he was content being alone, amusing himself. Someone always had to be there. And so the responsiveness that was Sharon's major reward also carried with it additional burdens. If she played with him, she was rewarded with loud, explosive laughter, but it took a lot of work to keep him entertained. He didn't stay with one thing for long.

When Jason was six months old Sharon returned to work, as she had planned. It was so strange getting up at 7:30, dressing for work, and leaving Jason with the sitter. He cried and clutched at her arm when she tried to leave. Even after she got into the car, she could still hear him crying piteously. All day long, that was the image that stuck in her mind: Jason crying and reaching for her. She quit at the end of the week.

Sharon told Stewart that she was too worn-out to return to work, and maybe it would be better if she stayed home with Jason. He said, "Fine, do what you want," but he thought she would feel better if she could get away from the baby for a while. Sharon stayed home but felt guilty because she saw so many other women who managed to work and raise babies, and because she never really believed that Stewart supported her decision.

Sharon wondered how Jason could have been so good in the hospital and so irritable and cranky at home. Maybe all babies were like this. Maybe she was doing something wrong.

◆

Why is it that while parents with easy babies think they are lucky, those with difficult infants usually worry that they are doing something wrong? Perhaps it is a testament to the average person's enormous capacity for self-criticism. It is also an out-growth of the abiding conviction that we can mold our children into anything we want. The parents I have spoken to worry most about their infants' fussiness, ease of feeding, regularity of sleep, fearfulness, and cooperation with others. Some parents say that their babies are always fussy, or always easy, almost as though these differences were there from birth. But they can't quite believe it. When things don't go well, they can't let go of the idea that they must be doing something wrong. Being a parent *is* impossible. We all muddle through, and we all feel guilty in the end.

One of the things that makes new parents unnecessarily susceptible to self-doubt and blame is the lack of general aware-ness that babies are born with wide variations in temperament. Many parents suspect that babies have innate variations in mood, but because they cannot shake the twentieth-century conviction in the catalytic power of social experience, they imagine that *their* infant's mood must have been influenced by something they did. "Maybe we should have held him more (or less) when he cried."

It is now becoming clear that some of a child's personality is due to inborn temperament. Alexander Thomas and Stella Chess, who are among the most respected researchers to look at infant temperament, concluded that babies are born with one of three dispositions: "easy to handle," "difficult to manage," and "slow to warm up to other people."[3] Jerome Kagan, summarizing the available evidence, concluded that two qualities persist from the first birthday onward.[4] Some children are *inhibited* ("restrained, watchful, gentle"), while others are *uninhibited* ("free, energetic, spontaneous"). As infants, inhibited children are more irritable during the early months. Moreover, this irritability seems to be related to higher levels of physiological arousal (which also leads to more stomachaches, allergic reactions, and other physical discomforts).

Parents can, of course, influence the direction that a child's predisposition will take. The final result is a joint product of the child's temperament and the parents' reactions. But this influence works both ways. An infant who is easy to care for and predictable makes life much easier for parents. On the other hand, a difficult baby like Jason greatly increases the stress of parenthood. Innately irritable infants tend to cry for long periods of time and are not easily comforted. So, in addition to the stress of the crying, parents are discouraged by their inability to relieve their babies' distress. Difficult babies resist the introduction of new people, new foods, and new routines, and their schedules are hard to predict.

All of this makes caring for a fretful infant extremely stressful. Studies by psychologist Carolyn Cutrona and researcher Beth Troutman demonstrate that bringing home a difficult infant frequently leads to maternal depression.[5] The link between infant temperament and maternal depression may arise from the mother's feelings about herself, Cutrona says. When a woman has trouble comforting her child, she feels less competent as a mother. She may develop ambivalent feelings toward her child, causing guilt and further lowering her self-esteem.

Although there is not much parents can do to alter their baby's basic temperament, they can lower the level of stress by working together to develop a network of support. Women who received high levels of support from their husbands, parents, or friends before their babies were born had more confidence as parents and felt less depressed three months after delivery, according to Cutrona and Troutman. A woman can help fend off the postpartum blues by cultivating supportive people and by realizing that she is not to blame for feeling stressed by a demanding baby.

"Support" is one of those vague words that often conjures up envy on the part of those who feel the lack of it, especially when they see others lucky enough to have plenty. I know several young mothers lucky enough to have lots of support, and the harder they work at it, the luckier they are. I don't deny that some women are fortunate in having friends or family, in some cases husbands, who freely and willingly help out. But for the most part, support, like love and friendship, is not something you "have" or "get"; it is something you create.

A young mother needs four kinds of support: emotional, informational, physical, and appraisal. If these supports are not freely available, she can become resigned or bitter, or she can do something about it.

Emotional Support

Feeling loved, cared for, trusted, and understood makes it easier to bear the stress of caring for an infant. A young mother can get this solace and encouragement from her husband, her own mother, and her friends. She may, however, have to work at it.

Husbands, too, find it difficult to adjust to being parents. Few of them have anywhere near the responsibility and burden of their wives, still most people become a little self-centered when they're under pressure. If you're not lucky enough to have a husband who senses your need for emotional support and gives it freely, make your own luck. Let him know you need him.

The same advice applies with regard to your parents and other members of your family. If you're having a tough time and could use some care and concern, let them know.

Perhaps the most reliable source of support for a young mother is her friends. Don't let the sleepless nights and constant stress make you turn in on yourself. You may not feel like entertaining, but let your friends know that you are under pressure and could use some attention. Despite your reluctance, friends usually like to help. Give them a chance. Most neighborhoods have a network of young women with babies—the modern equivalent of the extended family. If you live in the suburbs, you will likely be surrounded by other mothers struggling to cope with the same problems you are, and eager to find a sister to share their joys and concerns. If you don't live near other young parents, seek them out.

Informational Support

When should you start your baby on solid food? How many hours a night should the baby be sleeping? How do you heal sore, cracked nipples? Caring for a baby raises a thousand questions, questions that once might have been answered in the bosom of the family, by mothers and aunts and older sisters. Today, most young parents have to turn to experts for advice. Fortunately, there are a variety of readily available sources of information. There is your pediatrician, of course, and reading Dr. Spock. (If you can't talk to your pediatrician, get another one.) Another excellent book is T. Berry Brazelton's *Infants and Mothers*.[6] For questions about breast-feeding, call the La Leche League (look in the white pages of your phone book or call directory assistance). And don't forget that you can pick up a lot of information from talking to friends and family.

Physical Support

No matter how well-informed she is, or how much emotional support she has, a young mother still needs direct help with taking care of baby. All this talk about support may seem relatively obvious, but often young parents require considerable consciousness raising before they are able to take their own needs as seriously as they do their children's needs. Even though they are exhausted and overwhelmed, many young mothers think they should be able to do everything for their babies. Frankly, this is a damn shame. In the process of taking care of baby, too many parents neglect themselves—and each other.

I see far too many parents who use up their own energy and patience trying to be superparents, and not getting enough help. The more relief you get, the happier person and better parent you will be. If relief and assistance are not forthcoming from your family, consider hiring professional help.

There are now a variety of postpartum care services, some available through the Red Cross, others private agencies with names like Mother Care, Doula (from the Greek for "caregiver"), and After Baby's Arrival (check the white pages of the phone book). Commercial postpartum services charge between ten and fifteen dollars per hour, and prepare meals, do light housekeeping, keep up with the laundry, care for other children, and run errands. Women from these services also answer questions about breast-feeding, bottle-feeding, infant care, and personal postpartum care.

Appraisal Support

Parents want to know if they are "doing the right thing" from the first day they bring home the baby. Why not? There is no more important job than being a parent, yet most of us have to learn as we go. Still, too many parents (especially mothers) worry about being perfect. A good standard to strive for is "good enough" mothering. This means getting the job done but without hovering over your offspring, confusing your small fry with the crown jewels. When they are babies, the primary evidence of adequate parenting is that you learn how to soothe and quiet a crying baby and that the baby grows. For more reassurance, a young mother can obtain help to evaluate how she's doing from the same sources from which she gets information.

The job of bringing up baby is so consuming and the tasks so many and so demanding that it is easy to lose sight of the context.

We think of ourselves as individuals—mommy, daddy, and baby—rather than as a family unit. So, it is natural that when we think of change, we think of individuals changing. Since the baby changes so fast, we concentrate on that. At one month, the baby does this; at four months, the baby does that. There is no danger of parents losing sight of the baby's development (ask parents how old the baby is, and they will tell you in weeks). What we do lose sight of, however, is that having a new baby is also a stage in the family life cycle, and the family (as a unit) has developmental needs of its own.

THE FAMILY LIFE CYCLE

When we think of life cycles, we think of individuals, moving through time, growing and changing, mastering the challenges of one period and then moving on to the next. Boys and girls become teenagers and then young adults. Later on, somewhere off in the distant future, they will become middle-aged; and, what is harder still for young people to imagine, someday they will grow old.

Changes in our own lives often sneak up on us. One minute we are absorbed with the exciting pressures of starting a career and a family, the next thing we know we're staring middle age in the face, wondering what happened to all those years. Life is not static and growth is not steady, but life is long and change is slow, so it is easy to forget that we are always aging. Self-imposed limitations of perception and imagination seem to make it easier to keep us at the practical business of living. What's more, the longing for security makes some people reluctant to let go of the past in order to take hold of the future.

Life is change. Thanks to some excellent writing by Daniel Levinson (*The Seasons of a Man's Life*), Gail Sheehy (*Passages*), Roger Gould (*Transformations*), and others, we can now understand human life as a series of developmental stages.[7]

The cycle of human life may be orderly, but it is not a steady, continuous process. We progress in stages with plateaus and developmental crises which demand change. Periods of growth and change are followed by periods of relative stability during which changes are consolidated.

The life cycle view of human nature is more optimistic and practical than previous views. It suggests that we continue to develop throughout our lives, and that we are not condemned to live out the effects of traumas suffered at an early age, the so-called formative years. This is not to say that these early years are not important, only that they are not the last word. The life-cycle literature portrays life as a series of developmental stages, each with its own characteristic challenges. The good news is that life is not one long, uphill struggle. We reach developmental plateaus and can coast. The bad news is that we are never fully grown-up; we can never simply be who we have become without periodically reassessing and changing our lives.

Families, too, have cycles. By this I mean more than the parallel progress of parents and children. A consistent theme in the life cycle is the interconnectedness that reverberates between generations. Even when these connections are not apparent, they still exert a powerful, if unseen, influence. As parents move through young adulthood into middle age, their children metamorphose into teenagers, growing ever more willful and independent, until one day they are ready to leave home.

Changes in one generation often complicate the adjustment of those in another. A middle-aged father may grow disenchanted with his career and decide to become more involved with his family at the same time as his children are growing up and pulling away. His need to hang on to them may frustrate their need to be on their own, and can eventually lead to war between the generations. Or, to cite another example becoming more and more familiar in the eighties, just as a man and woman begin to do more for themselves after launching their children, they may find their children back in the house (after dropping out of school, being unable to afford housing, or recovering from an early divorce), and are therefore faced with an awkward, hybrid version of second parenthood.

The reason the family life cycle is something other than the intersecting story of separate lives is that those lives are joined together by more than conscious choice and habit. They are the product of an organization that includes and defines them. Remember that the family is a system whose basic properties are wholeness, organization, and patterning. From this it follows that: the whole is greater than the sum of the parts; change in any one part will affect the whole; and the whole is regulated to change only slowly, in order to maintain integrity and continuity.

Continuous, normative change takes place in each person,

each relationship, and the family system as a whole. The whole *is* greater than the sum of its parts. But it is difficult to think of the whole. As living experiments of one, we tend to be acutely aware of our own individual needs, and less aware of the reciprocal impact between ourselves and every segment of the family. Our relationships with our parents, siblings, and other family members go through stages as we move along the life cycle, just as parent-child and spouse relationships do.

At every stage, family members develop a patterned sequence of behaviors and interactions.

One property that families share with other complex systems is that they do not change in a smooth, gradual process of evolution, but rather in discontinuous leaps. Falling in love and revolutions are examples of such leaps. Having a baby is a little like falling in love and undergoing a revolution at the same time.

With the the birth of a child, the family undergoes a transformation far more radical than merely adding a new member. A man and a woman, already more or less wedded together, now become part of a complex organism. Their lives are now more bound together, and in a more complex way.

———◆———

Once they were married, Sharon and Stewart's lives took on an added complexity. Their relationship with each other and their involvements outside the marriage were reciprocal. The more time they spent together, the less time they had to do things alone. The closer they were to each other, the less they needed their own friends and independent satisfactions; the more distant they were, the more they sought satisfaction outside the marriage. Stewart was, for example, often torn between Sharon and his career. His own idea about how much time and energy to put into his teaching and writing had to be reconciled with his wish to be with Sharon, and with her claim on his time and attention.

Now that they had a child, they were more than a couple, they were a family. Stewart's involvement with his career was affected by Sharon and by Sharon's involvement with Jason. Because Jason was a demanding, fussy infant, Sharon needed more from Stewart. She hated seeing him go off to work. Here she was stuck at home with the baby—she was a mother. But he could be a father or not. He had an alternative. He could stay home or go to work. She had no choice. To Stewart, she seemed to demand constant attention and catering. He felt her demands on him; she felt his neglect. What they couldn't see was that every single thing that happened was now part of a triangle.

Sharon's relationship to Stewart was a function of her relationship to Jason. The more Jason wore her out, the more she needed from Stewart. The more stressed Stewart felt from work, the less available he was to Sharon. Nothing any one of them did would ever again be independent of the other two.

Jason's birth destabilized Sharon and Stewart's uneasy harmony. What had been a phase of relative stability in their relationship was interrupted by a new challenge, to which they would have to adjust. The addition of a new element is a *perturbation* to the system, which is destabilized and then must be reorganized into a new arrangement. In mechanical systems these changes are automatic; but the family is not mechanical. When the "new element" is a living child, and the "system" consists of two very human people, the "destabilization" brings uncertainty and anxiety. Because stress is highest at transition points, it is at these junctures that we tend to get stuck. The unhappy irony is that at precisely those periods when we most need to be flexible, we are least likely to be flexible. This is not only because as individuals we tend to fall back on familiar coping strategies (strategies that have worked in the past), but also because one family member's rigidity provokes an equally rigid reaction in others.

In response to the stress of caring for Jason, Sharon became more clingy; Stewart became more isolated. The more clingy Sharon was, the more distant Stewart became; and the more distant Stewart was, the more clingy Sharon became—et cetera, et cetera.

One of the things that makes conflict inevitable is that parents look at parenting from divergent perspectives. Each parent is different—cognitively, affectively, and stylistically. One has a shorter fuse than the other, and each of them responds to different triggers. He may get angry when the children make a little noise; she may not get angry until they start screaming. She may be more annoyed by the children fighting with each other than by their disrespect to her; he may not care about fighting, but may be unwilling to tolerate the slightest disrespect.

Even these differences in themselves are not what make

parenting so difficult. Contrasting styles are not static. Parents polarize each other, each one pushing the other to a more extreme position.

Imagine a little boy who scrapes his knee and runs to his daddy. The father wipes the scrape and tells the boy he's okay and should go back outside and play. His wife, watching on, may feel that the father was insufficiently sympathetic. She calls to the boy to come to her, and she gives him a little extra attention—bathing the scrape, applying first-aid cream, and inviting the boy to sit on her lap while she reads a story to him. Seeing this, the father may feel undermined and that the boy is being spoiled. In response he may try harder to toughen the boy up, or he may pull away (*If she wants to spoil him, let her*). Thus conflict is inherent. It is neither good nor bad, it just is.

The hardest thing about family life is not that we are different, but that we do not accept these differences. Some differences are hard to live with—how much time to spend together, how often to have sex, what temperature to set the thermostat at—but what makes them infinitely harder is thinking that one is wrong and one is right. Even before you find a way to compromise your differences, it helps to accept them: *Okay, so she thinks the children should take music lessons, and I don't. Fine. What are we going to do about it?* This makes it so much easier than *Ain't it awful!* or *What's wrong with her?*

So, the new organism starts in conflict. Then what? The first thing to keep in mind is the nature of the life cycle. The family goes through phases of stability, interrupted by transitional points (the addition or subtraction of new members, or a significant change in a member's status). At transitional points, the family's organization is first destabilized and then reorganized into a new arrangement. It is at these points that we must make active efforts to readjust, and change the way we interact—otherwise the family will get stuck.

Some people lose perspective and fail to appreciate transition points and the need for reorganization. In-laws may interfere with a new couple's adjustment by intruding into their relationship so much that the couple does not work out mechanisms for solving their own problems. A new husband may fail to recognize the need to spend less time doing things alone so that he and his wife can learn to do things together—even though he is married, he still acts like a bachelor.

Transitions, though disruptive and stressful, don't last long. If the appropriate adjustments are made, the family moves on to a new plateau in the life cycle. *But* the clock doesn't start until you begin to make the adjustments.

———◆———

One of my patients had a stormy relationship with her dependent, emotionally disturbed daughter. The daughter was unpredictable, impetuous, and erratic. She was given to sudden flare-ups of intense anger and impulsive outbursts of self-destructive and antisocial violence. Despite the girl's impossible behavior, the parents did everything they could to keep her in school, until at age seventeen the girl ran away to Miami, where she got involved in the drug culture and became a prostitute. When she was arrested and released to her parents' custody, they agreed to support her in an apartment near—but not too near—the town where they lived, until she could learn to be independent. When the daughter got to be twenty-one and showed no signs of supporting herself, the parents realized that they should "be firm" and stop paying for the girl's expenses so that she would be forced to get a job. However, because they feared the girl's impulsive outbursts and worried about her inadequacy, they kept prolonging their support.

These parents knew what they should do, but they just couldn't face their daughter's anger or the chance that she would fail. I told them that I understood their fears, but when they said they knew they "had to change," I gently but firmly told them no, they didn't have to change. They could go on as they were, until their daughter was twenty-eight, thirty, forty-five. If they did decide to stop supporting their daughter, I said, there probably would be a period of protest in which the daughter would test their resolve. Moreover, I said that period could last for several weeks, even a few months—but the clock wouldn't start until they made the change.

———◆———

The birth of a child requires a radical shift in the family organization—a shift for which one or both spouses may be totally unprepared. The spouses' functions must differentiate to meet the infant's demands for feeding and changing and bathing, and to adjust to the constraints imposed on the parents' time.

———◆———

For a helpless baby, Jason was pretty powerful. He was utterly and completely dependent on his parents' protection and care. As far as he was concerned, there was being alone—which meant sleep—or there was being caressed and nursed and petted and loved. Sleep, which he resisted, did not come upon him gently but overtook him as if by surprise. He woke demanding food. He wanted Sharon. If she didn't come right away, he was subject to flash rages.

Sharon tried to keep up with her son's fierce progress, but she also needed time alone. She tried to get him to nap, but never was there a baby who slept so little. She tried to find things for him to do while she read or just sat and rested. She put him in his playpen outside in the sunshine, gave him armloads of soft toys— but he didn't want to *do* anything; he wanted Mommy.

To the infant Jason, discovering his aloneness and helplessness, separation was unbearable, so he did everything in his considerable power to keep his mother near. Controlling her by crying out his need, he was a tiny bully, impossible to satisfy. When Sharon did put him down, he responded with fear and protest.

While parents are busy trying to keep up with the demands of an infant, one thing that invariably gives way is the couple's time alone together. With so much to do, so much anxiety and tension, and so little sleep, it's natural for parents to long for time to themselves—time to rest, time to relax. One thing Stewart made a point of doing for Sharon was taking the baby out for little trips on Sunday mornings, so that Sharon could sleep late and maybe read the paper.

Caring for an infant is so consuming that if parents think about themselves at all, they mostly think about getting a break. In the process, they lose sight of the marriage, which slowly dies.

2 + 1 = 2

According to a familiar song lyric, two plus one equals three: "Just Molly and me, and baby makes three; we're happy in my blue heaven." But the addition of a new baby can be calculated differently if we consider that the family now consists of two subsystems: the parent-child unit and the spouse unit. That parents are also a married couple may seen to fall into the category of things "everyone knows." The problem with basic truths that "everyone knows" is that we tend to lose sight of them when we, ourselves, are caught up in the anxious uncertainties of coping with a particularly difficult period.

The new addition is also a subtraction. No matter how much the couple cherish the baby, his arrival also threatens the fantasy of exclusive ownership and love. Not all young parents are consciously jealous of the attention their partners devote to the baby, yet inevitably these feelings are stirred beneath the surface of awareness. New fathers are especially prone to feeling displaced. Suppressed rivalrous and rejected feelings at this time propel many young fathers to overwork, to overeat, and to drink too much.

For Sharon, breast-feeding Jason rekindled archaic memories of the blissful time when as infants we are merged with our mother's tender loving. For Sharon and Jason it was a time of union, togetherness, bliss. She was everything to Jason. These were moments of happy fusion. But for Stewart, they were moments he could not share.

The father's exclusion from the magic circle of mother-child love, and the heavy demands of caring for the baby, may lead to an erosion of the couple's relationship. All too often, parenting swallows up the marriage. Too bad, because the marital relationship can be—should be—a haven that provides both partners with emotional support. More than almost anything else, a healthy marriage offers a refuge from the stress of life.

The most important ways to keep a marriage alive and vital are: paying attention to each other, doing nice things for each other, and spending time together. This may seem relatively obvious, but the demands of the baby and the attendant stress make many couples relatively insensitive of the need to work at preserving what brought them together in the first place—their intimate relationship.

Revitalizing their marriage is the greatest support young parents can give each other. After all, no one signed on to take care of anyone. They married because they were in love and wanted to be together. Early on, this may happen automatically. The trouble with things that happen automatically is that we don't learn how to work at them. Worse, many people don't like the idea that it's necessary to work at romance. It goes against our instinct, which tells us that love is something we "fall into." Indeed, that's the way it was with Sharon and Stewart. The infatuation of their courtship was more like a tropical fever than a relationship. Their love affair was filled with rich mysteries of emotion that simply descended upon them—as the song says, "It's Magic." It never entered their calculations that they might have to work to recreate this mystic sentiment.

If you would breathe life back into your marriage, you cannot do so by wishing, or waiting for your partner to initiate something, or even by taking advantage of existing possibilities to enjoy each other. You may have to create the possibilities. Before that, you may have to imagine them.

Try this little exercise. Close your eyes and think back to the time of your courtship. What are your happiest memories? Chances are you may remember going for long walks, opening up your hearts to each other, conversations that lasted long into the night, dancing slow and close, kissing for hours, watching the seasons change—just being together. You may even remember Johnny Mathis singing "Chances Are."

These tender memories can make your heart ache. What happened to all that magic? "Where Did Our Love Go?" Chances are the magic is still there, although perhaps submerged beneath a welter of dirty dishes, wet diapers, late nights, early mornings, and all the other facts of life that never figured in the romantic songs you used to listen to.

Even when things have cooled off or gone stale in a marriage, both partners know what *the other one* could do to bring the couple closer. The trick is to figure out what your mate would like from you, and start to recreate a warmer, more romantic relationship by giving to him or her. Think of it as getting the ball rolling. Giving attention means noticing the other person—how does your spouse look? feel? what has he or she been doing?—and acknowledging what you notice. Understanding can be as simple as recognizing that your partner looks tired, or asking about how the day went— *and* listening. Compliments are always a good idea, whether they are for something specific ("The dinner was delicious") or just for being ("I love you").

Another way to pay attention to your partner is to bring home surprises. Flowers are nice, so are special treats to eat or drink, magazines, books, socks, perfume, and so on. Greeting card stores have cards for any sentiment you might wish to express, as well as lovely cards to which you can add your own message.

In order for a couple with a new baby to enjoy doing things together, it's probably a good idea to get out of the house—away from guess who, and away from the atmosphere so filled with responsibility and tension. Hire a baby sitter or find friends with whom you can trade off baby watching, and get out. Go for a walk, go shopping for some new clothes, go out to dinner, go to the movies—get away, be together; enjoy yourselves. One of the nicest things young parents can do for themselves is to have a relative spend the night with the baby, so they can have a whole evening of peace and relaxation. Go out to dinner at a fancy restaurant and spend a restful night in a local motel. (Breast-feeding mothers can leave a couple of bottles of their own expressed milk in the refrigerator.)

It's more difficult to create an affectionate mood when you are around the house, but it can be done. Try holding hands, having wine and cheese by candlelight, giving your partner a backrub, taking a shower together (remember, it saves water); have dinner in a different part of the house, play Scrabble. You won't feel like doing these things all the time, but breaking the usual routine and closing some of the distance between you can be the beginning of a positive spiral that will regenerate tender feeling in the marriage.

Some unhappy couples are so bitter and resentful that they give up on their marriages and settle for a pale version of domestic peace. At least they can be decent parents, they think. Do not think that when a man and a woman drift away from each other, to the extent that all they share is their children, that they are likely to be good parents. On the contrary, the inevitable conflict about how to raise the children is heightened to a constant state of tension if the parents cannot escape from parenting long enough to enjoy each other's company without the presence of the children.

HEATHER'S BIRTH

By the time Jason was one-and-a-half, things settled down a bit. Neither Sharon nor Stewart forgot the sleepless nights, but as with other normal awful things, time blurred the feelings. So, they remembered . . . but not really. Besides, Jason was so cute now: a chubby, waddling, smiling miracle of their own creation. Every day there was a new astonishment of the heart.

Sharon didn't let herself think about having another baby, and she was surprised when Stewart brought it up. "I don't know," she said slowly. She didn't want to go through all that again, but she didn't want Jason to be an only child. What could she say?

Two weeks later she was pregnant, and six weeks after that she knew it.

Sharon was astonished, numb. It was all starting again, without her ever really having made up her mind. Stewart was elated. "Great!" he said. "Now Jason will have someone to play with." Sharon didn't dare tell him what she was feeling. Mothers weren't supposed to feel that way.

———◆———

The second baby was as late as Jason had been early. Sharon just kept getting bigger and bigger. Her due date came and went. Ten days later she went into labor. This time she was sure, and this time she waited as long as she could before calling Stewart. When she finally dialed his office at two in the afternoon, her contractions were coming every four minutes. He came home immediately.

Stewart was more considerate this time. He seemed more genuinely concerned about her. At least that's what Sharon thought. Maybe she'd finally gotten through to him. He didn't think so. He thought the change was in her—she wasn't as bewildered this time, or as demanding, or as critical.

Labor was quicker, easier. Jason hadn't wanted to leave her; this one couldn't wait to get out. It was only 6:00 P.M. when she finally finished panting and pushing.

"It's a girl!" Stewart shouted, tears streaming down his face. *That's nice*, Sharon thought. She couldn't see.

Heather was an easy baby, as peaceful and content as Jason was fussy and demanding. They didn't even look like brother and sister. Jason was a chubby baby, with a thick mat of dark curls. Heather was smaller, almost slender, and her wispy hair was reddish-blond. By some miracle, Heather slept through the night from her second day home from the hospital. Sharon's relief and gratitude for this blessing transformed her whole outlook. This baby was easy.

Another thing that won Sharon over was that Heather was

such a pliable baby; she liked to be hugged, and she was as flexible as a kitten mauled by a house full of kids. Jason, by contrast, had always been stiff when Sharon held him. He arched his back, grew rigid, and wriggled to get down as soon as he was able to crawl.

Everything was so much easier this time. Unlike Jason, who had always demanded attention, Heather seemed content to amuse herself. She'd lie in her cradle, her eyes wandering around the room, staring fascinated at her little corner of the world. She liked to play with crib toys and would do so until her eyes drooped shut and she drifted off to sleep. Sharon marveled at how much this baby slept. It was almost as if having paid her dues the first time, she had earned a respite.

Because they weren't worn out all the time, Sharon and Stewart were far freer to enjoy their second child. Heather was less demanding and seemed to need less attention, and so they could choose when to play with her and when to do other things around the house.

Jason was delighted with the new baby. Only once did he show his jealousy directly. When Sharon hung the mobile that had been his over the cradle, Jason climbed up on his little wooden chair and snatched it down. "What's that?" Sharon asked when she saw him take it into his room. "Mine," he said, only it came out more like "MINE!" Sharon made another mobile for the baby.

After that, Jason was very nice to his sister. He tried to help Sharon as much as he could with changing diapers. Even though he always fastened the adhesive tabs so loosely that they popped open, Sharon let him do it anyway. What he loved most was to hold the baby. At first Sharon was afraid Jason would drop her, but he was so happy with Little Sister in his arms that Sharon helped him sit down on the rug and then handed Heather over. At least the baby wouldn't have far to fall if Jason dropped her. When they went for walks, Jason pushed the stroller, and if Heather started to cry, he handed her a toy and said, "Don't cry, baby Heather, look at this."

Mommy's little helper was a good big brother but much more clingy. In one month he went from two-and-a-half to one-and-a-half. Now instead of walking he wanted to be carried when they went to the store. "You have to walk, Jason, Mommy has to carry the baby. You're a big boy now." Jason wasn't so sure he wanted to be.

On the whole, though, life was more peaceful. There was no repeat of the endless days and nights when Jason had been so irritable and Sharon felt so alone. As Heather got bigger, the two children kept Sharon busy, just by being children. She was never alone. Even when she went to the bathroom, she'd hear a knock at the door and then a little voice calling, "Mommy . . ."

Stewart liked to watch the children sleep. In sleep, their faces looked so heart-stoppingly tender. Jason's mouth made a little O, and his breath came gently. It was as still as he got. Heather, curled up in a fetal position, clutched Blankie in her hand and sucked her thumb. Stewart loved them. In those soft, warm faces was a quality of trust so absolute and pure it made him feel selfless. But he only watched for a minute or two.

There was no doubt in Sharon's mind that Stewart loved the babies, but he was so intolerant of what to her were normal, expectable changes in their moods. He always thought there was something wrong, something she should fix. When Heather got a little whiny, Stewart would say, "She's tired." He was always finding something. Either they were teething, or hungry, or tired. He could never just let them be little children with feelings, little children who needed a certain amount of tending and a certain amount of tolerance.

If he wasn't fussing at them, he was jostling them, taking them for walks, trying to distract them from their own games and their own moods. When they went out to supper, Stewart was in a constant state of anxiety. He was acutely sensitive to the reactions of other diners. Maybe they were only projected images of his own discomfiture. No matter.

One night he took the whole family out to dinner at Sharon's favorite restaurant, and the evening unrolled in its usual tense fashion. Stewart viewed the children as little bombs that might go off at any minute. To defuse them, he fed them rolls and let them drink from the little coffee-cream containers that restaurants so thoughtfully provided. He used all his ingenuity to find things for them to play with—quietly—at the table. He dangled his keys in front of the baby until she squealed and grabbed them. He gave Jason the spoons and taught him how to build things with them. He made puppets with the napkins and drew faces on them. Stewart was trying to be a good daddy, but he wore himself out.

When the food came, he expected the children to eat quietly. It was his turn. Between mouthfuls, he told Sharon about what was going on in the English Department. She listened, even though when she was tired the doings of Stewart's department were about as interesting as the marshmallow music piped in from the speakers in the ceiling. Jason felt free to break in. "Mommy, you have the same soup as Jason." "That's right," she said and then turned back to Stewart. But it was too late. He was sulking. He ordered a third Michelob and withdrew into himself.

Conversation grew tense, polite, strained. Sharon could tell that Stewart was mad, though he wouldn't admit it. "Would you please pass the salt." Then silence.

Jason didn't let the silence last long. Did he feel the tension, or just see an opportunity to seize Sharon's attention? In either case, Sharon seemed happy for the distraction.

"Can I get down now?" Jason asked.

"Wait a minute, honey, don't you want to finish your supper?"

"*No*, want to *get down*."

"What do you like best about coming here," Sharon asked, "the pretty decorations, or the soup, or the crackers, *or* the nice deserts?"

"You know what?" he said brightly, "I don't like anything!"

"Oh, honey . . . but what was the best part?"

Jason giggled. "No, nothing was the best part," he said happily.

This was a wonderful game. But Sharon took it seriously. She wanted somebody to have a good time. As a result, she ended up debating with a two-year-old.

"But honey, don't you . . .?"

Stewart continued to sit in stony silence, staring out the window. Heather just watched, her eyes round and clear.

When they got home, the tension of the evening hadn't dissipated. Sharon decided that she was overdue for calling her parents. "Jason, do you want Mommy to call Grandma and Grandpa?"

"No! *Jason* do it," he said, and with Sharon's help he placed the call.

RENEGOTIATING BOUNDARIES WITH GRANDPARENTS AND FRIENDS

Sharon's parents were, as always, delighted to hear from their grandson. The conversation went on for several minutes. Sharon listened as Jason babbled on, and wondered what her parents were saying.

Now that she had babies, her parents seemed more eager than ever to visit. It was nice. They fussed over Jason and Heather, who of course thrived on the attention.

Two things young parents don't like about grandparents is that they spoil the children and don't always take them seriously. Actually, these two problems are related, and they both strike a nerve.

Sharon's mother loved to give the children candy and take them shopping. The second of these Sharon didn't mind.

On one visit, Sharon's mother took Sharon and Jason shopping for children's clothes. They bought him two cute little shirts and a new pair of shorts. Then they went to the Junior Bootery for shoes. Sharon picked out three pairs of shoes she thought suitable, and then asked Jason to pick the ones he liked best. Her mother didn't approve of the ones he chose.

"Sharon, you shouldn't let him pick out his own shoes, he's only a baby."

"He has very definite ideas, Mother," Sharon said archly. "He is a person, you know."

Sharon was mad. *So, this is how they treat children,* she thought. *Act all nicey-nice, but don't really respect them. They're too wrapped up in themselves to recognize the children's real feelings. If they treat Jason like this, imagine how they must have treated me.*

◆

No one but a parent would believe that grandparents could fail to recognize how wonderful the children are, or ignore their autonomy. Grandparents dote on their grandchildren, but sometimes treat them more like domestic pets—to be cuddled and fed and spoiled—than like little people with minds of their own.

That grandparents spoil the grandchildren is, of course, news to no one.

Jason's grandparents spoiled him, and he ate it up. His love for his grandmother was absolute. Nothing was held back. She was mindless of discipline, so there were none of the hard feelings that complicated his love for his mother. Sharon, of course, resented this. It didn't seem fair. Her son, the child she did everything for, could be bought for the price of a candy bar.

Sometimes it seems that grandparents join with their grand-children against the children's parents. It's a way to strike at the things in their sons or daughters that they don't like.

Stewart thought that Sharon's parents undermined his discipline, and it made him furious. Sharon's biggest complaint was that her parents didn't take the children seriously.

———◆———

The underlying issue here is a boundary dispute. Will the grandparents recognize the boundary that separates them from their children as parents? And will the new parents recognize the grandparents' right to be grandparents? Young parents bristle when their folks don't respect their new roles as parents. They have certain rules they consider important—such as how much television to watch or what to eat—and they don't want anybody (not even, or especially, their own parents) to violate these rules. Parents must speak up about the rules they consider important, and ask their parents to respect their way of doing things.

On the other hand, parents can learn their first lesson in letting go by allowing the grandparents a certain amount of discretion in how they treat the grandchildren. Up to a point, let them do what they want. Some parents worry that their children will get confused if the grandparents let them stay up late and watch television, when they aren't usually allowed to do so. Stop worrying. Children learn, very quickly, to discriminate. Be clear about what you consider essential rules for your children. When they are with you, you are in charge. But when they are with their grandparents, let go—as much as you can.

———◆———

Having a baby to look after sometimes separates young couples from their friends, especially friends who don't have young children of their own. Some friends don't make allowances for the changed status of new parents. They don't understand why you spend so much time at home, and they may not enjoy your always bringing the children wherever you go.

Some friends, of course, will drift away—just as some friendships don't survive marriages. But it's a shame to lose friends, and some misunderstandings can be ironed out by talking about them. Explain to your friends how you feel about being a parent, what it's doing to you, and how you would like them to respond. If you don't feel like having people over because your house looks like Romper Room after a tornado, tell them, and tell them why. If you have friends without children, who feel slighted when you include the children in your plans, try to make accommodations, but if you don't want to leave the children at home, explain this to them and ask for their understanding.

This, too, is a boundary issue. Having children inevitably creates more distance between friends. It's hard, if not impossible, to be as close as you were before. But it is not necessary to give up your friends.

RECIPROCITY

Asked what's wrong with their marriages, most people are pretty generous in giving credit to their spouses. Oh, first you may hear something like "We don't communicate," or "We don't have many interests in common," but when you get down to why, it's likely to be: "He doesn't share his feelings with me," or "She's always nagging me about something," or "He never wants to do anything with the family."

What these complaints have in common is not just blaming the other person, but also a one-person psychology. What happens to us is a function of what someone else has done.

A causes *B*. With or without a way out, we have, at least, the sweet solace of feeling like victims.

Family therapists don't think this way. We see relationships as circular patterns of interaction, such that what one person does is a function of what the other does—and so on. Their behavior is reciprocal.

Reciprocity is the governing principle of every relationship. I do not simply mean the moral duty to return one kindness for another. This, by the way, is a happy view of human nature, but one based on the hope that doing nice things for others will always make them feel grateful and reciprocate.

By reciprocity I mean the descriptive principle that, in a relationship, one person's behavior is functionally related to the other's. A popular expression of this principle is "What goes around, comes around," meaning that meanness begets meanness. Another phrase that turns the same sentiment into a positive is "Give to get," meaning the best way to get love and understanding is to give it away. This comes under the heading of things most of us know, and most of us forget.

We generally consider the effect of our behavior on new relationships, but often lose sight of reciprocity in ongoing relationships. A woman preparing for a job interview is likely to dress carefully so as to create a certain impression. If she's anxious to be thought of as serious and businesslike, she may wear a dark, tailored suit, one she thinks downplays her femininity. Likely, too, she will make an effort to be friendly and to appear confident and knowledgeable. But the same woman falls into the habit of thinking that her husband (mother, child, boss, friend) behaves the way he does toward her because of the way he is.

Attributing consistency is something we do unto others more than to ourselves: "She avoids sex because she's frigid." "He spends all his time watching telelvision because he is aloof." But when asked to explain our own behavior, we refer to the stimulus of others. "He doesn't want to make love, he just wants a quick fuck." "I watch television because if I try to read, she always interrupts, and if I try to have a conversation, all she does is talk about the kids." Traits are consistent attributes that *other* people have.

The point is not to substitute self-blame for blame projected outward, but to get away from blaming altogether. Once you realize that behavior is linked in an ongoing circular pattern, you can stop worrying about who started what, and start thinking about what to do about it.

As a family therapist I frequently turn the burden of complaints back on the complainer.

> *Husband:* My wife's boring.
> *Therapist:* How do you approach her that she responds that way?

> *Mother:* It's our son, he's so immature. He doesn't even tie his own shoes.
> *Therapist (to the boy):* What does your mother do that keeps you so young?

Less often, but occasionally, family members blame themselves. This is just another way to deny connections, and avoid conflict. A lot of women come to therapy because they are "depressed." It's them. Something inside them. This is easier for some people than facing up to the fact that family life is disappointing, or that their spouses and children are depressing them.

> *Therapist:* What's the problem?
> *Wife:* It's me. I'm depressed.
> *Therapist:* Who depresses you?
> *Wife:* No one; it's just me.
> *Therapist:* No one in the family contributes to your depression? I don't believe it.

———◆———

The aim of these questions is to bring out the interrelatedness of behavior, to shift problems from something *inside* one person to something *between* two (or more) persons, and to provide alternatives to solutions that have been tried and failed.

Some people immediately catch on and see that they are agents in events they once felt victimized by. Others become defensive, or angry.

———◆———

Unfortunately, neither Sharon nor Stewart grasped the reciprocity in their relationship. The stress of caring for two small children heightened the emotional vulnerability that already existed in their relationship.

People have learned to be skeptical about the old bromide that having a baby brings a couple closer together. Actually, it does; but closer may be too close—closer than the spouses have learned to accommodate to each other. Jason's constant demands triggered anxiety in both Sharon and Stewart, making them emotionally reactive, each in their own characteristic ways. Stewart needed more time to himself; Sharon needed more help, and she needed to feel that Stewart was more involved and concerned.

BITTER FRUIT

When you have small children, colds sweep through the family like a plague, from child to parent and parent to child. If the spacing is right, the last person to succumb will give the cold back to the person who brought it into the house in the first place.

Heather and Jason both had colds. Heather was such a good baby, but when she was stuffy she couldn't sleep, and so she woke up several times in the night, scared and crying. The vaporizer helped some, but not enough. Jason was well enough to sleep through the night, but he complained constantly during the morning. "My throat hurts!" "Give me 'lozenger.' " "Give me aspirin." "I want some juice."

Stewart stayed as far away as possible. If he could only avoid getting too close to them for a couple of days, he thought, he could avoid getting sick and missing work. So it was Sharon who carried Heather around when she woke in the night, put drops in her nose, gave both of them Tylenol, and tried to get as much ginger ale as possible down their throats. In the middle of the afternoon, both children fell into fitful sleep, and Sharon plopped down on the sofa, exhausted.

Looking out the window into the back yard, she made an interesting discovery. Stewart had given her two dwarf apple trees for their first anniversary, and every year since then, each spring one of them flowered and then in the fall had apples. For some reason, the other one never bloomed or bore fruit. Looking at them now, Sharon could see that the tree that bore apples was much shorter than the other one. Apparently its strength had gone into producing fruit, for it was gnarled and twisted; the other one was taller and straighter, and much healthier-looking. All of a sudden, she started to cry.

Sharon cried a lot these days. She felt so vulnerable and isolated. Being a mother was sapping her strength, just like that poor little tree. She thought of how little Stewart did for her. As the days went by, she sank increasingly into bitterness and self-pity.

———◆———

Whenever we talk about "self-pity," it is usually said with disdain. Feeling sorry for yourself is a sin in our culture, combining as it does two things we're taught not to feel: our own human weakness and a "selfish" attention to our personal hurts and disappointments. It's okay to feel sorry for someone else; when it comes to ourselves, we're expected to be selfless and strong.

What's wrong with "self-pity"? "Pity" refers to the sympathetic suffering of one person, excited by the distress of another.

"Self" is the core of the person, the heart of the personality. Self-pity, therefore, means the suffering of a person excited by distress in his or her own inner being. It is a natural response to an injury of the self, and its purpose is to fill in the self-soothing comfort and consolation that isn't forthcoming from anyone else. There's nothing wrong with self-pity.

On a personal level, self-pity is adaptive and reparative, but in families it tends to freeze distance in place, especially when it is tinged with bitterness

———◆———

Sharon moved across a typical sequence from hope to despair. She expected marriage to bring intense emotional connection and sharing. When it didn't, she felt first disappointment, then hurt, then anger. These painful feelings lasted a long time. Having the babies—and most of the burden of caring for them—only made things worse. Eventually, she could no longer stand the vulnerability. It hurt too much. So, she moved to what family therapist Philip Guerin calls an "island of invulnerability."[8] She built a wall around her feelings, so that she could no longer be hurt or even reached emotionally.

When hope is abandoned, alienation sets in.

Once in a while Stewart surprised her by doing something nice. He liked to feed the children supper, and sometimes he took them for long walks, giving Sharon a chance to rest. But the good feeling from these small kindnesses didn't make the bitterness go away. She couldn't get her mind off all those times when he could have helped but just didn't.

Stewart felt sorry for Sharon. He looked at the girl he used to be in love with. She looked old, with permanently tired eyes. He felt sorry for her, but why did she have to blame him? Women had been raising babies for thousands of years, and with a lot less help from their husbands than she got from him.

It was as though each of them had an emotional vault in which they collected grievances. With every aggravation or disappointment, they put in a deposit. Interest was collected in the form of self-righteous resentment. By their preoccupation with the other one's past neglect, they both reinforced their own helpless passivity in the present.

Sharon and Stewart—Sharon *or* Stewart—could have put the

concept of reciprocity to good use by forgetting about who started their problems and shifting their attention to what they, themselves, were doing to prolong it. Instead of thinking of their problems in linear fashion (Stewart's neglect *made* Sharon bitter; Sharon's nagging *caused* Stewart to withdraw) they could begin to think of a mutual exchange, a circular chain of behavior *that can be changed at any point in the chain.* This helps combat the ever-present assumption that the other person must act first, and the unfortunate tendency to sink into a rut.

If he started thinking not about what he wanted from Sharon, but about what he was doing to provoke the anger he was getting, Stewart might have realized that he didn't take time to ask about how she was feeling physically and emotionally. He behaved as though her anxiety and depression infected him, and he couldn't listen without offering suggestions for things *she* should do to get over feeling what she was feeling. He could have started listening. Simply listening.

As for Sharon, she was in a vicious cycle: She was too tired to go out and too bitter to think about Stewart's needs—*and* the less she went out, the more tired she got; the less she considered Stewart's feelings, the less he considered hers. She knew what she wanted, what Stewart didn't give her, and that knowledge filled her heart with such bitterness that there was little room for anything else.

———◆———

What is it possible to give? How is it possible to divine what is helpful? It's not so hard. But first you may have to clear away the belief that thinking about how *you* can change the relationship isn't fair. *Why must it all be up to me?*

Fairness is not the point, effectiveness is. Both parties contribute to the problems in their relationship. Looking at your contribution—ironically—gives you power. Power to change the relationship. I'm not advocating one-sided or unconditional generosity. I'm talking about how changes in your behavior toward others lead to reciprocal changes in their behavior toward you. We continuously influence the "situations" of our lives, as well as being influenced by them, in mutual, organic two-way interactions. Too bad more people don't see it.

8

WHY CAN'T JASON BEHAVE?

*J*ason
was always an active child. From the day they brought him home
from the hospital he was a real handful. Sharon now no longer
remembered what those days were really like. All she had left
were some of the specifics. At most he slept two or three hours at
a time, then he was up, screaming, demanding to be fed, cuddled,
carried, tickled, and changed. He was adorable but consuming,
and Sharon was exhausted. The only peace she knew was sleep.
Yet even when she finally got to bed at eleven-thirty or twelve it
was with the knowledge that Jason's cries would jolt her awake in
a couple of hours. She hardly had time to dream.

When you are a new parent these things seem unforgettable
and at the heart of everything. But they slide away and are gone
sooner than you think.

After about eight months things settled down a bit, at least
enough for Sharon to start catching up on her sleep. Jason now

slept through the night, and he could sit up and amuse himself for a few moments while Sharon read the newspaper, one paragraph at a time. At about this time Stewart started taking an interest in his little son. Previously helpless as a newborn father, Stewart now took Jason for little outings every Sunday morning. It was a chance for Sharon to rest and for him to be alone with his boy.

It wasn't long before Jason could pull himself up to a standing position, and once he discovered this new trick he loved to do it over and over again. When Sharon and Stewart watched their pudgy little baby haul himself up to vertical, they knew he would soon start walking. Stewart tried to speed things up by putting his finger in Jason's tiny hand and helping him take a few halting steps. But practice or no, it was weeks and weeks between almost walking and the first solo steps.

Six months later it was hard for Sharon to believe she had been in such a hurry for Jason to start walking and talking. Now he was a little talking machine, and all over the house, into everything. He was cute but impossible to keep up with. If she tried to hold him back, he struggled free like a little animal. When she went shopping in the mall, he always wanted to get out and push his stroller. "Jason push!" If she tried to strap him in the seat, he cried and cried until she let him up.

As Jason got to be two and then three, Sharon discovered so many things to do for him. By this time Heather was born, but she demanded so little attention that Sharon still spent most of her time trying to please Jason. He loved to play dress-up and she was happy to provide him with a series of capes and hats and parts of Daddy's old Army uniform from the attic.

And there were so many things to buy. Cuddly blanket-sleeper suits, bright colored overalls, books, and toys—and toys, and toys. Hasbro, Playskool, Milton Bradley, Ideal, Child Guidance—they all made so many clever and charming things to play with. Every time Sharon went into the store, she saw something new Jason would like. Jason's favorites were the bad-guy toys: King Kong, Darth Vader, and later, when he got a little older, killer robots that transformed into innocent-looking cars or trucks. There didn't seem to be any bad-guy toys aimed at little girls. That didn't stop Sharon. When Heather was old enough, she bought duplicate versions of the same toys Jason had liked. But in spite of Sharon's efforts, Heather's favorites were Barbie and Ken.

With every new purchase Jason was briefly delighted. Once Sharon bought him a pair of gerbils and a cage with a series of clear plastic tubes for the little creatures to explore. Jason was enchanted. For two days. Then he wanted rabbits. Guess who got stuck feeding the gerbils and cleaning their cage?

Jason was the first grandchild. His birth was a magnet drawing admiring relatives; it was visible proof that Sharon had fulfilled her maternal role. He was so adorable, she loved to show him off. But he was cute only as long as things were going his way. When anything frustrated his whim, he turned nasty. Nasty? Sharon was ashamed for even thinking it.

The defenses that supported Sharon's wish for the family to be whole and happy had also supported a grand illusion: that motherhood was good and she was content. Emotions growing secretly in her heart since the baby was born now worked themselves to the level of conscious awareness. She started thinking about all the headaches. Everything that was supposed to be fun wasn't. Going to the park was a good example. If anyone had asked, Sharon would have said she loved taking Jason to the park. But when she thought about it, she realized that he always spoiled these trips. As long as she gave him all her attention he was happy, but if she wanted to sit on the bench and watch or read the paper, he'd start to shout, "Swing me, swing me!" And when it was time to leave he screamed and tried to cling to the swings. When she finally yanked him away he bawled until she promised him a treat when they got home.

He was so willful! She tried everything, but life with Jason was a constant struggle. Guilty and uncertain, Sharon thought maybe something was wrong. But how do you know? It was against her nature to go outside the family, but she had to do something, so she went to talk with a friend whose children were already teenagers. Emily was sympathetic. "Yes, little ones are a trial." But she agreed that things had gotten out of hand. "Maybe you should talk to your pediatrician, Jason might be hyperactive." Hyperactive? That would explain a lot.

At first Dr. Magruder was dismissive—"All kids are like that." But Sharon persisted. (Hadn't he said the spitting up that turned out to be an allergy to milk was nothing?) "Last Friday I was playing with him on the floor and I had to stop so I could cook dinner. So I bent down to kiss him, and he punched me in the mouth. I yelled at him—real bad—and said, 'Go to your room!' Then he came over and hugged me and said, 'Mommy, I'm sorry. I love you.' So I felt bad and I had to hug him.''

"Maybe you do have a problem. Perhaps you should call the child guidance clinic. I'll give you their number."

When Sharon finally got up enough nerve to call for an appointment, she was surprised that they wanted to see the whole family. Why all of them, when the problem was Jason?

FIX MY CHILD WITHOUT DISTURBING ME

The Simpsons went to the child guidance clinic unsure and scared. Each one had private reasons for being apprehensive. Jason, too young to formulate the idea clearly, worried that his parents were bringing him to another grownup in order to crack down on him. Even when you're sick, doctors hurt you; imagine what they do when you've been bad! Sharon was eager for help but felt that going to the clinic acknowledged her failure. Still, if the price for getting control was accepting blame, she'd pay. Stewart, quietest of the three, was also the most worried. His best hope was that this so-called expert would see things his way—it was Sharon's doing, she was too easy on the boy; he was spoiled, and it was her fault. His worst fear was that more would be asked of him.

The young doctor assigned to see them was an Indian, Dr. Singh, who was completing a dual residency in psychiatry and pediatrics. Sharon thought Dr. Singh seemed nice—but he was *so* young. Stewart couldn't help thinking of the Sherlock Holmes movie in which Basil Rathbone disguised himself as an Indian named Rajni Singh. This guy didn't look a thing like Basil Rathbone.

Speaking in a low voice, as though she didn't want Jason to hear, Sharon began, "Doctor, what we want to know is, why can't Jason behave?" When Dr. Singh asked her to elaborate, she burst out like a dam giving way to a springtime flood: "Since he was a baby he never sits still. He always has to be doing something, running around, getting into things; you just can't tell him no." Her voice rose and her eyes watered, but she held her emotions in check enough to continue. She wanted the doctor to have all the facts, but they were just words circling her feelings.

While Sharon continued to put the problem into words, Jason

put it into action. When they come to therapy, family members vie with each other to say what's wrong and who is at fault. The real story is how they interact together. Are the parents in accord or in conflict? Do they speak plainly to their children or do they give vague orders? When the children speak, do the parents listen, really listen, or only go through the motions? Sharon and Stewart and Jason demonstrated what their lives were all about. It took only a minute to see. Sharon complained endlessly about Jason's behavior, meanwhile doing nothing about it. Jason jumped from one activity to the next. He didn't appear to be having much fun, but rather seemed too anxious to settle down. Meanwhile, Stewart sat aloof, ignoring the chaos, counting his feet while Sharon complained.

Left to their own devices, Sharon and Stewart were passive and ineffectual. In order to test their flexibility, Dr. Singh asked Sharon to quiet Jason down. Half turning to him, she said, "Jason, honey, be quiet so the grownups can talk, okay?" Then she turned back and resumed her chronicle of complaints. Dr. Singh pushed: "He's ignoring you." Once more she said, "Jason, please go over there and play so we can talk, okay?" Two minutes later Jason was back again. This time Stewart said, "Jason!" But Dr. Singh put his hand on Stewart's arm and said, "Let her do it; she's the one at home with him all day." The problem-maintaining cycle was clear, now the doctor wanted to push for change.

Jason continued to interrupt and show off, determined to hold the center of attention and well-practiced at keeping his parents from conspiring against him. Meanwhile, Sharon continued to reason with him. It is tempting to think of the problem as her problem—she wasn't strict enough. We could even give reasons for Sharon's laxity: the bond with Jason was so important to her that she could not jeopardize it by forcing him to do anything against his will. But shifting the problem from one person to another, from Jason's "hyperactivity" to Sharon's "leniency," doesn't add much. The whole story involves the whole family.

Watching while Sharon tried unsuccessfully to control Jason, Stewart kept his mouth shut but his feet busy, fidgeting around, crossing and recrossing his legs. Finally he couldn't stand it any longer. "Jason! Get in the goddamn chair, and don't you dare make another sound!" Here was the mirror image of Sharon's reasonableness: Stewart's forceful threatening. First to respond was Sharon—"Honey, don't be so rough"—then Jason, who came over to sit in his mother's lap with a pitiful look on his face. Now the circle was complete. Father threatens, mother protects.

Dr. Singh saw the Simpsons only twice. In the second session Sharon and Stewart touched on the conflict they had been avoiding. He thinks she's overinvolved with Jason and too easy on the boy. She feels neglected by her husband, that's why she spends so much time with her son; she's afraid to be strict, afraid to be like Stewart, because she's afraid of his anger. Two things became clear in a hurry. Sharon and Stewart were using Jason to avoid each other, and his misbehavior was a product of their conflict over what to do about it. No small child can stand up to the united front of two parents in agreement over how to control him. The child who misbehaves always stands on one parent's shoulders.

Dr. Singh assumed a didactic role. Sharon's mistakes were so obvious that it was compelling to step in and offer suggestions— as though being a good parent was merely a matter of having good information. But without the wider perspective of family therapy, it's hard to see how her "mistakes" were embedded in the family system.

Even though Dr. Singh was not a family therapist, the conflict between Sharon and Stewart was too apparent for him not to comment on it. So, Dr. Singh talked briefly about how Jason seemed to be pulling his parents apart. "If you two don't start harmonizing—working as a team, yes?—it's going to be very difficult to get Jason to do what he's told." They listened, knowing what the doctor said was true but both hoping he wouldn't press them to open up all the painful feelings that had built up between them. To their relief, he didn't.

As far as Dr. Singh was concerned, the problems in the Simpson family were too minor to warrant further treatment. Besides, the parents seemed to understand what he had told them.

Did the conflict between Stewart and Sharon disappear—poof? No, of course not. But as we shall see, it did begin to change enough to make a difference. And maybe more important, Sharon and Stewart learned that their lives were linked together, and that they, *by themselves*, could affect the outcome of events they had previously felt victims of.

Sharon and Stewart began to learn how to harness the power of the family by going to a professional. But professional treatment is not always necessary or effective. What is vitally important from the family therapy perspective is that family members learn that they are interrelated, that no one person can act without affecting the others, and vice versa. Sharon and Stewart might have figured this out eventually, perhaps when they got a bit older. Unfortunately, by then it might have been too late. Not exactly too late, but late enough that they would be mired deep in patterns that become harder to change with time. In realizing that our lives are part of each other's, we do not lose our separate identities; the recognition of complex interactional forces gives us new power over our lives.

Our family lives are governed by a set of invisible laws, never ratified and rarely conscious. As a result, trying to solve family problems can be like trying to win at a game when you don't know the rules.

FAMILY RULES

If you asked Sharon what the family rules were, she would recite a set of *Do's* and *Don'ts* that she expected from Jason. *Do* brush your teeth at night, *do* get in bed by seven-thirty, *do* turn the lights out at eight; *don't* leave the yard without asking permission. When family therapists speak of *family rules* they mean something quite different—not what is supposed to be, but what is. The *rules hypothesis*, as it is sometimes called, is a descriptive term for recurrent patterns of behavior that characterize any social system, of which the family is a prime example. People in continuing relationships develop patterns of interaction which become regular and predictable. *Rules* describe regularity, rather than regulation.

The rules hypothesis was originally developed by a group of researchers in Palo Alto, including psychiatrist Don Jackson, who observed that families function as cybernetic systems.[1] Families, like other coordinated systems, tend to be homeostatic. That is, they aim to achieve relative constancy and preserve stability in the face of changing circumstances. The most familiar example of a cybernetic system is the home heating unit, which is regulated by a thermostat that signals the furnace to operate until the temperature reaches a preset point. Similarly, Jason could get away with murder until his misbehavior reached Sharon's rather high boiling point. Although the regulation in families is not mechanical, it almost seems to be. This is because family rules—what is, not what is supposed to be—are often arrived at through trial and error, and are generally not carefully thought out. The rules may be products of our own creation, but since they are complex and unspoken, we often become frozen in patterns not of our choosing. Furthermore, since no one ratifies the rules, they are hard to examine.

◆

From this new perspective we can see that the rules describing how things worked in the Simpson family were not at all the same as Sharon's official version. Take bedtime, for example. If we were to observe what actually happened, we would see that after she put the baby to sleep, Sharon usually told Jason when there were fifteen minutes until bedtime. Like most children, he tried to prolong the inevitable. Either he'd find something pleasant to do with his mother—"Mommy read to me"—which postponed bedtime for at least twenty minutes, or he'd whine and fuss, which mobilized Stewart to take over. When Sharon told Jason to go to bed and he defied her until Stewart yelled at him, an interactional pattern was initiated. If it is repeated, it may be perpetuated as a family rule: Sharon is incompetent at setting limits, so Stewart is the disciplinarian. The corollary is that Sharon continues to become closer and more affectionate with Jason, while Stewart, the disciplinarian, moves further to the outside.

In some ways Sharon is the archetypal mother of our time. Family life has become democratic. We believe so strongly in individual freedom that lines of authority are blurred, even, or especially, in the family. We believe in treating children with respect, and in many quarters it is fashionable to be aggressively child-centered ("Have you hugged your child today?"). Sharon accepted without question the rights of children and she was committed to togetherness. Togetherness is everything. Understanding and persuasion replace coercion. In earlier, less democratic times, things were harsh but simple. Children did things because "Mommy (or Daddy) said so," or "Because that's the way it's always been done." Today much more improvisation is necessary. As a result many parents get confused.

Modern parents conditioned by a fear of child abuse are even more afraid of their own anger. So they try harder "to communicate." In concept, increased communication should make for a more nurturant family. In practice, it means that the method of authority shifts from physical control to verbal control. Instead of spanking our children or sending them to their rooms, we argue with them. The result is ineffective parenting.

Sharon played out a controlling but ineffectual parent who could be manipulated and pressured, and who did not feel able to enforce limits or openly express anger. Any good child-rearing manual would spell out her mistakes. She gave too many orders ("Jason do this, Jason do that"), put them tentatively (". . ., okay?"), and failed to back them up. One could say a great number of cogent things to this mother about setting and enforcing clear guidelines. But she might not listen. If she did listen, she might find herself somehow unable to take charge. And like most mothers, she would blame herself. Until she sees it, the family triangle imposes invisible limits on her actions.

FAMILY STRUCTURE

Family rules are tenacious and resistant to change because they are embedded in a powerful but unseen structure. Rules describe the process of interaction; structure defines the shape of relationships within which the process takes place. Originally, interactions shape the structure, but once established, structure shapes interactions. Here's how it developed in the Simpson family: Sharon's solicitous overinvolvement with Jason moved her closer to him and away from Stewart, forming a triangle with two poles close and one distant. Stewart's contribution to this structure was his own lack of interest in, and involvement with, the baby. Sharon spent more time with Jason; Stewart spent more time at work. When Stewart started feeling lonely he discovered he had competition for Sharon's attention. Like any rival male, he responded by trying to pull Sharon away from the baby. But the new structure had already begun to coalesce, and the three of them were held harshly by a network of nebulous rules, constrained by the structure of a fixed triangle.

Once a social system such as a family becomes structured,

attempts to change the rules constitute what family therapists call *first-order change*—change within a system that itself remains invariant. For Sharon to start practicing stricter discipline would be an example of first-order change. The enmeshed mother is caught in an illusion of alternatives. She can try to be strict or lenient; the result is the same because she remains part of a triangle. As with all triangles, two people are close and one is distant. As long as Sharon remained close to Jason and distant from Stewart, she was unable to transform the nature of her interactions with Jason. Sharon and Jason were so much together and so much on each other's minds that they developed their own mutually defined relationship, in which the child conditioned the parent to accept limited control. (Army officers are forbidden from fraternizing with enlisted men in order to prevent the erosion of authority that comes from blurring hierarchical distinctions.)

What's needed is *second-order change*—a change in the system itself. Without some change in the overall pattern of their relationships, Sharon and Stewart and Jason would continue to be caught in an invisible network. First-order change usually appears commonsensical, but often turns out to be more-of-the-same. Suppose Sharon tried to be stricter with Jason. Instead of arguing with him, she tells him once what she wants and if he disobeys she makes him sit on a chair in the corner. Fine. But unless their overinvolvement with each other changed, Sharon would find it difficult to enforce the rules. Moreover, as long as parents are not united they will tend to undercut each other's authority. Second-order change involves a shift that transforms the structure of relationships, and it is sometimes counterintuitive, as in the following example.

————◆————

The Kolcheks were a family somewhat like the Simpsons. Rosie left most of the discipline to Arthur; she was enmeshed with the two girls, he was disengaged. This pattern, so common in middle-class America, is stable but unsatisfying. The mother's closeness to the children stabilizes the distance between husband and wife but does little to assuage the bitterness of love gone sour. If you wanted to find fertile soil for an extramarital affair, this is it. In the most common instance, the man has the affair. Eventually he confesses. She's hurt and angry (in varying proportions, depending upon her style) but forgives him—or at least takes him back. Chastened, like a naughty child, he keeps his eye from roving. She keeps her eye on him to make sure. They resume their former pattern, only now prepared to avoid future shocks.

There are, of course, at least as many alternatives as there are verbs in the above description—confess, forgive, resume. Now that most mothers also work outside the home, there is equally likely to be a change in the subject of "has the affair." That was the case with the Kolcheks. Rosie had the affair, and Arthur was about as able to understand as most men. After the divorce, Rosie wanted more time for herself and with her friends. She discovered how indulgent she had been with her girls. They expected her to do so much around the house, and they did so little. They loved her all right, but they didn't mind her. Now, absent the family disciplinarian, Rosie was it. She didn't have to think or plan or read a book about how to discipline the children. The change in the family structure led to a changed relationship between her and the children.

———————◆———————

Divorce is one form of second-order change, a revolutionary form. The trouble with revolutions is that you never know what will follow. Realizing that we are all embedded in family structures reestablishes the limits of "parenting" as a skill, susceptible to endless criticism and improvement. Family structure is not easily discerned. We see what "they" do, but not how the what-they-do is a function of what we do. We cannot change parts of our family lives without affecting the larger system. The first step in mastering the power of the family and turning it into creative living is to discover how families are structured.

A STRUCTURAL MODEL

One reason family life seems beyond our understanding and control is that families often appear as collections of individuals who affect each other in powerful but unpredictable ways. We can, however, bring order and meaning to the complex transactions that make up family life by understanding how families become structured. Salvador Minuchin's structural family therapy is perhaps the most widely used model of family functioning among family therapists, and I will draw heavily upon Minuchin's ideas in this section.[2]

Families, like other groups, have many options for relating. Very quickly, however, interactions that were initially free to vary become regular and predictable. As they are repeated, family transactions establish enduring patterns. Once these patterns are established, family members use only a small fraction of the full range of behavior available to them. The first time the baby cries in the middle of the night, new parents may wait, wondering if the other one will get up and bring the baby in to be fed. Soon they will stop wondering. What is at first uncertain quickly becomes routine. Perhaps Mom gets the baby—after all, she's nursing, so why not let Dad sleep? If she does so tonight, it's a safe bet she will do so again tomorrow and tomorrow. Less likely, but still possible, Dad will get the baby—she's tired, and although he can't nurse the baby he wants to help out any way he can. In either case, this is the first of many steps which will define their relationship as parents. If the mother starts getting the baby while the father sleeps, can they change this pattern three nights or six weeks later? Yes. Will they? Probably not.

Transactional patterns foster expectations that determine future patterns. Often these become so ingrained that their origin is forgotten and they are presumed necessary rather than optional.

Family structure is built up from the covert rules which govern transactions in the family. For example, a rule such as "family members should always protect one another" will be manifested in various ways depending on the context and who is involved. If a boy gets in a fight with another boy in the neighborhood, his mother will go to the neighbors to complain. This might make the boy feel better for a while, but cheats him of the opportunity to learn how to settle his own problems and may earn him the reputation of being a wimp. If an adolescent daughter has to wake up early for school, mother wakes her. If a husband is too hung over to get to work in the morning, his wife calls to say he has the flu. If their parents have an argument, the kids interrupt. The parents are so preoccupied with the doings of their children that it keeps them from spending time alone together. All of these sequences are *isomorphic:* They are structured. Changing any one of them may not affect the basic structure, but altering the underlying structure will have ripple effects on all family transactions.

━━━━━◆━━━━━

In order to understand family structure it is only necessary to begin with two basic concepts: *subsystems* and *boundaries*.

Families are differentiated into *subsystems*, determined by generation, gender, common interests, and functional responsibilities. The obvious subsystems—parents, or teenagers, or the younger children—may be less significant than covert groupings. Sharon and Jason, for example, formed such a tightly bonded unit that Stewart was excluded. Another family may be split into two camps, with Mom and the boys on one side and Dad and the girls on the other. Though certain patterns are common, the possibilities for subgrouping are endless.

Every family member plays roles in several subgroups. Sharon is a wife and a mother, also a daughter, a sister, and a niece. In each of these roles she is required to behave differently and exercise a variety of interpersonal options. If she is mature and flexible she will be able to vary her behavior to fit the different subgroups in which she functions. Debating important decisions may be okay for a wife, but it causes problems for a mother.

Individuals, subsystems, and whole families are demarcated by interpersonal *boundaries*, invisible barriers which regulate the amount of contact with others. Boundaries safeguard the separateness and autonomy of the family and its subsystems. A rule forbidding phone calls at dinnertime establishes a boundary which shields the family from outside intrusion. If small children are permitted to freely interrupt their parents' conversations at dinner, the boundary separating the parents from the children is minimal, and the marriage is sacrificed to parenting. Subsystems which are not adequately protected by boundaries limit the development of relationship skills. If parents always step in to settle arguments between their children, the children won't learn to fight their own battles or how to get along with peers.

According to Minuchin, boundaries vary from rigid to diffuse. Rigid boundaries between subgroups are overly restrictive and permit little contact with outside systems, resulting in *disengagement*. Disengaged individuals or subsystems are independent but isolated. On the positive side, this fosters autonomy, growth, and mastery. On the other hand, disengagement limits warmth, affection, and nurturance; disengaged families must come under extreme stress before they will mobilize mutual support. If parents keep their children at a distance, affection is minimized and the parents will be slow to notice when the children need support and guidance.

Enmeshed subsystems offer a heightened sense of mutual support but at the expense of independence and autonomy. Enmeshed parents are loving and considerate; they spend a lot of time with their kids and do a lot for them. However, children enmeshed with their parents learn to rely on the parents and tend to become dependent. They are less comfortable by themselves and may have trouble relating to people outside the family.

◆

Several years ago I received two phone calls on the same day, both requesting therapy for sixteen-year-old boys. In both cases I met with the families. Both mothers complained with equal concern about their sons. In the first family the boy was, according to his mother, a behavior problem: He rode his bicycle around the neighborhood sometimes for fifteen minutes past his 6:30 curfew; he often forgot to take out the garbage; and when he got mad at her, he slammed the door to his room. The other boy, whose mother was about equally concerned, was profoundly, suicidally depressed. He had been slipping into a deep depression for several weeks before his parents finally noticed. The enmeshed mother was so exquisitely attuned to her son's behavior that she was upset by the least sign of adolescent rebellion. The disengaged mother, while no less loving, was so distant from her child that she did not realize a problem existed until it became manifestly profound.

◆

Sharon and Jason were enmeshed. They spent an extraordinary amount of time together. But enmeshment is more than that. Sharon, wrapped up in Jason, could not see him as separate. She acted as though there was nothing he did that was not her business. Even when he was in the bathroom, she called out to him, "Jason, what are you doing in there?" She would say, "Children need love," but her version of love was symbiotic. Like most enmeshed parents she was unaware of the huge amount of interference and coercion that characterized her relationship with Jason. They were preoccupied with each other, and their intense mutual focus limited each one's participation in other relationships. The more Sharon was overinvolved with Jason, the less time and energy she had for Stewart, and the less freedom Jason had to be with his friends.

Remember that enmeshment and disengagement are descriptive, interactional concepts; they refer to patterns of emotional distance and they describe what is, not how it got that way.

———◆———

Among the common misconceptions about boundaries are that whole families are enmeshed or disengaged. This is only loosely accurate. Some families, especially from northern cultures, are generally more private and independent of one another, while in other families the members are about as independent as peas in a pod. But enmeshment and disengagement are most usefully applied to specific boundaries around discrete family subsystems. Was the Simpson family enmeshed or disengaged? Even if it were one or the other, so what? The fact that Sharon and Jason were enmeshed while Stewart was disengaged is not only more accurate but also more useful. If Sharon became aware of this pattern she could pull back from Jason as a way of getting Stewart more involved as a parent. Giving up control, asking for help, or simply being "unable" to do everything—these are more effective than nagging him to do more or criticizing his lack of involvement. If Stewart became aware of the pattern, he could change it by ceasing his interference with Sharon's discipline, move closer to her by suggesting activities they both enjoy (instead of making up excuses for why he can't do all the boring things she suggests), and spend more time alone with his son.

Another common mistake is to think of enmeshment as "close" in the sense of warm, loving, and affectionate. According to this thinking, the way to overcome disengagement is to bring people together in uncomplicated affection. This is simplistic and implies that people are dumb creatures of habit. No, human behavior is purposeful. Disengagement usually reflects a correct assessment that closeness means conflict, but a cowardly solution—avoidance.

When I describe enmeshment and disengagement, many people can't help thinking that, of the two, they prefer enmeshment. Isn't it better to be intimate than distant?

Enmeshment is not intimacy, it is a miscarriage of intimacy in which individuation is sacrificed to loyalty. Actually, people who are enmeshed are no more intimate than those who are disengaged. It's hard to be intimate if there is no room for privacy.

Other people wonder: Are disengaged parents better able to discipline their children?

Mothers who are enmeshed with their children, like Sharon and Jason, usually produce children who are well-behaved outside the home, in large measure because they are adult-oriented. By the same token, these children are somewhat more likely to have trouble-making friends. Children who become behavior problems at school often have a distant or unstable relationship with their parents. Disengaged parents are more likely than enmeshed parents to be indifferent or preoccupied than permissive. So, the children of disengaged families probably don't cause trouble (at least not that anyone notices) at home, while children from enmeshed families don't cause trouble outside the home.

———◆———

Although it is not possible to understand people without taking into account their social context, notably the family, it is misleading to limit the focus to the surface of interactions—to social behavior divorced from inner experience. The family systems concept of boundaries can also be understood in psychological terms. Remember that Murray Bowen's term *fusion* and Salvador Minuchin's term *enmeshment* both deal with the consequences of blurred boundaries, but they are not interchangeable. Fusion is a quality of individuals and it is the counterpart of the psychoanalytic concept of individuation. Enmeshment is not a quality of persons; it is a quality of relationships. Enmeshment is strictly a social systems concept; it is *between* people, and unlike basic personalities, it can be changed.

The concept of boundaries applies to the relationship of all of these systems-within-systems in terms of the nature of their interface. The individuality and autonomy of each subsystem (individuals, siblings, parents, nuclear family) is maintained by a semipermeable boundary between it and the larger system around it. In Bowenian terms, individuals vary on a continuum from fusion to differentiation; the structural family therapy equivalents are enmeshment and disengagement. Psychoanalytic theory emphasizes the development of interpersonal boundaries, while describing how individuals emerge from the context of their families. Beginning with the separation and individuation from symbiosis with the mother that characterizes "the psychological birth of the human infant,"[3] psychoanalytic clinicians describe repeated and progressive separations that culminate first in the resolution of oedipal attachments and then eventually in leaving home.

This is a one-sided emphasis on poorly defined boundaries between self and other. Psychoanalysts pay insufficient attention to the problems of emotional isolation stemming from rigid boundaries, and describe this preference for aloneness as an artifact, a defense against a basic lack of psychological separateness. This belief in separation as the model and measure of growth is another example of male psychology overgeneralized and unquestioned. The danger that people will lose themselves in relationships is no more real than the danger that people will isolate themselves from loving intimacy, which is part of the full expression of human nature.

We need a balanced view of boundaries. Problems result when they are either too rigid or too diffuse. Diffuse boundaries allow outside interference in the functioning of a subsystem; rigid boundaries interfere with communication, support, and affection between different segments of the family. To avoid the pain of conflict, Sharon and Stewart built up an invisible wall between them. The rigid boundary separating Sharon and Stewart kept them from talking over their opinions about how to discipline Jason. They were a team divided. Since they could not even agree to disagree, their unvoiced differences were acted out in passive defiance, using Jason as a pawn to subvert each other's wishes.

Another important point about boundaries is that they are reciprocal. Sharon's enmeshment with Jason is related to the emotional distance between her and Stewart—related as cause and effect. The less she gets from Stewart, the more she needs from Jason; and the more involved with Jason she is, the less room in her life for Stewart.

When I give workshops on family dynamics, I find that many people are bothered by the term *structure*. Using such a mechanical term may make it seem as though I'm saying individuals don't count, that we are just like cogs in a machine.

That certainly isn't my intention. *Structure* refers to the functional organization that regulates how family members interact. The reason for the architectural metaphor is that the relative positions of family members—their closeness and distance from each other—form a very powerful pattern, which serves to maintain family relationships unchanged. Individuals can, of course, change their roles in the pattern. The problem is that unless they consider the overall pattern, the structure, it can be very hard for them to change their roles.

People then ask; "Well, why do we become so fixed in these patterns?" Because the patterns are economical, both for the family and the individual. The human mind is thrifty and leads us along familiar paths. It sees its primary business as establishing effective channels for action, and resists altering a channel that has become established, to say nothing of constructing a new one that causes anxiety. Add to this the constraining force of other members of the family, who continue to influence us as they have in the past (whether or not we do what they want us to do, we do as they influence us to do), and you can see how powerfully set family patterns become.

BLUEPRINT FOR A HEALTHY FAMILY

What is the ideal structure for families? There isn't one. Families come in a variety of functional forms, reflecting cultural preferences (for example, child-centered families versus adult-oriented families) and unique demands (for instance, in single-parent families it may be necessary to invest considerable parental responsibility in the oldest child). Or, to cite another example, many couples without small children function quite happily even though they see very little of each other. Many commuter marriages only seem to be compromises with necessity, when in fact the practical "necessity" of working in different cities actually suits one or both partners' needs for a high degree of independence. The stability of these relationships depends less upon some abstract norm ("families should be together") than on whether or not the disengagement suits both spouses. However, although I have seen happy, successful commuter marriages and "companionate marriages" (where the spouses are like friendly roommates), the only place I have seen successful "open marriages" is in European films.

Although there is no single standard for optimal structure, healthy families do share three structural characteristics: clear boundaries, a hierarchical organization, and flexibility.

Clear Boundaries

Strong families manage to balance closeness and separateness, to satisfy individual and group needs, resulting in personal freedom as well as belonging and togetherness. Family members understand that the whole system must function for the individuals to prosper. This is a lesson that Stewart had to learn. Like other disengaged fathers, he sought satisfaction in activities and relationships outside the family. As a result, he got less out of the family and the family got less out of him. Sharon was the opposite. She looked for gratification almost exclusively within the family and was less trustful of the world beyond the family boundaries. This enmeshment deprived her of valuable sources of emotional energy and enrichment, as well as limiting her own and Jason's autonomy.

Sharon ended the constant power struggles with Jason by separating from him and moving closer to Stewart. *It did not happen because she tried harder.* Sharon had been trying as hard as she could for years. The problem was that her trying took place within a family system that crippled her initiative. As long as she was enmeshed with Jason and disengaged from Stewart, she could try all she wanted and still not achieve satisfactory results. She had to learn to put some distance between herself and Jason, to allow him to take more responsibility for his own thoughts and feelings and behavior, and to assume more authoritative control over those issues that were her responsibility. It wasn't easy. She had to tell herself, *I love this child enough not to give in.* For his part, Stewart had to learn that negotiating with Sharon was an aspect of being an individual within the family rather than an incessant compromising of his personal goals. When you negotiate in good faith with your spouse, you win by winning *and* you win by "losing." This cohesiveness is essential for healthy family life.

Strong families have *clear boundaries*. Like the membranes of living cells, their boundaries have enough strength and integrity to permit a highly involved interaction within, yet are permeable enough to permit an exchange of energy and information with the outside world. Members of healthy families are actively involved in the world beyond the family, relate to it with optimism and enthusiasm, and from their encounters outside bring varied interests and excitement back to the family.

Recently I spoke to a man whose wife was thinking about going back to work after six months of maternity leave. Naturally he was concerned about the balancing of household responsibilities that her return to work would necessitate. Still, he had no doubt that her working was best for all of them. "Sure, we can use the money," he told me, "but—more important—I just don't think she would be as happy or as interesting a person if she gave up her career."

Healthy families also have clear boundaries between members. They understand and respect that each of them is somewhat different. Dad likes Chinese food, Mom likes salads and seafood. Johnny likes swimming and ice skating, Suzie likes ice skating but prefers hiking. They do not attempt to establish a facade of pseudomutuality that says they must all like the same things. Yet they manage to work things out. Negotiation consists of accepting differences and working toward shared goals. In such a differentiated family group, individual choice is expected, family members speak up, and even the youngest children are respected as autonomous individuals with sovereign rights and responsibilities.

Hierarchical Organization

In healthy families there is a clear hierarchy of power, with leadership in the hands of the parents, who form a united coalition. There are clear generational divisions: Parents have more power than children, and older children have more responsibilities and privileges than younger ones. Though many decisions are shared freely, there is no question as to who is parent and who is child. Successful parents rule with good-humored effectiveness. They do not overcontrol their children, but neither do they feel obligated to disclaim their adult power. Only a weak executive subsystem establishes restrictive control; an excessive need to control occurs mostly when those in charge are ineffective.

Children are less overtly powerful than their parents, but their contributions influence decisions, and their power grows as the children grow toward adulthood.

Respect for individual boundaries encourages intimacy. Members of healthy families have the opportunity to openly share honest thoughts and feelings, experiencing each other as different but sympathetic. A child may be willing to talk over a problem with her father if the family is flexible enough to allow special time for the two of them, and if the father is willing to listen without taking over. If a woman knows that her husband respects her autonomy over her career, it will be easier for her to share her doubts and conflicts. Some of the worst marital conflicts arise where there is a blurred distinction between separate turfs. This may be unavoidable on issues that affect both partners equally, like whether to have another baby or what city to live in. But many arguments arise simply from a failure to respect each other's prerogatives. Over the years, I have heard many wives complain that their husbands won't discuss the one thing the husbands care about most: their work. The reason often turns out to be that the wives feel free to intrude with unwanted advice—and the husbands are too insecure of their autonomy to take it or leave it.

To some, the idea that families function best when they have a hierarchical structure and that there should be a clear boundary separating parents and children suggests that parents should be detached and aloof from their children. This distorted conclusion is particularly likely to be drawn by those people to whom the idea of boundaries is foreign and repugnant. Not liking the idea of separateness, they mock it: "Oh, you mean the parents should be like Marine drill sergeants, and that children should be seen and not heard? Well, sor-ree, Doc, we just aren't like that."

It is true that a clear boundary between parents and children makes room for a private relationship between the spouses, excluding the children from certain adult activities—making important family decisions, lovemaking, adult conversations. But what really separates the generations is not distance but modes of relatedness. Effective parents relate to their children from an unquestioned (and unself-doubting) position of authority. They are older, wiser, and stronger; they know it, and the children know it. At times, effective parents play at being equals with the children—tussling perhaps, or playing make-believe—but they are not equals. They know it and the children know it. They do not argue with their children ("I don't wanna . . ." "Yes, you do." "No I don't!"), and they don't burden the children unnecessarily with their own problems.

Moreover this appropriate mode of relatedness changes as the children mature. Infants need nurturance and little else. Some people lecture to their babies, but it's only practice—practice for future sermonizing and future deafness. Small children need nurturance too, but also discipline and control. When parents say in despair, "I can't control anything!" I usually ask them if their children run in front of cars. The point is, of course, that all parents teach their children to obey those rules they consider essential. Most parents could profit from making fewer—far fewer—rules. But there should be one superordinate rule: *The parents are in charge.* Too much discipline, control really, is as bad as too little. An excellent guideline is to let children learn for themselves the consequences of their own behavior. Some things, like running in front of cars, are too dangerous, and some things, like cruel treatment of pets, don't have consequences immediate enough for children to grasp. But an awful lot of what we nag children about, such as wearing sweaters on cold days, taking care not to break their toys, and eating supper, have consequences that the children themselves, if left alone, will learn from. Overuse dilutes authority.

Flexibility

In healthy families, social roles are clear yet flexible. Boundaries and alignments must be readjusted to accommodate to changes in the life cycle of the family. As we have seen in the Simpson family, a new couple must strengthen the boundary separating them from their parents in order to protect the autonomy of the new union. With the advent of children, a boundary must be drawn that allows the children access to both parents while excluding them from spouse functions. Some couples who do well as a twosome are never able to make a satisfactory adjustment to a group of three or four. And the familiar example of two people who live happily together for years but suddenly break up after they marry can be understood as a failure to tolerate the stronger boundary that marriage vows imply.

Raising children requires nurturance, control, and guidance.

What makes being a parent so damned difficult is not only the complexity of the task, but also the fact that the parenting process differs depending on the children's age. When they are young, children need little more than nurturance. Later, control and guidance become more important. The growing child's developmental needs tax the parents' capacity for flexibility. As children grow, their developmental needs for both autonomy and guidance impose pressures on the parental subsystem, which must be modified to meet them. One aspect of this modification is to strengthen the boundary between parents and children, which permits the children greater access to friends and school and other social institutions.

◆

When Jason was a baby, Sharon was a perfect mother. She loved him completely and tended his needs with love and devotion. When he got a little older, however, she had trouble shifting from a purely nurturant role to one of nurturance plus control. To think of this simply as Sharon's failure to exercise discipline is to ignore the context. Responding to the shifting demands of children requires a constant transformation of the position of family members in relation to one another. A parent's relationship to his or her chldren always reflects his or her relationship to the other parent, or in the case of single parents, the relationship to other significant adults.

If we understand the family as a social system in transformation, we get away from blaming everything on the mother and we get way from labeling the family as pathological. Instead, we can see the Simpsons as a family stuck in transition. Unfortunately, Sharon and Stewart responded to the strain of accommodating to a new member by increasing the rigidity of their transactional patterns and boundaries, avoiding and resisting any exploration of alternatives.

Problems of transition occur in a number of situations. They may be produced by developmental changes in family members, as in the Simpson family, or by a member's increased involvement beyond the family, as when a wife and mother begins to work outside the home. When this happens, family members may have to realign roles and boundaries in order to accommodate to changing circumstances. Another classic dislocation occurs when children enter adolescence. Teenagers become more involved in the wide world and less willing to submit without question to parental authority. If adolescents are to move a little away from the sibling subsystem and receive increased autonomy and responsibility appropriate to their age, boundaries must shift and parents must change. But it's easy to overlook the complexity of these changes. In order to change their relationship to children, parents must change their relationship to each other.

Sharon viewed the problems in the family from a subjective point of view, which did not include her own role. She saw that Stewart was distant from her and distant from Jason, but she tried to change him, not the relationships. Trying to change other people is an exercise in self-defeat. Still, Sharon kept trying. For years she organized her life around it—fighting to change Stewart, to make him the man she knew he could be. Eventually she gave up. Too bad she didn't know that the secret of changing a relationship is to discover your own role in the pattern, and then change that. The hard part is learning to focus on yourself, your part in the pattern.

Sharon told Stewart she wanted to spend more time together, yet she did not appreciate that her tight bond with Jason made it difficult for him to be with her. When he did try to talk with her, Jason was always around. By the same token, Sharon's enmeshment with Jason made it difficult for Stewart to spend time with the boy. When Sharon objected to the two of them going off to see an adventure movie ("He sees plenty of that stuff on TV") or gave detailed instructions for dressing the child, Stewart got mad and decided, *The hell with it; let her do everything if that's what she wants.*

Had she gone to individual therapy as a result of her unhappiness, Sharon would have discovered connections between these events and her feelings and her own family history. She might, for example, have learned that her efforts to be the perfect mother to Jason were founded on her own insecurity, which in turn stemmed from her parents' failure to take her seriously. But being insecure is a little like having a big nose or fat hips: How you got that way is somewhat irrelevant. In family therapy, Sharon would have learned a different lesson. She would have learned to see the connections among Jason's actions and Stewart's actions and her actions. What would have been most useful was thinking of the three of them as a triangle, so that if she wanted to get Stewart more involved she would realize that what she said was less important than that she make room for him. Specifically, when Stewart and Jason were together she might leave them alone. Once in a while she might even find reasons to be out of the house. In short, she could have started building a clear boundary between herself and Jason, which would have made room for Stewart to be more involved with him as a father *and* made room for Sharon and Stewart to have more of a relationship as a couple. Could have, could have. . . .

◆

The strength of a system depends on its ability to mobilize alternative transactional patterns when internal or external conditions demand its restructuring. The boundaries of the subsystems must be firm, yet flexible enough to allow realignment when circumstances change.

BUILDING YOUR CHILD'S SELF-ESTEEM

Because I introduced the concept of enmeshment with the example of Sharon and Jason, I have emphasized discipline and control. Ironically, though, effective discipline and nurturance go hand in hand. It is easier to sympathize with the children's wishes when you know you are in charge. It is also easier to accept their autonomous strivings if you do not depend upon their company to satisfy all your emotional needs. Ineffective discipline erodes a parent's capacity to be sympathetic and supportive. If we allow our children to become rival forces, the relationship is dominated by a struggle for control and our capacity for loving kindness is strained. It starts early.

If we cannot control their actions, we try to control their feelings. Parents who are unable to differentiate between accepting their children's feelings and acceding to their whims give in repeatedly, until they exhaust their ability to listen empathically. Once parents learn—or *decide*—to control their children's behavior, they can be more attentive to, and accepting of, the children's feelings.

Often when they express feelings, children are asking both to be understood and to be allowed to do something. A common example is bedtime.

———◆———

Daddy: It's time for bed.
Child: I don't wanna go to bed! I'm not tired.

———◆———

A father who never doubts that he is in charge can sympathize with the child's feelings. "I know, honey, you hate to go to bed. You wish you could stay up as late as you want, don't you?" "Yes." Little more need be said.

Parents who are threatened or doubt their control confuse the instrumental and expressive function of feelings, and they fight back. By the way, unless your three-year-old has very big muscles from lifting blocks all day, you can make her go to bed on time. If you have to. And you may have to. But only once or twice, *if* you start early. It should not be necessary to argue that a small child feels something she does not feel (tired) in order to get her to do something she does not want to do (go to bed).

Bedtime is especially likely to become a battlefield for parents who want the best for their children. In my practice I have seen dozens of young couples who have no peace or privacy in the evening because their toddlers "don't get tired" until ten or eleven o'clock.

Despite my flippant remark about the blocks, children usually control their parents by crying. Crying evokes primal anxieties. Especially after you listen to it for a while. My youngest child is now eleven, yet I still cannot listen to a baby crying without feeling a knot in my gut.

Unhappily, children who are punished or ignored when they express how they feel, learn to conceal and submerge their feelings. Eventually they no longer recognize their own feelings. Instead, they feel only the residues of suppression: boredom, anxiety, and apathy. When parents yell at them all the time, children get the idea that their feelings and impulses—and thus they themselves—are bad.

———◆———

Jason's mother was always there, but not always there for him. Her need was intense, so intense that she intruded herself into her child's autonomous experience, doing for him what he might have done for himself. In her way, she loved him completely. When he cried she held him, when he was bored she played with him. But her response was often a projection of her own moods and tensions. Once, for example, when they were playing together, Jason greedily took away all the blocks—"Jason's blocks, all for Jason! You don't get any." Instead of letting him play out his fantasy of having it all, she snapped at him, "You're a selfish brat!" Their enmeshment made her confuse being a mother with being a playmate.

Sharon's empathy was unpredictable and unreliable. She could be counted on to soothe and bandage hurts, to hold him when the shadows of night took on scary shapes, and to protect him from his father's anger. But—and this bewildered Jason—she scolded him for fighting, wouldn't tolerate his anger, and occasionally shrieked at him just for getting muddy. His early experience of her tenderness made him run to her with blind confidence, but sometimes he ran blindly into a wall of criticism.

As he got older Jason turned more to his father, but here too he was unlucky. He saw his father defer to her, steer clear of her, avoiding at all costs the fights in which, when they did occur, he quickly caved in before her shrill attacks. Jason never put it to himself in so many words, but he became aware that the father he loved and admired was a coward. Maybe that's the way men are with women.

Mommy's love was like a warm sweater on a winter night. But sometimes it was irritating. He wanted to go play outside, she told him it was too cold; why didn't he stay inside and listen to a story? Since she was always trying to control what he did, he didn't have a clear idea of the difference between her preferences and her rules. Sometimes when he was naughty she didn't notice; sometimes she screamed at him. This kind of high-volume denunciation had little measurable effect on his behavior but a far greater effect on his self-image. Later he would react with unforgiving rage; now all he felt was hurt and diminished.

❖

Suppose things have gotten out of hand; how does a parent regain some control over a young child who has become impossible?

By doing two things. First, by balancing discipline with affection. If you can use rewards to shape good behavior, so much the better. But even just starting to be nicer to your child for no special reason will help cement a positive relationship and make it easier for you to start setting limits. Sorry—*setting limits* is clinical jargon for making and enforcing rules. The second thing to remember is that parents *must* work together as a team. The essential point is not that they share equally in the parenting—though that certainly is a fine thing—but that they agree to support the same set of rules. Make sure your spouse agrees with you about what constitutes a problem. Talk things over. If you disagree, feel free to try to convince your partner, but be prepared to make some concessions yourself. Remember, only a united front will work.

Some experts say that parents shouldn't say to their child "You are a good boy (or girl)," but should instead praise only specific behavior—the things you want them to do more of. That's good advice for training behavior, not so good for building self-esteem.

It's impossible to overestimate the importance of trying to build your child's self-esteem. Praise your children lavishly. Keep your efforts to control and discipline them very specific and very forceful; don't let the relatively few things you need your children to do become battlegrounds. The best way to avoid that is to fight few battles, but when you do, get them over quickly. Teaching your children to treat their parents—and all adults— with respect is an investment in treating the children's own future selves with respect. If they learn to walk all over adults, what do they have to look forward to when they become adults but more of the same?

DISCOVERING THE STRUCTURE IN YOUR OWN FAMILY

If you are like most people, you see first the idiosyncrasies of others and none better than your spouse's. Since you've read this far, you have probably already come to a conclusion about whether he or she is enmeshed with or disengaged from: (a) you, and (b) the children. If a parent is enmeshed, most of his or her conversations are about the children, their problems, their accomplishments. Disengaged parents, on the other hand, spend relatively little time with the kids and get a glazed look in their eyes if you talk for long about children. You can diagram this as follows. Use a dotted line to represent a diffuse boundary, dashes for a clear boundary, and a solid line for a rigid boundary.

ENMESHMENT	FUNCTIONAL	DISENGAGEMENT
· · · · · · · · ·	— — — — — —	▬▬▬▬▬▬
DIFFUSE BOUNDARY	CLEAR BOUNDARY	RIGID BOUNDARY

If you think your husband is disengaged from the children, draw it as follows below. Remember if you are thinking of his relationship with the children, he is the father, not husband.

DAD

▬▬▬▬▬▬▬▬▬▬

KIDS

The trouble with this diagram is that it leaves out the other relationships, and it leaves out the only person you can change—you.

Put the rest of you in the diagram.

MOM   DAD

· · · · · · · · · |

KIDS |

Once you think of things this way, you can see that there are three ways things can change: by strengthening the boundary between Mom and the kids, by Mom and Dad moving closer together, and by Dad moving closer to the kids. Moreover, *any one of these changes will help bring about the others.* A clear boundary between parents and children exists when the parents allow the children a fair amount of control over their own lives. It's easier to be flexible and tolerant if you realize that they are them and you are you. Once parents accept a diminished need to manage their children's lives, most of their interactions take one of two forms:

discipline or nurturance. Disciplinary issues, however, will be short and sweet. When the parents are clearly in charge, battles are few and quickly settled.

Remember that breaking down a rigid boundary means moving closer emotionally. It means spending more time together and opening up whatever is being held back in the relationship. If you are disengaged from someone, it is usually best to begin to break down the distance by spending time together in as pleasant a way as possible. Real closeness may, however, require airing dormant complaints and working through conflicts.

Sometimes it is hard to tell if spouses are enmeshed or disengaged, because one seeks one pattern, the other the opposite. She calls him at work, he doesn't return the calls. Or he tries to get her to go out to the movies, but she always wants to bring the kids along. I will consider more fully in Chapter 10 the problem of a struggle to define the distance in a relationship. For now it may be best to decide what the predominant patterns in the family are.

Here is how to recognize the nature of boundaries: Who is the subject of your conversations? Your spouse's conversations? Do you talk about the kids most of the time, or rarely? How much time do you spend alone with your children, husband, friends, self? If you spend most of your time with someone, chances are you are enmeshed. The measure of the boundary between siblings is the amount of time they spend together and whether they are differentiated by age. If they each have their own friends, if the older one goes to bed later, then the boundary between them is probably clear. In general, the clearer the boundary between them, the fewer the squabbles.

Enmeshed parents respond to any variation from what they expect from their children with excessive speed and intensity. A common example is dinner table fights, where enmeshed parents get upset if their children don't eat their vegetables. Instead of establishing a simple rule ("No dessert unless you finish what's on your plate"), some parents argue with their small-fry as though they were equals. This only turns mealtime into a contest of wills—one that nobody wins. Most young parents know better than to argue with small children, but as in so many other areas of family life, what we know does not override what we feel.

Whereas enmeshed parents respond too quickly to their children, disengaged parents may not respond when necessary. Sometimes children of disengaged parents fall behind in school because no one makes sure that they do their homework. While children are still in elementary school, it may be necessary to check up on them, until doing homework becomes a habit and the children are old enough to feel the consequences of not turning in their assignments.

Consider a typical day. Do both parents wake up together? Who attends to the children in the morning? Are the children expected or permitted to make their own breakfasts? What is dinner like? Is everyone together, or is one parent always with the children and the other only occasionally? Where do people go and what do they do after dinner? Do the children spend the evening with their parents? Do the parents spend time alone? One of the simplest measures of enmeshment is open doors to bedrooms.

———◆———

In my experience, most people grow quickly impatient with explanations about how to recognize problematic behavior patterns. Right away they want to know what to do. Even though I have stressed that the only person you can change is yourself, many of you may be itching for advice about how to change the others in your family. My advice is to get as clear as possible about the structure of your family. Recognizing the structure gives us power as well as understanding.

Change doesn't exactly take care of itself, but it sometimes seems to. Unseen forces begin to lose their power once we become aware of them. Sometimes, however, patterns are ingrained and change is hard. The bad news is that the easiest patterns to see are the hardest to change. If, for example, your spouse is completely preoccupied with the children, the enmeshment will be easier to notice than to alter. *Don't criticize.* If you want results, try to discover your role in the pattern. Even if you didn't start it, you can change it.

THE TWO-PAYCHECK FAMILY

*I*t was raining the morning Heather was due to start first grade. Only September and already there was a chill in the air. From the kitchen window Sharon looked out at the rain coming down hard, swept sideways by intermittent gusts of a strong, early autumn wind. There was no light on the horizon of the gray, leaden sky. It would rain all day.

In the kitchen it was warm and bright. Jason was playing on the floor with his Legos while Heather finished eating her cinnamon toast. Because it was raining so hard, Sharon offered to drive Heather to school, but Heather wanted to ride the bus, just like all the other kids.

Sharon watched from the doorway as Jason dashed through the rain and onto the bus. Heather walked slowly, deliberately. In her slick, yellow plastic raincoat, she was a big girl. Big girls aren't afraid of the rain. Sharon's heart opened up and she started to cry, but only for a minute. She put on a big smile and waved as the bus pulled away. Watching as the bus disappeared into the rain, Sharon became aware of a strange sound in the house. It was quiet.

Now that the children were gone all day, Sharon felt like she had her life back again. The last few years now seemed a blur, from round-the-clock feedings and diaper changes to lugging the children everywhere, the cleaning up of a thousand messes. So much to do, and never enough time to do it. Now it was different. No longer were the children in charge of her days. She supposed she should feel liberated; in fact, she felt adrift.

Having small children is a little like being in the Army. Every aspect of life is regimented, but there is one great freedom: the freedom from deciding what to do. Sharon's little commanders didn't (usually) give orders, still they just as effectively set the agenda for how she spent her days. With Heather, Sharon had looked forward to this day. It meant that Heather would ride on the bus with her brother and go to school all day with the big kids. Sharon wasn't so sure what it would mean for her. Would she feel a little sad or just relieved? As it turned out, she didn't feel much of anything.

There was lots to do around the house. As long as the children were around it never seemed possible to catch up with the cleaning and fixing.

After finishing a second cup of coffee, Sharon stripped and waxed the kitchen floor. Then, after weeks of not getting around to it, she finally took the cracked basement window to the glazier for a new pane of glass. On the way back she stopped in at the library. It seemed strange not to go right to the children's section. She picked up three novels and leafed through some recent copies of *The New Yorker*. *My god*, she thought, *it's been years since I read one of these.*

Sharon knew how she felt about going back to work—she didn't want to. She would have been perfectly content to stay home. There were a lot of things to do. Besides, she didn't want to be away when the children came home. And what about the summer? What would happen to them in the summer if she were working? She could argue the case for staying home quite effectively with anyone who claimed that women *should* work. Still, in her own mind, she didn't feel quite right about it. Once again, though, Sharon didn't really have to sort out her ambivalence. She agreed with Stewart that they needed the money. They were just barely getting by now, and there was no way they'd be able to save anything for the kids' college expenses unless she took a job.

Stewart thought maybe she should go back to school, get a master's degree so that she'd have some real earning power. But Sharon didn't want to go back to school. She wanted a job, not a career, and she didn't want to work summers. That pretty well limited her to something at the college, and a friend of Stewart's in personnel found her an opening in the psychology department. It was a large department, with six secretaries, or "support staff" as they were now called. Sharon wouldn't exactly be a secretary—more like an assistant to the departmental administrative assistant, and she would be in charge of coordinating some of the professors' research projects. The salary wasn't much, but the job sounded interesting, and most important, the hours were flexible and she would have summers off.

Stewart was pleased. It was more than the money. He thought—though he would never say it out loud—that Sharon had regressed in the past few years. Taking care of children, she had become one. Working would be good for her. Get her out of the house, meet interesting people; let the children look after themselves for once. He knew there would be some changes around the house, but he could handle it.

The night before Sharon's first day at work, Stewart had a little talk with the kids. He told them that they'd all have to help out more now that Mommy was starting a new job. They'd have to keep their rooms clean and make sure to take their dirty clothes down to the laundry. Jason would have to start putting the dishes in the dishwasher and Heather would have to help set the table for supper. He, Stewart, would start planning the menus and helping out with the shopping and cooking. The kids nodded.

In the morning, Stewart and the children made a special breakfast for Sharon: eggs and yogurt and cinnamon toast. They were so sweet.

Sharon's first day was a mess. Everyone was nice, but nobody seemed to know exactly what she was supposed to do. So, she hung around a lot. Her hours were 8:00 to 2:30, so she got home just about the same time the kids did. Jason was very solicitous, very grown-up. "How did it go, Mommy?" Heather wanted to

know if she had done any "speriments" yet. "Not yet, honey."
When Stewart came home he was very mysterious. "Why don't
you go upstairs and read for a while, and we'll call you."

Forty-five minutes later Jason bounded up the stairs, calling
out, "You can come down now." Excited, impatient, he burst into
the bedroom and took Sharon's hand. "Close your eyes," he said,
full of mischief. He led her out to the back porch, where Stewart
was grilling lamb chops. On the table there were flowers and a
card. "Sit down, and have a glass of wine while I finish these,"
Stewart said. She could see that he had his hands full trying to
manage everything. Sharon opened the card. On the front was a
child's drawing of a woman with black hair driving a little red car
to a large gray building. Inside it said, *Happy New Job!* and it was
signed Jason and Heather and Daddy. Nice.

The first several days at work were hard for Sharon. Everyone
else seemed to know what they were doing; she didn't. Not only
was she new, but her job was ill-defined and she was supposed to
find things to do. When she told Carmen, one of the secretaries,
that she was confused, Carmen said, "Don't worry, you'll get the
hang of it. I was confused, too, when I first came." Carmen was
maybe twenty. It was disconcerting. Sharon had grown used to
being a mother, being in charge and in control. No one really
questioned her authority; when it came to her house and her
children, she was the expert. Now she was a beginner, starting
over—and asking a twenty-year-old for advice.

By the third week, Sharon was beginning to feel better. She
knew her way around the department, had met most of the
professors, and understood pretty much what was expected of
her. The thing she liked most about the job was working with
Alice, the departmental administrative assistant. Alice was so
organized. She kept the whole place running smoothly, and it was
a pleasure to see how efficiently she planned teaching schedules,
arranged meetings, and handled all the prima donnas.

The hardest thing for Sharon was getting up and out of the
house in the morning. She was used to coming downstairs in her
bathrobe and helping the children fix breakfast. After they left,
she would sit down with a cup of coffee and read the paper. In the
warm weather she sat out on the back porch where she could

listen to the birds; in the winter she sat by the window and looked out at the cold, happy to be inside. This brief period of unhurried solitude helped her ease into the day. Without it she felt rushed and tense. And that seemed to set the tone for the rest of the day.

Stewart and the children tried very hard to make accommodations. Stewart worked out a schedule for suppers, two weeks at a time, which included what they would eat and who would cook. He cooked as often as he could. Heather and Jason fixed their own breakfasts, and Jason helped Heather put together her lunch. These lunches consisted of more Fruit Loops and granola bars than Sharon liked, but she figured they would survive. All four of them were anxious about the change, and all four of them were on their best behavior. Sharon had planned to be home in the afternoon before the school bus, but once or twice a week she didn't quite make it. At the end of the second week, Jason, now eight, told her, "Mommy, I don't mind that you're not here anymore when I come home. I can take care of myself."

The easiest adjustments were the things Stewart and the children volunteered to do. It was nice to have their help with the meals, but nobody volunteered to help with the laundry or the cleaning. Sharon hesitated to ask, but after a while she just couldn't keep up. Why couldn't Stewart see that she needed more help?

Stewart thought everything was fine. He liked seeing Sharon dressed up for work in the morning—she looked more like the sophisticated woman he married than the middle-aged housewife she'd become—and he was rather proud of himself for doing the shopping and cooking. The first he knew something was wrong was on a night when he was particularly tired. He had just finished grading the last of twenty-six papers on Fitzgerald's portrait of Jay Gatsby and was lying on the couch watching a Humphrey Bogart movie on TV. Sharon came up from the basement and dropped a laundry basket stuffed to overflowing on the floor in front of him, and then stomped off upstairs.

Stewart's stomach starting churning. He could tell she was mad, but why did she have to slam things down without saying anything? He went back to his movie, trying his best to ignore her. He'd be damned if he was going to give in every time she had an infantile tantrum. But after a few minutes he could hear her sobbing in the bedroom, and he decided to go up and make peace.

Unfortunately Sharon was ready for war. She screamed at him: "You said you were going to help out; you don't do anything except sit there in front of the *goddamned television*, while I do six loads of your dirty laundry. You're a fine one when it comes to making big speeches, but you don't *really* help out. Once in a while you cook supper—when it's convenient for you—but what about everything else around here? Who does the laundry? Who takes the kids everywhere? Even when you do condescend to clean up, I have to go around and clean up after you. You put dirty dishes in the dishwasher and I have to scrape them off after the crud is all baked on. You don't have an ounce of compassion in you! *You don't give a damn about anyone but yourself!*"

Stewart tried to listen, but he couldn't stand it—her yelling and exaggerating everything all out of proportion was more than he could take. When he said, "I'm sorry," and reached out to put his arm around her, she slapped him. "Don't touch me, you bastard!"

He was stung, livid. He got up and walked out of the bedroom in a cold fury, down the stairs, out the front door, and into his car. Once he got into the car he wasn't sure what to do next. He was scared of leaving, but too angry to go back into the house, so he drove off to the bar across the street from the university. This wasn't him. He'd never walked out before, and he never went into bars, but he didn't know what else to do. He sat there nursing a beer and thinking about all the awful, unfair things Sharon had said. Sure it was hard with both of them working, but why did she have to blame everything on him? If she couldn't cope with working, he could be sympathetic; why did she have to take it all out on him?

For the next two days they avoided each other. Silence is a common power play. Who will give in first? Stewart was angry and hurt, too upset by Sharon's yelling to take in what she had said, and definitely too mad to discuss it. Sharon was hurt and angry, determined to wait for Stewart to come to her. After all, he was the one who walked out. After a couple of days of nursing his resentment, Stewart calmed down and thought about what Sharon had said. She was exaggerating, of course, but maybe he *could* do a little more. Half out of a sense of fairness, and half just to appease her, he decided once again to try to make peace. He began as he usually did, with an apology. "I'm sorry, honey." Sharon didn't say anything. She just waited to see what he would say next. "I know you have a lot to do, and I'm sorry if I'm not doing my share. What else would you like me to do to help you out?"

For a while things were better. Stewart did help out more, though Sharon couldn't help noticing that he asked a lot of questions about things he could have figured out himself. She'd be trying to read to the children and he'd interrupt. "Honey, where does this go?" She wanted to scream.

Another source of resentment was looking after the children. He could not seem to do as much for the children as she did. When they fussed about doing their homework, he might ask them what was wrong or he might just tell them to quiet down; it never seemed to occur to him to help them. The same thing with cleaning their rooms. If they cried and started banging things around, he yelled at them to cut that out and get busy. He didn't seem to understand that little people need help. They have feelings too.

One rainy morning when everybody was running late and the kids were cranky and whining, Sharon asked Stewart if he would mind driving them. "No, I can't," he said. He had an article to edit before he went in. Besides, it was their job to catch the bus. Another time he promised he would be home in time to drive Jason to a skating party, but he called at the last minute to say he couldn't make it. By then it was too late.

Sharon found herself incredulous at Stewart's letting them down. She thought he was acting out of a selfish, stubborn unwillingness to be a fully sharing member of the family. Stewart wanted to do more. But in his life the consistent payoff was for succeeding at work. There, he got raises and plaudits. No one cheered when he helped out at home. In fact, it infuriated Sharon that he expected to be praised just for doing his share. They rarely argued about the children, though. By some kind of mutual agreement, differences about the children were consigned to the realm of Things Not Safe To Discuss. That left housework as the primary subject of active contention.

They seemed to fall into a pattern. For a while after a blow-up, Stewart would do more. Then he'd start slipping. Forgetting to do certain things, lapsing into the old habit of expecting Sharon to take care of everything. She tried not to say anything. She didn't like their fights any more than he did. But after a while she'd get to the point where she couldn't stand it any longer and just seemed to explode. There'd be another fight, and another cooling off. Promises made, and promises broken. They seemed to go in cycles. And they both thought these arguments were unique to them. The truth is that Sharon and Stewart were struggling to adjust to the new family form of the eighties.

THE TWO-PAYCHECK FAMILY

In the early 1970s, the women's movement put the traditional nuclear family on trial and found it guilty of oppression. Full-time housekeeping and child care were described as numbing drudgery, and homemakers were thought to be little more than domestic slaves. Radical voices focused on women as victims of a patriarchal culture, and even moderates like Betty Friedan claimed that the average middle-class household was a "comfortable concentration camp."[1] At the same time, a corrosive cycle of inflation and recession made it increasingly difficult for most American families to subsist on only one income. The rising divorce rate and the fact that women are still overwhelmingly awarded custody has created a legion of single mothers who suddenly find themselves dropping out of the middle class into poverty. As a result, more and more mothers are now working outside the home to support themselves and their families.

It is important to note that most of the increase in women working for pay has occurred among married women with husbands and children present in the home. Victor Fuchs, an economist at the National Bureau of Economic Research, notes that among single women ages twenty-five to forty-four, four out of five work for pay, and this proportion has not changed since 1950. Divorced and separated women have also traditionally worked, and their participation rates (about 75 percent) have grown only slightly. The really revolutionary change has taken place in the behavior of married women with children.[2]

For most American families, arguments about whether or not women should work, and why they do, are just so much rhetoric. Regardless of their politics, in most families two working parents is simply a fact. The two-paycheck family has become the new American norm.

Despite the hopes of feminists that entry into the sphere of production is the ultimate road to women's liberation, so far it has proved just the reverse. The problem is, of course, that most married women who work carry a double load. Like their husbands they work all day, but when they come home at night they do not find what their husbands once did: tended children and a warm familial refuge from work.

At the end of the day, most working mothers have no time for decompression. With chores to be taken care of and children clamoring for attention, a working mother hardly has a chance to change her clothes and read the mail, much less go for an evening run or relax with a drink. Study any working parent's schedule, with its taxing list of obligations and its tight restrictions on personal freedom, and you have a surefire formula for stress. Once we considered stress a problem—"You need to take a rest, you're under too much stress." These days stress is part of the human condition.

Given the fact that many busy people feel compelled to keep going despite overwhelming stress in their lives, how can you tell how much is too much stress? Some of the symptoms of too much stress are restlessness, fatigue, boredom, worry, and impatience— all much more frequent than in the past. Decision making is harder. You procrastinate more and find that more time passes with less produced. You become forgetful of little things, like appointments and umbrellas. You become increasingly susceptible to minor illnesses, allergy flare-ups, and mood swings. You spend more and more time in escapist activities, such as watching television, drinking and eating, or reading romance novels.

A lot of people daydream of a vacation when they feel overworked. The visions are tantalizing: lying on the warm sand beneath a cloudless sky, watching the waves break on the beach; or relaxing in a mountain inn, sitting by a warm fire after a bracing hike through the fall foliage, breathing deep the clear mountain air. Vacations are fine, but it seems a shame to live for them—to think of everyday life as drudgery that must be endured for a brief reward somewhere off in the future. Living only for the future is one sure way to squander the present.

Many people slog through weary days only to narcotize themselves at night with regressive indulgence in alcohol, ice cream, and television. There's nothing inherently wrong with this. People who work hard *do* need some way to relax—though it may be more genuinely relaxing to go to a little extra trouble and to find activities that give back more energy and allow family members to interact, like going for walks, playing games, reading together, even getting out of the house to go to a movie. Whatever form relaxation takes, however, it is only a way to endure stress; it does nothing to address the source of stress. If overwork is making you into a couch potato, you may need to reassess what you are doing. You'd think any reasonable person could figure this out. But there are forces at work on us that nullify reason.

In *Turning Forty in the Eighties* I described how "careerism swallows life" when people become obsessed with achievement, as though success could overcome self-doubt and compensate for insecurity.[3] But even though we may not be chasing grandiose dreams of achievement, many of us are stretched to the limit just trying to pay the mortgage and put aside a little for the children's college expenses. Between work and chores and the kids, most of us are worn out. There is much to do but little to enjoy; overwork chokes our zest for life. If we lived alone, we would have only the systematic self-restriction of our own particular brand of neurosis to keep us from taking a hard look at what we are doing with our lives. Working couples are not alone. Sadly, though, instead of providing support and enrichment for each other, many couples find the stresses of two careers driving a wedge between them.

Instead of pulling together, many couples find that stress pulls them apart. At the end of a long day, working spouses come home to partners also worn down by their private quotas of stress, which strains their capacity for sympathy. This is the sad part. Personal stress inevitably puts a strain on our relationships. Since both partners are tired and frustrated, both need comfort.

When both parents are busy working, leisure is often the first thing to go. Here, too, the burden falls disproportionately on women. A UNESCO study showed that working mothers around the world have less than two-thirds of the free time enjoyed by their husbands.[4] Working mothers have little time for reading and sewing and letter writing and sports. This is unfortunate because, as I've said, one of the most important ways to keep stress from leading to exhaustion is to take time to relax. Sitting down in the morning with a cup of coffee for a few minutes makes a big difference in your frame of mind. Few working parents have, or take, this time.

Tired and busy, working couples get into a rut and stop having fun. Despite the familiar rationale about not enough time and not enough money, in many cases working couples don't get out because they don't want to be alone together. Their inertia is doubled because if one spouse is tired, neither one goes out. Since one or the other is usually tired, they fall into a pattern of staying home, or going out only when they feel they have to—to after-school activities or shopping with the children. Too many spouses respond as though they are chained to their partner's moods and habits. Part of the rut is assuming that your tired spouse *never* wants to go out, or that you can *only* go out together. Instead of wallowing in apathy and resentment, try asking yourself, *What do I really feel like doing?* Once you focus your vague discontent on some specific goals, you will find it easier to achieve them. Once in a while, you might even consider, *What would he (or she) really like to do?*

This simple advice—figure out what you'd really like to do and start doing it—will work only up to a point, the point where more than inertia and lack of imagination stand in your way. If you found yourself blocked from doing what you'd like to do, a good therapist would ask, "What gets in the way?" and perhaps explore these (real or imagined) impediments. If you would be your own therapist, ask yourself this: What's getting in the way of your doing what you should? And since we're talking about systems interaction, in what way is your behavior—say, avoiding going out, assuming your spouse won't go, responding only negatively to her suggestions rather than making your own—an example of how you automatically react toward others? Distancers may find that they'll have more fun by initiating what *they* want to do, instead of always fending off unwelcome suggestions from a pursuing spouse. In order to start figuring out what in your relationship is holding you back, you have to be able to be somewhat objective, to look at the pattern of interaction instead of just feeling your own resentment.

A further cause—and effect—of resentment in many two-career marriages is the deterioration of a couple's sex life. They are too tired and too tense and their schedules conflict. It is wives who are most often "too tired" for sex, and what usually makes them "too tired" is the housework. It's not so much the physical effort of having to do it all, as the enormous resentment that builds up. Moreover, once they are working, many women feel they have earned the right to say no when they don't feel like it.

Sex is one of the many things couples are reluctant to discuss. Most of us are pretty good at avoiding certain painful realities, even better at not discussing issues likely to lead to an argument. Some couples are expert at conflict-avoidance, but even those who are not normally so reticent lose their appetite for broaching difficult subjects when they're tired. At the end of a long day, who wants to argue?

We avoid bringing up tough issues because we anticipate a critical or angry response. If you think your spouse will become defensive or critical if you voice your complaints about sex or housework, you're probably right. The mistake many people make, though, is thinking only about the other person's response, rather than their own reactions. Conversations go downhill, not because of what the other person does—acts hurt or angry or whatever—but because of how we (a) approach and (b) react to them. Think of the difficult conversations as a pattern of what-you-say and what-he(or she)-says, and so on. You probably know how it goes (if you don't, it's easy to find out, just pay attention). Try anticipating what usually happens and control your side of the discussion. If one person changes, the system changes.

Suppose, for example, that you avoid asking your spouse to shop for groceries because every time you ask he gets annoyed. Take a look at the pattern. Perhaps you wait so long to ask that you are exasperated and "asking" comes out as complaining. Remember, one of the tricks to getting what you want in relationships is to avoid making the other person wrong. Instead of saying, "Why don't you ever help with the shopping?" or "I'm always the one who has to do all the shopping" (in other words, "I'm right and you're wrong"), try saying, "I have a problem and I need your help."

Suppose you ask without criticism or attack, and he still gets mad. Fine, what can you do about it? Try letting him be right ("You're right, honey, I know you have a lot to do") and still asking for what you want ("But I can't keep up and I need your help").

One reason we allow anticipation of an antagonistic response to keep us from complaining is that we are conflicted in our own minds about our right to complain. The average working mother's guilt makes her reluctant to push for more help. Changing roles is thought to cause her guilt. Maybe, but in many cases changing roles doesn't cause guilt; it only allows the enormous guilt most people carry around inside them a point of focus.

SHOULD MOTHERS WORK?

Much of the voluminous writing about the two-career family has focused on the strain on women's lives and the problems of inadequate day-care facilities. An extraordinary amount of the literature on working mothers is addressed to the question of whether or not women *should* work. There are countless studies of how placing children in day-care affects them. The studies show that working mothers spend almost as much time with their children as women who stay home all day, and that children placed in day-care show no pattern of any deleterious effects. Therefore there is sufficient ambiguity to allow free play to those who want ammunition to support whatever course of action they have chosen. "See it *is* better for me to be at home." "Research shows that working makes me a better mother."

Most analyses of the two-career family have emphasized economic and political causes, and psychological effects; much less has been written about the dynamics of the family. This is unfortunate because without some understanding of the overall structure of the family, we may be trying to cope disjointedly with a new set of conditions that requires a coordinated response from a unified family system. Moreover, the dynamics of the family may be relevant to whether, and when, a wife and mother goes back to work in the first place.

Mothers return to work for many reasons; for money, yes, and for their own fulfillment as well. But in some cases a woman may be propelled to look for work partly in order to compensate for her husband's lack of emotional availability. This is not necessarily right or wrong. The point to keep in mind is this: The relationship between a wife and a husband and her job is another triangle. In this triangle, there are two things to look out for. The first is whether or not a wife (or a husband) becomes overly involved with a job as a means of escaping a frustrating marriage. Once again, this isn't necessarily awful. Outside of fairy tales, no marriage can satisfy a person's every need—and let's face it, many marriages are only tolerable. But you should at least be aware of the degree to which your investment outside the home is negative—to escape your spouse—because most relationships have more room for improvement than people think.

The second problem with the couple-career triangle is the response of some husbands who criticize their wives' involvement outside the home (job, friends, volunteering, sports, whatever). Husbands and wives must give their spouses room to grow, or incur the resentment that is the lot of jailors. Many people are all too ready to blame their partners for their own failed aspirations; no need to give them any extra ammunition. Those who do have trouble letting go should identify their own dependence and explore the feelings of loss they are experiencing. If you sense that your spouse is running away from the relationship, instead of pouting or criticizing try looking at your role in driving him or her away.

One of my patients complained that his wife avoided him. "She's selfish and cold." It turned out that when they were together, he dominated the conversation, talking about himself—his job, his headache, his day, et cetera, ad nauseam. Once he became aware of this and made a concerted effort to ask about her day and how she was feeling, somehow she became less "selfish and cold."

For a more complete understanding of the family dynamics involved in the two-career family, both spouses should focus on interlocking triangles, which may take them back to their families of origin to understand the source of their scripting. Some women who return to work are fleeing from images of their own mothers as victimized examples of old-fashioned femininity—injured, stunted, helpless, accommodating, self-sacrificing. Some women become aggressively career-centered, and in an effort to split themselves off from the "bad" femininity sacrifice the good aspects of femininity—nurturance, empathy, compassion. Obviously, the same can be true of men.

There's nothing wrong with taking your parents for models, positive or negative. We do certain things because our parents did them that way and it seemed to work out. In other areas, we look at the lacks in their lives and try to make our own lives better. The problem is that if you are so busy not being your mother (or father), there is no room left to be yourself. Try to decide what's best for you and your family, what you want and what you think is right, and try to differentiate this from what your parents did or did not do.

Questions of why both spouses work are largely academic in most households. Whatever the reasons, most people just do. What they really want to know is how to cope with all the stresses inherent in this new model.

Every family is unique. Some families, likely younger, have always had two working spouses. They expected to, they did, and they are used to it. They may not be without their problems, but these problems are less likely to be basic to the structure of the family.

As we shall see, there are enough similarities among most middle-class American families to offer some general guidelines for accommodating to the demands of two working parents—and I shall discuss them—but you must also give some thought to the structure of your own family, and whether and why it has failed to adapt to a transition.

THE NEED TO RESTRUCTURE THE FAMILY

The family is not a static entity; it must change to accommodate to the growth and development of its members, and it must change in response to new challenges from outside the family. A long-range view of any family would show great flexibility and many stages of reorganization. Yet in between these periods of reorganization are steady states during which family members are beguiled into thinking that the current structure of the family is the permanent structure of the family. Alternative patterns are available within the system, but any deviation that goes beyond the system's threshold of tolerance elicits mechanisms that reestablish the accustomed patterns.

———————◆———————

Before Sharon went back to work at the college, the Simpson family had evolved a style of living together that worked. Stewart's disengagement and Sharon's enmeshment, though not ideal, made up a functional parental unit. Likewise, Stewart's being the sole breadwinner allowed Sharon time (and made her feel it was her responsiblity) to do the vast majority of household chores. Sharon's return to work destabilized the system. Stewart was dismayed to discover how many little things he now had to do for himself. Going to the dry cleaners, taking his car in for tune-ups and repairs, buying birthday presents for his mother—these were just a few of the myriad services Sharon had provided, services he had taken for granted. Sharon had one foot in the fifties, one foot in the eighties.

Trying to be wife and mother as well as a working woman, Sharon kept having the feeling she was supposed to be in two places at once. Trying to do both jobs, she was afraid she'd succeed at neither.

When Sharon demanded a transformation in the family rules, the remaining family members resisted. Fluctuation, either internal or external, is normally followed by a response that returns the system to its steady state—people always resist change. Stewart tried to help out more, but frequently forgot some things and outright refused to do others. Jason and Heather knew Mommy was working, and knew they weren't supposed to rely on her as much as before, but old habits are hard to break. When Mommy is around, children just naturally go to her when they want something. And Sharon, though she wanted things to be different, tended to pick up the ball when Stewart dropped it. She didn't know how to say no to the children. The family organism, proceeding according to its own rules, was stable enough to persist with a structure that no longer fit the circumstances.

———◆———

If we think of the two-paycheck family as a static entity, we are liable to evaluate it as more or less successful. By thinking instead of the family as a social system in transformation, we highlight the transitional nature of certain family patterns. Most families who feel stretched to the limit when a mother returns to work are average families in transitional situations, suffering the pains of accommodating to new circumstances. Some, in the face of stress, increase the rigidity of their transactional patterns and resist any exploration of change.

Even when it comes to housework, some couples cannot seem to compromise. According to wives, husbands do it wrong—they buy expensive groceries, do a half-assed job of cleaning Junior's room, and they don't separate the laundry properly. According to husbands, wives are too critical. So, the wives take over and the husbands (why not?) let them.

In some cases, like death or divorce, the need for reorganizing the family is obvious. It is harder, however, to recognize the necessity for restructuring the family when a wife and mother takes on a new job. Sure, the family recognizes the need for some changes, but these changes often amount to tinkering with the family structure rather than reorganizing it. Though it may be difficult to recognize the need for new structure as absolutely imperative when a mother returns to the job market, the change is analogous to the death of a wife.

A wife is a very good thing to have. She takes care of your home and your kids, and is there to soothe and sympathize when you come home from a hard day at the office. Few women, unfortunately, have wives. And as more and more women are now working, fewer and fewer men have wives in quite the same way they used to.

Of all the disruptions caused by the transition from the traditional marriage to the two-paycheck marriage, perhaps none is felt as keenly as coming home at the end of the day and not finding someone there waiting with a sympathetic ear. Men miss this, of course, but so do women. I don't think it matters how grown-up you are, how long you've been on your own, or how long you've been the one waiting to greet a spouse returning from work. If we were coming home to a roommate, we wouldn't expect to be taken care of, but living in a family evokes old longings. Maybe coming home at the end of a day of work stirs up the kind of feelings we had as kids—when we came home from school we wanted cookies and milk.

With both spouses working, neither one feels like serving cookies and milk at the end of the day. They're both tired, they both wish they could come home to a refuge and perhaps be fussed over a little—but they both know that isn't going to happen.

I have talked about the difficulties families go through in adapting their structure to changing developmental needs. In a similar way, the model of the family itself is in transition from the stable (though perhaps limiting) form of the traditional, complementary marriage—with a division of labor based on well-defined sex role stereotypes—to a new form, the symmetrical marriage.

The traditional division of labor allowed each partner to concentrate on his or her own special activities. Conflict was minimized because interaction between roles was minimal. The spouses divided roles—men were strong, aggressive, career-centered (and, incidentally, a little selfish); women were soft and sensitive (and perhaps a little too selfless for their own good). Complementary relationships tend to be stable, like two inter-locking pieces of a puzzle that hold each other in place. The trouble was, the division was unequal. We had stability without fairness.

Symmetrical relationships are what we find in a friendship of equals, where the friends take turns. When one friend needs help, the other one is there to give it. When one feels weak, the other is strong. Symmetry is the family's response to the inequality that existed in complementary relationships. Both parties play similar roles, but these ventures tend to be more unstable, because when a married couple tries to switch from a complementary to a symmetrical relationship, they try to share and take turns, but often resent doing so, and may drift into competition instead of cooperation. They resent doing so because they are still bound by an old set of expectations, a set of values that belongs to a different society, one in which the divisions between the family and the extrafamilial were clearly delineated. The adherence to an out-moded model leads to enormous pressures on the contemporary family. Today the American family, like American society, is in a transitional period. Who knows what final form the American family will take? Meanwhile, though, families are caught in the crunch of change.

Incidentally, married partners who were complementary in sibling postion may have an easier time balancing in marriage. Sharon and Stewart, both the younger of two children, had somewhat similar expectations. They were both the babies of the family. They expected to be doted on. But an older sister who is used to taking care of others might be quite compatible with someone who is a youngest brother. How does this pattern work out in your marriage?

Once you understand the meaning of the terms *complementary* and *symmetrical*, there is probably little doubt in your mind what kind your own marriage is. Complementary relationships are more traditional, and often more stable. To illustrate this, try taking the following simple test. First answer these questions, and then ask your spouse to. (For each question, your percentage plus your spouse's should add up to 100 percent.)

1. What percentage of the housecleaning (excluding that done by hired help) do you do?_____
2. What percentage of the food shopping do you do?_____
3. What percentage of the child care do you do (things for the children and with the children)?_____
4. What percentage of the cooking do you do? (Exclude going out to dinner.)_____
5. What percentage of washing the dishes do you do?_____
6. What percentage of the laundry do you do?_____
7. What percentage of the yardwork do you do? (Exclude what you pay to have done.)_____
8. What percentage of making plans and arrangements for family entertainment (engaging baby-sitters, planning outings) and health care and education (making doctors' appointments, arranging for tutoring or after-school programs) do you do?_____
9. What percentage of the arrangements for repairs and servicing do you make?_____
10. What percentage of the family income do you earn?_____

The more symmetrical the relationship, the more your percentages approach 50–50, though in fact 70–30 is more equal and symmetrical than most couples with children would score. What may prove even more interesting are the discrepancies between your ratings and your spouse's. Discussing these differences may (depending upon your relationship) create more acrimony than understanding, but thinking about them may help you to understand each other better.

Traditional sex role stereotypes allowed couples to achieve complementarity, but at the expense of fully rounded functioning for each spouse. A traditional husband may have been something of a privileged character in the family, someone who did not have to change dirty diapers or worry about how to get the children to all their activities; however, the price for these "masculine" prerogatives may have been that he was not allowed to cry, never learned the pleasure of cooking a special meal, and did not fully share in the joys of caring for his children. A traditional wife may not have had to earn a living or open her own doors; however, she may have had to submerge her independence and live in the shadow of her husband.

Once, wives complemented their husbands' personalities, careers, even friendships. A "good" wife was expected to socialize with the wives of her husband's friends, whether she liked them or not. (Few women will put up with this kind of crap anymore.) The problem in many modern marriages is how to strike a balance between shared activities and friendships, and those each spouse pursues separately. Exaggerated complementary roles can detract from individual growth; moderate complementarity enables spouses to divide functions, and support and enrich each other. One's permissiveness with children may be balanced by the other's strictness. When one spouse gets sick, the other takes over.

When a wife and mother returns to work, complementarity unravels and a new balance must be created. It needs to be more equal, but "equal" does not necessarily mean "the same." What is needed is a rebalanced interdependency, with the couple operating as a coordinated team.

The most successful two-paycheck couples I know have a division of functions. That is, they achieve a more symmetrical, more equal relationship not by sharing the same chores, but by dividing them up. They don't cook together and shop together; they alternate some of these chores, and some are his, some are hers. This is sometimes confused with equality. Don't kid yourself. In most families, particularly middle-class families like the Simpsons where the wife returns to work when the children reach school age, the problem is to get a husband who hasn't been doing much of anything around the house to do a little. Equality? Most working wives would settle for 70–30.

Equity—a sense of fairness—is achievable; equality is rare and elusive. Moving toward equality may lead to a better balance, but insisting on complete equality is likely to produce frustration and bitterness.

As I have said before, communication does not solve very many family problems. Action, not talk, is what really counts. However, talking things over is usually a good place to start. It is, for example, when you are trying to rebalance the housekeeping and parenting after a mother returns to work. What's needed is a revisiting and renegotiating of previous issues of power and sharing. It's time to update the marital *quid pro quos,* the (largely implicit) patterns of exchange in every marriage. These discussions work best if you can avoid the following aggravating expressions: *You should, It's not fair, I always, You never*—okay, you get the idea. Start with your feelings: "I'm too busy and tired to do all the shopping," or "I can't keep up with everything." Then make specific requests—requests, not accusations or guilt-trips. (Save those for emergencies.)

As social psychologists discovered years ago, one of the most effective ways to change someone's attitude (and then behavior) is to elicit and then listen to that person's point of view. To change an inner tube it is first necessary to let the air out. Likewise, a person's unspoken (and perhaps unexamined) attitudes are harder to change until they have been voiced, and heard. If you want to change your spouse's behavior, find out how he or she feels: "I know you're busy, too. How do you feel about doing more?" Be realistic. If you want him to do more, you will probably do best to ask him what he'd be willing to do. You may not end there, but you might start there.

One thing that holds couples back is the logical but false assumption that marriage is a zero-sum game—a competitive relationship in which a gain for one must result in a loss for another. "If you win, I lose; and if I win; you lose." Stating this unfortunate assumption so baldly makes its falsity obvious, yet many of us secretly think this way. Take doing chores, for example. Many husbands feel that since whatever they don't do their wives will, the less they do the better. Another common assumption is that since she's always nagging for more help, it doesn't matter how much he does, she'll always want more. Both of these assumptions are false, though many people will never discover this *because they don't test their assumptions.* The truth is that if one person makes a significant and consistent change in a relationship—enough to unbalance the status quo—the relationship will shift.

When it comes to family life, men have trouble taking hold, women have trouble letting go. If a woman wants her spouse to take more responsibility around the house she has to give it to him. Some wives refuse to cede authority that would enable their husbands to assume responsibility. I keep coming back to this point because it's important. It helps to remember that you aren't just asking someone to help you—the way a child helps a parent— you are trying to shift the relationship toward symmetry. *You* have to change so that he will change. Ask for the help you want, then back off; don't give too much "helpful advice" about how things should be done, and don't be too quick to take over if your spouse fails to do his share. Try to wait long enough to let him feel the consequences of not living up to his agreements. It's better to let the kids miss one or two doctor's appointments, or even not to have anything ready for supper a couple of times, if that's what it takes to make it clear that if he doesn't do his share it won't get done.

Wives, try a little "strategic helplessness." It's harder to argue with *I can't* than *I won't*. Most husbands, incidentally, are experts at strategic helplessness—they must give classes in the subject to bridegrooms.

———◆———

So far I've been talking primarily about the couple and their need to shift from the traditional complementarity to a new, more symmetrical balance. The limits of this analysis are due to taking the couple out of context. This is a mistake many people make when talking about family life—looking at one part of the family, while ignoring the whole system. The husband and wife are the architects of the family and they are the ones with the greatest capacity to change the system. Remember, though, husbands and wives are also parents, and unless they change in relationship to their children, as well as to each other, change may not last.

The major transformation required when a mother returns to work is from a diffuse (......) to a clear (————) boundary between mother and children. This, in turn, permits and encourages the father to move closer to the children. Families, like all of nature, abhor a vacuum.

A family realigning its boundaries to accommodate to a mother returning to work looks like this:

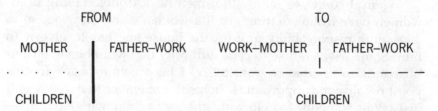

FROM   TO

MOTHER | FATHER–WORK   WORK–MOTHER | FATHER–WORK
. . . . . . | – – – – –|– – – – –
CHILDREN | CHILDREN

As you see, changes must be made in the boundaries between both parents and their careers. He needs to be a little less involved, she more involved. Both of these modifications require complementary shifts in each of their relationships with the children. He needs to be more involved, she a little less.

In many families, the subsystem of the children should be subdivided; children of different ages should be differentiated, given different rights and responsibilities. This can be diagrammed as follows.

```
WORK–MOTHER    |    FATHER–WORK
               |
_ _ _ _ _ _ _ _|_ _ _ _ _ _ _
               |
OLDER CHILD    |    YOUNGER CHILD
```

The point to keep in mind is that all of these changes are interrelated. A concerted effort to change only one boundary—say, that between husband and wife—may create a ripple effect and alter the whole system. A more likely possibility, however, is that change begun in one part of the family will not take hold if other subsystems resist and block the new patterns. The most effective way to restructure a family is to keep the whole system in mind and coordinate efforts to change on several fronts.

"Restructuring the family" may sound a little grand, and some people are understandably put off by any suggestion that change is simple or that life is easy. In fact, life is so sticky with problems that often the best we can do is to exert a little effort in the right place, and to move ahead, one foot at a time.

Although we are looking at matters for which theorizing brings no easy remedies, many people needlessly add to their problems by trying to make changes without taking the whole family system into account. Restructuring the family may not turn a sour marriage sweet or make the daily grind into a day at the beach, but even a modest change in the overall structure of the family will make things a little easier and shore up the cohesiveness that provides a basis of security for all family members.

◆

Even when we understand the need for changing the system, our own personalities make it hard for us to follow through. When it comes to family life, the average man has trouble with closeness, the average woman has trouble with distance.

Fathers find it hard to back off from work and get more involved at home. This is due not only to male reticence, but also to the way our society is structured. Greedy occupations may resist a working father's efforts to become more involved with his children. Some men, confident of themselves and their abilities, will draw a boundary between work and home to safeguard their commitment to their families. Others, conditioned by competitive anxiety, may find it difficult to resist the pressures of their careers. Sadly, many of these men never have the chance to learn that giving a little less—concretely, spending a little less time and energy at work—need not diminish job performance or success.

Mothers have trouble backing off from the kids. (This is a secret known only to mothers, and their children, and their husbands, and their employers.)

While people worry about the effect of a working mother's greater separation from her children, no one worries more than working mothers themselves. Nevertheless, the most important single factor in being a good parent is the nature of the parent's interaction with the children. It matters how much time children have with their parents, just as it matters whether or not children suffer losses and deprivations, but it matters more that the adults in their lives understand and accept what the children are feeling—and convey their understanding in a way that helps the children feel good about themselves, and the selves they are becoming.

Maternal separation can be a problem, but so too can maternal overinvolvement, and with it the children's lack of autonomy and incapacity to deal with being separate and independent.

———————◆———————

Restructuring the family may be what's needed, but no one is completely successful at this. Many families suffer a heavier emotional toll than is necessary, getting by, enduring life but hardly enjoying it. However successful at reorganizing you are, there is one essential but neglected ingredient to make life more bearable for beleaguered families.

EMPATHY

At the end of a long day, we are tired and want to go home. Instead of a place of refuge and relaxation, however, many working parents come home to a household in disarray, and a host of noisy claims on what little energy they have left. There isn't a whole lot you can do about that. Unfortunately, many spouses also come home to partners equally worn out by a grinding routine that strains their capacity for sympathy.

In unhappy families people are cut off from kindness and compassion. These people develop whole reservoirs of feeling they believe their families don't know about and don't care about. Resentments fester and become a preoccupation. However much family members are concerned about and involved with one another, they are still largely preoccupied with their own agendas: successes and failures of the day; deadlines met or unmet; hurts and slights at the hands of co-workers, bosses, and friends; and more to be done, always more to be done. The persistent pressure of these private concerns works a strong claim on the mind. As long as feelings and desires go unshared, they separate the individual from the group.

The uninvolved husband or cold wife isn't just "not participating"; he or she is actively engaged in feeling something. As long as your partner continues stewing in unspoken resentment or anxious worry, there will be little room in his or her heart for anything else.

Shared experience, on the other hand, is the first step toward mutual understanding. Sharing emotional experience helps us regulate our feelings. Unhappy feelings don't just go away if we talk about them, but it is impossible to overestimate the soothing comfort of talking over the upsets of the day with someone who cares enough to listen. The sharing of emotional experience is the most meaningful and pervasive feature of true relatedness.

Most of us are not inherently self-centered, not really. We are fully capable of empathy—that is, until our own personal resources are depleted. We become more and more preoccupied with our own unhappy feelings when no one seems willing to listen. Those others? The ones who don't seem willing to listen? They want what we want—to talk about their hurts and have someone listen. Someone needs to go first.

Empathy starts with listening, but doesn't end there. Listening is a strenuous but silent activity, rare in busy families. Most of the time we are too eager to get a word in edgewise, or get off by ourselves, to really hear what anyone else is saying. Foremost among the obstacles to listening are those that stem from our need to "do something" about what is being said: defend ourselves, disagree, or solve whatever problems are described.

One popular technique for fostering empathy is to have couples take turns talking and listening. First one talks while the other listens, then they switch roles. This device is useful, but does not of itself teach empathy. It teaches taking turns. Taking turns is fine, but it is not empathy.

Empathy has as much to do with understanding as with dialogue. Open conversation and empathy are related in circular fashion, one begets the other. But ordinarily we achieve empathy for other people when we think about them, not just when we talk with them. Ironically, sometimes it is while watching strangers that we begin to develop empathy for those closest to us. A woman sees male emotional reticence portrayed in a television drama and begins to understand that her husband may be more shy than cold. A man sees a child in a playground, anxiously looking for someone to play with, and realizes—perhaps for the first time—how much his children need him.

Empathy—understanding what your spouse is feeling *and* showing it—helps counterbalance all the time apart and all the conflicting tension about dividing up the housework and child care. The emotional availability of family members to one another may depend less on their personalities than on the quality and timing of their work, such as how stressful and fatiguing their jobs are. I have seen several families destroyed by moderate levels of interpersonal conflict because the spouses were so overtaxed by hard work and economic hardship. These are extreme examples of the overwork and conflict that we all face. Not all family conflicts are resolvable. But if we can at least understand the people we live with—what they really want, what are their private feelings, what drives them to do what they do, and what are the fears holding them back—a great deal has been accomplished.

How do you empathize with a husband who doesn't shoulder his share of the household burdens, or a wife who is always giving you the cold shoulder? How do you empathize with a child who wants more than whatever you give? Part of the problem is mistaking sympathy for empathy.

Empathy is often confused with sympathy, but there is a crucial difference. Sympathy is more limited and limiting; it means to feel the same as, rather than to be understanding of. It is an emotion that makes us suffer *with* unhappy people, and that feeling motivates us to avoid them or try to do *for* them. Here is a small example that caused my wife and me needless friction for years. She loves to talk about fixing up the house. For years she would describe her plans for knocking out this wall or that, putting in cabinets here, and buying new furniture there. These conversations made me very uncomfortable. *Why do we need to do that?* I'd think, and, *Where's the money going to come from?* I had no patience for these discussions and she knew it. But like a lot of people we refused to discuss what seemed obvious: She wanted to remake our house from top to bottom and I didn't want to hear about it. In fact, my wife just likes to imagine most of these projects. Oh, maybe someday in the next century, when we can afford it, she might actually remodel the place, but for now she just likes to daydream. It hurt her that I wouldn't listen. After all, doesn't she listen to my hopes and dreams? My unwillingless to listen stemmed from an unfortunate but common confusion about where her dreams ended and my responsibility for fulfilling them began.

During courtship, if your partner becomes depressed you are not likely to take it personally, assuming that it may well have nothing to do with you or the relationship. This assumption of not being responsible makes it easy to be empathic and supportive. Marriage tightens the relationship, making it harder to empathize because we assume responsibility for each other's troubles—and assign responsibility for our troubles to each other. We extend our feelings of obligation far beyond real responsibility, because of emotional fusion—a blurring of the boundary between you and me.

Feeling a burden of obligation to do something about it if your partner is depressed or discouraged makes it hard to listen to feelings. This blurring of boundaries may lead to your avoiding each other—or at least avoiding emotional topics. We avoid certain subjects because we don't want to be blamed. We don't want to hear about it, because he (or she) won't take our advice.

Over the years of married life we learn to hide away our feelings. Not all of them, of course, but enough. These silent areas fester and assume more than their share of importance, eventually perhaps becoming preoccupations. We retreat into our own personal and subjective worlds, hiding away our real feelings, sometimes even from ourselves. As a result, everyday family life is taken over by obligation and habit; real feeling is strictly controlled and limited, and the people we say we love are kept at a distance and seen through a curtain. We get by, but intimacy slowly dies. To meet, truly meet, means that we must open up part of ourselves, feel our feelings and share them.

Will empathy solve a family's problems? No, that only happens when Walt Disney writes the script. Empathy does not extinguish conflict, but being understood makes conflict bearable. We all need allies to cope with stress. In the absence of empathy, everybody loses.

WHAT PRICE DRUDGERY?

Restructuring the family to accommodate to a mother's return to work makes the family system more functional, more stable, *and* better able to meet the emotional needs of its members. This, in turn, makes it easier for family members to empathize with each other, which further strengthens the structure of the family. It is a positive spiral. This is part of what we need to take the stress of modern family life and turn it into creative living. Still, we cannot break the iron limits of circumstance. Even strong and cohesive families have to perform so many chores that it is hard to keep the burden from squeezing the zest out of life.

Among the most obvious but underused resources are practical ones. Many middle-class families are more able to buy their way out of drudgery than they realize. There are housecleaning services and lawn-care services; there are people who will blacktop your driveway in the summer and shovel snow in the winter; and with a little effort you can find a teenager who will help you clean the attic, sort the laundry, wash the windows, and watch the kids. These are just some examples of ways to buy your way out of drudgery. Yet few families take advantage of these services. Why? Guilt is one reason, being stuck in a rut is another.

Many people think of household duties as their DUTY, even though their time may be worth considerably more than what it takes to pay someone for assistance. Caroline Bird, author of *The Two-Paycheck Marriage*, cites surveys which show that even highly paid professional couples with two careers don't often hire paid help, not even for housecleaning.[5] This is much more likely to be the case with older couples in which a mother returns to work. Younger two-career families know better.

In the 1970s young working wives created a new kind of rich. Couples newly graduated from college and doing well in their chosen professions could easily be earning two big salaries before they had babies, mortgages, fuel bills, and debts. Young, childless, and fancy-free, these young urban professionals were a new breed and they opened up a gorgeous variety of luxury markets. What would you have said twenty years ago to someone who predicted that young people would be buying designer-label ice cream for $2.50 a pint, and Godiva chocolates for $20 a pound?

Stores opened on Sundays to serve couples who had no other time to shop (in the process, destroying our national, noncommercial day of rest). Time became precious, creating customers for microwave ovens, automatic coffee makers, fast food, and beds "made" with comforters that didn't have to be tucked in to look neat. Buying convenience items is somehow easier, less personal perhaps, than hiring someone to work inside your home.

When you calculate the relative value of your time and the cost of paying someone to wash the floors or rake the leaves, take into account whether or not these activities are a drain on your energy and spirit. Ask yourself, too, how many of the things you feel you "should" do really need doing? Do the floors really have to be spotless? Does it really matter whether or not your lawn looks like it belongs in *House Beautiful?* Some of these things *do* matter, of course. The trick is to prune away the ones that don't. Learn to say no. Simplify. Delegate.

Busy parents, with little time and energy to play with their children, also have diminished resolve to make the children do chores. Some of our overindulgence is guilt-induced, some is due to just plain tiredness. It's often easier to feed the cat or make Johnny's bed yourself than to keep after the children to do their chores. Try not to get caught up in short-term thinking. Once children learn they are expected to help out—and that rewards and punishments are attached to their performance—they will learn to accommodate. Besides, it's good for them.

Overindulged children don't learn what it feels like to participate fully in a family and to share the load. Love your children enough to put demands on them.

In this section I have focused on the underused potential most working parents have to save time by hiring more help. I believe that hard-pressed working couples can and should reduce as much as possible their share of drudgery. There is, however, no substitute for spending time with children. Earlier, when I spoke of the need to restructure the family, I concentrated on the parents' need to move toward equality and to become more like partners—for their own good. But what about the children, what about *their* own good?

SHARED PARENTING

Given the limited availability and high cost of day care, families are faced with a real choice about whether or not it's worth it for a mother of preschool children to work. But this problem solves itself (more or less) once the children enter school. I say more or less, because even though school resolves the problem of who will look after the children from morning until afternoon, that is only part of the job. Too many men continue to think of caring for the children as their wife's problem. Fathers are as responsible as their wives are for finding a way to reconcile their professional ambitions with the interests of their children.

The dominant demand heard from people concerned for the welfare of families with working mothers has been for better child care for women. Notice how this takes the heat off men. If men were the primary caretakers of their children, child care would now be in place. If both parents are going to work, then both must share the burden of looking after their children. The solution to the instability created in the family once the mother goes back to work is to move from the traditional family setup, in which the mother is the primary parent, toward shared parenting.

The advantages of shared parenting include: (1) relieving women of the dual oppression of being a paid worker and the sole parent; (2) liberating women from full-time mothering to pursue other interests; (3) affording the opportunity for more equal relationships between men and women; (4) allowing men more access to their children, and vice versa; (5) enabling children to be parented by two nurturing figures, and thus freeing them from enmeshment with one overinvolved parent (and alienation from an underinvolved one); (6) breaking down gender stereotypes as role models; (7) putting pressure on political, economic, and social structures for changes, such as paternity and maternity leaves, job sharing, more equal pay, and freely available child care.

The advantages of shared parenting range from the purely practical—having two people working together to do a job that is virtually impossible for one of them to do alone—to changing the way children are brought up, and even to leading the way toward social change. Normally, we think of social change as proceeding from society to the family. Families are conservative, homeostatic systems; they follow social change, dragging their heels.

Thinking of change as proceeding from society to the family is, of course, a form of linear thinking. In fact, change is circular. In the case of the two-paycheck family, economic and political changes are fueled by inflated material expectations and dissatisfaction with traditional roles in the family, which have propelled more and more women into the workforce, which in turn creates pressures on the family to change its structure. No doubt, economics could make a case that the primary causes of change are economic, and members of other disciplines could make similar briefs for the priority of their own particular domains. My claim is that at present the cycle of change is stuck in the family.

Now families can take the lead. The crisis of the two-paycheck family is a result of trying to adjust to new demands with an outmoded and unchanged family structure. Like individuals, families cling to the familiar and resist precisely those solutions that mean breaking old habits. But the untapped power of the family can transform society as well as the lives of individuals.

Constructive change occurs when one or more individual family members develop new perspectives that lead them to new actions. What often blocks change is that most people underestimate the conservative structure of family systems. A woman who returns to work may, for example, assume that her husband and children will make adjustments to accommodate to her changing role. Good luck. The rule of change in families is that one person's attempts to change will be tolerated only within a limited range. If an individual's behavior violates existing family rules or extends beyond familiar boundaries, the family system will resist—or, to put it in more human terms, the other family members will exert pressure on the individual to change back.

A mother who takes a job outside the home may not be

breaking the rules, but even couples who try to move toward sharing the physical tasks of parenting have trouble reversing the rule that says Mother Is In Charge. The system—embodied in the expectations of both parents and their children—will resist significant change. No matter how much Dad does, in the final analysis it's up to Mom to make sure that someone takes the kids to the dentist, that they have clean clothes, and that they get to their after-school activities. This perception is also shared outside the family.

One morning when I was home writing, the elementary school nurse called and asked to speak to Mrs. Nichols. I said she was at work; I was Dr. Nichols, could I help her? She then asked if she could reach my wife at work? I said again, could I help? She said that our son, Paul, had gotten sick and threw up in the boy's bathroom. Could she have Mrs. Nichols' phone number at work, so she could call her to come and take Paul home? I said I'd come. Oh, she said.

The sexual division of labor remains intact, embedded in the American way of life, and in the hearts and minds of most mothers and fathers. Years spent in female-dominated households have led many to believe it cannot be otherwise. Motherhood is a woman's "natural" calling, and it is her sphere of influence and power. Recently, women have challenged the belief that the home is their rightful place, and they have sought power and influence in the workplace. Most of these women did not, however, abandon their aspirations to have families; they thought they could have everything if they worked at it. This is an attractive vision, one that holds an extraordinary power over the imagination.

Privileged young people in the seventies thought they could lead the way to more egalitarian marriages and families. Young women graduated from college not wanting to be trapped in the narrow domesticity of their mothers. Encouraged by the rhetoric of the women's movement, many of them put careers first; families would come "later." They wanted equal opportunity, they wanted challenge; they wanted to "have it all." They were pursuing an attractive but untested image, the image of the Superwoman. Theirs was an individualism that underestimated the conservative forces in society and ignored the conservative structure of family systems.

———◆———

The essential benefit of family systems thinking is that it offers a fresh perspective, a new way of looking at things. Our lives are coordinated within our families such that what "they" do is a function of what we do. It is an enormous insight, and one that puts us in charge of our own lives. The man who complains that his wife spends all her time with the children can stop complaining and get more of her attention by approaching her through the children; his spending more time with them frees her to become available to him. To "get it" in family therapy is to realize that while we are inescapably bound together, we are ultimately free— free to get what we want and need out of family life *if* we understand something about how families function and what we must do to bring about change in the system.

You can make significant changes by keeping in mind that in families (and other systems), change is a three-step process: (1) someone initiates change, (2) the system (other people) resists and exerts pressure on the person to change back, *and then* (3) the one who initiates change either gives up and changes back or persists until the system shifts.

A simple example of this three-step process is trying to make your children more responsible for themselves. Suppose you are tired of matching socks for a ten-year-old daughter, or waking up a fifteen-year-old son in time for school in the morning. (1) You change. Simply stop sorting the socks, or acting as an alarm clock. (2) The child will resist the change. She may whine about not having any clean socks; he may yell at you for not waking him up, and may even be late for school. Step 3 is then up to you. If you persist, the system will shift.

Restructuring the family to accommodate to two working parents is a more complicated application, but the basic principle remains the same. Decide what changes must be initiated, work to bring them about—in cooperation with your spouse if possible, or by yourself if necessary—and then be prepared to persist in the face of inevitable resistance.

THE BEST OF INTENTIONS

Sharon and Stewart tried to become more equal as parents, but despite the best of intentions, they gradually slipped back into familiar roles. Their relative failure is instructive because it illustrates the trouble men and women have changing their approach to parenting.

Stewart tried to become more involved with Jason and Heather because he felt he could do some things—like enforce discipline and teach the children to be more adventurous—better than Sharon, and because he thought that freeing Sharon from some of her burden would make her a happier and more agreeable person.

Stewart started coming home early on Friday afternoons and taking Jason and Heather on outings. One week it was hiking in the woods, the next week it was teaching them how to throw a football. On school nights he made more of an effort to get after them to do their homework, pick up their rooms, and put away the dishes—things Sharon usually spoke to them about.

One evening after supper, Stewart told Jason to pick up his dirty socks from the living room floor and put them in his room. Jason snapped at him, "You're getting to be an old nag, just like Mom." Stewart was furious. How dare Jason speak to him this way! "Pick up those goddamned socks and get up to your room. Don't you ever take that tone of voice with me, young man!"

Stewart wondered what happened to make Jason react like that. Was he losing his authority?

In contrast to the children's overtly conflict-laden relationship with their mother, their relationship with their father is usually smoother because it's diluted. He is a once-in-a-while, feared and idealized figure. That's why fathers are often better disciplinarians. They aren't around enough to get housebroken. Stewart was around more now, and the kids tried to mold him to their way of doing things. It didn't work. He wouldn't bend.

Daddy's Friday afternoon outings with the kids started getting cancelled. Usually, it was something at work that got in the way. It's hard to be really involved with your career and your children. Few men manage it.

Most successful careers require some backup at home—a supportive person who frees the career striver to concentrate on the demands of work. Traditional men had this support from their wives. When a man came home at the end of a long, hard day, his wife was waiting for him with a drink and a sympathetic ear to listen to the latest skirmishes in the office wars. By the time he had a chance to relax, dinner was ready. If he had to stay late for a meeting, all he had to do was call and dinner would be delayed or waiting to be warmed up in the oven. Sharon could no longer play that part, even if she wanted to; Stewart couldn't get this vision of marriage out of his mind.

So, they muddled along. Stewart continued to help out in some ways—washing the dishes, mowing the lawn, and, when he remembered, planning the menus. He wasn't really satisfied with these contributions, but he felt he couldn't do any more. With the children, he did what he felt like doing. Sharon did what had to be done. (Sometime go to the waiting room of a pediatrician or an orthodontist and count the number of fathers sitting there waiting for their children.)

Sharon wanted more help from Stewart, but it was hard for her to give up the control necessary for him to feel comfortable as an equal partner.

———◆———

We get into touchy matters here. On the one hand, we must recognize that it is hard for women to surrender control over their traditional female realm. On the other hand, it is important not to blame the victim for her plight.

Although ethical questions do not disappear, they sometimes recede in importance when we adopt a systems point of view. Instead of asking ourselves whose fault it is that men and women have trouble sharing parenting, we can focus on why it is hard to restructure the family system.

In the wake of feminism's angriest period, we are rediscovering that, even as they move (slowly) toward equality, men and women are different. One of the biggest differences is the way they parent. Mothers get more involved with the children in their world at home. Fathers take their children on outings. They are more able to distance themselves from squabbles and peer conflicts because they are less emotionally involved. Mothers join their children; fathers usually expect the children to join them.

When they need something, children turn to their mothers— and they are socialized to do so. Outside their own father, close friends, and relatives, young children meet few men in their everyday life. The women they meet—teachers, their friends' mothers, and their mother's friends—interact with them. The men they encounter are usually busy doing something else.

Fathers could learn to pay more attention and be more responsive to their children, but usually don't if their wives are around. Many men learn to be better fathers only after they get divorced. Sad, isn't it?

———◆———

Shared parenting seemed to elude Sharon and Stewart not because their intentions were ignoble, but because old habits are so hard to break. They were often at odds about the children and had difficulty understanding each other's position. Stewart often put his own needs ahead of the children's and he couldn't understand why Sharon didn't do the same. "Parents have to take care of themselves," he told her. "Satisfied adults make good parents." To Sharon, it sounded like just another excuse.

———◆———

It isn't easy to run a family when both parents work. But it can be done. Although strain is inevitable, it is possible to work together as a team if changes are thought out, discussed, made, consistently applied, and reexamined with some regularity. Remember that patterns take time to shift; persisting in new, more equal, roles is the most important step. And don't forget that a little empathy for each other makes a difficult situation bearable.

10

THE OVER-INVOLVED MOTHER AND PERIPHERAL FATHER

*W*hen did it happen? Sharon's life was consumed by two small children, and though she was married she might as well be a single parent. She did so much, and Stewart did so little. Is this the way it's supposed to be?

Some days all she seemed to do was chauffeur her kids around—soccer practice, swimming, Sunday school, piano lessons, skating parties. Why was everything so far apart? On the rare occasions when Stewart drove, he expected to be thanked profusely, as though he had done something wonderful. Husbands sometimes "help out," but that's a lot different from sharing. He seemed to resent the children's needs. It scared her. If he could not love them, he could leave. But this thought, only vaguely apprehended, just made her mad.

She hadn't wanted kids. Never really saw the need for them. She wanted him. He wanted kids, seemed to think they were essential, and his certainty overruled her doubt. Besides, she thought he would make a fine father. He was so boyish and playful. When they visited friends with kids, he loved to play with them. But things didn't turn out the way she expected.

The day they brought Heather home from the hospital he was at work before lunchtime. She did not, as he accused her, resent his work. What she did resent was the way he used work to rationalize his lack of involvement with the children. He usually managed to show up for the really important events, like birthdays, but even then he was likely to come late or leave early. He was not a loiterer. His many entrances and exits were justified in the name of work. "I'll be a little late, honey, I have to tie up some loose ends before I can leave the office." He never let go and gave himself to them. She wanted more, but learned to live with less, less of him at any rate.

By the time she was thirty-five, Sharon was used to doing everything for the children. They trained her well—Jason and Heather, and Stewart. She might get annoyed at having to drive Heather to play at Tammy's and then take Jason to the other side of town for Cub Scouts, but she rarely bothered asking Stewart, and never really questioned the need for all this driving. In fact when she did say no she felt guilty. Once when she didn't feel up to driving Jason to The Great Escape amusement park, she got into a big argument with him. Afterwards, Jason went off to play and forgot completely about The Great Escape; still, Sharon couldn't stop hearing his accusation, "But all the other kids are going."

Most of the time she enjoyed doing things with the children: reading to them, listening to them read, going to museums and concerts, taking them on picnics and field trips, and helping out with special events at school. In the winter they went ice skating and sledding; in the summer, there were outdoor concerts and rock collecting expeditions. Stewart was usually busy working.

When she did succeed in dragging him away from his separate

existence, the results were mixed. Sometimes he was agreeable, even fun, but you couldn't count on it. When the kids were exceptionally good, or if they played while she listened to him talk about his job, they could have a nice time. But even when she planned things the way he liked, time together could turn sour. One Friday she took the kids to meet him after work at T.G.I. Fridays. It was the kind of thing he liked to do—a drink after work. He always expected the children to conform to his preferences rather than the other way around. He could be so intolerant. Jason was a little cranky and couldn't decide what he wanted to eat. So, Sharon gave him a little of the attention Stewart couldn't seem to share. That was it! "These kids are so spoiled, why don't you leave them at home? We can't ever finish a conversation with them around." And that was that. They sat languishing in an expensive restaurant over a speechless meal. She sometimes thought he saved his sourest moods for their most expensive outings.

Lately she was tired all the time. Thirty-five years old and only now did she finally feel grown-up. Grown-up but tired. Too much work, too much stress, and not enough sleep. Once she daydreamed about men; now her fantasies involved taking a vacation in the sun. She would love to go to one of those resorts they showed on "Lifestyles of the Rich and Famous." Maybe Club Med. Seven days of sleep would set things right. No doubt these measures would restore some measure of well-being, at least temporarily. But the real problem was emptiness, not overwork.

Sharon's counterpart, the peripheral father, is a familiar role, so familiar in fact that it evokes a stereotyped image: the unfeeling male, obsessed with his work, not caring about intimacy or about his family, except as an obligation. Like many stereotypes, this one is simpler and thus more commonplace than the truth. It reduces an unhappy interaction to the problem of one person, and suggests that the person is willful and selfish. The truth is somewhat more complicated. Like most problems that occur in families, a father's remoteness can be understood on three levels: *monadic*—his personality; *dyadic*—the interaction between husband and wife that maintains or exacerbates the problem; and *triadic*—her tight bond with the children and his overinvolvement with work that stabilizes the distance between them.

◆

Stewart's life was about loneliness and privacy. As a young man, he had his privacy and with it plenty of loneliness. He did not choose solitude. Who would? He learned it from his mother, who taught it by example and by leaving him to his own devices much of the time.

In college he shunned dormitory small talk and noisy fraternity parties. Why did everything have to be so loud? Besides, he didn't have time. His program of serious purpose kept him busy working, studying, while at the same time masking his anxiety and covering his insecurity. He felt himself too sophisticated to join in, so he stayed outside. With Sharon it was different. She cared about music and art, seemed genuinely interested in him, *and* she was gorgeous. He married for many reasons but perhaps none so compelling as to escape from loneliness. He thought she'd always be there when he wanted her. But it didn't turn out that way. She didn't always want the same things he did. Sex, for one thing. The painful discovery that she was a being in her own right, separate from him, a being who refused to submit to his whims, made him depressed and resigned. At other times he felt she had no life of her own and tried to live off his, wouldn't give him any room to breathe. Once again the thing he sought was privacy.

He thought she spent too much time with the kids. Yes, he had some intuition that she turned to them because he was too independent to suit her. A few years ago he'd welcomed that, felt that because of the kids she left him alone more. But now he and Sharon were older, calmer, more flexible. Maybe they could be closer—except that the kids were always in the way. She let them interrupt whenever they wanted, she hardly ever wanted to go out without them, and Stewart felt they couldn't plan anything on weekends because there was always some children's activity going on. There were soccer games and little league baseball and swimming lessons and puppet shows and children's theater and birthday parties and school outings, and on and on. Work often kept him from going, but he didn't always regret missing these outings.

He didn't exactly plan to be so busy. He just was. And when he did have some free time he wanted to relax. He loved Heather and Jason, but he had little to give them at the end of the day. Sharon didn't seem to understand that. Without trying, she was more open to the children and more sensitive to their needs. As a woman she was more ready to connect with them, even when she was tired. So she had little patience with Stewart's unwillingness to do the same. She thought he was acting out of malice—a stubborn refusal to be a fully sharing member of the family, a kind of selfishness she couldn't understand. Take, for instance, the night she asked him to go to one of Jason's Cub Scout meetings.

That night Stewart was riding home in heavy traffic, hurrying to Jason's elementary school for the Cub Scout meeting. He hadn't thought about it, hadn't questioned the need for him to be there. But now he was resentful. It had been a long and tiring day. He loved his son and enjoyed their time together. But this was different—Cub Scouts—an organized activity, "for boys," maybe, but conceived and run by adults. Hell, adults ran these kids' lives! Even little league baseball wouldn't be so bad if they didn't let the parents come around. Tonight he was tired. He wanted nothing more than to have a drink or two, eat some supper, and then maybe watch a movie or a ball game. It might be nice to have a drink with Sharon, tell her about this and that. Fat chance. He didn't even feel that he could tell her he didn't want to go to this stupid pack meeting. So he went, and left early with a reluctant Jason.

And what was it that Stewart worked so hard to insulate himself from? Certainly not physical pain. No, he even sought that out, like when he ran hard on a hot day. Something about unstructured, unplanned, everyday family life just made him uneasy. He'd always been like that, though when he was single he hadn't really noticed. His habits were carefully constructed to isolate him from casual social contacts. People who didn't know him confused his cultivated reserve for aloof uncaring. It wasn't that, really; more that he liked to pick and choose when to socialize. This pattern of privacy may work for a single man; it does not work for a married one. In order to be this isolated from everyday intrusions, small talk, and children who want attention, it's necessary to keep busy. Stewart kept busy at work.

Stewart's investment in his career was not just negative—

avoiding family life—it was also positive. Like many people, he enjoyed what he did, and thought it was important, or at any rate he used to think so. More to the point, it made him feel important. It wasn't just work, it was also the nature of the relationships at work. At work, people share the same professional interests, and they are always at their best. Social relationships on the job are usually brief encounters, either intense or superficial. The level of involvement is always under control. Well, almost always.

Like many workaholics, Stewart was too self-involved and preoccupied to drift along with the currents of everyday family life. His schedule absorbed his time and energy, so that daily family events, moods, and irritations were not inflicted on him. He liked to choose when and where to let down his guard. Otherwise, events—human events, that is—penetrated too far into his fragile self-esteem. He depended primarily on hard work of a particular kind—hard work in pursuit of achievement and success—for rejuvenation and maintenance of morale.

Workaholics settle for excellence in one endeavor and admit they are inept and uninterested in other things. Long ago, Stewart stopped trying to be a handyman around the house, and he no longer tried to keep up with the gardening. His excuse, that he didn't have time, was true as far as it went. But it was also true that these activities didn't feed his insatiable need for recognition, and hanging around the house exposed him to leisurely family life.

He knew how *he* felt, but what about Sharon? There was a part of her he could not fathom. In fact he was not really interested in her at all, except as someone who listened sympathetically to his problems and whose face lit up with his triumphs. He wouldn't like someone putting it that way, though. He tried. And there were times when a terrific feeling of love for her washed over him, especially when she wasn't around to mess it up. Most of the time, though, he thought she was too demanding, too dependent, and *way* too committed to togetherness. Why did she always want to do everyting together? The truth was that outings with all four of them usually ended up in quarreling and bickering. Why couldn't she understand?

———◆———

It is good to understand Stewart and Sharon's separate psychologies—her need for togetherness and his craving for privacy. If only Stewart and Sharon could understand each other, then they could begin to get over their resentment, and learn—try at least—to relax the drive to change each other. How about you? What is the other person feeling, that cruel monster who selfishly withholds the little sympathy you crave? Maybe that person feels neglected and is also hurt and angry. Maybe he or she isn't deliberately hurtful, just different, driven by deep longings long ago stamped in the heart.

Sharing often eludes us not because our intentions are ignoble, but because of differences in our core identities. Women generally have more permeable boundaries, and are therefore more readily able to connect with children. A man's self-image is built around himself and his accomplishments; being a father is important, but not *as* important. She has problems with separation; he has problems with connection—problems that make themselves felt in relation to the children, just as they do in relations with each other. She moves toward him for connection; he moves back for separateness. She feels shut out; he feels overwhelmed, intruded upon. Husbands and wives are often at odds because they have difficulty understanding each other. But people can change some things without touching the structure of personality.

If you aren't getting what you want, consider yourself as a stimulus. You may not be able to stop *feeling* like a victim, but you can take time to think about what you might be doing to bring about the reaction you get from those around you. The point is not to substitute self-blame for blame projected outward, but to get away from blaming altogether. Instead of thinking that X (his avoidance) causes Y (your hurt feelings), think of a circular relationship where your behavior and his behavior are linked in an ongoing circular pattern: X—Y—X—Y—X, and so on. It doesn't matter how these things get started; what matters is what to do about them. "Not fair," you say? Okay, all those who want fair can stop reading now; those who want results, read on.

Remember that human problems are created and maintained on three levels: monadic, dyadic, and triadic. Stewart's emotional distance from Sharon reflected: his personality, the couple's pattern of interaction, and their other involvements—hers with the kids, his with work. If Sharon wanted to get closer to Stewart—if she wanted results—she had to act counterintuitively. She had to stop trying to pull him toward her. First she needed to see the pattern of their relationship. Understand first, change second. As we shall see, Sharon's understanding of the dynamics of the relationship led to the painful but liberating discovery that she could change him by changing herself.

PURSUERS AND DISTANCERS

The pursuer-distancer dynamic is so common that even if you have never heard the phrase, you may immediately recognize the pattern. The more one partner pursues, and asks for more communication, time, and togetherness, the more the other distances—watches TV, works late, or goes off with friends. Sound familiar? It probably does, because at various times during your life you have experienced this dynamic. Sometimes it's transitory, such as when a young man's eagerness is matched by a young woman's coyness, and other times it seems so natural that you take it for granted, like when your mother (or Aunt Rose) calls too often to complain you call not often enough. In marriage this reciprocal pursuit and withdrawal often becomes set into a chronic and troublesome pattern. The pursuer feels neglected, lonely, cheated; the distancer feels crowded, pestered, and smothered. The more neglected the pursuer feels, the more he (or she) pursues—asks, demands, cajoles, and entreats the partner to come closer, or criticizes the partner for being selfish. And the more demanded of the distancer feels, the more he (or she) withdraws. From a distance the pair resemble two ponies on a merry-go-round—one chases the other but never catches up. Up close it hurts too much to be objective, so both continue to play out their parts.

———◆———

For years Sharon tried to get Stewart to spend more time with her and the children. At first she just assumed he would help out with the responsibilities of parenting and share in the fun. The only trouble was, Stewart didn't agree with her about what the responsibilities of parenting were or about what constitutes fun. He didn't think they should enroll the kids in so many activities and then have to drive them here, there, and everywhere. And Sharon's outings to museums and concerts and art galleries weren't exactly his idea of fun.

Sharon tried so hard. She tried asking him nicely to come along. She tried having the kids ask him. When nothing else seemed to work, she screamed in frustration at him. These unhappy outbursts usually got his attention. For a few days he would make an effort to spend more time doing things with her and the kids, but then he would revert to his usual disengaged self. From her point of view, Sharon tried nearly everything. But notice how her various strategies all revolved around a common theme: her attempt to pressure him to change his lack of involvement.

Stewart played out the other half of this complementary pattern. When they were first married he felt a tremendous pressure coming from her. It was awful. She seemed to have no life of her own. She never did anything by herself—"Why should I go by myself, we're married aren't we?" She objected to his playing volleyball—"How come you have time for that when you never have any time for me?" She criticized his friends, and she always wanted to know what he was doing—"You never tell me anything! Why are you so secretive?" Usually he caved in. He felt humiliated, hurt, attacked—all of these were safer than experiencing his underlying fury. So, he stopped playing volleyball and gave up most of his friends, except one or two whose wives Sharon happened to like; in short, he stopped having fun. It had nothing to do with his own conflicts about enjoying himself, of course; it was her fault. Neurosis recruits accomplices.

He promoted her complaints about things he liked to do without her into an ironclad, blanket prohibition. It was a negative, grudging compliance. Since he felt criticized and controlled, he made little attempt to enjoy being with her. He felt trapped. The one place he could escape was work.

Things changed a lot after the kids were born. Gradually, as she became more involved with them, she demanded less of him. Over the years they evolved into a stable pattern: Sharon and Jason and Heather did all the everyday things together, while Stewart was busy working. Once in a while the four of them went to a movie or, more often, Sharon insisted that they all go to a show at the museum or a concert. Her insistence that Stewart join them on these occasions which he so disliked only served to reinforce his wish not to. No more, though, than his own failure to suggest that they do things he liked. Sometimes he felt guilty about not being more involved with them. Occasionally he planned little trips for the whole family. What seemed to put him in the mood were periods during which didn't see them at all for a couple of days—business trips, or when Sharon took the kids to visit her parents. Most of the time, however, he felt like a prisoner, too busy longing for escape to consider relaxing and enjoying himself.

———◆———

Sharon's relationship with Stewart fits such a familiar pattern that we may be tempted to take it as natural. Stewart was independent, concerned more with professional accomplishment than with everyday family life. Sharon was the opposite. For her, family life was the number one priority; she respected hard work and achievement but thought that doing things together as a family was equally important. Are we really talking about masculine autonomy and feminine relatedness? No. Stewart's separateness was not autonomy, it was isolation. He was not so much self-sufficient as he was reclusive. Unlike Stewart, the truly autonomous man can be himself, and flexible and self-possessed, in relationships. Stewart was not independent of others; in fact he was quite dependent on Sharon to look after the house, the kids, and him. What he was, was allergic to intimacy. He disengaged himself to create a protective wall of distance. Failing to acknowledge his reliance on Sharon, he lived under the illusion of independence.

In pursuer-distancer marriages, the pursuer is often, though not always, a woman. Perhaps "often" because of culturally induced values. However, autonomy and relatedness are not essential aspects of male and female nature, but depend upon the pattern of relationship as much as personal history. True, most women are more relationship-oriented than most men. But all couples tend to polarize each other on this dynamic of the relationship, as on others. Even small differences evolve into complementarity during courtship, and once the couple is married such patterns tend to become exaggerated and stabilized. By the way, the pursuer-distancer pattern may reverse at different times in the relationship. Many husbands, for example, ignore and take their wives for granted until they become jealous of their own children. It's not at all uncommon to see a father competing with his children for his wife's attention. Often this happens while she's too busy cooking dinner to pay much attention to any of these supplicants.

The pursuer-distancer pattern may also vary in different aspects of a couple's relationship. Stewart, for example, was the pursuer when it came to sex. When he and Sharon were first married sex was pretty good. The only thing was, he seemed to be in the mood more often than she was. Gradually he got the feeling that she always made up excuses; she felt like he was always after her. So, he "courted her" and she "avoided him"—or she "wanted a more balanced relationship" but he "had a one-track mind," depending upon whose point of view you take.

———◆———

Sharon made discoveries that many of us make when we calm down, though maybe you have to get to a certain age before you relinquish the habit of waiting for others to change to make you happy. Your relatives don't have any tricks up their sleeves. Their actions only surprise you because you keep looking for them to do what you wish they would do, or what *you* would do. They do what *they* do. Once you learn this you can stop being so surprised and upset. You can let them be who they are. You might as well— they will anyway.

Sharon discovered the pattern of pursuit and withdrawal that she and Stewart were locked into, but the discovery came about in stages. The first real change occurred when she gave up on him. She stopped trying to figure him out, stopped underlining passages in self-help books for *him* to read, and started looking after herself. Focusing on herself rather than on the man in her life helped Sharon develop a healthy self-interest, and as she took more responsibility for her own life, she felt a diminished need to control him. Instead of trying to make him into the man she needed, she let him go to discover the man he was. She gave up on him changing, and contented herself with the kids and her friends.

———◆———

With no one chasing him, Stewart stopping running. He had always been interested in self-improvement—as though his self was all and always in need of improvement. So, he decided to go to "est," a popular encounter-group program that promised to help participants get more out of life. Sharon didn't want to go, but she hoped it would do him some good.

The friends who encouraged (!) him to attend wouldn't tell him exactly what goes on at est—part of the effect depends upon surprise and spontaneity—but they did prepare him for the austere restrictions. Two long weekends, with no trips to the bathroom or meals except those few scheduled by the staff. When the appointed weekend came, Stewart took the train to New York on Friday afternoon and checked into the cheapest hotel he could find. After all, why pay for a fancy room that he would only be using for a few hours? He went to Chinatown for supper with friends, but he was too apprehensive about the next day to enjoy the evening fully.

The first thing that struck him when he arrived at the training site was the incredible regimentation. Everything was organized. Everything. He found his nametag, deposited his watch with one of the assistants—participants were not supposed to keep track of the time—and took a seat in the auditorium. For the first time he felt really anxious. Two hundred wooden chairs were packed closely together in a small room, and Stewart suddenly realized that he was going to be trapped in close quarters with a large group of strangers for two whole weekends. He liked people, but he also liked to keep his distance, and he liked to get up and leave when he wanted to. And that was fairly often.

Just about then, one of the assistant trainers strode up to the front of the room and read off the rules. It sounded like the Army: Don't do this, don't do that. Stewart was bored and annoyed. He knew this stuff already. But some people apparently didn't; dozens of them stood up to question, protest, and challenge the rules. "But what if I *have to* go to the bathroom?" someone asked. *That's asinine,* Stewart thought; *if you have to go, you have to go.* Someone across the room rose to say, "This is bullshit! Nobody's going to tell me when to sit and when to stand; these rules are stupid and unnecessary!" After each question or argument, the leader simply repeated the relevant rule, as if to say, "This is the way it is, take it or leave it." But the haggling went on and on. It seemed as though everyone in the auditorium had to stand up to declare that he or she was special, and to try to find some way around the rules.

Stewart was getting more and more irritated. *Why don't these people sit down and shut up so we can get on with it?* But they didn't. More and more people got up to say that they didn't like this or they didn't like that, and why do we have to do these things, and you can't make us. Then it hit him: *These people are me! The only difference between them and me is that they are willing to say what they feel.* Then the trainer came in and helped spell out the significance of what was happening by connecting the rules of the training to the rules of life, which are often just as arbitrary, just as unfair. And as he listened it struck Stewart how much of his life was devoted vainly to struggling against the rules—from running yellow lights to wanting Sharon to be a more independent person. How much easier it would be to accept things the way they are and deal with the world as it is, rather than to piss and moan because life isn't the way it should be.

Not all the rest of what followed was equally powerful. Some of it was interesting, some of it was annoying, and some of it was just plain boring. But there were moments. One of the most powerful came quite late on the second Saturday night. The trainer introduced a group exercise wherein the participants were supposed to confront their inner fears. Normally, people don't even have access to their inner fears, much less are they willing to confront them. But the long hours and lack of familiar routine had worn away several layers of defensiveness.

When the exercise started, Stewart didn't expect much. He wasn't afraid of many things; besides it was only an exercise. Following an elaborate set of preliminaries, which acted as a form of hypnotic induction, the participants were guided into a vivid fantasy. They were to imagine walking into a dark city alleyway and then coming face-to-face with a desperately violent criminal. The effect was further enhanced because the room was absolutely dark and all around people were screaming. At first Stewart couldn't really get into it; maybe if he lived in the city he too would be scared of dark alleyways, but he didn't and he wasn't. Then something happened. *Holy shit!* Instead of some criminal, Stewart saw Sharon and the kids coming toward him. They were reaching out their arms to him—he could see that they loved him—but he was scared out of his mind. He screamed and tried to shut them out, but he could still see their faces. In that instant he knew that they loved him, really loved him. And he knew that he was terrified. Stewart kept on screaming, but now tears gushed down his face and he was wracked with aching sobs. He couldn't stop crying. *They love me . . . all they want is for me to love them back . . . and I keep running away.*

Tired as he was after the session ended that night, Stewart didn't go to sleep. He kept going over and over it in his mind. That was about all he could do—he kept seeing the sweet faces of Sharon and the kids, and the love in their eyes. And he thought about all the ways he contrived to keep his distance from them. Somehow Stewart had confused these people, who only wanted to love him, with something dark and sinister that lurked in an alleyway, something that wanted to suck him dry. Now he knew he didn't have to run away from them. And he didn't.

Love that blooms in the hothouse climate of an encounter weekend usually dries up on Monday. Remarkably, though, this change stuck. Stewart didn't give up anything to spend more time with his family, as many men dutifully do. He just started feeling that they loved him, and that they didn't want anything from him but to be with him. The change wasn't easily noticeable in the amount of time he spent at home, but it was different. Now, when he was with them, he was with them. Occasionally Stewart lapsed back into his old self-sufficient, introverted self, but then he remembered that there was nothing to be afraid of.

◆

Years of practicing psychotherapy have made me skeptical of sudden transformations. They occur, all right, but usually don't last. More often than not sudden changes are originated in changed circumstances or conscious resolution. Someone gets a sore throat and quits smoking. Another person learns he has high blood pressure and decides to cut down on salt. A man hears his friends describe the benefits of running and so he becomes a runner. Or perhaps a woman reads a book on child-rearing and decides she will no longer do for the children those things they can do for themselves. Change that is initiated by circumstances or conscious decision will last or not depending upon two underlying factors: character and family structure. The man or woman who takes up running needs a certain amount of self-discipline and compulsivity to keep at it. Moreover, the person will also require sufficient distance from the children and the spouse to support this separate activity.

The change in Stewart's involvement with his family stuck because it was consistent with a receptive family structure. Part of what I mean is that Sharon and the children wanted Stewart to spend more time with them. But there was more as well. The rigid boundary separating Sharon from Stewart was unstable because Sharon was always willing to change, and the diffuse boundary between Sharon and the children was still flexible enough to permit Stewart's participation. In some families a parent and the children are so close that there really isn't room for another parent. This often occurs when a divorced parent remarries but cannot allow the stepparent sufficient say over the children for that person to effectively become a parent. Sharon did everything she could by letting go. Many people are afraid to let go, and thus keep doing more of the same things they've always done. By avoiding experiences that are threatening we fail to learn how to cope with them. Besides, it's hard to relinquish the doubtful pleasure of blaming your spouse and waiting for him or her to change.

———◆———

So much of what we experience in relationships is clouded by our natural human inclination to be judgmental. Instead of observing carefully, we often note only enough to decide who's right (us) and who's wrong (them), and what's fair (very little) and what isn't (plenty). If you do become interested in learning about family dynamics, my advice is to take up the attitude of an anthropologist. Instead of ignoring the commonplace, these curious observers note everything. An excellent place to observe *Americanus middleclassus* is in the neighborhood shopping mall, America's living stage. Here adults come with their young to hunt for trinkets and clothing, or merely to escape the boredom of long afternoons in their nests. You will see tired parents threatening their children—enough to hurt the children's feelings, but not enough to keep them in line—and you will see spouses tugging at each other and pulling away.

If and when you're ready to try to be objective about your own role in the family pattern—by now you know whether you are a pursuer or a distancer—the best laboratory for further study is your parents' home. If your spouse is on hand to find fault, unspoken or otherwise, you may be too defensive to discover much. Moreover, you won't notice much about your parents' relationship when you are busy relating to them yourself. Your best chance to observe the people who trained you for marriage comes when you can watch them interact over a prolonged period of time. What follows is an incident that occurred when Stewart took his son Jason to visit the grandparents.

———◆———

They were, at least their marriage was, aging gracelessly. Since Stewart's father retired the two of them were much together. Still, they both kept busy and spent very little time in the same room without protective diversions. This Sunday was different, however, because they had agreed to drive into the city so that little Jason could visit the aquarium. Forced to interact without the familiar distractions of everyday routine, they drove each other crazy. She wasn't busy puttering around the house, therefore he figured she was fair game. So, he talked incessantly. Either he was oblivious to the pointed lack of response or it spurred him on to more talking. In either event the result was the same. He talked and they stared out the window.

Entering the city brought up the question of directions, and with it issues of who was right, who was wrong, who was self-sufficient ("I've driven this way many times without your help") or privy to special knowledge ("Well, Margaret told *me*. . . ."). If either of these people were to strangle the other, a good case could be made for self-defense.

But here's the really sad part. Each one of them, in his and her own eyes, was completely innocent, completely helpless to influence the other. Grandpa simply could not get the others "to engage in civil conversation." No matter what interesting and thoughtful subject he brought up (how he used to . . ., or the time when he . . .), they either "did not hear" him or willfully "chose to ignore" him. Still, he didn't get mad. He was patient and long-suffering—too bad, because that way he only prolonged theirs.

Stewart's mother tried to keep busy talking to her grandson. He, a little overtired and a little overexcited, was busy being silly. Still she needed him: "Jason, look at the beautiful cathedral." He was silly but responsive. He at least understood that she wanted something from him and that he should try somehow to oblige. Meanwhile the more she tried to discourage her husband from talking constantly by not responding to him, the more annoyed he grew and the harder he tried to engage her. What could she do?

Finally Stewart, who could not bear the constant quarreling, stepped in. "Mom, why don't you take Jason to the aquarium, while Dad and I go for a walk and have a drink." "Fine." It was a familiar role, the rescuer, something he used to do all the time. Only now he knew what it was, and he felt ashamed, like when he took a drink to calm his nerves. Triangulation may be a bad habit, but like taking a drink, it does settle things down for a bit. Unfortunately, however, after the long, contentious drive, he too was sick of listening to the old man. As soon as they sat down, Stewart made up some excuse about needing to buy a present for Sharon and hurried off for a little solitude.

So. Each of them was alone. The grandmother wasn't exactly alone, of course, but the boy was no trouble—he wouldn't try to penetrate her inner reserve. Stewart's father was brooding. Going over the afternoon in his mind, making sure that things hadn't changed. *She was irascible and stubborn. Always had been and always would be.* At first Stewart felt like an escaped prisoner. Then it struck him: He was playing his mother's part. He could see the pattern his parents played out, like two tired old fighters clinching in the late rounds. In the past he had seen one of them as the good guy; which one varied over the years. When he was young he thought his father was a windbag. In his twenties he thought his father was interesting, his mother was cold and unsympathetic. Now, although he tended to sympathize with his mother, he could see that the two of them just polarized each other. Dad *was* a windbag around her—the more she ignored him, the more desperately he tried to recruit an audience. And Mom *was* cold to him—the more he babbled on, the more she refused to respond. More important, Stewart also began to see how all this had affected him.

He was a little like both of them. Like his father, he wanted attention. Like his mother, he wanted solitude. When he was courting Sharon, she was special, an outsider rather than a family member. This meant that her attention was special and their time together was special. He could prepare himself. After they were married, however, all the old reticence took hold, revived and reinforced by Sharon's emotional demands. Life may be playing grown-up, but we revert to childish roles once we establish our own families. From his mother Stewart had learned to be a specialist at avoiding everyday family relationships. From his father he had learned to crave attention. He saw how his parents played out this pattern—and he began to see the way he played out a similar scenario with his own wife and kids.

Becoming more objective about the forces that shaped us frees us from blindly acting them out. Insights like this don't automatically lead to change, but they help us stop fooling ourselves. The mechanisms of illusion are known and destroyed by self-consciousness. Stewart might not always be open and receptive to Sharon and the children, but after seeing how he had learned to handle relationships from his parents, it would be harder for him to deceive himself that his way was *the* way and anything else was wrong.

SELF-DEFEATING CYCLES

Unhappy people are keenly aware of what others do to make them that way. "My boss takes me for granted." "My friend never invites me to do anything." "My husband always gives me a hard time when I ask him to do something with me and the children." Looking outward keeps them stuck. In psychotherapy, the therapist asks, "How do you *feel* about that?" This attempt to get at the personal equation emphasizes unresolved emotional reactivity. A family therapist would ask, "What do you *do* about it?" The first question—"How do you feel?"—may lead to new understanding; the second leads to a new relationship. The oversensitivity will take care of itself if you transform the relationship.

The "What do you do about it?" question is designed to uncover the cycle of interaction that exists around all family problems. Who does what, when, where, and how? When I first ask my patients to look at what they have been doing in attempting to get what they want, many of them immediately reply, "I've tried!" The response is part defensive—it really *is* the other person's fault—part naïve. The naïveté comes in thinking that, like a rose, trying is trying is trying. In fact, the attempted solution often exacerbates the problem.

A woman once called me on a talk show to ask for advice about her husband, who, she said, at age forty-two was losing his sex drive. For years he used to want to make love far more often than she did. Now the pattern was changing. He was less and less interested. I suggested that if she wanted more romance she try acting more romantic, but before I could explain what I meant, she interrupted to say, "Oh I've tried that." What she had tried was chasing him around the bedroom. Never pursue a distancer.

———————◆———————

It has been claimed that relatedness is part of a woman's nature, the source of her capacity for nurturance, her rich emotional life, and her empathy and intuition. What some people call "female dependency" is actually a combination of strengths and weaknesses. It is a capacity for affililation, a nurturing disposition, a sense of responsibility for others. The underside is clinging to a powerful partner, craving the approval of others, feeling guilty and selfish when not deferring to or caring for others. In the extreme, it means fearing the loss of a relationship as if it were the loss of self.

Robin Norwood described one form this pattern takes in her excellent book, *Women Who Love Too Much*.[1] Norwood writes of an obsessive love, rooted in fear—fear of being alone, fear of being unlovable, unworthy, empty, on one's own with no meaning or purpose. It is a moving, touching account. Yes, some women are like that. The truth is, though, that all of us are a little like that. Dependency, like autonomy, is basically transactional. It has meaning primarily in relation to others. To say that someone is "dependent" means that their dependency needs are not being met. Maybe some people "are" more dependent than others, but in the context of a long-term relationship, like marriage, the interaction is more important than the personalities.

Still, most people are prone to think in individual terms. "It's his fault!" Angrily: He's "cold," "alienated," "selfish," "narcissistic." More generously: He's "shy," "insecure," "needs his space"; he's "just a private person." Beneath the blaming you'll find guilt. "It must be me." "I'm not really very interesting." "I'm not smart enough, pretty enough, or talented enough to hold his interest." "It's our sex life; if only I were a better sex partner he'd be more concerned about me." How we torture ourselves!

We can break many of our self-defeating cycles by subjecting them to a two-part analysis. The first reevaluation involves applying the principle of circular causality; the second is to consider the principles of reinforcement and shaping. I explained circular causality in Chapter 1, but this concept is so central to understanding family life that I want to review it here. The terms *linear causality* and *circular causality* sound technical, but they are really quite simple and useful. Linear causality is the way we normally think about events: *A* causes *B*. "I'm critical because he ignores me." From the perspective of circular causality any delineation of before and after, or cause and effect, is purely arbitrary. Instead, behavior is seen as a series of moves and countermoves in a repeating cycle. A distancing husband may be convinced that his wife's nagging (cause) makes him withdraw (effect). She is equally likely to believe that his withdrawal causes her to nag. From a family systems perspective we see their behavior as part of a circular pattern: the more she nags, the more he withdraws, *and* the more he withdraws, the more she nags. Yes, but who *really* started it? It doesn't matter. Once underway, the system,—the circular interaction—is perpetuated by both of them, and *either one of them* can break the cycle.

As soon as you realize that your behavior is inevitably related to what other family members are doing that bothers you—the minute you recognize the circular chain of interaction—then you can figure out how to change things for the better.

By thinking in terms of *reinforcement* and *shaping*, you can maximize your chances of getting more of what you want. The principles of reinforcement are quite simple. The likelihood of a particular response being repeated depends upon its consequences—what happens after the response. If the response is followed by positive reinforcement, it is more likely to be repeated. If the response is ignored or punished, it will gradually be extinguished. Reinforcers come in the form of biological rewards—food, for example, or sex—and rewards that have acquired a positive value through social learning, such as praise or simply attention. Punishment can take the form of aversive responses, such as yelling or spanking, or withdrawal of positive responses, such as having to sit in the corner or being "grounded."

So? The principle of reinforcement—whether you call it that or not—is so obvious that it doesn't seem to add much. It does if you look at *your* part in the patterns that trouble you. Whatever your words might be intended to convey, interactions function either as positive or negative reinforcements. Yelling at your husband, "You're not part of this family! You're never around!" is aversive. It doesn't work. At first glance it would seem unlikely that family members reinforce undesirable behavior. Why, for example, would parents reinforce temper tantrums in their children? Or why would a wife reinforce her husband's withdrawal, when it appears to cause her so much pain? The answer is not to be found in some kind of convoluted motive for suffering, but in the simple fact that people often inadvertently reinforce precisely those responses that cause them the most distress.

As to the "convoluted motive for suffering," I believe that the concept of "female masochism" is a myth promulgated by men. That some women buy it only testifies to the magnitude of their own self-doubt. For some women the continual cycle of pursuit helps ward off certain painful feelings and experiences. On the surface it might appear that a woman's relationship with a distant man is a negative experience, something missing, or absent. Actually it can be quite involving. All her time and energy is focused on him: wanting him, thinking about him, dwelling on how awful it is that he isn't around more. The relationship, bad as it is, absorbs her consciousness, and in this way it functions like an addiction. (Who says people only become addicted to things that make them feel good?) The relationship is addicting because it relieves pain—it detracts from the need to pay attention to and deal with other aspects of her life. She uses her obsession with him like a drug to avoid her own pain, emptiness, fear, and anger. The more painful it is, the more distracting it is. She may not know who she is, or what she wants, but as long as she is embroiled with her unsatisfied longings for him—and it continues to be "his fault"—she can avoid holding still and finding out who she is and what she wants.

———◆———

Though she yearned for closeness with Stewart, Sharon didn't know much about true intimacy. She grew up in a family with plenty of closeness but little intimacy. What kept her parents together all the time were duties, obligations, social functions, family tradition, and habit. They did everything together, to be sure, but "everything" did not include opening their hearts to each other. In fact, when she was a teenager Sharon felt all the pain and tension of this constant but shallow togetherness. All she wanted then was to get away. What made Stewart so attractive was that he seemed quieter, more serious, and less demanding. But after they were married she automatically recreated the same environment she was accustomed to. We spend years fighting our heredity, but eventually it breaks through.

◆

Pursuers help create and maintain the very distancing that they complain about by resorting to *aversive control*. I have already explained how pursuing a distancer is only likely to make him feel pressured, which leads to anxiety, which leads to withdrawal. Never pursue a distancer. But there are even more specific solutions that make things worse. One is criticizing someone you want more from. Nagging him to come closer works about as well as kicking your car when it won't start.

In unhappy marriages spouses react to problems with attempts at aversive control—nagging, crying, withdrawing, or threatening. Rarely do these couples think to shape positive alternatives, and so the spouses feel more and more negatively about each other. If someone yells at you to stop doing something, you will probably feel upset and anxious; you may understand what the person wants, but you certainly won't feel like going out of your way to please that person. Of course. When I put it like that anyone can see the point. And probably you can readily identify all the aversive things your spouse does. The aversive things you do are harder to see, because, naturally, no one means to be aversive and because what we do is often driven by feelings more than rational consideration.

Consider the wives who doggedly pursue their disengaged husbands. The distant husbands make them disappointed and angry. These feelings propel certain actions—hurt withdrawal alternating with bitter complaining. Part of what perpetuates the problem is that they follow the dictates of feeling. Part of what enables us to solve problems is our ability to act counter to what feelings dictate. Over the years, I have counseled many spouses to change their part of the pursuer-distancer pattern. It usually begins to work, but many start to complain, "It isn't fair," and "Why should I have to do all the work?" The person who asks such questions probably does not want to hear the answer. But the answer is simple: Family patterns are circular; it doesn't matter who started what, or even what's fair and what isn't; what matters is that one person can change the system.

Here's how you can apply this principle in your own family. If you are a pursuer—if you want more from your spouse, more time, more attention, more communciation—the first thing is to recognize that pursuing only pushes him or her away. *Letting go is the most important thing you can do.* Once you stop the self-defeating pattern of pursuit you may begin to experience unhappy feelings that pursuing others wards off. Many people pursue their spouses rather than feel their own depression. Feel your feelings. Own them. Try not to blame them all on him or her. Get past thinking that one pattern is wrong and one is right. They are just different. Realizing that your spouse is just trying to keep his or her insides calm may help you to take it less personally.

Even if you have trouble getting over the idea that it is the spouse's fault and it's not fair, at least get one thing clear. The person you married is the person you're married to; he or she is not going to become a different person. Only by accepting that fact and acting accordingly can you begin to get what's available in the real world.

If you are an unhappy wife (or husband), do you really need one man (or woman) to satisfy so much of your need for companionship, communication, and recreation? Make friends. (Most men need this advice more than most women.) If you have friends, spend more time with them. Learn to spend time alone. Pretend that life is now, not some time in the future. Consider what things you like to do, and then do them. Consider all the obligations and commitments you have. Which ones are really necessary? Which ones are done out of the habit of doing things for others in hopes that they will reward you with appreciation? (Most women need this advice more than most men.) Upon reflection you will probably decide to continue many of these "obligations"—but probably not all of them. One theme underlies my advice to start doing more things that energize and enrich you and fewer things that numb your spirit and drain your energy: learn to do for yourself what's right for you, rather than doing, and not doing, things because he this . . . and they that. . . .

Ironically, pursuers get more of what they want when they stop trying so hard. Like a baseball player who learns to relax and swing the bat smooth and easy, you will get more closeness by relaxing your frantic pursuit. Letting go creates the space for other people to come closer *of their own accord*. Still, this may not solve the whole problem. Here's where the principle of shaping comes in. *Shaping* means using rewards to bring about desired changes in small steps. If an animal trainer can teach a pigeon to ride a bicycle by shaping its behavior, think of what you can do if you switch from aversive control to positive reinforcement. For example, instead of asking your reluctant husband to do what you and the kids normally do, then criticizing him if he doesn't, think of what he likes to do. Maybe he prefers hiking in the woods to sitting in a concert, or vice versa. You don't know what he likes? Ask him. Some of the things he might enjoy doing—hiking, adventure movies—you and the kids can do together with him. Other things might be just for the two of you. The point is not whether "he gets to do everything his way" and you "have to make all the sacrifices." The point is to break the cycle of pursuit and distancing.

Some changes require negotiation at the start, but whether or not they stick may depend upon your willingness to accept gradual improvement *and* your willingness to relax your expectations and standards. Here is an example from a working mother!

> *Last fall I decided I was taking on too much responsibility for the day-to-day functions of running the household: food shopping, meal planning, cooking, organizing and planning activities for the children, for the whole family, and for Fred and me. I discussed this with Fred, who agreed that I was doing too much. He agreed to take on some of these tasks and we chose to work on dinner. For about two weeks he remembered his night to be responsible. Then he forgot. I would bail him out, and be angry. After all, the kids had to be fed, I'm well-organized and can whip up a well-balanced meal in minutes. We talked again and he agreed to be more reliable—but the same pattern repeated itself. I felt like giving up, but this is too important, so I have learned not to bail him out. That, by the way, turned out to be unexpectedly hard for me. I have to try very hard to stop worrying about the children being fed according to my standards, and about the time when supper is actually served. Fred would eat out of a can; I prefer at least a paper plate.*

In order for an overinvolved mother to make room for greater participation from her husband, she may have to surrender control over what has been thought of as the traditional female realm. Differences in the way women and men parent, especially in terms of how much to do for the children, are related to boundaries of the self. Women tend to be more observant and sensitive to the children's needs. Fathers could learn to pay more attention—but they generally don't if their wives are around, unless the wives learn not to step in.

The children also must learn to readjust their expectations. They may demand more from Mother at first if she tries to stop doing it all. The children will learn to look to Dad, but not right away.

———◆———

Sharon got sick and tired of always having to be the one to buy clothes for the children, so she let Stewart know that Jason needed some socks. "No problem." The next day Stewart came home with two packages of socks. It was great for Sharon because the socks were her size, not Jason's. It wasn't hard for her to avoid making him feel worse by criticizing him—especially since she thought it was funny. The hard part was not going out for him to get the socks. "Don't worry, I'll exchange them tomorrow," Stewart said. The next day he forgot, and the next. Sharon waited; she was not going to say anything. It was astounding to her how hard she had to try to ignore the holes in Jason's socks. When Jason finally came to her to complain, she didn't make an issue of saying that it was Stewart's responsibility; she just told Jason, "Ask Daddy."

———◆———

If you are a distancer it may be even harder for you to bring about the changes you want. Maybe you've grown sour on the relationship and just want to be left alone. Okay, but you will find that you are freer to spend time alone if you begin to volunteer to spend a little time together. (A little giving makes a big difference.) One other thing, that feeling that it's awful when you are together—she (or he) nags, criticizes, complains, bosses, and bores—is partly a product of the process of getting together. She has to pressure you, feels you don't want to be there—and you don't. What I'm recommending is breaking the pattern. Switch from passive, grudging, defensive, reactive compliance and defiance to actively initiating contact. It goes a long way. You will reap two rewards. First, by initiating getting together you will lessen the pressure, demands, and criticisms you (both) have lived with. Second, if you initiate doing things you like, you may discover that being together isn't so bad after all.

There are, of course, those who question the idea that some people have an affinity for more closeness and that others prefer more distance. One woman might seem to be one way with her husband and children and another way with her parents. This is a valid and important observation. Although most people have a predominant style, a person's style can vary from relationship to relationship. That's what makes us able to change this dynamic— it's a product of the relationship, not fixed in our character.

Another question often asked is, "Okay, but how can I change how I feel?" This is one of those "questions" that sounds more like a statement. If you really want an answer, I'd say first notice that your behavior is automatic in most relationships. And that it is often part of a complementary pattern. Then all you have to do is experiment with changing the pattern. If you are pursuing a distancer, try backing off, spend more time with your friends. If you are a distancer, try initiating surprise contact with the other person. See what happens. You may begin to feel that you have an enormous ability to regulate the pattern.

Finally, some people complain, "It sounds good, but I've tried moving away and it doesn't work." There's a big difference between *planned* distance and *reactive* distance. If you move away when you're angry, your partner knows it and he (or she) feels a great deal of direct pressure. Planned distance is different. If you create more space when things are relatively calm, the other person won't feel obliged to come and make amends, he or she will just start to miss you.

Another thing: If you are a pursuer and you move back, then you must try to accept any movement toward you, even if it's done in anger. Some pursuers say they want the other person to express more feeling, but what they really mean is positive feelings. If you want the person to move toward you, to be more involved in the relationship, you may have to begin by putting up with some long-avoided complaints.

One final note about my suggestions. Try out one or two changes at a time, and stick with them. If you try a barrage of variations in rapid succession, they may cancel each other out.

11

FAMILY FEUD

"*L*ast one to the car is a rotten egg!" Stewart shouted, then raced off through the parking lot. Jason, now ten, was not far behind, running as fast as he could. Heather, panicky at being left behind, bolted in front of a car. The driver braked in plenty of time, but it was close enough to make Heather's heart race.

Stewart slowed his pace a little to let the kids catch up. Then, when they were almost to the car, he put on a sudden spurt and got there first. He ran around to the driver's side, yanked open his door, and jumped in. "Ha!" he said with a grin.

Two seconds later, Jason slapped the hood with his hand, just ahead of Heather. "I win!" he yelled triumphantly. "Stupid, you ran right in front of that car, and I still beat you. Guess who's a rotten egg?"

Heather looked miserable. "Yeah, sure, but you got a head start. Besides you're older."

"So what? You're a rotten egg, and you stink."

"*Kids*, come on, it's *only* a game. Don't take everything so seriously."

When they got home, Sharon wanted to know, "How come you two look so grumpy?"

"It's Heather, she's such a big baby. We had a race and Daddy won, and I came in second, and Heather lost. Now she's being a fuss-face."

"It's not fair," Heather said, close to tears. "Jason got a head start, and then he was teasing me."

"Is that right, Jason? Were you teasing your sister?"

"No! She always says that. She's just a big baby."

At that, Heather broke into tears. "Leave me alone!"

"Jason, you apologize to your sister, right now."

"No, I won't. Why does she have to be such a baby? And you always take her side."

Sharon was furious. "I don't take *anybody's* side. *You* are constantly tormenting her. You seem to take delight in picking on her. Why can't you be nice to each other? I'm sick and tired of you always arguing and fighting. You're getting to be selfish and mean; and I won't have it!"

Stewart watched, full of anxiety, as Sharon screamed at Jason. He felt he should stop it, but he didn't know how. To his surprise, Jason screamed right back at her.

"*It's not fair!* You never listen to anything I say."

"That's it, young man. Go to your room."

Jason stomped up the stairs and slammed the door to his room.

"And don't come out until I tell you," Sharon shouted after him.

Stewart was upset. As far as he was concerned, Sharon only made things worse by trying to settle all the kids' arguments. *Let them work it out by themselves,* he thought. But as usual, he didn't say anything. He didn't like to get yelled at any more than Jason. Maybe less.

If children learn to fight by watching their parents, then Jason and Heather had little to go by. When Sharon vented her pent-up frustration on Stewart, he rarely fought back, at least not openly.

A half hour later when Stewart went upstairs, he was surprised to see Heather in Jason's room. They were sitting on the floor playing Chinese Checkers, as friendly as puppies.

It was amazing. How could they do that? Stewart wondered. One minute they were at each other's throats, the next thing they were playing together happily. Maybe that was part of the problem. They spent too much time together. That, Stewart was convinced, and the fact that Sharon was always trying to settle their disputes, instead of leaving them alone to fight their own battles, made a bad situation worse.

What he didn't realize was how he fostered competition by

making invidious comparisons ("Why can't you be neat like your sister?"); playing one against the other ("I sure like it when you help me cook supper, Jason—you're a lot more helpful than some people I know"), and making everything into a contest ("Last one up the hill's a stinkpot!").

Whatever the causes, Stewart and Sharon were suffering the effects. At least once a day, Jason and Heather got into a major fight. There didn't seem to be any way to predict or control them. The least little thing would set one of them off, and pretty soon there'd be name-calling, and then tears. Going out to supper or to the movies used to be something to look forward to. But now, an escalating series of battles between the children took all the fun out of being together.

"Sibling rivalry." Everybody knows about it. People joke about it. Parents are reluctant to complain—friends dismiss it as "normal." So it is, but so too are auto accidents.

SIBLING RIVALRY

Sibling rivalry is one of those concepts about family life whose familiarity has rendered it a cliché, robbing the term of emotional impact. "The kids are fighting? Don't worry, it's only sibling rivalry." Friends and grandparents smile when they say "sibling rivalry." Parents don't.

The constant bickering, arguing over who's going to get what, and acute sensitivities that flare into tearful battles whenever the family is together can drive parents crazy.

Why do brothers and sisters fight so much? This familiar question, which has plagued legions of frustrated parents, has a familiar answer. Siblings fight because they are jealous. Every child wants the exclusive love of his or her parents, and with less and less parental time available in busy households, there is all the more reason for siblings to quarrel.

The seeds of sibling rivalry are sown when the new baby comes home from the hospital and gets so much attention. The regression we see in older children at that time is partly an involuntary reversion to more infantile modes of behavior, partly an attempt to get taken care of.

Most parents could tell at least one anecdote like the following, related to me by a friend.

"It's a story my mother loved to tell, about the afternoon my infant sister was sleeping and the house was suspiciously quiet. She checked the nursery at just the moment when my brother, a mere thirteen months older, had climbed up the side of the crib and was about to lower his rubber tomahawk on his baby sister's head. Mother swooped down, picked up her son and, cuddling him, explained that he couldn't hit Fran on the head with the tomahawk because she was just a little baby. My brother looked up at her and replied, 'But I just a widow baby, too.' "

No wonder the arrival of a new baby provokes intense jealousy: The older child's entire life is changed. It seems that the infant has number-one priority for mother's attention. This impression is partly true and partly an artifact of the universal tendency to be more aware of when we don't get our fair share than when we do. Despite this, we expect the displaced child to be pleased with the new arrival and, after a brief period of mild anxiety, to share the parents' enthusiasm. But even a child who was convinced he should await a baby brother or sister with happy anticipation may feel cheated after the baby's birth. The little sibling can't play, doesn't talk, and is little more than a nuisance. Children aren't kidding when they ask whether the parents can give the baby back.

While older children are jealous of the attention given the baby of the family, the second-born's sustaining passion is to be the equal of those who are already grown-up. Younger children are envious of their older siblings, who seem to have so many privileges and who gain attention through their accomplishments. Envy may spur children to attempt feats beyond their capacities and lead to additional frustration.

Sibling rivalry is a theme that occurs several times in the Old Testament. The rivalry between brothers for their father's blessing—and not incidentally, to inherit his estate—led Jacob to drive a hard bargain with the starving Esau and cheat him. Jacob later was deprived of his favorite son, Joseph, when his ten older brothers united to get rid of their rival. And most ominous of all, Cain's murder of his brother, Abel, stands out as a sinister warning of the consequences of fraternal jealousy. This story dramatizes the danger of unchecked human impulses and under-scores the need to keep them under control. The message of these cautionary tales is clear: Rivalry between siblings is evil. Equally clear is the implication: Such feelings should be repressed.

With such dire warnings, it's easy to forget that there is a value to all the fighting between brothers and sisters. Sibling rivalry is a natural occurrence, and it takes place throughout the animal kingdom. Rough-housing and spirited play, whether between monkeys or kittens or puppies, or your own young monkeys, builds speed and agility. Incidentally, when animals play-fight they send signals that it isn't serious. So do children, though their parents often don't get the message.

This tussling is valuable training, teaching youngsters how to fight for a place in the world. As they get older, animals (including *Homo sapiens*) engage in slightly more serious struggles for dominance. Although many parents worry about fighting, it's a good idea to keep in mind that some fighting is inevitable. Competition is natural, and it is a major force in evolution. Battles for dominance occur among all creatures of nature. But as anyone who watches nature programs on television realizes, the vast majority of these conflicts are ritualized encounters in which no one gets hurt.

Attempts to establish dominance, among friends and between siblings, makes kids tougher, more resilient. And if you'll notice, kids, like puppies and kittens, have their own ways of keeping their fights within safe limits—especially if they realize that there is no one around to step in and call foul if things get out of hand. Fighting teaches children how to assert themselves, defend their rights, and—if the scraps aren't interrupted—how, eventually, to compromise. Verbal sparring is one way for children to learn the difference between being clever and being hurtful. Even jealousy—the green-eyed monster—teaches children how to compete, which can spur them on to greater achievement.

Much depends, however, on the parents' response. The way parents handle sibling rivalry often determines not only how brothers and sisters get along, in childhood and beyond, but also how they feel about themselves and their parents.

———◆———

One patient of mine, a middle-aged woman, came to see me because she was depressed. Silvia White was the epitome of the long-suffering, self-sacrificing wife and mother, always ready to do something for anyone in need, rarely thinking of herself. Now she was fifty, her children were growing up, and she felt empty. She wondered why it was so hard for her to enjoy herself, and why she was—in her words—"such a sucker for everyone else." Although her daughters, ages nineteen and twenty-one, were living in their own apartments, she continued to buy groceries for them, and she regularly did their laundry.

Like many patients, Mrs. White came to therapy with an idea of what she needed to do to improve her situation: learn to say no occasionally to requests for help, and start doing some things she enjoyed. She tried to use the sessions as morale boosters, telling me who was now demanding what and how she shouldn't give in. Only thing was, she couldn't seem to stop taking care of everybody. She knew what she needed to do, but her habit was more than habit; it had been programmed in childhood, and would be hard to change.

Silvia was the youngest of three daughters. When she was four, her father had three successive heart attacks, and for the remaining ten years of his life he was an invalid. The atmosphere of the house became that of a sick room. Silvia's mother, worried about the effect of any stress on her husband, cautioned the children not to make noise, not to argue, not to do anything that might upset their father. For a young child raised in such an atmosphere, the lesson is indelible: *Don't make trouble.* At least that was the effect on Silvia. Her older sisters were not as affected by their mother's warnings; they continued to make noise, to look after themselves, and to quarrel with each other—in short, to act like children.

Silvia's mother, cut off emotionally from her chronically ill husband, turned to her "good girl" for solace and sympathy. She complained to Silvia about the thoughtlessness and selfishness of her older sisters, and came to rely on Silvia for help around the house. Silvia complied and became a little Cinderella—trapped every bit as effectively by love and duty as by threats and punishment.

Too bad Silvia's mother allowed her own need for solace and support to separate Silvia from the world of her siblings and turn her into mother's helper.

———◆———

Another of my patients was a young man who became acutely anxious when he entered graduate school. Despite being bright and having achieved a fine record as an undergraduate, Dennis was afraid that he had overreached himself. He was, he thought, an impostor who had gone too far and now would be found out. He was convinced that he was inadequate and that he would fail. Whenever he was called upon to speak in class, he suffered all the symptoms of a panic attack.

One of the things that struck me about Dennis's accounts of graduate school was how he constantly compared himself to his fellow students. He felt they knew more than he did and that he could neither compete with them nor be accepted socially. It wasn't hard to discover the roots of these feelings.

Dennis was a little brother. His big brothers, two and four years older, were intensely competitive; instead of treating Dennis like a little guy who needed support, they treated him like a rival, one who because of his age was always easy to defeat. It seems that Dennis's mother was always tired and preoccupied with various aches and pains, and therefore unable to fulfill the maternal function of supporting and protecting her youngest. He may not have needed her to interfere, but he did need her to sympathize. Hungry for attention, Dennis turned to his father. He was not lucky there either.

Dennis's father was a rough, aggressive battler, a successful businessman who believed that the world was a jungle and only the tough survive. He encouraged his boys in sports and taught them that winning was everything. Dennis couldn't win. Love was conditional, and the condition—defeating his two older brothers—was impossible. No wonder he grew up thinking he was inadequate, and faced with any serious challenge, he was bound to lose.

The rivalrous conflict that is almost certain to occur, particularly between siblings spaced less than three years apart, creates friction, which, like a squeaky wheel, gets a lot of attention from parents who seek whatever means of lubrication they can find to restore calm and quiet.

Most parents develop a repertoire of predictable responses to their children's competitive quarrels, responses based on intolerance of fighting and an exaggerated sense of the parents' duty—and capacity—to control their children. These responses, which usually begin with reasoning with the little adversaries and end with threatening them, interrupt squabbles before the children have a chance to settle them, or allow the quarreling to continue until it goes beyond the parents' rather low threshold of tolerance, at which point they once again step in, attempting to control what they cannot.

Ironically, the same parents who try to muzzle their children's fighting contribute inadvertently to the rivalry. Parents who foster competition, either deliberately or without thinking, or lock their children into roles (such as calling one "serious" and the other "outgoing") fan the flames of rivalry and resentment.

Parents foster competition blatantly, by challenging one child to outdo the other, and subtly, by making comparisons.

Parents aren't stupid. Few of us ask younger children to perform as well as their big brothers or sisters, and few of us goad older ones to defeat the little ones. Each child is different—in age, size, and capability—and therefore should be treated differently. This makes sense, but feelings are not always sensible.

Sometimes we pit one child against another playfully. "Come on, Billy, let's see you beat your sister out to the raft." "Who can build the biggest snowman?" Men do this more than women. Many of us are highly competitive ourselves, and although common sense tells us not to encourage one child to succeed at the expense of another, in play we often drop our guards and turn a good time into a contest. I don't happen to agree with those people who think all children's games should be noncompetitive. My point is simply to encourage parents—especially fathers—to be aware of turning play into a time where the only way for one child to win is for the other one to lose. If you aren't concerned about sibling rivalry, don't worry about it; if you are, notice how often you say things like "Okay, let's see who can be the first one to . . . ."

We also slip up and set our children in competition with each other when we get upset (company's coming and we ask the children to see which one can clean up the most) or when we are very anxious about the outcome (getting good grades in school, behaving politely at important social events, making "the right" friends). Often, we set up these competitions "in secret." "Don't tell your brother, but . . ." (Don't tell one child anything "in secret" that you don't want repeated.) We wouldn't play these games if we thought about it. The problem is, sometimes we don't think. Although most parents have pretty good instincts, it helps to be clear that competition fosters rivalry, and to remind ourselves what's going on when anxiety floods our reason and clouds our judgment.

Like competition, comparisons turn family life into a contest: In order for one person to win, someone else has to lose. Favorable comparisons ("I wish your brother was as helpful as you are") can give one child a vested interest in surpassing the other. Unfavorable comparisons ("Why can't you be as neat as your sister?") can prompt one child to decide that if he can't be the best, he can be the worst; to resent the "good" sibling; and to go through life measuring himself against others.

Whether you are praising or rebuking, describe your child's behavior without reference to a sibling.

"Honey, it's so nice when you help me with the cooking. I really enjoyed working on the supper with you."

"Your floor is covered with Legos; please clean them up, now. I'll be back in fifteen minutes to see if you did a good job."

———◆———

One of the more insidious ways we foster rivalry among our children is by casting them into different roles. If one child is "the baby" and the other is our "big girl," the older child may be jealous of the attention lavished on the little one. Instead of feeling more grown-up, the older one may long to be babyish. By typecasting children we thwart their development. For every positive image any role carries, there are, by implication, negative consequences—all the other roles that seem to be ruled out. When we label our children ("my studious daughter," "the family athlete," "the serious one") we are often projecting our own strengths and weaknesses onto our children. This not only limits the development of the child—pushing him or her in *our* directions—it also polarizes the siblings. Putting one child into a role tends to cast the other into a complementary role. If one is "neat," the other is "the slob"; if one is "bad" (wild), the other is "good" (tame).

When my brother and I were growing up, he was the "big boy," I was "the baby." I always felt that gave me an unfair advantage. In any competition, he couldn't win. If he did learn to swim before me, so what? After all, he was older. But if I did something first, how come he let "the baby" beat him? He was also "the brain" and I was "the athlete." In fact, I'm sure he was as athletic as I was (which he is demonstrating in his mid-forties in triathlons), and I was probably as smart as he was. But these self-images, more imposed than discovered, had powerful consequences. In sports, I was always an overachiever, trying my best to be a star but never quite making it. My brother didn't even go out for any teams. And in the brains department, I withdrew my application to my first-choice college (an Ivy League school) at the last minute, because despite good grades and high SAT scores, my image of myself was that I wasn't smart. Perhaps you can recall what role or roles you played in your family, and how your parents fostered those roles. Try to remember; it's a good antidote to repeating the same stereotyping with your own children.

———◆———

Talking about the ways parents unintentionally heat up sibling rivalry by making comparisons, fostering competition, and putting their children into categories may, unfortunately, exaggerate the impact parents have on their children's behavior. Much of this is good advice, but it tends to be too specific, as though there were correct responses needed to control every aspect of our children's lives. This, by the way, is often what people want to hear—"What do I do when my children get jealous?" "How can I keep my children from fighting?" The do's and don'ts are appealing (they give us something to do) but suggest that we can control every situation, some of which we should stay out of.

Once again, we have the irony that the most involved and concerned parents can make a difficult situation worse. Sibling rivalry is natural and inevitable. Most of the time your children have to work out their own quarrels. Intervening itself can be a problem.

ENMESHMENT

The biggest mistake many parents make in dealing with sibling rivalry is not being ignorant of some specific technique of child rearing; rather, it is being overinvolved in their children's lives. Enmeshment, not poor parenting skills, is the problem.

Remember that the family is made up of subsystems surrounded by semipermeable boundaries, which partially separate their functioning from other segments of the family. Unless the boundary around a subsystem is clear, the members of that unit will not learn to relate effectively. As we have already seen, when a new couple marries they must establish a clear boundary around themselves in order to work out all the problems of adjustment. Similarly, young parents who fail to maintain a boundary around their relationship as a couple may lose their marriage. At least as important as these boundary issues is the need for parents to respect the boundary around the sibling subsystem in the family.

Without a clear boundary between generations, the parents' executive functioning will be impaired. If everyone is the same, no one is in charge. Children must be taught to respect their parents. But parents must also respect their children. Parents who try too hard to *teach* their children to get along violate the boundary around the sibling relationship, and cheat the children out of the opportunity to *learn* to get along.

Parents, unlike practitioners of other complex callings, learn mainly through on-the-job training. Being a parent is easy—like learning to ice skate in the dark. You just push off into where you cannot see, and have never been before, and go on your nerve. The ice is thick, you hope. Keep going and watch out for heartbreak.

By the time our children have grown up and left home, most of us are experts on how to raise kids. We may not know much about children when we begin, but we learn a lot, mostly through trial and error. Trial-and-error learning, as you probably know, works through reinforcement. We try several approaches, keep those that work, and drop those that don't. This is the same way that white mice learn to negotiate laboratory mazes; they keep exploring until they find the cheese. If one alleyway doesn't have cheese at the end of it, the mouse will try another one. The difference between human beings and mice is that we have more complex brains. For this reason, we pursue certain paths for years, even though there's no cheese. Maybe next time.

In family life, we are sometimes rewarded for making mistakes. Consider the following familiar scene. A harassed mother arrives at the supermarket checkout line and her small son reaches for a candy bar. The mother tells him it's too close to dinner to have candy, and the little darling starts to wail. Now she's mad: "If you think I'm going to buy you a treat when you make such a fuss, you have another thing coming, young man!" This only escalates the tantrum, and the little boy shrieks louder and louder. Finally, exasperated and embarrassed, the mother gives in, saying, "All right, if you quiet down *right now*, you can have a cookie."

Obviously, this mother is teaching her child to demand what he wants; she is reinforcing his temper tantrums. Less obvious, but equally true, is that her own behavior is also reinforced. Giving in leads to peace and quiet. Behaviorists call this *reciprocal reinforcement,* and it is one of the major ways we maintain spirals of undesirable behavior.

I deliberately chose to introduce the concept of reciprocal reinforcement using the example of temper tantrums, because almost everybody knows that it isn't a good idea to give in to temper tantrums. When it comes to fighting between siblings, we aren't so clear. Parents, especially enmeshed parents, interfere too much. Unfortunately, their interference leads to reinforcement. The problem is that sometimes we get reinforced for interrupting a problem, without solving it. Here's a typical example.

Just as the family is about to sit down for a holiday dinner, the children start arguing over who's going to sit where. "I'm going to sit next to Daddy." "No, I'm sitting here." "No, me!" At this point, their mother interrupts. "If you're going to fight, go up to your rooms." The argument subsides, to be resumed later. They always are.

The best thing to do is stay out of the children's arguments. Let them settle it.

———◆———

Development of interpersonal skills is predicated on a subsystem's freedom from interference. The sibling group is a laboratory in which the children learn—or don't learn—how to get along. Some children learn only how to fight in the presence of an overactive referee.

Most parents suffer from an illusion of control. We think we can mold our children, protect them, shape them, that we can get them to do whatever we want—what's best for them. When they're little, we *can* control them to a large extent. Using bribes and threats, we bend them to our wills. Some parents never let go. Most of us, however, slowly learn to draw the line between what is theirs and what is ours. We let them pick out the color of a new shirt, we let them choose the pictures to hang on their walls, we may even let them name the family cat. But when they fight, we get upset and step in, offering a number of solutions that only make things worse. We tell them to "be nice," "share," "take turns,"—if we are really brave, "fight fair." As long as we attempt to control the children's battles with each other, we prevent them from developing their own competence.

In order to respect the boundary around the sibling subsystem, it helps to clarify what belongs in their relationship with each other and what concerns their relationship with you. What time they go to bed, who goes to bed first, whether or not you will tolerate yelling in the living room while you're trying to read— these things necessarily involve their relationship with you. Who called who what on the playground, who gets to sit in the front seat of the car this time, and the well-known Who Started It— these things are their business. Stay out of it. Let them learn to negotiate with each other. You may have to tolerate a little noise once in a while, but if you remember to respect the difference between their relationship with each other and their relationship with you, it will be a little easier.

"Yes, but what if they start screaming and yelling and cursing?" They will. If they expect you to intervene, they know that no matter what they do they are safe. If they have come to rely on you to interfere, they will escalate their arguments with impunity. They know they won't get hurt or be held accountable, because they know you will step in. Once you start interfering, the kids will always try to involve you. They will run to you with their complaints—"Kerry hit me!"—and they'll never learn to work out their own rules for negotiating as long as you keep doing it for them.

If your children start to argue or come to you with complaints about each other, the best thing you can do is to express faith in their ability to work things out, and leave the room.

> "Mommy, Mommy, Tommy came in my room and took my flashlight, and now he won't give it back."
> "I did not! That was *my* flashlight; yours is in the basement."
> "See? I told you. Make him give it back."
> "I'm sure you two can work this out. I'm going to finish cooking supper."

There may be times when the fighting seems to be getting out of hand—the little one picks up a rock to throw at the big one—or when, for reasons of your own, you just want them to be quiet. So, when and how should you intervene? Adele Faber and Elaine Mazlish wrote an excellent book, called *Siblings Without Rivalry*, which contains some very good suggestions about what to say in particularly trying situations.[1] I recommend their book highly. But I also recommend that you not worry too much about trying to find the perfect solution for every situation. The main thing is the general principle: Respect the boundary between children and parents, and try to stay out of your children's squabbles as much as possible.

One of the worst mistakes parents make is trying to decide "who started it." For one thing it is almost impossible to figure out who started it. When did "it" start? When Jessie called C.J. a "dick head" or when C.J. came uninvited into Jessie's room? Older siblings have an uncanny ability to torment their younger siblings in ways that are invisible to parents. It must be genetic. They all know how to give that special look. You know, that sneering glance of mockery, flashed faster than a human parent can see. *I know*, I was a little brother. As far as I know, younger siblings (especially younger brothers) don't do anything to provoke the older ones. At least nothing I can remember.

Another mistake is to hold one accountable rather than hold all of them accountable. Even if you *could* figure out who started it, that's not the point. If you must step in, punish the entire subsystem. That way they'll learn that they are all in it together, and they'll have an incentive to learn to work things out. If you pick out one kid as the bad guy, you are teaching them, not to work things out with each other, but to find a way to appear innocent to you.

———————◆———————

Enmeshed parents also tend to blur the boundaries between their children. They try to be fair, and in the process, they treat unique individuals as though they were the same.

Sometimes a parent who has been traveling will happen to see a perfect gift for one of the children. It might be a souvenir T-shirt for the oldest boy or a poster for the youngest girl. Most parents then feel that they have to find something of equal worth for the other children. This may mean a long, anxious search through gift shops at the airport, or, just as often, deciding not to buy the serendipitously discovered present for the one child.

Forget about being fair. Rather than trying to give equal measured amounts, give to each child according to individual needs. If you buy a present for one child and not the others, explain to them that you saw this one and thought it was perfect; next time, you may find just the right present for them. Children will accept this; they don't mind taking turns. It's only grown-ups who worry about giving every child a gift if one gets one.

Trying to give "equally" to children actually encourages rivalry—"Hey, Sara's piece is bigger than mine!"—and it may blur the distinction between the children. Recognize the difference between older and younger children by giving older ones more privileges—larger allowances, later bedtimes, more latitude in the neighborhood—and giving younger ones additional support and leeway. In the following examples, my point is not to tell parents what rules to make for their children, but merely to illustrate differentiating between siblings.

> It's Friday night and the family is watching television, when "Miami Vice" comes on. Mother tells Derek [age eleven]: "This show is not for you, you'll have to go upstairs and read." Derek protests: "What about Amy [age fourteen], how come she gets to watch?" "Because she's older, that's why."

> Michael [age eleven] wants to know, "How come you always help Raymond [age eight] with his homework, and you tell me to figure it out myself?" "Because he's only eight, that's why. You're eleven, it's time for you to start figuring out your own assignments."

> With some chores, parents can't win. If a mother lets Eleanor [age fourteen] use the snowblower to plow the driveway, she may hear complaints from Teddy [age nine], "I want to do it, too"; and Eleanor, "Why do I have to do all the work?"

Once you realize that the children are different (some are older, some are younger) and have different needs (one may need extra help with school work, another may require more, or less, structured activity), answering these questions becomes easier.

What do you say if one of your children asks you, "Who do you love best?" Most parents answer: "I love you both the same." This rarely satisfies the child. A child who asks such a question is expressing feelings of self-doubt and asking for reassurance. See if you can help the child put into words what's bothering him or her—"What makes you ask that, honey?"—and then explain what's special about him or her. "I couldn't love you any more. You're my special boy, with that wonderful smile of yours and your friendly way with people. You're terrific."

◆

Some enmeshed parents try to control not only their children's relationship with each other but also that with their friends.

A lot of kids complain that their parents want to choose their friends for them. "How come you're not friends with Katie? She plays the piano and she gets good grades."

We care so much about our children, and we want the best for them, including the best friends. We think it's important that they play with certain children and wish they would avoid others. So, we push them and try to arrange their social life. The result of this well-intentioned interference is that when we disapprove of our children's choices, they feel we are disapproving of *them*. Moreover, trying to make your children play with other children usually has a paradoxical effect. By blurring the boundary between you and them, you are intensifying their relationship with you, not with their friends.

It's not what we say to them ("You should make more friends." "Would you like me to call Cheri's mother and ask her to bring Cheri over?") but what we do and who we are that has the greatest effect on whether or not our children make friends.

Children without friends usually have parents without friends. This is because children follow their parents' example, and because parents with no friends of their own are more likely to intrude into their children's lives. Instead of separating ourselves from our children and developing our own friendships, we can't stop worrying about them, and worrying for them. We coach and coax, and usually get the opposite of what we want.

Accept the fact that your children are different—from each other and from you—and that they have their own preferences. You may not like or approve of all your children's friends, but respect their right to choose, and their right to fight their own battles.

◆

I once treated a family who called because fifteen-year-old Roger was depressed. It seemed that he didn't have any friends and he was lonely. His mother responded by trying to make friends for him and by trying to get the neighborhood kids to stop teasing him. Roger had complained to his mother that as a new kid in the neighborhood, he got teased a lot at the bus stop. But he was horrified when his mother came to the corner in the morning and told the other kids to stop picking on him. All she accomplished was giving them more ammunition. Now, in addition to calling Roger a wimp and a nerd, the kids called him "momma's boy." We can't fight these battles for our kids, nor do they want us to. Listen to their complaints. Sympathize, but don't interfere.

◆

One mother I know feels that her own children should be best friends and play together. When they go outside, she watches to see if everything is okay. Often she's out there with them, acting like a social director, trying to orchestrate what they do. "Let's play Alphabet Soup," or "Why don't you two come inside and play with trains?" When the kids are playing in the backyard pool, she thinks she has to be the policeman. "Don't splash." "Let Suzie have a turn." On and on. Now the other kids in the neighborhood don't play over there anymore. Her own children are well-behaved but don't seem to have much spirit.

◆

By now I think my message is clear. Just as it is essential for parents to create a hierarchical boundary that sets them apart from their children in order to carry out such executive functions as decision-making and disciplining, this same boundary is essential to allow the children room to work out their own relationships with each other and with their friends.

Because we love our children and want everything to work out, we are tempted to intercede in their lives in countless ways, often crossing the boundary between what is our responsibility and what is their business. When enmeshment develops, we need to do less, not more.

There is, however, one potential problem with this analysis. In talking about the problems of enmeshment, I may seem to be dumping on mothers, favorite targets of psychological and socio-logical analyses. Mothers willingly accept the blame. They are used to being criticized, and used to taking all the responsibility. Enmeshment is *not* something mothers do. It is a *family* pattern. Mothers don't become overinvolved in their children's lives be-cause they are intrusive and controlling. They become overin-volved with the kids to the extent that their husbands are underinvolved—with them and with the kids.

Disengagement on the part of one parent (usually the father) is not only part of a general family problem, it also has a specific destructive effect where sibling rivalry is concerned.

DISENGAGEMENT

Stewart reached for Heather's hand and held it tight as they walked down the aisle—past displays of pastel sweaters, designer jeans, and then a long row of color televisions, all tuned to the same game show—on their way to the bicycle section. It was a long time since he'd shopped in Sears and he was struck by how big the store had gotten, and how it had changed from a store of practical, serviceable goods he remembered to a glittering array of the fashionable and entertaining—keeping pace with the times. When they got to the bicycles, there were a lot more to choose from than he had anticipated. There were three-speed commuter bikes, ten- and twelve-speed tourers and racers, dirt bikes, free-style bikes with nobby wheels for doing spins and tricks, and something called a "mountain bike," which was a more rugged version of the ten-speed. And the prices! Stewart had thought he'd be able to buy something nice for well under a hundred dollars, but the prices seemed to start there and go up, and up.

This was to be Heather's first new bike. She had finally outgrown the one she'd inherited from Jason, and Stewart wanted to be the one who bought her this special present. "This is a big day," he told her. "You're getting to be a big girl, and Mommy and I are very proud of you; you deserve your own bicycle." He was excited, proud of Heather and happy to be able to show it.

Heather was excited, too, but she held it in. In return for this special treatment, she tried to be what she thought her father wanted—appreciative but not too eager, hopeful but not too demanding. After they had seen several bikes, Stewart asked her which one she liked best. Heather said they were all nice, but Stewart could see that her eyes kept drifting over to a lavender and white street-style bike. Stewart had seen one like it before. Heather's friend B.J. had one, only hers was red and a little smaller. B.J.'s father was a vice president at Marine Midland Bank. The bike Heather had her eye on had coaster brakes and hand brakes; it also had a removable white wicker basket, *and* a price tag of a hundred and nineteen dollars, well over the limit Stewart had set.

"You really like that one, don't you sweetheart?"

"Yes, but they're all nice, Daddy."

Stewart put his arms around this sweet child of his and held her tight. "Daddy loves you very much, Heather." And then, to the salesman: "We'll take that one," pointing to the lavender and white.

"Oh, thank you, Daddy! Thank you, thank you, thank you!"

With the salesman's help, Stewart put the new bike in the trunk of his car. When they were settled in the front seat, Stewart asked Heather where she'd like to go for supper. That was the plan, first look for a bicycle and then go out to supper. It was Stewart's favorite way to spend time with the kids.

Heather said she didn't care where they ate, maybe Chinese—which she knew he liked, and he knew she didn't.

"Honey, maybe you'd like to skip supper and go straight home so you can ride your new bike. I could call up and order a pizza."

"Oh no, Daddy, I want to have supper with you."

Halfway to the Golden Dragon, Stewart said, "Let's go home, sweetheart; I bet you'd really like to ride that bike."

"Yes, I really would," came the eager reply.

In Stewart's family, if you wanted a glass of water, you said "No, thank you" three times, and then, having proved that you were no bother, it was okay to say "Yes, if it's no trouble." Like father like daughter.

The minute they wrestled the bike out of the trunk, Heather hopped on and sped off down the block, eager to find B.J. Stewart watched her peddle off, happy for her, happy with her, happy to have given her this moment.

Half an hour later Jason burst in the door, shouting, "Goddamn baby!" Heather, two steps behind, was in tears. "Daddy, Jason won't let me put my bike in the garage."

Now what? Stewart didn't mind the swearing so much (although Sharon didn't permit it), but why did they have to drag him into their fight? Why couldn't they just play and enjoy themselves? Why did they always find something to fight about? Goddammit!

"Heather took my spot. I always put my bike between your car and Mommy's, and Heather stole my space."

"There wasn't any room. Besides, you don't own it."

Stewart didn't want to hear any more of this. He was annoyed that they still expected their parents to settle their arguments. He didn't intend to intervene, and so he wasn't about to listen. "I'm sorry, but you two will have to settle this yourselves. Now go away and leave me alone."

Jason and Heather knew when their father meant business and so they left the room. But they didn't settle anything. There was nothing to settle. It was over. There was room for both bikes. What wasn't over was their upset.

What were they feeling? Stewart didn't have the slightest idea. He didn't think about it. The main thing was that they learn not to depend on anyone else to solve their problems, that they learn to work things out independently. That was the main thing. Wasn't it?

Jason was upset because Heather was always getting into his stuff. Ever since she was old enough to crawl into his room, she'd been getting in the way. And he couldn't do anything about it. Mom and Dad were always protecting her, telling him to share, telling him she was just a little girl, telling him not to pick on her. What about him? How come she was always picking on him?

Heather was upset because Jason called her a baby in front of B.J. He *always* laughed and made fun of her. She didn't come to Daddy to ask him to make Jason move his bike, she told him herself. But it's hard to act grown-up with a brother who knows how to torture you and make you cry in front of your friends.

Both kids went up to their rooms and slammed their doors. Separately, they shared the same feelings. Both were angry and frustrated, and both felt cut off from understanding and sympathy. Heather picked up a book and tried to forget about how misunderstood she felt. Jason pulled his blanket over his head and went over the whole thing again in his mind, brooding about how misunderstood he felt.

◆

There's such a thing as not enough space, and there's such a thing as too much. Sharon didn't give the children enough room to work out their own difficulties. She wrapped her love around them like a big blanket. It was warm and comforting, but sometimes it chafed. Stewart was the opposite. He gave the children more room; he wanted them to lead their own lives—and he wanted to lead his. But his distant position was not taken in a vacuum. Seeing Sharon so engaged with the children made him pull back, from her and from them, even farther than he otherwise might have. Sharon reacted to his distance by increasing her own involvement. Think of it as polarization, or as a circular, mutually reinforcing pattern. The result is the same. From Sharon the children got too much interference; from Stewart they got insufficient understanding.

◆

A clear boundary between parents and the sibling subsystem means maintaining enough distance to allow them to develop their own competence at settling disputes, but unless the boundary is inappropriately rigid, it also means permitting the children access to their parents to get comforted when they're upset.

When Jason and Heather ran up to their rooms after the fight about the bikes, what were they feeling? Stewart didn't know, and the truth is that the children didn't really know either.

Although we usually speak of feelings as though they were clear and specific, they don't start out that way. Young children's feelings are inchoate, vague. Small children know little more than that they feel pleasure or pain. It takes time, and parents who help by understanding, for children to differentiate between feeling angry and feeling depressed, between excitement and nervousness, or between fear and guilt. You may know people who grow to adulthood unable to make these distinctions—the woman who only feels (is aware of) feeling bad when she's attacked, or the man who instantly transforms hurt into anger. We don't *teach* children what they are feeling. We help them discover what they are feeling, by listening and showing understanding. This lets the children know that their feelings—even "bad" feelings—are natural, and it helps them differentiate chaotic affects into articulated emotions. (This is, by the way, one of the reasons we read novels: because the novelist helps to articulate what we have felt in our own lives.) The understanding an upset child gets from an empathic parent takes the sting out of unhappy feelings. Unless this happens, siblings may continue to harbor resentments and jealousies toward each other, which fester and grow all out of proportion.

When your children argue with each other, try to stay out of it. But when one of them comes to you crying or complaining, listen sympathetically and let the child know you understand. This is much easier to do once you realize that you aren't going to settle the argument.

When I first started teaching, one of the hardest things for me was listening to students who came in terribly upset after an exam because they got a low grade. "Dr. Nichols, you gave me a C, and that means I won't get a fellowship." I found these discussions extremely painful and tried to avoid them. Then I realized that I was confusing two things in my mind: the students' upset and my responsibility for it. Once I decided that my exams were fair and that I wasn't going to change any grades (unless my arithmetic was wrong), it became much easier for me to listen and show my sympathy. "Gee, I'm sorry you got a C. That's a shame. Does it really mean that you won't be able to get a fellowship? What can you do about it?" It was implied, but rarely necessary to say, "That's the grade you earned, and I'm not going to change it."

When siblings come to their parents complaining about the other one's pestering or teasing, what do parents usually say? "She didn't mean it." "Find a way to get along." "Ignore him." "Share." "Shut up and leave me alone." As far as solving the problem, some of these suggestions may appear more or less useful. But "the problem" when kids come to their parents is two problems: working out the disagreement and the child's upset feelings. Most of our responses carry the message *Don't feel that way*.

Acknowledge your children's unhappy feelings about their siblings. This is another example of the enormous importance of empathy. Separate feeling from action. Leave the action to them; help them understand their feelings, and let them know you understand and accept what they are feeling. "You hate it when she does that, don't you?'' "Sometimes you wish that he would disappear, don't you?'' "Yes, I know, when he teases you in front of your friends it's really mean." "She knows just what to do to make you mad, doesn't she? And she can do it in such a way that Daddy and I can't even see it—by making mean faces when we aren't looking."

These empathic comments actually help resolve the feelings. Once spoken, and heard, unhappy feelings lose some of their sting. Unspoken, they fester and leave little room for positive feelings.

Perhaps even more important, when we listen to what our children are feeling and let them know we understand, we are inoculating them against shame. Children who aren't allowed to talk about "bad" feelings grow up ashamed of their feelings, and of themselves.

Is that really all a parent should do? Listen to the children's feelings when they get mad at each other, but avoid settling their disputes? What about protecting them from each other if they are about to do something dangerous? Common sense will tell you to stop one of them from swinging a baseball bat at the other one, but as long as they don't expect someone to intervene, children rarely attack their siblings in a dangerous way. On the other hand, it is a good idea to discourage destructive, hurtful battles. Let the children know you disapprove of violence—and here parents have to clarify, and reach mutual agreement about, their own limits.

If you see a fight getting out of hand, separate the children and send them to their rooms for a cooling-off period. But don't make the common mistake of paying attention only to the aggressor. When we concentrate on the big sister who hit her little brother, we are rewarding her with attention (even critical attention is better than being neglected), and depriving the little one of sympathy. Don't ignore the fact that the injured child feels bad, and don't try to decide who started it. Sympathize with whomever is hurt or upset; but if you need to separate them, send both of them to their rooms.

———◆———

By now it should be quite clear that I think general principles of family dynamics are a better guide than specific prescriptions.

The reason is that most people are enormously creative, and it is better to release their natural instincts than to chain them to a dependence on advice from experts. The general principle at the heart of all that I have had to say about raising children is to maintain a clear boundary between generations—firm enough to keep the parents in charge, and open enough to allow the children plenty of freedom to come to the parents.

At least as important, though, is another principle, one that is a little harder for most of us to accept, and harder still to put into practice. In technical terms: two heads are better than one. Most of us are inclined to be either a little too pushy or a little too permissive, too intrusive or too distant. Unfortunately, as we have seen, parents have a tendency to polarize each other rather than join together in a harmonious blending of strategies. Instead of a team, built out of compromise, many parents cling to their separate ideas about how to raise the kids—perhaps because they never learned to achieve compromise by arguing out their differences when they were growing up.

BROTHERHOOD AND SISTERHOOD

"I'd like my children to be friends someday." These words have been spoken by so many parents, often with longing and regret. Behind the deadlines that preoccupy us, and the work that consumes us, lurks loneliness. When we slow down, it catches up. We wish we could be closer . . . to our spouses and our friends, to our parents, and often, to our brothers and sisters. We want more for our children. We don't want them to be lonely. We want them to be friends.

They can be. Only, we can't make them. We can only avoid putting obstacles in their way, and hope for the best.

Family . . . As we grow older, this homey word takes on the evocative power to conjure up so much feeling, much of it a yearning for something missing. Toward the end of young adulthood, when the flames of ambition and desire begin to cool, many of us long for more intimate relationships. One place we turn to is family. When we get older, and somewhat detached from our parents, we think about our brothers and sisters. Siblings now turn to each other, more so than in years gone by. Brothers and sisters help each other out with their own children, trading cribs and hints. And maybe more—closeness and caring. Our conversations may be about today, but they are enriched by recollections of a shared past. Where there is a residue of misunderstanding, we may have an urge to reconcile and reclaim the love we once knew. How successful we are at making connections depends to a large extent on seeds of intimacy sown a long time ago.

We can help make it possible for our children to be friends by offering them access without intrusion. Unlike Stewart, we can try to understand and sympathize with their feelings. We can make ourselves available so that there is less need for them to compete for our attention.

Sibling competition may be as much a function of access to caring adults as of the inherent rivalry of children. If your family is, like the Simpsons, almost a single-parent family, then competition for attention is needlessly intensified.

Sharon's mistake was the opposite of Stewart's. Like a lot of people, she confused intimacy with affection and harmony. As long as the myth of normal family life as placid and cheerful holds sway over the imagination, parents fret needlessly about their children's quarrels. Their fighting and bickering may obscure how much they love and need each other. They may fight to keep from getting too close, or to mask their dependency on each other, or to define their separate identities—or just because they get mad. A relationship with no room for angry confrontation is like a dance without touching, gyration without contact.

Fighting is part of intimacy. Real intimacy requires fighting through the inevitable anger that arises when people are close enough to feel genuine warmth and affection. The sanitized vision of brothers and sisters playing together cooperatively—"nicely"— without jealousy and anger, and without working out these feelings between them, is a desiccated version of intimacy. Kinship without conflict is kinship without passion.

If we teach our children to keep the lid on their conflict, to hide the truth of their feelings, we are preparing them for cowardly and constrained adult relationships, lived out within a truncated range of emotion. Blocking your children's quarrels prepares them for a future of conflict-avoidance, and a lasting difficulty sustaining and resolving disagreements.

Brotherhood and sisterhood don't end when one of the children reaches eighteen and leaves home. Sibling relationships continue throughout life, ebbing and flowing, but always there.

There are, however, many strains on this bond. Too often, siblings put their relationship with each other second to all others. Many of us are cut off from our brothers and sisters if our boyfriends and girlfriends, lovers and spouses, don't get along with them. For this reason, brotherhood and sisterhood may recede into the background in our twenties and thirties. When the chips are down, as for example in a family crisis, siblings come together. But how close they come may be limited by a history of third parties coming between them.

As parents, the best contribution we can make to the sibling bond is negative—the absence of interference. Let them work out their own relationship. Don't compel them to "play nice," or even try to make them play together at all. Let them play if they want, and let them fight if they must.

12

LOSS OF
INNOCENCE

*I*t
was Sunday morning, a little before noon. Outside, the day was
pearly white, the soft light from the sky reflected back by the first
snowfall of the season. The clean, dry, granular snow clung to the
branches of the long-needled pines and the stubby fingers of the
spruce. The snowfall that lasted all through the night was over
now, though when the wind stirred the trees, little clumps of
white drifted to the ground, making it seem that the storm wasn't
quite over.

Stewart and Sharon sat in the living room reading *The New York
Times*. From his position on the couch, Stewart could see the
remains of brunch in the dining room.

Stewart was reading the book review section, hoping to find a
new novel that would be fun to read, hoping not to find any
"important" literary biographies, which he'd *have* to read. Sharon
was leafing through the travel section. He glanced over to see
what island in the sun she was daydreaming about.

Sharon tossed the travel section on top of the growing pile of
papers on the floor and walked over to the window. She stood

there looking out at the snow; he was ten feet or so away from her, but he felt the distance. Something he couldn't put his finger on. Neither of them spoke. There is a kind of silence that is almost as loud as a shout. Stewart heard it. It was all around them, thick and hard.

Now, there was nothing to indicate that she didn't forgive him for his affair. But he didn't know. She didn't say. He didn't ask.

What he did know was that he felt a chill every time an incident of infidelity cropped up in a movie or a television program. Did she, sitting next to him, feel the same? She must.

He tried to avoid television shows that might bring back memories of what had happened, but it was impossible. Sex, infidelity, they were everywhere, portrayed in movies, miniseries, cop shows, situation comedies . . . everywhere. To most people, dramatized infidelity was titillating—it must be or they wouldn't show so much of it—the sex more real to most viewers than the pain. He imagined that Sharon felt the same, but he could never be sure. One more thing they didn't share.

The aftermath of his infidelity was like a divorce; they divided the spoils. Sharon got the hurt, the anger, the humiliation, the betrayal, and the self-doubt. She consoled herself with her innocence, but worried about the future. Stewart got the guilt, the shame, the sense that he could no longer hold his head up as someone who was at least honest, faithful—and he got the memories of the most thrilling sex he'd ever known.

And what about their relationship? They stayed together, but it seemed that there was a permanent wall between them. Before, they didn't always talk much, but they could. Now, it seemed they couldn't. Sharon changed the pattern of her sleeping, so that she went to sleep later than Stewart and stayed in bed until after he was up and dressed. All to avoid him? It wasn't obvious; he couldn't be sure. And if so, why did she stay with him? Was it love or need?

Stewart tried not to think about the affair itself. *Affair*—he hated that word, but he didn't know what else to call it. It was too painful. From time to time he'd think: *If only I could go back to before it happened! If only I knew then what I know now, I could have prevented all this grief.* Then, often as not, his mind betrayed him. *Yes, but what about that incredible sex?* He'd never had it like that before, and he knew he never would again. His obsessive ruminations felt like a shameful version of the old saw: "Is it better to have loved and lost, or never to have loved at all?"

◆

Six months ago Stewart would have said that, for him, being unfaithful was impossible. He couldn't imagine it, and didn't. He was embarrassed when his friends at work made comments about female students. They talked about graduate students, even undergraduates, using crude expressions that made Stewart flinch. This one had "a nice ass," that one had "big tits." Driving back through campus with his regular lunch companions, Stewart was annoyed at all the sexual cracks, which became especially frequent in the springtime, season of renewal, season of halter tops and shorts.

One time, when they stopped on the way back from lunch at Colson's News and Variety Store, Pete and Don opened up a copy of *Penthouse* and said, "Hey Stewart, look at the boobs on this one!" He looked but felt humiliated. How could they do this in public? Maybe they didn't find these big-breasted, slutty-looking women as disturbingly fascinating as he did. When he looked, he did so in secret, full of shame.

It was late spring when the new secretary was hired to replace Margaret, who was retiring at fifty-seven. Her name was Angela. She didn't seem to fit in with the academic atmosphere, its sterile concrete corridors inhabited by students and faculty dressed for adventure by L. L. Bean. It was the early seventies, feminism's agressive age, and most of the women downplayed their femininity. Mostly they wore trousers and sweaters in subdued colors. There was nothing subdued about Angela. She wore her blond, corn-silk hair straight and long, and she dressed very carefully, a little more showy than most women, but Stewart liked that.

She wasn't exactly pretty—her nose was crooked and she was tall enough to be self-conscious about it—but she had a good figure. Although she was slim, she had prominent breasts, and she made no attempt to hide them. Her previous job had been downtown in a law office and she continued to dress stylishly, even though she was now in a very different milieu. She wore slinky dresses in rich colors, and silk blouses with straight skirts, and a little more make-up than anyone else in the office.

Pete and Don made the expected cracks about the new

secretary—"I wonder how *she* got the job"—but Stewart sensed that Angela was too flashy for them. Not for him. He couldn't keep his eyes off her.

For all the attraction Stewart felt for the new secretary, he kept his distance. Whenever it was necessary to ask her to type an exam or look up a student's folder, he was brief and businesslike. He probably seemed aloof, uninterested. The truth is, he was intimidated by her sexuality. But after she had been there for about a month, all of that changed.

One Monday morning, Stewart noticed that Angela looked depressed. She kept busy at her desk, but everything took her twice as long as usual, and her smile was gone. She was wearing a stylish knit dress but hadn't bothered to put on any make-up, and her nail polish was chipped. Stewart could tell she was unhappy about something, but he was too shy to say anything.

The next day was the same. She looked miserable. Finally, late in the afternoon, Stewart came over to her desk and asked what was wrong. "Nothing," she said, "I just have a touch of the flu." Oh, so that was it.

The following day was Wednesday, the day Stewart had to stay late to teach his graduate seminar, Contemporary American Fiction. He liked this course, because it gave him a chance to read and reread his favorites. Saul Bellow, of course, and Ann Tyler, and Toni Morrison, and his favorite, Philip Roth. He enjoyed explaining why he thought Philip Roth was so much better a writer than the overrated John Updike. He liked the course but hated staying so late. It made the day too long. So, at lunchtime he sat in his office with the door closed, eating tuna fish on rye and escaping with the latest Dick Francis thriller. It was just getting interesting when he heard a knock at the door. Now what?

"Come in," he said, trying to sound polite.

The door opened and in walked Angela. "Do you have a minute?"

"Of course," Stewart said. "Sit down."

Angela's eyes met and held Stewart's for a moment, but then she looked down. Her nearness was exciting. Stewart struggled uneasily with his feelings.

"I hate to bother you, but I don't know who else to talk to. You're so different from the other people around here . . . more serious . . . more sure of yourself. You were so nice to ask about how I was feeling, and . . . well, my boyfriend moved out—and I don't even really understand why. He said something about not wanting to get too serious, but we've been living together for over a year. It's not like I asked him to marry me or anything. . . . I just feel awful." At that she started crying softly.

"Gee, that's lousy," Stewart said. Suddenly, he was no longer intimidated by her. Instead of a sexy woman, Angela now seemed like an unhappy girl. He felt on more familiar ground.

Stewart listened sympathetically as Angela described how she had met her boyfriend; how at first she hadn't wanted to go out with him—he was too unconventional—but had eventually been won over, and then gradually came to feel that they were committed to each other. Now he was gone, and she was alone.

Stewart felt sorry for her, and angry at the man who had dumped her. He guessed the guy must have found another woman and was just not honest enough to say so. Otherwise, why move out? This he kept to himself.

After a few minutes, Angela wiped her eyes and blew her nose. "I don't know why I'm boring you with all this," she said. "I know how busy you are."

"Nonsense! I'm glad you felt you could talk to me. Please, feel free—any time."

"Well, thanks, Dr. Simpson."

" 'Stewart,' please," he urged.

"Okay—Stewart—thanks for listening."

Stewart stood up as Angela rose to leave. He became aware again of how attractive she was, and he was uneasy standing there. She said good-bye and Stewart took inventory of his feelings. Now that she'd broken the ice, he felt more at ease with her. Sure, she was attractive, but she wasn't at all stuck-up. He didn't think he'd be uncomfortable around her anymore.

As it turned out, Stewart and Angela became friends. It began by him inviting her to walk across campus to get a cup of coffee. Once or twice, he invited her out to lunch. Mostly they talked about what was happening with her boyfriend. She made attempts to get back together again, but it didn't work out. Stewart was comfortable playing the same avuncular role he adopted with his students. He liked seeing Angela but he was always a little tense. She was so sexy. Sometimes, while she was talking, he couldn't help dropping his gaze from her eyes to the front of her blouse. He tried to be unobtrusive about it; he was certain she'd be insulted if she noticed.

One Friday afternoon, suffering from a late-summer attack of spring fever, Stewart asked Angela to go out for a drink with him. "Let's go someplace swanky," he said, and so they went downtown to the fancy bar at the Hilton. Stewart was nervous, like a kid playing hooky, but after a couple of gin and tonics he started to loosen up. Angela asked him how he got to be an English professor, and Stewart started talking about how he had always loved books and wanted to be a writer, but how, in college, he felt that he didn't have the talent and so decided to go into teaching. As he talked on, Stewart found himself really opening up. It had been a long time.

Angela seemed really interested and asked all the right questions. Her eyes were tender and admiring. Stewart reveled in the attention. He was astonished to realize that a man of his intellect could depend so much on other people's approval. Sharon couldn't remember what he told her yesterday.

When Angela excused herself to go to the bathroom, Stewart looked around the bar. This was unfamiliar territory. The room was now crowded with elegantly slick young men and women, aggressively pursuing the serious business of being friendly. They looked like predators and prey, circling. The singles scene. Stewart began to feel uneasy. He didn't belong here. Then he noticed the time and realized he was late. His heart was thumping when he called Sharon to say that he had gotten held up and would be home in forty-five minutes.

"Stewart . . . is anything wrong?"

Could she hear his heart beating? "No, nothing. What makes you ask?"

"I don't know, you sound kind of funny."

"It's been a long week. I guess I'm tired, that's all."

"Well, you come on home and I'll fix you a drink, and then we'll have a nice supper."

Stewart drove Angela back to where her car was parked on campus and then went home. Inside the house he felt relieved. Safe. Secure.

———◆———

After that, Stewart avoided Angela. He didn't trust his feelings. Oh, he said hello, and was perfectly friendly, but he didn't think he should be going out to lunch or having a drink with her. Instead, he put his energy into finishing his book on F. Scott Fitzgerald. He'd written the first half with such enthusiasm, then got bogged down. Now, he got back to it and found he had a lot of things to say.

About a month later, on a Tuesday afternoon, the department had a wine and cheese party for one of Don's students who had successfully defended her dissertation. Stewart hated these things. The faculty stood around like priests at a church social, while the students clustered around like worshipful parishioners, eager for an audience, eager to break down the usual barriers—and, who knows, perhaps to receive a blessing. Stewart went late and left early. Two glasses of wine and a couple of brief conversations, then back to his office to work on his book.

Angela intercepted him on the way out. "You're not leaving already?" she asked breathily. "Yes, I'm afraid so. I've got a lot to do." "Too bad," she cooed, "I'll miss you." Now, what did she mean by that?

Later, absorbed in his writing, Stewart didn't realize how late it had grown. It was 6:45 and everyone had gone home. He was just finishing up when there was a knock at the door. Before he could answer, in walked Angela, and with her the heady aroma of wine and sweet-scented perfume. She was wearing a yellow silk blouse and a black leather skirt. She seemed edgy. Stewart's heart quickened and his breathing grew labored. Between the two of them there arose a sudden agitation, a breathlessness that was almost painful.

"Dr. Simpson—Stewart—I want to go to bed with you."

Stewart couldn't breathe. Shocked, unable to think, he answered on instinct. "Oh, Angela, that's very flattering, but I'm married . . . happily married."

"I don't care. I still want you. *Please.*"

"No, I can't. Really, I can't."

Angela just stood there, only now she was sobbing. Stewart's mind raced. She seemed so unhappy. Why on earth had she developed a crush on *him*? He wanted to comfort her; he wanted to hold her. Gingerly, he put his arm around her shoulder. "Don't cry, *please.*"

She moved into his arms and pushed hard against him. Stewart was beyond logic. All he could think of was how badly he wanted to touch her. He slid his hand from her shoulder down to the front of her blouse. Trembling, he began to stroke and cup and caress her lovely soft breasts through the yellow silk. She wasn't wearing a bra. Angela gasped with pleasure as he traced a fingertip across the hardening peaks outlined against the fabric of her blouse. Stewart slipped his hand inside and slid it over the satiny skin of her breasts. Oh, God, he was hot! Angela reached down and fumbled with the buttons, opening her blouse for him, but not bothering to take it off.

Stewart lowered his mouth to her breasts, now hard and taut, and flicked his tongue over the hot skin of her nipples, making her tremble with desire. She closed her eyes and whimpered with pleasure. With his free hand, Stewart reached down between her legs, gently stroking the inside of her soft, warm inner thighs. Slowly, he glided his hand up to her panties, and without bothering to push them aside, he slid his finger back and forth across the moist, soft material. Angela reached down and hiked up her skirt and spread her legs.

Stewart felt like a teenager, hot enough to melt. Still, he knew he should stop, so he pulled away. "We have to stop this," he said. "This is crazy."

Angela stood there, her blouse wide open but still hanging on her shoulders. Her eyes were lidded, her mouth was open, and her lips were wet. She was breathing heavily, full of desire, full of confidence in her sexual power. Stewart was shaking, uncontrollably aroused. He couldn't keep away from her. He reached under her skirt and slid both hands around behind her. Grasping and clutching her buttocks, he pulled her toward him. She moaned softly as he ground himself against her.

Stewart couldn't stop, but he couldn't go on. He didn't know what to do. Angela decided for him. She unzipped his pants and pulled out his penis. "God, it's beautiful," she said. Stewart couldn't believe it! Sharon never looked at him, refused to touch him. Now, here was this exciting woman, standing here with her breasts lewdly exposed, stroking his penis with her long, cool fingers, sending electric thrills all the way through him. She bent down and Stewart felt the warm, surging moistness of her mouth.

Stewart thought he would go crazy. Her mouth felt so wet and warm and soft. Her hot kisses were an unbelievable pleasure. His breath was coming faster and faster. He started to pull back, and she reached down and stroked him with both hands while he shook with a series of tremendous spasms.

When it was over, Angela smoothed her skirt down and buttoned her blouse. "I'd better go," she said. "Okay," Stewart replied. Those were the only words they exchanged.

Stewart slept badly that night. His stomach was knotted up so painfully that he had to keep his knees bent. Still his intestines felt like a living thing on fire, writhing and burning. Lying there, trying to sleep, trying not to think, his mind attacked him. *What if I get syphilis or herpes? How would I ever tell Sharon?* He wasn't entirely sure if venereal diseases could be transmitted by mouth. He had to find out.

He got up early, and as soon as he reached his office, he locked the door and called Dr. Weis. On the second ring, he banged down the phone. Better play it safe, he thought. So, he picked the name of an internist out of the Yellow Pages. He told the nurse who answered the phone that he was afraid he might have contracted VD and wanted to arrange for a blood test. They were able to take him that afternoon, and after drawing out what seemed like a lot of very dark red blood into a tube, the nurse told him they'd call tomorrow.

Another sleepless night. The next day, when the call came from the doctor's office, Stewart was immensely relieved. He'd been foolish, he'd been weak—but he'd been lucky, given a second chance. Now all he had to do was make sure there would be no recurrence.

Angela was not at work all that week. She had said something about taking personal leave to go on some interviews for another job downtown, but Stewart wasn't sure. The following Monday Angela was back at work, and Stewart told her that he needed to speak to her. Could he buy her a cup of coffee that afternoon?

When it came time to go for coffee, Stewart was too nervous to sit, so they went for a long walk. Even though they walked very slowly across the open campus, Stewart's heart was speeding and he couldn't catch his breath. He told Angela that he'd made a terrible mistake. He was sorry. It could never happen again. Never. To help her understand that he didn't mean for anything to happen—why he had lost control—he told her he had sexual problems in his marriage. "My wife," he said, "is frigid."

Stewart had never confided in anyone about this before. Not only was it private, it was a lie. In his heart, Stewart thought the real problem was him: He was inadequate. Sharon had been hot enough before marriage, and if her passion had cooled afterwards, it must be his fault. Looking back on this time with Angela, Stewart would feel that this was the worst thing he had done. Rather than admit his own feelings of inadequacy, he had blamed Sharon—betrayed her and then blamed her. Well, he hoped his explanation would make things easier.

Angela didn't say much. She seemed nervous too. She did say she understood, and, anyway, she had decided to try again as a legal secretary. The work was less interesting, but the pay was so much better. She'd be leaving in two weeks.

For the remaining two weeks, Stewart avoided Angela. Then she was gone. So. That was the end of it.

"TO TELL OR NOT TO TELL," THAT IS THE QUESTION

As H. L. Mencken once said, "For every complex question, there is usually a simple answer. And it's usually wrong."

Most people are way ahead of me on this particular complex question. They *know* you should keep your affair to yourself. The vast majority of men and women in Shere Hite's reports on sexuality felt—even aside from being afraid of their partner's reaction—that it is "more civilized, more polite, simply to keep their extra relationships secret and save their spouse's feelings."[1] Others believe, with equal conviction, that you should bring it out into the open. Frank Pittman, one of family therapy's wisest voices, believes that unless affairs are brought out into the open, they remain a secret source of poison to the relationship.[2]

I don't know. What I do know are some of the ramifications of either confessing or remaining silent, and I will mention a few of these consequences.

An unfaithful spouse who decides to end the affair—to choose the marriage and fidelity—may feel that it is dangerous and unnecessary to burden the partner with a confession. Dangerous because the cuckolded spouse may become enraged and demand a divorce; unnecessary because one person's mistake shouldn't be the cause of another's grief.

Men more than women feel the agonizing need to confess. Confession casts the unfaithful husband in the role of a naughty child, and his wife in the complementary role of a parent with the power to forgive. Some men resist the urge for absolution, taking responsibility for what happened, choosing not to dump their anxiety onto their wives—and avoiding the risk of their anger.

Married women are less likely to confess infidelity than their husbands. And with good reason. Wives are better than husbands at forgiving—not forgetting, forgiving. A wife who confesses her affair takes a great risk. Men are extremely threatened by their wives' infidelity. If a man "cheats" on his wife, she is likely to feel that the relationship has been betrayed and jeopardized. Husbands may feel this too, but are also likely to feel that they, themselves, have been betrayed—emasculated. A man may be devastated by his wife's infidelity because he takes it as proof of one of the greatest male fears—sexual inadequacy. This is why the cuckold has traditionally been an object of scorn. Men often react violently to the discovery of their wives' affairs, as though someone had stolen their property. And, as women fear, their husbands may not want the stolen property back.

Choosing to remain silent is choosing to handle the problem oneself. It is a vote for silence and suppression.

Confession tests the strength of the relationship. It may produce a crisis that brings the couple closer together, creating an opportunity to close the distance that made the affair possible in the first place. Trying to avoid a crisis, you succeed in perpetuating the distance, reinforcing the wall between you with guilt and anger. A permanent secret may stand as a permanent barrier, fixing a limit to intimacy and closeness—and honesty—in the relationship. It is a lie that makes possible future lies.

Make no mistake, confessing infidelity is almost certain to lead to a firestorm of emotional turbulence. This fiery confrontation may, however, make it possible to forge a stronger bond by discovering and addressing problems in the relationship.

For most people the question of whether or not to confess their affair resolves itself. In the throes of conflict and ambivalence, they manage to get found out. Some of these discoveries may be completely accidental (it *is* hard to commit the perfect crime), but it is often hard to imagine how the careless guilty party could be *so* careless, unless he or she somehow couldn't bear the burden of guilty secretiveness. I've heard some remarkable examples of blundering self-revelation from some otherwise very careful people.

There are, of course, the phones hung up when the wrong spouse answers. I knew one couple, a married man and single woman (more trusting than realistic), who saw each other on the sly once or twice a week. When they couldn't meet, she—at his request—dialed his house and let the phone ring once, to let him know she was thinking of him. This went on four or five times a week, for years!

Husbands leave love letters in pockets of clothes they give their wives to take to the cleaners. Absent-minded? How often do wives find twenty-dollar bills in their husbands' pockets?

Some enterprising souls even leave love letters on top of their bureaus. I suppose that way there's less chance that the writing will come out in the wash.

Once caught, some people have amazing excuses. My favorite was that of a businessman who was staying over at a friend's house out of town. He was in the bathroom when—before he had a chance to defend himself, poor fellow—a friend of the friend's girlfriend burst in on him, seized his penis, and started committing a sexual act involving oral contact with the male genitals.

———◆———

Stewart wanted to tell Sharon what had happened, but couldn't bring himself to. This was a turning point in the marriage—a chance for Stewart to risk more honesty, to face the music, and perhaps, to put the relationship on a more intimate footing.

He felt as he had when he was a boy standing on a cliff over the lake. His friends were standing beside him. They jumped. He was terrified, equally afraid of diving in or turning around in shame to walk back. He stood, poised to jump, wanting more than anything to prove himself, but he couldn't. He was too scared. Now, Stewart the man could no more risk the disclosure standing between him and greater intimacy than Stewart the boy could take that dizzying leap into space to prove his courage.

As the weeks passed, Stewart's anxiety slowly diminished. He still felt guilty, but less so. Yes, he was ashamed of what he had done, but how many men in his position would have acted differently? At least he had finally done the right thing. Only he couldn't get the image of what had happened out of his mind.

Stewart was totally unprepared for Angela's call. He had no intention of ever seeing her again, yet when he heard her voice at the other end of the line a shiver ran through him. "I have to see you," she said, "it's important." Of course, he said no. "But I have something to tell you." Stewart's thoughts were in utter turmoil. He wanted to forget about this woman. And yet, something in her tone made him afraid. If she got mad enough, she could tell Sharon and ruin his marriage. So, he agreed to find out what she wanted. She suggested meeting for a drink after work. "No, that's impossible," he said. Instead, he agreed to meet her for lunch downtown. "I'll only have a few minutes, so let's make it McDonald's."

Stewart arrived early. He ordered some food and sat down to wait at a booth in the corner.

Angela arrived right on time. She must be making more money, he thought. She was wearing an expensive-looking wool suit, dark brown, with a red satin blouse. She looked good.

Stewart took a sip of his chocolate shake but he was too nervous to eat. Her eyes caught and held his; her smile was warm and eager. He waited for her to say something. She waited for him to ask.

"What was it you had to tell me?"

Her voice was shaky. "I want to see you again. I think I'm in love with you."

"That's impossible! You don't even know me."

She was hurt. "Don't say that! I *do* know you and I think you're a wonderful man. I don't care if you're married, I want to see you again." As she spoke, her voice got a little loud, greatly adding to Stewart's embarrassment.

Stewart's ears were ringing. He was visibly shaking. "Is there someplace more private we can go to talk?"

They went to Angela's apartment. Vaguely, Stewart knew they were going to do more than talk. But his thoughts were far from clear. Maybe they could just fool around a little.

This time was like before, only this time there was no stopping.

When they had finished, Angela excused herself to go to the bathroom. She returned a couple of minutes later wearing nothing but a pair of silky red panties. By now Stewart was ready to leave.

"Can I get you something to drink?" Angela asked.

Stewart's mouth and throat were dry and so he agreed to have a Pepsi before he left. As he was finishing the soda, Angela slid up next to him. She leaned over and blew her warm, moist breath into his ear, then she snaked her tongue around in that same quiet, private place. "Is there anything special you like?" she whispered. "I'll do anything you want."

Stewart couldn't believe it. No one had ever said anything

remotely that exciting to him. His mind went immediately to a scene from a pornographic movie. In it a beautiful woman had made love to a man. He didn't have to do anything, just sit back and enjoy it. First the woman did a kind of striptease. She unbuttoned her blouse, very slowly, and then let it slide to the floor. Underneath she was wearing a lacy black bra, which she opened at the front but left on. She didn't bother to take off her skirt, just pulled it up slowly, sliding it past the tops of her dark stockings, and then slowly inching it up to reveal black satiny panties—not the bikini kind but fuller ones, "tap pants" they were called.

Stewart had never seen anything so erotic. He didn't say so, though. He said only, "I like to watch you undress." Even that, he thought, was too much. That meant there would be another time.

There *was* another time, and another. He felt no tenderness for Angela. It was pure desire. She was of no real importance to him. Just a human being with blood and brains and emotions. But Stewart didn't think about any of that. If he had, he might not have allowed himself to feel such intense desire. He tried to bring that same desire, teased out of hiding by his unrestrained passion with Angela, back home into his own bedroom. But Sharon was put off. "Why do you always have to grab my breasts? What makes you think I feel like making love after spending the whole day working and the whole night picking up after you and the kids?"

Stewart was hurt, and angry. *The hell with her,* he thought. *If she doesn't want me, I know who does.* So, he plotted his further infidelity with the self-righteous air of an injured party.

Stewart's anger at Sharon gave him an excuse to put off ending the affair for a few more weeks, but he knew he had to stop. This time when he told Angela it was over, he was more definite. There was no doubt in his mind, and he made that fact very clear to her. She became unreasonable, told him she loved him, and then, weeping, told him he was a bastard. Stewart was firm. It was over.

That night the phone rang at eleven o'clock. Sharon picked it up but heard only a click. Stewart was panicky, but the phone didn't ring again, and that was the last he ever saw of Angela. (A month later he overheard one of the secretaries mention that Angela had moved back to the Midwest.)

The following night Stewart and Sharon were sitting in the

living room watching *Annie Hall* on television. He'd been a fool to
disturb the simplicity and good sense of familiar routine. He had
run a terrible risk, but now domesticity triumphed. Custom
crooned its soothing rhythm, and Stewart felt safe, secure. Diane
Keaton telephoned Woody Allen to come over and catch a spider
in her bathroom. She was terrified of spiders, and her call gave
Allen the chance to be her protector. Then a commercial came on,
and Sharon asked him, "Are you having an affair?"

Stewart froze. He couldn't say yes, but he couldn't say no. Just
an instant of hesitation, and that was that. Sharon became
hysterical, weeping and wailing and cursing him all at the same
time.

ALL HELL BREAKS LOOSE

We have seen how terrified Stewart was of confrontation. For
him the first few minutes following Sharon's accusation were a
time of unspeakable anxiety. He tried to lie, but it was hopeless,
futile. And so he unburdened himself. It was the wrenching
confession of a heart laid bare. He told Sharon everything, or
nearly everything. Never had he been so afraid, never had he felt
so craven. His worst fear was that Sharon would leave him. She'd
throw him out, and there he'd be: alone, homeless. He would lose
her and his children. How little he knew her.

There comes a point in moments of crisis when you know
you're going to make it. The car is skidding at high speed on an icy
road, but you narrowly miss crashing and drift toward the safety
of a soft embankment. You're caught in a small boat in a storm,
and you *know* in your bones that you are about to capsize. But then
the storm begins to subside, and you realize that you will not
drown. Stewart told Sharon what happened, assured her that it
was over, burst into tears, and pleaded for forgiveness.

Sharon was devastated, furious. She lashed out at him like a
wounded animal, shrieking, screaming, demanding to know what
happened, how it happened, why it happened. If she did not
bend, the marriage would break. When Stewart could no longer
bear his torment, he asked her if she wanted a divorce. "No," she
said. "I don't want a divorce." At that moment, Stewart knew he
would not drown.

Over the next few days, the storm gradually subsided. Sharon
and Stewart lived every moment with the knowledge that some-

thing dreadful had happened to their marriage, but they knew the marriage was going to survive. And although neither one of them would have said so, there were moments when it felt that the something dreadful had happened to both of them—that they were in this crisis together, and that they were surviving it together. Stewart needed very badly to feel this way. Looking back, he knew he was in the wrong, and so now he had that bitterness as well to swallow. Still, somehow he felt relieved, better than he had for months. He still had his marriage, his home, his security.

Sharon tried to put away her feeling that Stewart had done this to her, and she did—for a few days at a time. Then all the hurt and bitterness would storm up inside her, until she felt she was drowning in her own private anguish.

There was at these moments no love. Her heart was tormented with grief and anger—ugly, awful emotions that crowded out hope and happiness.

So, how does the certainty that your husband was sleeping with another woman feel? Not wretched, worse than that. Sharon knew what Stewart had done, but she couldn't get her mind around it. She could no more let the image of him naked with another woman into her mind than she could have eaten a decaying rotten fish. It was sickening. Eventually, when she could no longer contain her feelings, she would lash out again at Stewart.

◆

Extramarital affairs are epidemic in our society. Sex researchers estimate that between 50 and 60 percent of American husbands and 45 to 55 percent of wives become extramaritally involved by the age of forty.[3] When you consider that in many couples only one spouse is unfaithful, this means that the number of families affected may be three out of four. Despite the high incidence of infidelity, few people think it will happen to them. Somehow, we cling to the illusion of safety. The discovery that your spouse has been unfaithful usually comes as a shock—totally unexpected and often devastating.

The aftermath of an affair is one of the most wrenching and painful turning points in marriage. The whole family is rocked and its structure is undermined by the shock of betrayal.

What can you do until the immediate crisis passes? Hang on. Once the secret is out, expect all hell to break loose—inside you and between you. But know this: Infidelity is a common problem, and one that can be resolved gradually. Those involved—the guilty, defensive adulterer and the wronged, angry victim—may be so nearly overwhelmed with intense and painful feeling that they entertain a variety of desperate courses of action. It is not uncommon to imagine murder, or self-murder, or running away.

There is no need for immediate action. Wait until you calm down.

◆

At this most difficult of times, Stewart and Sharon could have used a therapist, not merely to bear up under their upheaval, but to turn it to creative advantage. The emotional turmoil that is so hard to bear also has a positive potential. It shakes up the system, unfreezing old patterns, making it possible to create new ones. A marriage jolted by an affair can be put back together again; the distance that made the affair possible in the first place can be closed. But two very difficult things must be accomplished: The couple must be able to talk about their feelings, and they must be able to negotiate changes in the relationship.

Stewart tried to listen to what Sharon was feeling, but it was too much for him. Together they survived, but they made all the usual mistakes. Sharon had trouble bearing her hurt, and so she showed Stewart only her anger. Too much anger and denunciation feels like excessive punishment, and may set the stage for future affairs. Even if it doesn't, it drives a wedge between the partners.

Sharon tried to tell Stewart how awful she felt. He tried to listen. His eyes with tragic intensity would meet hers for a second, but she always went too far. He would turn abruptly, slam his private door on her, and walk away, feeling like a whipped dog. Instead of hearing her, instead of sensing the hurt behind her attacks, he felt only the peevish shame of the persecuted. And so he never even considered taking the next important step, which would have been talking about the dissatisfactions that led to his infidelity and then asking for some changes in the relationship. He hardly even thought about it.

Empathy, at this painful time, works wonders. But Stewart and Sharon couldn't imagine how the other one felt. Their own private suffering was too awful and too absorbing. There was no room in their hearts for understanding.

"WHY, WHY, WHY?"

One of the most unproductive questions people ask about affairs is, "Why?" Betrayed spouses often ask endless questions— What happened? When? Where? How often? and Why, why, why?—tenaciously pressing for details, hoping to undo the feeling of vulnerability to the unknown and unpredictable. This is a game without end; don't play it. Once the secret is out, the unfaithful spouse should be fairly candid about what happened. More lying, at this point, is intolerable. The betrayed spouse, on the other hand, is ill-advised to ask for a blow-by-blow account of all that happened. The real motive for these questions is to find a way to still the unbearable doubt and confusion. It's better to talk about these fears directly than to try to put them to rest by asking for endless details. Relentless inquiry about the particulars makes the unfaithful spouse feel like a criminal undergoing the third-degree, and is likely to provoke some half-truths and some outright lies. Let there be an end to lies.

It isn't details that are needed at this point, but finding a way to address two kinds of hurt. The first hurt is a loss, like a death— the death of innocence, the loss of trust. Dealing with this loss is like dealing with any other. The healthy course is to feel the feelings—the pain and the anger—and then to go through a period of mourning.

The innocent, injured party will not be able to put aside her or his feelings of hurt and betrayal. Repression doesn't work. If you are the betrayed spouse, you will need to remember and feel all the bad feelings. Expect that, count on it. However, you should be aware that your partner—the guilty party—will only be able to listen to so much of this. It's hard to listen, because your partner feels guilty. Every time you bring it up, he or she feels attacked.

When the ugly images come up, face them; when the awful feelings arise, feel them, and find someone to talk to about what you're going through. The guilty spouse (the one who did something that he or she is ashamed of), however, has a limited capacity to hear these feelings without becoming defensive.

A common mistake is confusing guilt with shame. Guilt is the painful awareness of damaging someone you love, and regretting it because of the risk of losing that person's love. Shame is a deeper, often more painful, feeling that results from damaging one's own self-image. The reason most unfaithful spouses cannot tolerate much criticism is that they feel more shame than guilt.

If you tell a friend or a therapist that you feel terrible about what happened, that person can listen sympathetically. If you tell the person who feels responsible, that person may tell you: "It's time to put this behind us," "Why do you keep dwelling on this?" "I'm not the only one," and so on. Don't overestimate your spouse's ability to listen to your hurt and angry feelings, *but* don't try to submerge them.

The second kind of hurt is wounded pride and damaged self-esteem. *What's wrong with me?*

A few people don't ask this painful question; it hurts too much even to allow it into consciousness. And so some people keep their self-doubt buried beneath a smoke screen of angry blaming. But for most married people whose spouses have an affair this is the hardest part of all—feeling rejected, feeling that there must be a reason for it, and feeling that the reason is their own inadequacy. Look inside yourself for this feeling. If you find it, face the feeling, but try to put it into perspective. At a deep level, all of us feel profoundly insecure and inadequate, so don't expect the feeling to disappear or try to talk yourself out of it. On the other hand, is a spouse's infidelity really a confirmation that something is wrong with you? Who elected that person The Great Arbiter of Human Worth? If you lined up in a row all the people who really know you well, would they say you are worthless? If they knew about the affair, would they say it must have been your fault? I don't think so.

———◆———

Then there is a different kind of Why, not the obsessive search for reassurance, but a sober exploration of the reasons for the affair.

If there is an extramarital affair, there must be something wrong with the marriage. Everybody knows that. If one partner sought solace in sex outside the relationship, there must have been problems in the relationship—not enough sex, too much bitterness, or just plain monotony. The trouble with this analysis is that all marriages have problems. Blaming the marriage for the affair is like blaming nationalism for war.

As a family therapist, more interested in the future than the past, I find it less useful to worry about the individual's motivation for an affair than to look at the relationship for the reasons it was not prevented and the potential for a possible recurrence.

What a person does is up to him or her. Often the adulterer—such a harsh and powerful word—is the weaker spouse, the one who is unhappy but not honest enough or strong enough to say or do anything about it. Many affairs are mutinous rebellions against a spouse who is perceived as a controlling and depriving parent.

The likelihood of an affair is a product of three things: opportunity, the strength of desire, and the power of defenses. The magnitude of unsatisfied desire is related to the fulfillment found in the marriage, and also to the fulfillment found, or not found, in other outlets for energy and satisfaction. Although there are people who pursue sex outside of marriage because their personal standards permit it, I think more of these people are found in popular fiction than in real life. Far more common than the willful and calculated adulterer is the person who is unprepared to defend against a temptation that he never really thought about.

Affairs come in endless—well, great—variety, from single one-night stands to a chronic pattern of philandering, and from purely sexual dalliances (the Zipless Fuck) to passionate romances. But perhaps the most common of these is the unpremeditated and brief affair, the sort that Stewart had.

There are many motives for infidelity: anger, frustration, rebellion, boredom, jealousy, revenge, curiosity, need for acceptance, and of course, unsatisfied sexual desire. We look for two sets of needs to be gratified by our spouses: sexual and emotional. Over the years, there is much disappointment. Love—the soul-searing, dizzying kind—can last forever if, like Romeo and Juliet, the lovers die at the height of passion. In real life, romantic love fades. Some people don't like that; some can't accept it. And don't underestimate the role of sexual problems—not only the missing satisfaction but also the feelings of being undesirable or inadequate.

Marital sex is dulled by familiarity and complicated by bad memories. Among men, sex is often the conscious motive for infidelity; the wish for emotional closeness and the need for affirmation are equally powerful, but less likely to be conscious. For women the reverse is true. The relationship comes first, sex follows.

Men and women today are exposed to much more talk about open sex, and we are titillated by explicit eroticism on television and movie screens. These images may fuel our fantasies and heighten our dissatisfaction with our own sex lives. But most of us distance ourselves from this sex—we may not turn away our eyes, but overexposure numbs our shock and makes us underestimate the risk of our own potential involvement. We want to be loved exclusively, and most of us don't plan affairs. They just happen.

At the time he met Angela, Stewart was a prime, and unsuspecting, candidate for an affair. He and Sharon had drifted further and further apart. He was frustrated and angry about the lack of sex in the marriage. His own sense of inadequacy and frustration were compounded by anxieties and self-doubts about his career—anxieties and self-doubts that festered within him. Finally, although like Jimmy Carter he had lusted after women in his heart, he never really imagined acting on his fantasies *and*, even more important, never imagined having to say no to a woman who made the first move.

Stewart's affair was his affair. "Eve Tempted Him?" Sure, and he was tempted, not only by sex, but also by the need to shore up a faltering self-image. The nature of the marital relationship may be more important in determining whether or not the affair continues and what happens afterward. Initiated by sexual desire—which, once ignited, became a fire out of control—Stewart's affair was fueled briefly by hostility toward Sharon. Most affairs that last are sustained as much by this hostility as anything else.

In *Women and Love*, Shere Hite points to a similar motive as the prime reason married women have affairs. Most married women, according to Hite, are emotionally alienated from husbands who are unable to give women what they most desire, intimate connection. It is this emotional hunger that drives married women into the arms of other men. "The basic cause of women's search for love and enjoyment outside of marriage has to do with women's emotionally alienated state within marriage."[4] This is common wisdom. It blames the relationship—and blames the other partner for that. It is linear (A causes B) and one-sided (*he* causes *her* loneliness and longing). Bad marriages cause infidelity. What about the other way around?

Hite concludes: "Having an affair can put new love and humanity into one's world, enabling one to go on living."[5] In other words, the affair "props up an inadequate marriage"—as though the marriage were a thing that existed outside the control of the person who is unhappy. This is a remarkably pessimistic and passive view of the possibilities of marriage.

I have treated several married women who had sustained extramarital affairs, and all of them expressed similar motives. They felt stifled and stagnant in their marriages. The affairs made them feel more alive and appreciated. This is precisely the motivation Shere Hite is talking about. She claims that women in our culture don't get their needs met in marriage, and that it is therefore understandable for women to have affairs. That may be, but in the cases I treated there was some confusion about where the problem lay.

Where is the problem: in the relationship, or in the person? All of the unfaithfully married women I have treated began their affairs in their thirties or early forties. All were unhappy with their lives. They had been in a rut and were in the process of finding themselves. Some discovered, or rediscovered, dormant artistic talents, others found new life through athletics and sport. It was at this time in their lives, this time of emerging from a cocoon of self-denial and drudgery, that each of these women met her lover. The men were art teachers, writing instructors, karate teachers, and others involved in some newly discovered activity. And like most partners in extramarital sex, they were opposite sorts of people to the spouses—not better, different. The lover was part of the process of renewal, but was the affair cause or effect?

I think these affairs are partly the result of a personal reawakening, and that the same energy might be applied to revitalize a stagnant marriage.

It is said that an affair can revive an empty marriage, reawakening one partner's sexual desire and creating a crisis that brings up dormant conflict. Sounds good, but it is equally likely for an affair to keep a bad marriage going or destroy a good one. Affairs are still the most widely accepted justification for divorce.

The stories in Shere Hite's book of married women's unhappy lives are remarkable—remarkable for the recurring theme of loneliness and emotional distance, but remarkable, too, for the lack of appreciation that marriage is a relationship between two people and that both partners might have a role in the problem. And remarkable as well when unfaithful wives compare their feelings toward their lovers with their feelings toward their husbands. A woman in love is like a man in love, temporarily insane. It's crazy to compare a lover to a spouse. One woman in Hite's study remarked upon how nice it was that her lover didn't care whether or not the ironing got done. So? Most of us felt the same kind of passionate love toward our spouses before we got married. If you must compare, compare that.

MOVING ON

The causes of extramarital affairs are complex and varied, enough to provide ample opportunity for anyone (author or participant) to emphasize a pet theory of what purpose they serve—a means of assuaging a sense of insecurity, a way to strike out at the spouse for years of no sex or months of no conversation. Discussing the whys and wherefores of infidelity is further complicated by the fact that infidelity takes so many different forms— open or secret, one-night stands or a consistent pattern of casual affairs, or continuing romances. There are compulsively promiscuous philanderers, partners in open marriage, homosexual liaisons in heterosexual marriages, and relative innocents (free of experience, not free of responsibility) like Stewart. I have emphasized the example of Stewart's brief, unpremeditated, and secret affair not because it is the only kind, but because if may be the most common.

As I have already said, affairs are a product of drives and defenses in the individual, and of the balance of forces in the marriage. An individual may be trying to shore up flagging self-esteem, desperate for sex, compensating for career setbacks, looking for love, or tired of looking after everyone else. As a family therapist, my approach to helping couples move on is to ask: "Why couldn't these dissatisfactions be contained and dealt with in the family?" The point is not that we lose personal responsibility and initiative just because we are members of a family, but that strengthening the family is often the best way to enrich the lives of its members.

Once it's over, it is productive to consider the affair a symptom of missing satisfaction in the relationship, and then to find ways for both spouses to work together to achieve greater satisfaction.

From a family systems perspective, an extramarital affair is related, as cause and effect, to an overly restrictive, rigid boundary between the spouses: the rigid boundary makes the affair more likely, and more possible; the affair makes the boundary more rigid; and the rigidity of the boundary affects the outcome of the affair.

Married and in love, the couple begins family life very close.

$$H : W$$

In time, however, tension and conflict enter the relationship. Even the best relationship.

$$H \approx\approx\approx W$$

Despite their efforts to resolve these tensions, most couples begin move further apart, strengthening the boundary between them as a way of avoiding the pain of conflict.
Perhaps both move apart. Or they may establish a distancer-pursuer pattern.

$$\leftarrow H \mid W \rightarrow \qquad\qquad \leftarrow H \mid\leftarrow W$$

Over the years, the rigidity of this boundary makes it more likely that competing relationships will become more intense. If the couple has children, the boundary between one or both parents and the children will be diffuse, and the boundary between one or both spouses and outside interests will also be diffuse.

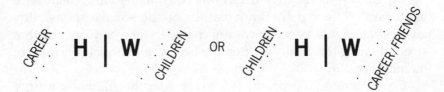

Among these "outside interests" are extramarital affairs.

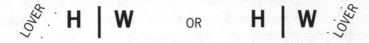

From this perspective, the immediate goal is to redraw the boundary around the couple, and then move them closer together.

The first priority is damage control; keep the marriage afloat by ending the affair. If the unfaithful spouse promises to end the affair but does not, the marriage may turn into a game of "Who is lying and who is crazy?" The hardest thing to forgive is an unfaithful spouse who promises to end the affair but then is discovered to have been lying, again. The betrayed spouse feels doubly violated. If the spouse having the affair is openly unwilling to end it, it may be wise to separate. Often the spell of an affair is broken during a separation. Unfortunately, by then it may be too late for the marriage.

Are separations sometimes a good idea? Maybe. In my practice, I usually refuse to treat a couple if there is an ongoing affair or a separation. My position is that I cannot help the couple work on a marriage where there is insufficient commitment to the relationship, or too much emotional energy concentrated elsewhere.

Drawing a boundary around the relationship involves strengthening the couple's commitment. "Commitment" is one of those much-used words that have taken on the status of clichés. If you're like me, you may start nodding off when someone talks about commitment. Nevertheless, commitment is one of the essential ingredients in a strong marriage. (In fact, it is the single best reason to legalize living together with a marriage ceremony.) Commitment is never more important, and never more difficult, than in the aftermath of an affair. It is the glue that holds the family together when not all of them feel like staying together.

Commitment is another name for the boundary around the

couple that protects the relationship from excessive outside interference and destructive involvements. The same boundary—
commitment—protects the relationship from dissolution during
hard times. With insufficient commitment, there is little pressure
to face each other, and little protection against dissolving the
relationship if (when) hard times come again.

Note well: Moving closer to a spouse you have been avoiding
means surfacing buried and avoided conflict. Couples don't
distance themselves from each other without reason. The reason is
conflict, and it must be addressed or the distance will not be
bridged.

Moving closer—breaking down a rigid boundary—requires
speaking up and listening. You must voice your resentments and
negotiate your unsatisfied needs if you are to feel like moving
closer. And, you must be open and receptive to your spouse's
feelings, complaints, and requests—if you want that person to feel
like being close.

Most people are intuitively aware of the need to address
unsettled old business before they can move on to a more
satisfying and stable relationship. But most people have great
difficulty avoiding the same pitfalls that drove them apart in the
first place—blaming instead of asking for changes, withdrawing in
the face of attack instead of speaking up.

It's a good idea to take turns talking about your feelings. And
the best way to do this is for you to listen first. Wait for another
time—a time when tempers are cool—to speak your piece. Otherwise, these "discussions" turn into contests of cross-
complaining, with each spouse too anxious to press his or her
concerns to hear what the other one is saying.

Communication involves *talking* and *listening*—but it's hard to
do both at once. What passes for communication in many couples
is both parties talking, either taking turns or competing for the
same turn. This kind of spontaneous give-and-take may work
when you are discussing relatively (!) safe subjects, like movies
and restaurants. It is almost impossible with emotionally charged
topics—the gut issues of marriage.

So, take turns, but *take your turn*. Some spouses listen, usually
half-heartedly, without getting—or taking—a turn. If you're
lucky, your spouse will invite you to say what's on your mind; if
not, invite yourself.

Bringing up, talking over, and getting through conflict is the most important step in opening up a rigid boundary between married partners (or anyone else). Believe it or not, human beings are naturally loving, kind, and interesting. We tend to enjoy each other's company unless something gets in the way. However, in some couples, even after the partners have cleared away some of their unresolved conflict, there is little left. Over the years the marriage has petrified—a living thing has turned to stone.

It may, therefore, also be necessary to work at creating a renewed vitality in the relationship. Open yourself to the possibility of being interested in your spouse. The greatest secret to finding interesting people is to be interested. Express your care, and love, and concern—even if you have to work at creating them. Your partner will find your interest as refreshing as a sudden shower on a hot day.

Find ways to spend more time together. This, too, may take some work—the shackles of habit don't just melt under good intentions. Make a list of ten of your favorite activities. Then note when the last time was that you did each of these things. You may be in for a shock.

Compare lists. Scheduling time together to do those things you both like is the easiest place to start. Then consider taking turns joining each other in your individual preferences. Maybe one of you likes outdoor activities, such as camping, canoeing, hiking, picnicking, stargazing, playing outdoor games, bicycling, walking, running, swimming. The other may prefer movies, restaurants, concerts, and dancing. Try to strike a balance between doing things together, just as a couple, and doing things as a whole family. Strong couples balance their time alone with time for the children.

Stewart and Sharon got over the affair. Time passed, life went on. Their marriage survived.

Stewart realized that he had been bitter and angry about the lack of sex in his marriage. And so, when things calmed down, he was more intent on asking Sharon to make love. But instead of trying to make friends with Sharon, Stewart waited for his chance to rush into passionate sex. That was his way, holding himself in until his sexual self-control reached the breaking point, and then making a nervous, pushy assault.

At first, Stewart was on tenterhooks. He watched Sharon very carefully, looking for a sign that it was okay to make a sexual advance. That had always worked in the past. A month went by. Stewart grew more frustrated and more anxious, but since he didn't want to make the wrong move, he didn't make any move. He didn't hug Sharon, or hold her hand, or even kiss her good-bye. Exercising what he thought of as self-restraint, he gave the impression of being cold and uncaring.

Then one night the barrier between them seemed to melt. After dinner with candlelight and wine at Luigi's, Sharon asked him, on the spur of the moment, if he wanted to go to the movies. Surprised, he said sure. Sitting there in the dark, watching a prettier version of life flicker past on the screen, Stewart felt Sharon reach over and take his hand. Suddenly, he was warm all over. After a few more minutes, he moved his hand in hers to Sharon's lap, and she held his hand with both of hers. Later, when they were in bed, Sharon came over to curl up beside him. He was excited, but lay there stiffly, wondering what to do. After a few minutes of holding himself back, he grabbed her roughly and started making love feverishly.

Sharon had been ambivalent, uncertain. She wanted to end the cold war but needed more time before opening herself up to sex again. Stewart misread her signals and pushed through her ambivalence. She complied. What else could she do? To turn him down now would only lead to more hurt and withdrawal, and the wall would come up again. But the result was a repetition of what had happened on their wedding night.

It had been late, very late, and they were both very tired. Nevertheless, Stewart felt they had to consummate the marriage. It was a bad idea. Sharon went along, but it was the beginning of trying to do what she didn't feel like doing, and it was the beginning of the end of her passion for Stewart. It was their wedding night. She did it. It wasn't very good. Compliance had been a mistake then; it was a mistake now.

Sharon felt used, turned off. After that, sex between them dropped off once more, and again Stewart started avoiding her. Guilty and angry, he pulled away, in the bedroom and in the relationship. Soon Sharon was again feeling emotionally deserted, and again she responded by pursuing and attacking. Now Stewart was no longer willing to hang his head and slink off—but he was no better able to listen. He just started fighting back.

The arguments were more frequent now, every few days. Loud shouting matches, touched off by a thousand things. Jason and Heather were older now. They heard everything. They hated it, each in their own way. Jason was angry. Heather was scared.

13

DIVORCE, REMARRIAGE, AND STEPPARENTING

*L*ate one night Heather awoke, hearing her parents arguing. Their voices were loud, ugly, mean. It was scary. Heather tried to shut out theirangry words. She pulled the covers over her head and mashed the pillow around her ears. But even though she couldn't make out what they were saying, she could still hear the noise. It seemed to go on forever.

Finally the door slammed and the shouting stopped. The only sound Heather could hear was her mother crying. *Maybe they'll get a divorce*, Heather thought. So many of her friends' parents were divorced.

Sharon and Stewart Simpson did not divorce. Oh, they thought about it all right, but something held them together.

When we hear that someone we know is getting divorced, sometimes we say, "I'm not surprised." But sometimes our reaction is, "Them?" It's hard to predict who will and who won't divorce. No matter how well you know someone, it's rare that you really know what their marriage is like. One friend of mine never says a word of complaint about his wife. Never. He never talks about his marriage at all. The only thing I know is that they do very little together. How happy they are, or how content, I have no idea.

On the other hand, I know another couple who fight all the time. Going out to dinner with them inevitably means listening to their sniping and carping at each other. It's been that way for over twenty years. I think they're just one of those couples who do most of their fighting in public, where the presence of other people will keep them from really hurting each other. These weary wranglers have survived several crises that would break up many marriages. He had an affair with his secretary that became embarrassingly public. She's had a serious drinking problem. When he lost his job, they had to move to a city neither of them wanted to be in. Still, they stay together.

After all the years that I've treated people with troubled marriages, I've given up predicting who will divorce and who will stay together. It isn't just a question of how bad the marriage is. Some people just stay together, no matter what. It's not really a rational thing—though a lot of people do a lot of thinking about the consequences—nor is it a question of morality. Some people appear predisposed by character to stay married. Or so it seems.

People who stay married often imagine that they've had as many problems as couples who divorce, but they feel that they've tried harder to work them out or that they've managed to put up with more. In their hearts, they believe that people who get divorced are taking the easy way out. Perhaps. Yet many of the divorced people I know divorced only after long and painful struggles to stay married. Many of them—people of courage and determination, believing in family, believing in marriage—tried to hang on to their marriages as long as they could. In some cases this meant fighting and struggling to keep the marriage alive. In other cases it meant blinding themselves to their own unhappiness and to the severity of the problems in the relationship. Many of the divorced people I spoke to were like Ed and Kathleen, who did everything in their power to keep their marriage from breaking apart.

◆

They met at the University of Wisconsin. Ed was a freshman; Kathleen was studying to be a physical therapist. She was a green-eyed girl who'd glanced up from a cup of coffee in the student union to find a ruddy, handsome boy staring right at her. She looked away. But he wasn't shy. He came right over and started talking. That's how it started.

He saw her as buoyant and outgoing. "She was a lot of fun. She looked very Irish—I felt comfortable. And she was a staunch Democrat—that made me feel close. We both had liberal political values, though personally we were very conservative."

Kathleen thought Ed was very smart. "That's always been very important to me. And he was sensitive, more gentle than most of the boys I knew. But he was strong, too. He seemed very sure of himself, and very outgoing. He certainly knew how to have a good time. I guess I liked that because I was so shy. Don't get me wrong. He wasn't cocky or vain . . . more like secure. That's the word, secure."

Their courtship was a stormy one, with plenty of fights. According to Ed: "Sometimes we had a great time. But at the big events—parties, dances—we'd have problems. Big fights. If I paid attention to anyone but her, she'd feel rejected and withdraw, and that would spoil everything." At social gatherings Kathleen was uneasy. She needed Ed to be close. When he seemed to want to talk to everyone but her, she felt he didn't care.

One time the two of them went off with their friends on a skiing weekend. Kathleen thought Ed was flirting with his roommate's date, so she went to her room and wouldn't come out to join the party by the fire. She felt he wasn't paying enough attention to her. At the time, he thought she was a big baby. "I was just being social." He didn't realize that he was open to other women, but she could see it. They had their worst fight ever. "I should have known then," Ed told me, "that we weren't right for each other."

Many unhappily married people look back to unresolved differences that cropped up when they were dating as warning signs they should have heeded. But other forces—powerful yearnings, conscious and unconscious—kept them going.

Sometimes things were wonderful. Ed recalled a formal dance

at the Palmer House in Chicago. Kathleen was visiting her folks in Green Bay, and a big snowstorm hit. "I thought the weekend was off. But she drove down in her father's pickup truck. All that way! And she looked sensational—voluptuous. She wore a black strapless gown. God, she looked just like Ann-Margret."

It wasn't only passion that propelled these two into marriage. Ed didn't hesitate for a moment when I asked him when he decided to get married. "I always wanted to get married, and have a family. It was never a decision. It was just a matter of time." They both romanticized marriage—candlelight dinners, all that passion. Ed thought once he had her there with him, he wouldn't think about other people. Kathleen thought, *Once we're married it will be just us.*

When Ed was in graduate school they came close to breaking up. Kathleen was working as a physical therapist in Eau Claire, a small town in northern Wisconsin. She loved it—loved the town, loved her work, and loved the feeling that people looked up to her and depended on her. When she visited Ed for a weekend in the fall, they had another of their fights. By now Ed was sick of it. When she left, he thought, *Good riddance.* Neither one of them called or wrote. Then, on Valentine's Day, Kathleen sent Ed a red terry cloth bathrobe with a hood. It opened his heart. In an excess of loneliness for her, Ed drove to Eau Claire, and it all started again.

"We talked about getting married," Kathleen remembered, "but the big question was where to live." That question, however, and all it involved was pushed aside by the need to plan the wedding. It was a big wedding, lots of family. Both of them were happy. And yet, here too, there was a moment.

Ed was upstairs in the hotel with his best man, getting dressed to leave for the honeymoon. Looking out the window, off into the trees in the distance, his eyes unaccountably grew watery. Why he didn't know. He was happy and sad at the same time. His best man said, "Hey, bridegroom, you look like you're gonna cry." They both laughed at the preposterousness of the idea.

When Ed got a job in Milwaukee, Kathleen agreed to go. After all, a physical therapist (or whatever the woman's career is) can find a job anywhere. Kathleen hated Milwaukee and hated her job. She put on weight and was upset and depressed much of the time. Ed was not very sympathetic. Looking back, he said, "I put too many expectations on her. She should always be in a good mood, always look her best, always be socially gracious, and most of all, she should always be concerned about me. I wasn't even conscious of these demands." Still, Kathleen felt them.

In the second month of their marriage, Kathleen became pregnant. When is the best time to have a baby? I don't think there is any formula, but this was probably too soon. Before the couple had a chance to work out their own relationship, they had another adjustment—and another distraction.

Ed fell in love with the baby right away. "Those were the days when they didn't let the fathers in the delivery room. I remember going to the nursery and seeing all of those babies. And then her. She was right up front, with her cute little pink face, all smiles. In front of her was a sign: 'Girl O'Brien.' She was mine."

That year was a good one. What made it good were more distractions. They kept busy, doing something every weekend— trips to Chicago, attending plays at many of the local colleges— and they kept up a very heavy involvement with their families. Kathleen said, "We added excitement and other people to our relationship."

Would Ed and Kathleen have been able to forge a stronger relationship if they had built a stronger boundary around themselves? I don't know, but without it there was less of a chance.

Often after the very worst moments in their marriage, Ed and Kathleen experienced a sudden release from their torment as they forgot themselves in some new venture. The baby, the hectic social life—later on there would be other things. "We had so many distractions, we didn't think about our relationship," said Kathleen. "We just assumed everything was all right." Ed remembered this as a time of feeling fulfilled, happy. Most of his memories, however, were of the baby. "I remember walking her down the street every Saturday morning in the stroller. Everybody admired her. And I'll never forget that morning when I was feeding her and I stuck the spoon in her mouth and heard a little clink. It was a tooth! I was so thrilled."

The next distraction was moving to New Haven, where Ed was going to graduate school. Only it was more of a distraction for him than for Kathleen. Intellectually, he came alive. She felt stuck, stagnant. Ed remembered that she complained a lot. "She said she wanted to do something, maybe take some courses, but she never did anything about it." His achievement made her feel inadequate. And she became jealous of Ed's fellow graduate students, especially the women. According to Ed, she had no reason. Again, there were scenes. Like the time at Maggie's party. Ed said, "Maggie invited me—I mean us—to a party. Everyone was there. But Kathleen felt out of place. They were all my friends, and she felt jealous, hurt."

Kathleen began to resent being treated as "Ed's wife." Ed was in his late twenties, living in the stimulating atmosphere of a great university, surrounded by interesting people. As he put it, "I was in my glory." Kathleen felt more and more left out. The marriage went from bad to worse. Kathleen got depressed and began seeing a psychologist. The psychologist insisted that Ed come too, but he refused. He thought, *I'm happy; she's the one who's miserable. Let her go and get herself straightened out.* This touched off one of their worst fights. Afterwards, Kathleen said she was thinking of moving out.

To his surprise, Ed was terrified. He had taken her more or less for granted and to a considerable extent ignored her while he got on with his career. But losing her was unthinkable. He thought about all the financial problems and what would happen to the baby, and he was convinced that he would never find anyone else to love him. Considering how he had blinded himself to problems in the relationship and how little either of them got out of it, I thought this was an odd reaction. Perhaps the heart of the matter was that, to Ed, the idea of being a whole person was tied to being married and having a family. It wasn't so much Kathleen he was afraid of losing, it was the fact of being married.

He pleaded with her not to go. Unfortunately, he did nothing to resurrect the love he had once felt. At this point the marriage may already have been dead, but it took a long time to bury it.

Since it isn't really stamped in the genes, what are the factors that make some people stick out a difficult marriage? There are, of course, practical considerations: What will happen to the children? and how will the separated spouses support themselves? Cultural influences and religious beliefs also play a part, as does the model of one's parents. As Ed put it, "The idea of divorce was contrary to the way I was raised; it signaled failure."

When their marriage is in trouble, most people turn for comfort to family and friends, or maybe to a therapist. Other people are full of advice—whether they give it directly or in the form of subtle hints—but perhaps more important than the advice is the sense of support the person gets for his or her decision. One man I know, who comes from a very conservative background, sought refuge in his parents' home during the worst of many marital separations. When he told his parents that he couldn't stand it any longer and was thinking about divorce, they did not try to change his mind (as he had expected). Instead, they told him that they loved him and would stand by him whatever he decided. He went to a lawyer the next day.

◆

Because Ed refused to go to therapy with Kathleen, much of the advice she got concerned how to make herself less unhappy, rather than how the two of them could improve their marriage. Few therapists ever take a direct opposition to a marriage, but when one spouse goes alone there is inevitably the danger that his or her dissatisfaction will become magnified. Individual therapists say, "Be yourself. Be honest; find your own satisfaction."

At about the same time she started therapy, Kathleen became receptive to some of the anti-men thinking that was part of the angriest phase of the feminist movement. She went from trying (in vain) to live through Ed, to becoming self-absorbed, bitter, and hostile.

Since Kathleen had raised the threat, Ed had to confront the possibility of divorce in his own mind. When he did so, he had to face his own dissatisfaction. So he turned to the coping mechanism he had always relied upon: self-improvement. He started working out in the gym to improve himself, really to make himself stronger. It's a thing men do.

Then something shifted. Now he wanted out. But he couldn't find a way to tell her. Finally, he told her in an awkward, roundabout sort of way. She cried. She was confused, unsure of what was right. Finally, she conceded maybe he was right. Ed was unaccountably upset. That was not what he wanted to hear. Though he hadn't known it, he was hoping for a declaration of reassurance.

That same week, Kathleen found out she was pregnant with their second child. When she told Ed, it was the first time she'd ever seen him so happy. That discouraged her. She didn't really want another baby, and besides, his reaction made it clear that it wasn't her he cared about, only the baby.

Kathleen had a miscarriage in the third month. The doctor told them there was no way it would have ever gone full-term. "It just wasn't meant to be."

Once again they got sidetracked. Ed finished graduate school, and they started making plans to move to Madison, Wisconsin, where he got a job in the state government. Talk of moving and houses brought them together; this one was one of the few conflict-free areas of their conversation. Some couples can talk about a lot of things—the children, their jobs, friends, politics, whatever. Others quickly get into arguments about any one of these things. The number of subjects that two people can discuss openly is one measure of the strength of their relationship. Kathleen and Ed could talk about houses and furniture.

For a time they were content. But then the same old things began happening. Ed's job consumed him. Night and day. He worked from early until late, and then brought work home with him. Is overinvestment in one's career a cause or an effect of marital problems? Maybe a little of both.

Kathleen became depressed again, only worse this time. Her jealousy increased. She was convinced that Ed was having affairs at work, and he couldn't persuade her otherwise. It got so that he didn't want to come home at night. "When I finally did, I had to put up with Kathleen's bitching and screaming. One night when I came home, I heard my daughter say, 'Uh-oh, Daddy has that mean look on his face.' I was crushed."

Kathleen talked more and more about moving out. She kept complaining about being saddled with a house and a child, and she had trouble finding a job she felt really satisfied in. She blamed the marriage for holding her back. Ed still wanted the marriage. "I still cared about her. I realized that my earlier doubts were self-doubts."

She went to a lawyer, then they went together. "Get yourself an attorney," Kathleen's lawyer told Ed. "I don't want a divorce," was his answer. "I'm sorry, but your wife does," she said. At first they agreed she would leave in order to reestablish herself professionally and to find the freedom to move ahead with her life. But then Kathleen changed her mind. They couldn't resolve it. How could they? Two years went by. Two years of cold war.

Then Ed got a chance to spend a month in Ireland, and he took it. There was no question of Kathleen's going, they were that alienated. Her absence was nice. Now he could think. There is so little thinking in families, normally such a jumble of need and conflict. In Ireland he wandered around. Kilkenny, Tipperary, Galway, the Aran Islands. He saw so much beautiful countryside, and everywhere ancient villages, traces of the past. Ed fell in love with the timelessness of the landscape, and he began to think about his marriage now in a more detached way. He realized he wanted a divorce.

When he came home, he saw a lawyer and sued for divorce. It was going to be ugly. It was an extremely painful time for both of them. Still it dragged on. Months went by before they could get a court date. Kathleen wanted to tell Meagan, now twelve. Ed wanted to put it off as long as possible. "Wait till we know what all the arrangements will be." Finally he agreed to tell her. Meagan knew, of course, about all the tension, but kids don't want to believe their parents will actually split up. He fumbled for words. She sat silently, her back to him. While he told her, she just sat there, fiddling with one of her stuffed animals. He tried to keep from crying. She asked only one question, "When?" Then she said she didn't want to talk any more about it, and went down to watch cartoons on TV. He followed her. "How about if I make us some popcorn?" "Good idea."

Still more months went by before they could get the case on the docket. It was a time of agony. Whenever Kathleen was served with legal documents, she stalled as long as she could. A whole year went by. Finally their lawyers set up a joint meeting with the two of them. "Can't you two work this out?" Kathleen refused to negotiate. She filed countercharges.

The trial *was* ugly. Each of them had to say hateful things—lies, too—as if the truth weren't bad enough. The judge was Catholic and very conservative. He called Meagan into his chambers. "Who do you want to live with?" Is there a more cruel question to ask a child? She said either one, but she wanted to stay in her house. Then the judge called Kathleen and Ed into his chambers. "You two should be ashamed. You have a wonderful daughter. Why couldn't you work out your differences?" It was a stupid and mean thing for him to say, but it was what they were feeling, too.

"After considering all things, I'm going to award you joint custody; but Meagan shall reside in the home with her father."

Ed felt a tremendous rush of relief, like a steel spring unwinding. Kathleen didn't flinch. That night, Meagan stood at the top of the stairs and watched her mother pack. Kathleen took a lot of furniture. After she was gone the house looked bare.

◆

Some people stay in difficult marriages because they are too dependent to strike out on their own, or they are afraid of anger, their own and the spouse's. One woman I spoke to said that she stayed with her husband because she imagined that if she told him she was leaving, he would tear the house apart. Certainly this woman had other, more complicated reasons for staying with him, but it is surprising how many people are conditioned by fear to avoid saying what is on their minds. Some people who put up with what they themselves think of as lousy marriages just seem willing to endure. Often these people compensate for the emptiness and frustration by finding satisfaction outside the marriage— in their careers, children, friends, or even hobbies. In my experience, more people stay with a disappointing marriage because they can put up with it than because they feel they can create a positive change in the relationship. Not that people don't try. Many men and women do their damndest to improve things in their marriages. Unfortunately, though, as we have seen, most people act within a limited range of alternatives.

I could go on trying to explain why some people stay married and others don't, but I don't see the point. When things get bad enough and people think they're prepared to deal with the consequences, they get divorced. When that happens, some people make a lot of mistakes. Divorce is not something that people have much practice at.

◆

As for a lot of couples who make each other's lives miserable and then finally divorce, many of them are still stuck. They have never made the transition from being married to being divorced— separate as man and wife, cooperating as parents. Much of the trouble in many divorces is due to a blurring of the distinction between marital and parental subsystems. "Ex" and "former" refer to the marital relationship, not the parental one. Letting go of the former means getting past anger and giving up secret hope for reunion.

One man I know had been surprised and pleased that his family understood and accepted his divorce. He was equally surprised to discover how his friends deserted him. "No-fault" applies only to the legal process; it is not a concept congenial to most families and friends. Even when family and friends don't make unkind judgments, they often behave cruelly because they are confused. Torn by divided loyalties, they don't know how to react. Many divorced men and women feel bitter about being deserted by their friends.

The problem may not be so much in the friends as in our culture. We still think of divorce as a pathological event. Not everyone fixes blame on one of the mates, yet we all tend to think of divorce as an aberration. "Broken families," "stepfamilies," "estranged spouses," "dismembered families"—these terms suggest that something is wrong, that the family is deformed. Despite all that has been said and done, we still think of the traditional nuclear family as the norm and the ideal.

Divorce is like a death. In both, there is a profound loss, a wrenching upheaval, and a need to remake one's life. But unlike death, divorce carries with it a sense of willful abandonment, personal failure, and humiliation. In death there is not the personal sting of having somehow been inadequate, no narcissistic injury, and no secret rage. There is only loneliness and longing. The death of a mate is a brutal loss, but one that is surgically clean, clear-cut, and final, and one that carries with it no stigma. In divorce, the family is severed by a blunt instrument, and nearly everyone gets bloodied in the process.

Divorce may be *like* a death, but it is not a death. Divorce is not an ending, it is a transition. In divorce, the family must change the nature of its boundaries, establishing a firm separation between husband and wife, but permitting access to both parents—by the children, and by each other.

Families take many forms; the divorced family is one of them. Families do not get broken, ruined, or stepped on, but they do change shapes. Unfortunately, the transition from being together to being divorced is a road without maps. No wonder there is so much pain and confusion.

FAMILIES IN TRANSITION

Let there be no mistake, divorce can be, and usually is, a wrenching, painful process. Unfortunately, the common perception that divorce implies a defect in one or both partners and that divorce means the break-up of the family only makes things worse. Getting divorced does not mean that the partners are frivolous or irresponsible. People who end up getting divorced usually married just like those couples who stay together—soberly and in good faith. Most people are thoughtful and sincere. If they marry unwisely, it is because they fall in love under the predominant influence of unconscious forces. We all do. Sometimes the combination of luck, goodwill, and hard work makes things work out; sometimes not. Perhaps the major reason that a marriage doesn't work out is that irrational forces of attraction impel two people into an alliance that cannot meet their needs.

Perhaps it's no longer necessary to dwell on the point that people who get divorced don't necessarily suffer from individual pathology, or social deviance, or a failure of nerve. There is, however, another myth about divorce that retains its force. Given the increased prevalence of divorce in this country (in recent years, there have been almost as many divorces as marriages), some journalists have begun writing about the "Death of the American Family."

The family is not destroyed with divorce, it is transformed into a new family form—one that may be arrived at after several transitional stages. Please note: I'm saying something more than that divorced parents still need to take care of their children. I'm saying that the family survives and takes on a new form. Even marital attachments don't end with divorce; rather, they change form and intensity.

Divorce can be a creative attempt of family members to develop a new shape. For husbands and wives and children, divorce may be a loss and a liberation. For the family, it is the transformation from an old pattern into a new one. The family system has to maintain some subsystems, shed others, and develop new ones. Boundaries between couples must be strengthened to facilitate the individuation of the divorced spouses, boundaries between both parents and their children must be kept open enough to allow contact, and new relationships will require further complex boundary-making. Many divorces don't work out, or take a hell of a long time doing so, because the family is unsuccessful at letting go of the old structure and establishing a new, functional structure.

It is no longer true that the intact nuclear family is the norm, with all other forms deviations from it. Family life is change. We must all restructure our families at various points of transition. Or to put it in more human terms, the family must grow and change shape as its members grow and change. Divorce is a radical change, but by recognizing that it is a transition that calls for restructuring, we will be better able to explore the creative possibilities of the new forms. New transitional forms are experiments in living.

There is no magic formula that can change the fact that "breaking up is so very, very hard to do." Making divorce work is like any other activity, you have to put in the hours. Courage and goodwill cannot be put into a prescription, but having a description of the process may help. To begin with, it's useful to realize that there are actually two processes in the divorce transition: separation and reorganization.

UNCOUPLING

In the process of a marital separation, almost everyone goes through periods during which they cannot seem to manage. Their feelings are a jumble of griefs. Anger and bewilderment alternate with relief. They may not be able to devote enough time to their children, and they catch themselves yelling at the kids for no particular reason. One person feels guilty, one feels victimized; both feel responsible. Although this process is inevitably disorganizing, it helps to have a conception of going through a transitional process. At times, everyone involved will be confused—unsure of what the other person intends to do, unsure of how to respond, and unsure of where all this is heading. Thinking of separation as a transitional process provides a framework of understanding, like a bobsled run on a snowy hillside. You may slide in and out of it, but at least you can see its outlines there to guide you.

Separation can be divided into three major phases: deciding to separate, physically separating, and restructuring the family to stabilize it during the separation.

The decision to separate often seems to be made primarily by one person. It seems that way and it feels that way, but one person's decision is usually preceded by a long period of heightened ambivalence during which one or both partners withdraw their investment from the relationship. Meanwhile, the other one may make desperate attempts to reinvest the relationship with life—perhaps moving to a new house or having another baby. It can be confusing to figure out who wants what, as the following two examples illustrate.

———◆———

Glenda was a twenty-four-year-old graduate student who quickly outgrew her husband. It was easy to see that they were a poor match. Jack was handsome and had a good heart, but was poorly educated and primarily interested in having a nice house and a family. Glenda was a creative intellectual whose talent and interests soon took her a long way from the lower-middle-class neighborhood where she met Jack. Within two years after they were married, Glenda had grown entirely dissatisfied with her husband, but somehow couldn't do anything about it, directly. Having dinner at Glenda's house meant getting a well-prepared meal but also listening to the hosts squabble. I'm not sure which was worse, Jack's inane conversation or Glenda's cruel, cutting remarks.

At the time, I was sympathetic to Glenda. Jack *was* boring. Glenda was lonely, she felt neglected; as time went on, she acted out her fury toward her husband. She stayed away for two or three nights at a time, she was blatantly insulting to Jack in front of company, and when he complained in private, she laughed at him. After about six months of Glenda's calculated abuse, Jack announced that he wanted a divorce. Friends were surprised. They wondered why Jack wanted a divorce. They weren't surprised to see the couple break up, but they were surprised that it was "Jack's decision."

———◆———

In another case, Mitchell had a midlife crisis at about age thirty-seven. He was unhappy, life was no fun, and he blamed his marriage. When he came to therapy, he asked his wife, Audrey, to make some changes. He wanted to have more fun, get outdoors more often, go sailing, play tennis—enjoy life. What's more, he wanted his wife to do all these things with him. Audrey agreed to spend more time with him and do more of the active things that Mitchell liked. Still, Mitchell wasn't sure he was happy, and he felt that Audrey was not as openly expressive with him as he wanted. (What he wanted her to "openly express" was sexual passion, which she did not feel.) What made Audrey somewhat reserved was that while she was sympathetic to Mitchell's unhappiness, she was annoyed that he put it all on her. However, she did not think this was a good time to express her dissatisfaction with all his demands.

Because things weren't quite right, Mitchell moved out to think things over. To help him think, he went into individual therapy. As a result of his thinking and consulting, Mitchell decided that he wanted to be happy and wanted to keep his wife. He told her this and gave her a list of demands, ways she would have to change to make the marriage work out. During the separation, however, Audrey had discovered her own ambivalence. At first she thought that the separation was her fault: She had failed to keep her husband happy. After a while, though, she realized that wasn't true, and that they had never been terribly happy. Audrey would have liked to preserve and improve the marriage, but she saw Mitchell's demands as putting all the responsibility on her. She did not want a marriage where all the change would be unilateral, so she told her husband, "No, if that's what you want, I want out." A week later, they were separated. Who left who?

———◆———

So far in this chapter I have described three marriages that came apart. I'm not sure that any of them could have been or should have been preserved, but they might have had a better chance if the spouses had taken ownership of their own ambivalence, instead of passing it back and forth like an unholy hot potato. If you are unhappy about your relationship, acknowledge your feelings and voice them. Then maybe you can try to do something about them. If you try to make things better and it doesn't work, it doesn't work—at least you tried. One of the most destructive pressures on marriage is the feeling that it's too fragile to think (think, not daydream) about the possibility of separating and therefore that it isn't safe to make demands.

The actual process of uncoupling usually begins as a private, unilateral decision. One person broods over hurts and mulls over the possibilities of what to do about them. By keeping these dissatisfactions secret, the unhappy partner initiates a breach between the two. Secrecy promotes the unhappy person's ability to explore and assess, but deprives the partner of the chance to understand—and the opportunity to respond. Getting the message across that you are unhappy is important for negotiation, which cannot begin until both partners understand that a problem exists.

Unfortunately, most people who are seriously unhappy with their marriages turn away to other alternatives. They may put additional time and energy into their careers, or they may search out some new interest. It's not just a matter of finding something else to do. This new, or newly invigorated, interest involves the discovery of self-worth and adds missing satisfaction to life. These outside interests can shore up a failing relationship—careerism and hobbies enable many people to endure loveless marriages—or enhance healthy ones. Outside interests are more likely to contribute to separation if the partner is shut out. We shut out our partners not only by excluding them from participation but also by not bringing home our enthusiasm and sharing it in conversation. In time these other activities become more important than the relationship.

At some point, the spouse who is more actively dissatisfied tires of pushing for (or hoping for) change and begins to view the relationship as unsalvageable. He or she wants out. Now the unhappy spouse accentuates the negative, reversing the earlier process of idealization. Instead of seeing only the beloved's virtues, now he or she sees only shortcomings. The spouses move in and out of bad feelings. One person wants more, the other feels bewildered and begins to think, "Nothing I do is good enough; everything I say is wrong." This dissatisfaction is often magnified by seeing other alternatives that look better—other marriages that seem happier, the possibility of having an affair, or the lure of the freedom and excitement of the single life. (The joys of single life are often especially clear to married people.)

What to do? Most unhappily married people go through a prolonged period of trying to decide whether or not to separate. The obstacles that the spouses conjure up entail more than separation anxiety. There are many practical concerns about the consequences and how to manage them.

Most parents think hard about their children's well-being. Should they stay together for the children's sake? Should they postpone divorce until the children are older, or do kids fare better when parents separate, instead of prolonging an unhappy home atmosphere?

In the early 1970s, as the divorce rate was beginning its upward spiral, there was a shift in thinking about the effect of divorce on the children. The conventional wisdom that parents owe it to their kids to stick together at all costs was replaced by a new—and more convenient—cliché: that miserable parents make for miserable children.

It's something most of us have said. Someone comes to us in great distress. The marriage is terrible; they're suffering, but they tell us they cannot get a divorce because of the children. What do we say? Often we say, "Maybe the children would be better off . . . ." Friends, family, therapists want the miserably married person to stop suffering and we wish we could relieve them of their excessive guilt. If we care about someone, we actually feel their pain. So, instead of simply listening with understanding, we often suggest some form of action. When the dilemma is a marital crisis, this well-intentioned advice is a form of triangulation.

Thinking about leaving a marriage is a crisis that raises anxiety, and whenever anxiety is high in a relationship people tend automatically to triangle someone else in. Unhappily married people turn to friends, therapists, and lawyers for advice. Often they seek out people who will tell them what they want to hear. Sometimes one spouse will push the other toward someone who will help ease the separation. I remember once, for example, that a young couple came to see me about a marital problem. When I asked what the problem was, the man said he was in love with someone else and he was leaving. He wasn't kidding; he got up and left! He didn't have a marital problem, he had a separation problem—a problem which he handled by leaving his depressed wife in my hands, so that he could wash his.

When we're in trouble, it's natural to look for help. In fact, when a married person is moving from the decision-making stage to the physical-separation stage, it's a good idea to talk to a lawyer. You should know what your rights are, and you might want to know whether moving out of the house or being seen in public with a boyfriend or girlfriend will adversely affect a divorce settlement. When, therefore, is triangulation a problem, and when is it part of a functional process? It is almost always the case that if sources outside the family intervene in a way that undermines family functioning, it is detrimental to the resolution of family problems.

If you are in the process of deciding whether or not to separate, consulting an individual therapist can create problems, depending partly upon the therapist and partly upon how you use the consultation. If you don't think you can get what you want from your marriage and are thinking of leaving, the wisest thing to do is: First, try to get what you want. This is an interpersonal solution, more likely to be fostered by a family therapist (or marriage counselor) than an individual therapist. Trying hard to create the satisfaction you want in your marriage can lead to two possible outcomes. Either the relationship will improve, in which case you may decide to preserve the marriage, or things won't improve at all, in which case you have more reason to believe your decision to leave is the right one.

Lawyers, too, can be part of the problem instead of part of the solution. In structural terms, there should be a clear boundary between the spouses and their lawyers. (*Yes,* two lawyers.) Don't say, "My lawyer made me do it." Formulate your needs before going to see the lawyer. Define for yourself what you need, what you would like, and what you would be willing to settle for in terms of money and custody. A protracted legal struggle consumes energies that would otherwise be available for new beginnings.

The lawyer should be your advisor and representative, not someone who pushes you where you don't want to go. Avoiding this pitfall begins with selecting the right lawyer. (Lawyers are like members of any other profession—about a third of them are highly competent.) Ask around for the names of experienced matrimonial lawyers. If you happen to know a lawyer (or a marital therapist), ask for a recommendation. Don't just ask for the name of a lawyer, describe the type of person you want to advise you. And unless you're looking for a bloodbath, avoid anyone with a nickname like "The Barracuda."

Although most states now have no-fault divorces, the division of property and awarding of custody are still adversarial processes.

This greatly adds to the stress on the family. If the spouses convert their anxieties into anger—as many do—they will make accommodation twice as difficult. Furthermore, warring spouses frequently miscalculate the impact their actions will have on their spouses. If, for example, a lawyer convinces one party to ask for more than he or she wants, this may only intensify the opposition, leading not to compromise but to a tortuous struggle for parity.

———◆———

Marriage is a process in which two individuals restructure much of their lives into a unit: The Couple. Friends invite The Couple over for dinner, the IRS taxes The Couple, The Couple accumulates belongings, mail comes addressed to The Couple. Separation is a reversal of this process, in which two members of a couple gradually redefine themselves as individuals, disentangling not only their belongings but also their identities.

Separation plunges both partners into an intense state of social and emotional *anomie*—literally, normlessness. New patterns are called for, but until these patterns are established, events rather than individuals are in control. Before the separation, family tasks were more or less routinized. Things may not have been pleasant, but they were predictable. Uncoupling shatters these routines. Thus, the emotional shock of separation is compounded by such hard practical realities as reorganizing finances and arranging for baby-sitting. Even cooking meals can be complicated.

Confusion inside the family is matched by confusion outside. Separated spouses feel rootless, without their old identities and without established roles to guide them. For example, if you are separated, do you go to your office Christmas party alone? If the school requests a conference, do you tell your spouse? If your friends know that you are separated, do they invite one or both—or neither—of you to a dinner party? If they invite one, which one?

When you are separated you need support from family and friends. Unfortunately, they may be confused about how to behave. Old friendships are often based on the couple. I've heard many separated spouses say bitterly, "Now you find out who your real friends are." Well, your real friends may be just as confused as you are. Tell them how you feel and ask them for whatever support you want.

Friends and family represent not only problems but resources. Confusion, blaming, and ambiguity won't disappear, but they can often be reduced by direct dialogue. In-laws are confused. They want to support their own child but may not want to alienate their child by marriage. They certainly don't want to lose contact with their grandchildren. A mother-in-law may wonder who to invite to Thanksgiving dinner. Talk to her. When you do talk to your family and friends, remember to take into account that they may feel divided loyalties. Tell them how you feel and what you want, but understand that they may be torn.

◆

Once the decision to part has been made, physical separation requires a restructuring of the family. When a parent leaves the family, three subsystems are radically altered: the spouse unit, the parental unit, and each parent's relationship with the children. The most functional structure at this time entails building a clear boundary between the spouses while maintaining the parental subsystem as a problem-solving unit.

Suppose we look at what happens to a family when a husband leaves his wife:

H W	H/W
F M	F M
– – – – – – –	– – – – – – –
CHILDREN	CHILDREN

The fact that husband and father (and wife and mother) are the same person make this adjustment easier to diagram than to achieve.

In a good marriage there is a clear boundary between the couple as spouses and the couple as parents. In a failing marriage, however, when the couple unit ceases to meet the needs of both partners, it may decrease in importance or become so emmeshed with the parental subsystem that the boundary between them is quite unclear. When these functions become emmeshed, it is difficult for separating spouses to define where their spousal relationship ends and the parental relationship begins. Boundaries must be clarified.

When a couple with children separate, the children's welfare should get priority. Rules defining when and how each parent will relate to the children are essential to the children's understanding of the separation process and their adjustment to it. It's not easy for couples to preserve their parenting relationships while dissolving their relationship as husband and wife. Those who succeed manage to establish a structure that enables them to preserve their continuity as a problem-solving unit.

When the possibility (real or imagined) of reconciliation is present, reorganization of responsibilities is done tentatively. Separation requires different—less rigid—boundaries than divorce. If a husband leaves his family, they must readjust; if he returns, these changes must be reversed. If he was disengaged, the separation and reentry may solidify the coalition between mother and children. If instead of reconciliation the separation leads to divorce, structural changes can be stabilized. Separation is disorganizing; divorce is reorganizing.

REORGANIZING

Divorce is the formal confirmation that the marriage is definitely and finally over. The partners have now shifted from participants in to observers of each other's lives. They see the other person reconstructing a new life, perhaps even with someone else. What they see brings a sense of loss and exclusion. Even when the marriage was unhappy, these feelings can be exquisitely painful.

After a divorce people need to let go of the marriage and get on with their lives. Negotiating this transition demands psychological work and it requires reorganizing the family system. Achieving a psychic divorce requires that the loss of the relationship be mourned. The mourning process can take as long as a year. The interval of grieving doesn't start, though, until the reality of the loss is accepted. I have seen many sad cases of depressed spouses who prolonged their suffering needlessly because they could not accept the fact that the relationship was over.

The mourning process is a wrenching transition; it takes time to get over any loss. This seems obvious, doesn't it? Most people feel terrible, lonely, deserted, empty, worthless. Unfortunately, some people are impatient and self-critical, which only makes things worse. That awful pain, I'm afraid, must be endured as part of the process of working through the loss.

It may help to think of the mourning process as consisting of three phases. First is a period of shock, numbness, and a sense of disbelief—"This can't be happening." Denial at this point—"This *isn't* happening"—stalls the process. The second phase of mourning is a time of intense pain. Weeping. Despair. Anger. Guilt. There is little to do but feel the feelings. Try to remember that the pain of mourning is a healing process; don't attempt to subvert it.

The third phase of mourning is completion—recovery, acceptance, adaptation. It brings hopefulness, the ability to enjoy life, and a renewed vision of the immensity of human possibilities. This is the time to let go of strong feelings, including bitterness and blame. One way to get some perspective on your bitterness is to think about who in your family is a bitter person. In other words, get over thinking that bitterness is something inflicted on you by your spouse's cruelty and realize that it may be partly that, but also partly a result of a family pattern of feeling victimized.

Once they give up bitterness that has been consuming a substantial part of their emotional lives, people are liable to feel depleted and drained. Rootlessness is hard to bear, but it may help to realize that this feeling is part of the process of uncoupling from old dependencies and becoming one's own person again. The guilty breaking of the contract to be a whole family and the tearing up of roots seem a necessary price for what may be waiting just ahead, a happy life with an undivided soul. If divorce is a destruction of order, it is also an optimistic reaching for authenticity, a rebellion against emptiness.

———◆———

Viewing the post-divorce family as a reorganized family system helps us recognize the importance of clarifying boundaries and establishing clear and separate roles for subsystems. Each parent and his or her children comprise one subsystem. There will be two households, but only one family system. Family therapist Constance Ahrons has suggested the term *binuclear family* to describe the post-divorce family that spans two households.[1] The nature of the two households is defined by custody agreements, the clearer the better.

In the 1980s, joint custody has emerged as the favored disposition. Several states have recently enacted legislation that makes joint custody a presumption. That is, in order to have some other arrangement, divorcing parents must prove that joint custody is not in the best interests of the child. Regardless of what type of custody is awarded, two things are essential for the welfare of the children: a stable and predictable arrangement, and access to both parents. Joint custody requires a high level of cooperation and mutual support. Couples who cannot stop battling will have trouble with this arrangement. Custody arrangements need to be flexible enough to accommodate to the needs of the children as they grow older. To begin with, however, it is important to create as clear a structure as possible.

Although joint custody is becoming popular, it is still more common for one parent to have the children, at least most of the time.

The custodial parent and the children make up one subsystem of the post-divorce, or "binuclear," family. This unit is often called a "single-parent family," but this is not strictly accurate, because in most post-divorce families both parents continue to be involved. Still, this subsystem must be capable of functioning independently. The biggest problem for this unit is learning to cope with being understaffed. There are fewer people to do more work. Parenting is more difficult because one must carry the whole burden. Yet parenting is also simpler because there is no longer any need to negotiate two different perspectives. Furthermore, some uncoupled parents find that they can be a lot more flexible. Instead of having to serve dinner at seven o'clock every night, they and the children can eat any time they want.

Divorced parents seem to have less time and therefore must learn to manage it better. Make a list of those activities that have to be done at specific times—your job and the children's lessons, for example. Try to eliminate things that are optional and draining, then consider what time you have left and how you can spend it wisely. You may discover that there are alternatives for even some of what you consider essential activities, such as making dinner and doing laundry. For example, you can cook meals ahead, when you're in the mood, and then freeze them to reheat on days when you come home too tired to cook. Perhaps your children can help by loading and unloading the washing machine and spending an hour or two on the weekend helping you straighten up and clean. Children may (will) initially resist accepting additional responsibility, but hang in there, they'll get used to it. It's important to strike a balance between giving the children more responsibility and making them "parental children"—little grownups who get cheated out of childhood.

When I consult with family therapists at various agencies, one of the most frequent questions I hear is, "How do you treat a single-parent family?" My answer is that the so-called single-parent family is the same as any other family. Let's look for a moment at the structure of this unit—custodial parent and children.

CUSTODIAL PARENT

_ _ _ _ _ _

CHILDREN

This diagram is as incomplete as the following one is for an intact nuclear family.

MOTHER

_ _ _ _ _ _ _

CHILDREN

Obviously, the father is left out. Whether he is involved or disengaged, he still belongs in the picture. If he is disengaged, then that may suggest important changes for the family—namely getting him more involved with his wife and children.

MOTHER | FATHER   MOTHER ← FATHER
               | ↓
_ _ _ _ _ _ | _ _ _ _ _ _ _

CHILDREN | CHILDREN

A single parent and his or her children have similar structural needs, namely that there should be a clear boundary between parent and children, and the parent should develop sustaining involvements outside the children—with friends, family, probably a job, and perhaps a boyfriend or girlfriend.

		FRIENDS
MOTHER	MOTHER →	FAMILY
	⤳	BOYFRIEND
	— — — — —	CAREER
CHILDREN	CHILDREN	PARENTS WITHOUT
		PARTNERS

A great deal of research has now demonstrated that loss of access to the noncustodial parent (usually the father) is associated with greater problems in children's adjustment to divorce,[2] while loss of access to the children is associated with problems of adjustment for fathers.[3] Much of the research on divorce is on "father-absent" families, as though he were married and present, or divorced and absent. We have already seen how inaccurate this is. In addition to the problems for fathers and their children, mothers with sole custody report more depression from the overwhelming burden of taking care of the children without help.[4] To prevent—or minimize—these problems, divorcing parents must remain civil enough to coordinate whatever version of shared parenting they have chosen.

The parental subsystem after divorce is a limited partnership. A clear boundary is best. Distance helps reduce anxieties and expectations, making it possible for the divorced spouses to get along better. Some people ask, "Can't we be friends?" It's not harmful to be friendly; it is harmful to be enmeshed. Enmeshment may take two forms: Either the partners try to preserve the loving, husband-wife relationship, or they continue battling with each other.

If parents fight after they are divorced, older children often withdraw from both of them; younger children may choose sides. When this happens, no one wins. When you fight openly with your divorced spouse, realize that you are putting your children in a bind. If you must argue, don't do it in front of the children.

Having two households can actually be a positive, enriching environment for children—if the parents don't make one regime "right" and the other "wrong." They also have to make sure that the transfer back and forth between households is handled with as little contention as possible.

Permissiveness often becomes a special problem for divorced parents as children grow older and learn to exploit inconsistencies between households. Parents may be demoralized. It's difficult to assert parental authority when you are confused and lonely, especially if you depend on your children for companionship. If each household is clear about rules and roles, children can switch back and forth comfortably. Some parents allow their guilt over what has happened to make them give in or make big speeches when the children say, "*Daddy* lets us watch whatever we want on TV." Clarity, not symmetry, is most important for the children's adjustment.

Most kids long for a natural relationship with both parents. Don't create loyalty conflicts for them by criticizing the other parent. It's up to you, if you're not the everyday parent, to keep your relationship with your kids alive and intimate. Pick up the phone and call them, often. If you're far away, write to them. If they are under ten, make the letters fun. Bring the words alive by cutting out pictures from magazines and pasting them on the page. Don't let your feelings about the divorce get in the way of your feelings for your kids.

Noncustodial fathers who were involved with their children before the divorce cope with the loss by seeing the children often. Unfortunately, many of these fathers stop visiting after a couple of years because they find that periodic contact is too painful to maintain. Living in another house, or even a different city, the divorced father can no longer share the everyday pleasures of watching his children grow up. He may console himself with the notion of "quality time," but there is no substitute for being there.

Because divorced fathers tend to think of themselves as visitors, they often feel pressure to entertain their children. Uncle Dad. A father can arrange special activities for his visits—roller skating, movies, expensive suppers—but he can't program "meaningful" conversation. Children talk about things that are important to them when they feel like it, not on some particular schedule. One very important way to prevent contact from decreasing over time is for fathers to have their own living space and establish routines that enable them to behave and feel like family. Routine activities such as cooking meals at home and doing homework together help keep the relationship natural.

Guilt and distance combine to make many noncustodial parents doubt their moral authority. Some are prone to sermonize. Seeing less of the children, they have less opportunity for long discussions and often try to cram everything in with heartfelt lessons about life. Many noncustodial parents are insecure and wonder if the children will hate them for the rest of their lives. This makes them overly sensitive and overly reactive, as the following example illustrates.

---◆---

Barry was divorced for two years and was living with Jeanette. Every other weekend Barry drove 245 miles to pick up his children and take them to his apartment for the weekend. Both he and Jeanette worried excessively about the children's feelings and were ever alert for any signs of insecurity. One Saturday night Jeanette told Markie, age eight, that it was time for his bath. When Markie started to fuss, Jeanette told him sternly that it was time for his bath—whether he felt like it or not. Markie ran upstairs crying. Barry went into Markie's room, and after finding out what the problem was, comforted his son by saying that he shouldn't worry, "Jeanette and Daddy love you." ["What's love got to do with it?"] From downstairs, Jeanette could hear Barry talking to Markie and she felt excluded, so she went upstairs and began a lengthy—and unnecessary—explanation of what had happened.

Hearing this story, I felt sorry for all three of them—all that anxiety. If I were in a similar position, I hope I could remember to continue to treat children as children (let them complain if they want, but expect them to obey) and not be so insecure as to worry that they would stop loving me if I spoke firmly to them.

---◆---

Finally, there is one other family unit, the siblings subsystem, that can help stabilize families of divorce. Siblings can band together, not only to support each other but also to help manage their parents' relationship. Children who are loyal to both parents can stick up for a parent who is attacked in absentia, and the children can also encourage their parents to negotiate with each other. As the following diagram illustrates, the siblings can be seen as a subsystem that remains in the center of the divorced family. When one sibling is pulled toward one parent, the other can keep the system from becoming unbalanced.

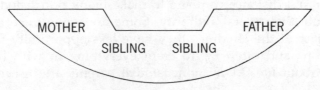

There is little evidence that the rise in divorce rates indicates disillusionment with marriage. The high incidence of remarriage suggests that divorce represents dissatisfaction with a particular marriage, not marriage as an institution. According to the U.S. Census Bureau, 45 percent of the marriages registered in 1981 involved remarriage for at least one of the partners. Another, even more striking, statistic from the Census Bureau is that 80 percent of divorced adults remarry within three years. When one or both partners in divorce remarry, they open up new possibilities, but these possibilities bring with them a host of hard problems.

BLENDING

Any child can tell you the word that modifies *stepmother* is *wicked*. Hoping to soften this unfortunate connotation, many family therapists substitute the phrase *blended families* for the more familiar *stepfamilies*. It's a nice solution—verbal magic. With equally swift strokes we can transform the elderly into *senior citizens*, orphans into *foster children*, and homosexuals into *gays*. The message is clear: It's not good to be old, orphaned, homosexual, or a stepparent.

As many as 40 percent of second marriages end in divorce within five years, and the presence of children from previous marriages is a major factor in making a second divorce more likely. The opposite is true for first marriages—having their own children means a couple is *less* likely to divorce.[5] This fact supports other research indicating that remarried families have more stress and are less cohesive than nuclear families.[6] These statistics can be misread to support the idea that stepfamilies are an aberrant form that doesn't work. The truth is that stepfamilies fit neither the Pollyannish image of television's "Brady Bunch" nor the dismal picture of Cinderella's family.

What stepfamilies do suffer from is stress—the stress of having to create a new family form, with more misconceptions than useful information, and often with the residue of unresolved messy divorces.

Before they can get on with the complicated business of developing a new structure, with new rules and new traditions, stepfamilies must deal with unfinished business from the past. Stepfamilies are born of loss—death or divorce. Homes may be disrupted, old schools and old friends may be left behind.

Children are often hurt and angry. They need assurance about their well-being and time to mourn their losses.

Children do a lot of scary thinking. They have seen their parents stop loving each other. For a child, that can be like seeing the earth open up beneath your feet. Children of divorce are at high risk to develop problems with intimacy—making and sustaining close relationships. But this is not, as some people think, because they have seen their parents break up; it depends more upon the nature and continuity of their relationship with both parents. It isn't seeing the parents break up that's the worst thing, it's the fear of being abandoned.

Tell your children that they are not responsible for the divorce, that both parents will continue to love them, and that they will continue to be cared for. Don't blame the other spouse when talking to your children. Doing so blurs the boundary between parent and child. Parents should try to avoid dumping their problems on the children—treat them like kids, not confidantes.

Perhaps the most important thing for remarried parents to keep in mind is the need for a clear structure. Children need security and predictability. They need to know where they are going to be next week, at Christmas vacation, and during the summer. Like any organization, the family is under great stress whenever anyone enters or leaves. At divorce and remarriage, it is important to establish a clear structure with specific and agreed-upon rules and regulations.

In order to develop and maintain this clear structure, it is essential for the children's parents to work together as a team. Unless the parental subsystem is able to function adequately, the parents are liable to triangle in the children or a new spouse. New spouses usually know how much emotional energy is used up carrying on a vendetta with "the ex"—although if they are insecure they may be relieved to perpetuate a bad guy as a repository for unresolved bad feelings and as a scapegoat for future conflict.

At the same time as they are forming new allegiances, children must also be allowed to preserve old ones that are still important. Wherever possible, remarried parents should help their children maintain contact with their relatives and friends. Most important, children should not be pushed into instant love with their stepparents. Where is it written that stepparents and children will love each other?

Kids hate it when one divorced parent refers archly to the other as "your father" or "your mother." To them, it's still "Mom" or "Dad"—or whatever they've always called that parent. Similarly, it isn't fair to expect them to call a stepparent—a stranger—Mom or Dad. First names are easier.

Perhaps the biggest mistake that stepfamilies make is trying to model themselves after the traditional nuclear family. Having suffered through the upheaval of divorce, it's understandable that reconstituted families would want to shut the doors and draw the shades, but it doesn't work. Someone is outside—and that someone is a mother or a father.

Stepfamilies must go through the same kind of accommodation and boundary-making that new families go through, but they must remain open to the noncustodial parent. Each household will have its own rules and rituals. Remember that clarity is more important that similarity. Different rules are not hard on children; they can adjust to two sets of expectations *if the expectations are clear*. It's harder on the adults, who must learn to respect the other parent's autonomy.

Adjusting to this new family form takes time—at least two years, often five. Avoid pseudomutuality—acting as though everyone is one big happy family. The wish for "instant love" is often driven by guilt over the divorce and the wish to make up for the children's pain. Attempts to force intimacy or to deny conflicts only make a difficult situation worse.

"You're Not My Father!"

When children complain that a stepparent isn't their real parent, they're right.

Ninety percent of stepfamilies are made up of a custodial mother and a stepfather. Mothers in these families feel pulled, engaged, worried, and eager to please. Stepfathers often feel rejected, ignored, and competitive with the children. This is natural and takes time to work through. The divorced father—or even a deserting father—will never be replaced in the minds of his children. Trying to replace him only sets up loyalty conflicts. A stepfather (or stepmother) should not try to be a father. The children already have a father.

What works best is for the biological parent to be in charge of his or her own children. He or she is the only one with the moral authority to handle discipline. The stepparent should begin as an assistant parent and should be given time to ease into a more fully sharing role. Initially, the stepparent should support the decisions of the biological parent and should not attempt to assume a major role in discipline.

Support goes both ways, though. Although the natural parent remains primarily in charge, he or she should teach the children to respect the rights of the stepparent. In one family I treated, the father, who was a Latin, assumed full responsibility for the discipline of his two children from a previous marriage. What brought the family to therapy was the stepmother's complaints that the children were rude and disrespectful to her. Not being in the role of disciplinarian, she was not sure what to do. My advice was simple: I suggested that the father tell his children, "This is my wife; you will treat her respectfully or you will answer to me." That seemed to work.

The most difficult role in a remarried family is likely to be that of stepmother. Custodial fathers often try to turn over the care of the children to their stepmother. After all, mothers take care of children, right?

In any family, parents have two major tasks: nurturance and discipline. In biological families, there is a natural sequence; nurturing takes precedence with infants, limit-setting develops as the children grow. Limit-setting is especially difficult for stepparents. Not only do stepparents enter a family that has preestablished rules, but also the way has not been paved for the children to care about—and want to please—the stepparent.

The best way to develop a relationship with someone is to spend time alone with that person. However, it's best not to push children.

Initially, the child's time alone with the stepparent should be brief and casual—perhaps a walk to the store, or going to a movie, or playing a game together. Look at it from the child's point of view. Suppose your parent falls in love with someone new. Suddenly you're competing for your parent's time and affection with a stranger. How would that make you feel? If we give the children understanding and don't rush them, these thorny problems are easier to bear.

"It's Got to Work This Time."

Having "failed" once, remarried parents often feel a tremendous pressure to create a happy family the second time around.

The biggest danger is not respecting the natural boundaries of the family. The boundary around most stepfamilies must be permeable because the children often spend time in two households. This much is obvious. What may be equally obvious—that the new couple needs time alone together—is, unfortunately, easily lost in the pressures of dealing with the children.

In first-time families, parents have time to forge a bond before they must learn how to deal with children. In stepfamilies, this may be a problem. The newly married couple must accommodate to children at the same time as they are accommodating to each other. It is very important that the couple establish and maintain a clear boundary between themselves (as husband and wife) and the children. Without sufficient shared loving time alone together, the new marriage may wither like an unwatered flower.

One of my cases was a couple married after the man was divorced for the second time. He was filled with guilt over the possible harm his divorces might do to his children, and consequently acutely concerned about their needs. His wife, married for the first time, was equally aware of the children's sensitivities, and very eager to be accepted by them. Both members of the couple were so worried about the children that they were reluctant to exclude the children from any of their activities. The result was a kind of anxious, driven stuck-togetherness. The children didn't have time to be children, and the couple didn't have time to be alone. Until I pointed this out, and they were able to use therapy to help them draw a boundary around their relationship, they were in danger of letting their fears—another traumatic dislocation for the children—become a self-fulfilling prophecy.

Children may be the most important and vulnerable members of the family. In fact, it could be argued that the family is an institution for raising children. Nevertheless, it's important to remember that the life of the family depends on a strong couple bond.

14

SEX, DRUGS, AND ROCK 'N' ROLL: THE REBELLIOUS TEENAGER

*T*ime
is funny, isn't it? You're waiting in the airport on a rainy night for a delayed plane, and fifteen minutes seems like forever. Then one day your birthday catches you by surprise. Years have slid by, and suddenly, instead of being eighteen, you're thirty or forty, wondering where all those years went.

Sharon could hardly believe that Jason was sixteen. Her little boy had grown up so fast. Not long ago he was a mischievous little elf; now all of a sudden he was a hulking adolescent. Almost overnight, it seemed, her smooth-skinned little boy sprouted hair on his face, and his baby fat hardened into broad muscles.

358

Heather, too, had changed. The once cheerful and slender little girl had become a moody teenager, unable to conceal, but not quite ready to accept, her developing curves.

As striking as these physical changes were, even greater changes had taken place in the children's attitudes toward their parents. Heather still spent a lot of time with her mother; they went shopping together and sometimes even exchanged clothes. Sharon liked to joke that they were "best friends," but Heather often lapsed into periods of gloomy self-absorption. She had her father's talent for withdrawal.

The change in Jason was even more dramatic. He had grown from a whiny, willful little boy to a defiant and demanding young punk. He fought Sharon over everything—clothes, chores, curfews, drinking, homework, grades—everything! Nothing was easy. Sharon began to feel she was living on the raw edge of nervous collapse. She was worn out, sick and tired of all the arguments. But she was afraid to relax her grip, afraid that Jason was too cocky to exercise good sense in the wide world of adolescent temptation and adult risks.

When the children were little, the house was large enough to provide islands of privacy. Now, Sharon felt that they had taken over, and there was no room left for her to be herself. The four of them were like cats in the city, too crowded together to stay out of each other's territories. The inevitable result was a series of battles. Fur flew and there were plenty of shrill, shrieking caterwauls; but nothing ever got settled.

It had all happened so fast. Looking back, though, Sharon could see that there had been early warning signs. Take mealtimes, for example. By the time Jason was thirteen, Sharon found that nothing she served for supper pleased him. He picked at his food, and if she told him to eat, he complained that it was lousy. He preferred a snack when he came home from school and was never hungry when the family sat down for supper. Sharon worried about his health. "You've got to eat," she told him. The problem was not really food; the problem was that Jason was challenging the rules that governed their relationship. He was getting to be more independent, more defiant. But Sharon still expected him to accept her choice of what he was to eat. She reacted to his defiance with a mix of resentment at his behavior and anxiety that he wouldn't get the proper nourishment. As she intensified her efforts to make him eat a decent supper, he escalated his refusals to comply.

It was a "game without end," in which the solution—making him eat—became the problem. More control produced more rebellion. In Jason's eyes the relationship should have become more one of equals; in Sharon's eyes, Jason was a big boy, but he was still *her* boy.

All parents go through this struggle with their children. The only things that vary are the personalities and dispositions of the parents, the temperaments and inclinations of the children, the relationship between the siblings, the parents' different reactions to different children, the influence of the children's peers, and the parents' relationship with each other. That's all.

After Stewart's affair and the couple's brief, abortive attempt to resurrect their intimate union, Stewart pulled further away from the family and Sharon tightened her grip on the children. Heather accommodated; Jason rebelled fiercely. He grew angrier every year, frightening Sharon and Stewart with his defiance and recklessness. Some nights he stayed out until one or two in the morning, and once he didn't come back until dawn. They tried all the usual punishments—grounding, taking away his allowance, making him do extra work around the house—but nothing seemed to work. Besides, Sharon wasn't sure punishment was the answer. She began to think that something was wrong with Jason.

He was so changeable. One day he'd steal ten dollars from her purse and then lie when she confronted him; the next day he'd come to her for a hug and tell her that he needed her to act like a mother and not always be picking on him. Sharon was never sure who she'd be talking to when Jason walked into the room. He was tearing away from the restraints of who-he-thought-he-was-supposed-to-be to the freedoms of who-he-thought-he-wanted-to-be, trying on a succession of identities. Half the time, he seemed to be at war with himself. Some of the qualities Sharon loved in him—his tenderness, wit, and open expression of feeling—were under heavy attack from some kind of bombastic, macho ideal. One minute he was as appealing as John Travolta, the next minute he was a brutal, defiant Rambo.

A person is made up of many and diverse strivings, likes and dislikes, moods, wants, and fears. The search for a self—the famous "identity crisis"—comes from the effort, not to create something, but to find harmony and integration among these strivings, purposes, wishes, and ideals.

———◆———

Heather was going through the same struggle to discover who she would become, but she kept the questions about herself and doubts about her parents' values to herself. She was as quiet and docile as Jason was demanding and unyielding.

People often ask, how can two children from the same family be so different? The fact of the matter is, they aren't born into the same family. Jason was born into a young family, one in which the father was totally preoccupied with his career and the mother was full of energy and enthusiasm, eager to become intensely involved with her baby and willing to keep up with his restless demands for attention. Both parents were unprepared for the strain of caring for such a demanding infant, and that strain divided them. Heather was born to a somewhat more experienced couple. Her mother was tired, less willing to do everything for the new baby. Her father was aware that he could not abandon his wife to all the burdens of child care, and so he helped out a bit more.

Then, too, there were the differences in temperament. Jason was fussy, Heather was placid. Even where such differences are slight, they aren't static. Instead, like so many complementarities of family life, the differences are polarized. When the first child comes along, the parents create a cognitive niche for him. Jason was Sharon and Stewart's "lively" child—demanding and assertive, but also energetic and forceful, a boy who was going places. All through childhood these definitions are confirmed by the family's actions. Whatever Jason did that did not fit this image was not acknowledged. Thus is formed a powerful persona that convinces a child: *I am this and nothing else.* That role having used up certain of his parents' aspirations and expectations, the next child is given a different role, based partly on the child's behavior but often more on whatever needs and fears were not already projected onto the first child.

Sharon was willing to have an aggressive, outgoing son, but her own sense of femaleness dictated that Heather should be less demanding and more helpful. Sharon did not want her daughter to become another source of aggravation in her life, and especially did not want her to grow up to be as defiant and ungrateful as her brother. Stewart was happy to have a vigorous son and an affectionate daughter. Jason was his frisky puppy, Heather was his cuddly kitten.

And of course, the children have a polarizing effect on each other. Jason, who was jealous of Heather's easy affectionate ways, thought of her as a goody-goody, and stiffened his resolve to be tough. Watching his little sister cuddle up with Mommy made Jason embarrassed by his own dependency wishes. Heather, the younger sibling, was even more profoundly affected by watching Jason's progress through childhood.

The older sibling's legacy is a morality play interpreted by the younger child's observations of her parents' reactions. So frightening to Heather were Jason's fights with her parents that she made a secret vow always to be good. As a spectator to Jason's noisy struggles, she was a witness to the wounds suffered by her parents, and by Jason. In the wake of her big brother's hurricane, Heather would be the calm. She controlled her passions to avoid the fights, but her overcontrol of hostility led to apathy and withdrawal. When she was little, she put on a mask of passivity; as she got older, the mask became a prison.

Adolescence can be a time to correct the narrow reality of the family—to discover and actualize dormant potentialities of the self—but for this to happen the child must venture far enough to be exposed to wider realities. Heather stayed pretty close to home.

Heather learned not to confide in her parents because she didn't want them to be hurt or disappointed. She felt inadequate because she couldn't meet what she thought were their expectations, so to please them, she pretended to be whatever they wanted. Stewart made a point of praising Heather, even when she brought home B,'s and C's on her report card, and Sharon reassured her that she was popular, even though Heather knew she wasn't. But being human, Sharon and Stewart had a subtle way of letting her know when they were disappointed, and Heather could read these clues like a twelve-year-old Sherlock Holmes.

So exhausted by Jason's escapades were Sharon and Stewart that they took Heather for granted. She never seemed to get into any trouble, so everything must be okay. Beginning at about age eleven, she began to slip away from them, retreating more and more inside herself. By fourteen she would be a mystery to them, still showing a compliant self on the outside, but deeply troubled within.

Heather's feelings about her parents were all jumbled up. As Sharon grew more distant from Stewart and more antagonistic toward Jason, Heather sensed more and more that she was her mother's only pleasure, that her sympathetic understanding was her mother's comfort and her necessity. Heather's love for her mother was still the dominant force in her life. It was absolute, and yet . . . it was mixed with pity and fear. Heather had witnessed the effect of her brother's defiance and her father's coldness. She'd seen the fury of her mother's anger, and she knew she never wanted to risk that.

Sometimes when she watched her father and mother arguing—each of them so mean to the other!—Heather thought, *They* couldn't *be my real parents.* She didn't belong in this family, she must have been born into it by error. Her father didn't usually argue back; Mom just yelled at him, and he just sat there. He yelled plenty at her and Jason, but he generally didn't say much to Mom. Every once in a while, though, he'd lose it. Mom would be nagging him about something or other, and he'd explode, screaming at her at the top of his lungs, calling her all sorts of names, until she couldn't take it anymore and ran out of the room crying. Heather watched with scared eyes, afraid the storm might engulf her. They didn't see her, though—as if she wasn't even there.

When this happened Heather would go to her room and close the door. She still felt safe in her bedroom—her special place, her refuge. She would carry the cat up with her. Sally. They'd had Sally since she was a frisky little white kitten. Now that she was older, she pretty much ignored the family. She hunted for mice and fought to keep other cats out of her yard at night, but during the day she just lay around. If she stretched twice in the same hour, it was a major event. Heather loved her anyway. Sally was supposed to be the family cat, but Heather knew different. Sally was *her* cat. Who else loved her so?

Heather would lie down on her bed and put Sally on her stomach. Gently, she stroked the soft, silky fur—she had to be very careful or Sally would hop down and walk off, looking for someplace to sleep undisturbed. Heather petted her very slowly, very softly, hoping Sally would fall asleep, or at least stop twitching her tail, and condescend to stay. Heather didn't want to be alone.

———◆———

Things got worse and worse between Jason and his parents. The angrier he got at them, the more he sought refuge in the great preoccupations of American teenagers: sex, drugs, and rock 'n' roll.

Parents rarely know very much about their children's involvements with these things. They have their suspicions and their fears, but as to what's really happening, they have only clues. Often these clues match what the children are most conflicted about, things they seem to want their parents to discover. When the Simpsons came to me for therapy, I was to get two sides of the story of Jason's wildness. To his parents, Jason seemed a reckless, defiant, and self-destructive boy. They saw him strutting and bragging, fighting with an excess of spirit against their "few and sensible" rules. They were concerned that he might be experimenting with drugs, but they weren't sure. They were even more worried about his deteriorating performance in school. Their confusion about what they should and shouldn't try to control made it doubly hard for them to respond effectively. According to Jason, he was just doing what all the other kids did.

Sharon's version of events was pieced together from what she discovered and what Jason chose to defy her about. Once she began finding well-worn copies of *Penthouse, Forum,* and even *Hustler* in Jason's closet, her greatest concern was pornography. Stewart was less worried than Sharon. He said it was just a phase, don't worry. Sharon was furious. She thought her son was ruining his life—and hers too. She yelled down for him to come upstairs, and when he finally clomped up to his room he was mortified to see what she had in her hand. But she was so mad, she couldn't see that. She screamed at him, scalding him with her vituperations. Jason couldn't stand it, and he stormed out of the house.

Jason didn't come home for dinner and he didn't call. When he finally walked in the front door at two o'clock the next morning, Sharon thought he looked drunk. "You've been drinking," she said, trying to sound more certain than she felt.

"So what?" was Jason's reply.

This was new. His denials were bad enough; she could no

longer tell when he was telling the truth and when he was lying. But this was different. "So what?" was worse than a refusal to tell the truth; it was a scornful mockery of her authority as a parent.

Sharon's fury was choked off by a feeling of impotence. She managed to make "Go to your room!" sound angry and disgusted, but she was scared. If only things between them hadn't locked into a pattern so stubbornly wrong, which had not, not any of it, been her fault.

THAT AWFUL, AWKWARD AGE

Hell, with all its famous inconveniences, is only slightly more intimidating than raising a teenager. We've all been warned: "Just you wait." But somehow our own children's adolescence still sneaks up on us. The years between when they enter school and reach adolescence are not uneventful, but they have a slow, steady sameness. These are the years Freud called "latency"—the calm before the storm. Nothing changes radically. In fact, as the children learn to care for themselves (tie shoes, help with chores, scramble eggs) and spend more time with their friends, parents become more invested in their own lives, their own work, and their own friends and leisure pursuits. Preteenagers need you less and less, and you have more time to yourself.

Teenagers, on the other hand, seem to demand more time. Sometimes they seek out their parents, wanting to talk. Other times their behavior demands attention.

Adolescence is supposed to start with puberty, but even that is hard to predict. Most parents begin to notice a change in their children a little before they turn thirteen: The children start to become sarcastic, they answer back, they begin to look more like adults, and they are more threatening.

I remember, for example, that when my own daughter was twelve she began, on occasion, taking a tone with me that I found very hard to accept from my little girl. Once she was looking for her hairbrush and asked me if I could see it in the living room, where I was reading. I couldn't find it, and said, "I don't know, honey, I don't think it's in here." She replied in a voice I was completely unused to, "Then *where the hell* is it!" I was shocked, speechless. It wasn't the "hell," it was that tone.

These early signs of "defiance" and "disrespect" are the hallmark of adolescence, and the parents' response is critical.

As parents, we do what we do. Sometimes we think a great deal about what we *should* do. We may even ask friends for advice, read books, or consult experts. Much of the time, though, we act on instinct. Whatever we do, we underestimate the influence of our behavior on our children. We worry about how to cope with what they're doing, but it is very hard to recognize that much of what *they* do is in response to what *we* do.

When we worry about our children, we see them doing this and then doing that. What we miss is the *circularity* of parent-child relationships. There is a spiraling interaction of their behavior, our response, their response to our response, our reaction to that, and so on. We see our dear, sweet children turning into sneering, ornery adolescents. What we overlook is our own failure to accept their growing autonomy. What's really ornery is their insistence on growing up; instead of remaining children, they're becoming people. When communication breaks down, we see them developing a "listening problem." What we don't see is our own "lecturing problem."

We underestimate the mutuality of our interactions with our children because we overlook the systemic nature of the family. Teenagers and parents are, of course, separate individuals, but they are also part of a unit. Each member of this unit is torn by competing forces—one force pulling in to preserve the integrity of the whole, another force pushing out to establish the autonomy of the individual.

The individual is both a member of the family and a separate person. At various times of their lives, some individuals are more related to contexts outside the family than to the family. This diagram depicts the Simpson family at the time Jason entered adolescence. You can see that some family members are more completely contained within the family than others.

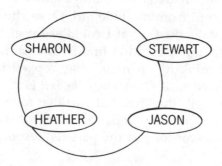

What the diagram suggests is what family members assume: that the family is static. Like Sharon and Stewart, the diagram overlooks the reality that the family unit is unstable. Jason is moving away.

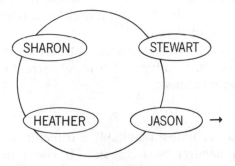

Jason pushes for autonomy, his parents pull for stability. Teenagers struggle against the family's constraints. Their parents struggle to maintain family cohesion and to enforce the family rules (the old rules, the ones that used to work). Together they are a family in transition. Conflict is almost certain because the parents want to slow the transition, while the teenager wants to speed it up.

The range of permissible behavior is still regulated by the family organization, in the form of rules and expectations. Breaking the rules carries strong emotional consequences (remember Stewart's affair, for example), including guilt, anxiety, and in some families, even damnation and banishment.

———◆———

I once treated a family in which the presenting complaint was the sixteen-year-old daughter's "defiant" behavior. This defiance turned out to be almost laughable: She sometimes stayed out thirty minutes past her deadline, she had to be reminded to clean her room, and when she got mad at her parents, she walked out of the house and slammed the door!

This was a family with eight children. The three children who were younger than sixteen were very close to their parents, and very obedient. *Very* obedient. The four older children were out of the house; none of them was on speaking terms with the parents. The youngest of the oldest (nineteen) had recently been banished by her mother. Her crime? She had married a boy she met at a church social. The mother liked the boy and approved of the marriage. Her only reservation was that she felt three months between the engagement and the wedding was too short. Her daughter insisted; she wanted a June wedding. Each of them hardened her position, until, as had happened three times before in this family, the mother told her daughter that if she didn't obey, she'd have to get out.

If this example seems extreme, that may be because it is. The dynamic, however, is universal. A family structure that does not bend, eventually breaks.

———————◆———————

Adolescence is almost inevitably a difficult time for the whole family, but it needn't be a disaster. If you remember that the family is a system, with all of its members interconnected in such a way that one person can change the system, and if you understand adolescence as a transitional period—for the teenagers *and* for the entire family—you can minimize conflicts and manage those that do arise.

Normal adolescence can be less violent, less anxious, less filled with conflict, and less wounding than we have come to believe. It can be altogether more pleasurable, even exhilarating, for everyone in the family. The adolescent is a conduit to the world at large, bringing new styles, new attitudes, new information—even a new language—into the family. Our adolescent children help keep us up-to-date; they keep us informed and they keep us on our toes. Often, however, the infusion of new ideas is unsettling. The adolescent becomes a critic—challenging our beliefs, exposing our hypocrisies, and undermining our long-standing prejudices. Although it is possible for us to accept and appreciate this challenge as good for them and good for us, many parents are threatened and fight back. This often begins an escalating series of conflicts, which in many cases are never settled, only broken off when the children leave home.

Too bad, because our children need us. For all their opposition to their parents and breathless enthusiasm for the adventures of adulthood, adolescents still need their families. Family is a refuge to return to from time to time when they are discouraged, hurt, or simply worn out.

Normal parents react to their children's adolescent transition in two ways. Parents are resentful, jealous, even competitive, but at the same time they also feel joy and pride in their children's developmental achievements, their growing autonomy, their vigor, and their assertiveness. The secure parent will grasp the fact of having become a target for the child's challenging self-assertion and will respond in a tolerant and respectful manner. When an angry teenager demands to know *why* he has to be home by midnight, an understanding parent will ask the child to express his point of view *and* will listen to it. Then, after hearing the child's opinion, the parent will rethink the rule—not necessarily change it, but not automatically maintain it—re*think* it, taking into account the child's growing ability to make his own decisions, but reserving the final decision for the executives of the family. This is a shift from a complementary position ("Because I'm your father, that's why!") to a more symmetrical position ("Because I worry about you when you're out. Why, what's your proposal?"). What's decided should make sense to adolescent children, even if they don't like it.

Joy and pride—these are the mature, self-confident parents' responses to their children's growth and development. While these important responses are comparatively silent, especially when deep-rooted and genuine, they are nevertheless pervasive. They are an expression of the parents' relative self-sufficiency as individuals and relative cohesiveness as a couple. The adolescent child is the beneficiary of his or her parents' emotional maturity and marital stability. Parents who are secure as individuals and united as a team will welcome their children's adolescence—despite its anxieties and conflicts—as a joyfully accepted reality.

What is the result? How does a child who is the recipient of these wholesome responses experience adolescence? It is still a time of turmoil and confusion; but the child who is anchored in an accepting family faces this turmoil with a sounding board, a testing place, a home base. Having a stable, supportive family makes it easier to venture out into the world, knowing that home is a safe harbor to return to when necessary for emotional refueling, as well as a source of identity and pride. At the same time as the adolescent is creating an individual identity, he or she also retains a sense of belonging—a family identity. A boy like Jason, on the verge of adulthood, is discovering what it means to be Jason, but he is still a Simpson.

———◆———

Coming back to the family's role in all this, families can err in either of two directions: by letting their children go too early and too easily, thus depriving them of support; or by holding on too tight, too long, and thus becoming a force against which to rebel. Does this sound like a Catch-22, in which whatever the parents do they are wrong? That's the way parents sometimes feel, but the answer is to establish and maintain clear boundaries between parents and children. In adolescence, clear boundaries give children enough room to explore, but provide enough contact for support and guidance.

Two guidelines to keep in mind are: (1) that the limits of effective control end at your front door. Since you cannot enforce what they do away from home, don't squander your authority by trying; (2) while attempting to strike a balance between too much and too little control, make every effort to minimize the extra stress *you* put on your children. Those children unlucky enough to be driven even harder by ambitious, controlling parents find the perfect defiance in passive-agressive nonperformance, and the perfect escape in drugs.

A tremendously pressured environment leads to pressure-releasing activities. For quiet, inward children like Heather, escape takes the form of passive, soothing pursuits—in her case, television, romance novels, and dreams, endless dreams. For lively, outgoing children like Jason, escape takes the form of drinking, partying, and staying out late.

What do kids do when they stay out so late? Most parents would love to find out. Few do. If asked, the teenagers usually say they are going over to so-and-so's house. Sometimes they do, sometimes they don't. Sometimes they go over there and stay, sometimes they leave. Bolder children may tell their parents that they just hang out. But where, and with whom, and what do they do? The three things parents fear most are drugs, sex, and drunk driving.

Dating practices have changed. Teenagers rarely date, at least not in the same sense we did. They don't go out two by two, they go out in groups. Sometimes a group of kids will get together to go to a specific event, such as a dance or a rock concert, but more often they simply arrange to meet and hang out at the local shopping mall. What they do after their parents drop them off varies tremendously. Some kids cruise the halls, sample fast foods, and go to the movies. Others succumb to pressures and temptations to defy authority by shoplifting, taking drugs, and experimenting with sex. They make out in secluded corridors or in the parking lot. Many kids leave the mall and seek out places where they can be alone together. Relationships tend to be brief and nonbinding, one result of which is that there is likely to be an increased number of sex partners.

However, there is so much variation among individual teenagers that it is hard to generalize about patterns of sexual behavior. Later we will see, in the case of Jason, how some teenagers pair off to experiment with sex. Kids take drugs for the same reasons they engage in sex play (and sex serious)—to defy authority, to be cool, to satisfy their curiosity, and because it feels good.

The exposure to drugs can start at any age, but the pressure to experiment often begins as early as junior high school. If a kid doesn't feel good about himself, he can find someone to sell him something that will make him feel good, at least for a while. Probably the main reason teenagers take drugs is to transcend their experience—to escape from stress and frustration, and to liberate their imaginations. The motivation for getting high plays a part in determining the drug of choice, which can be anything from beer to cocaine. Often, however, the particular drug a kid plays around with is only an accident of circumstances. It's not necessarily what they want to take, it's what's available.

Most kids sample beer, many with their parents' approval. (Lots of parents believe that "if you can't lick 'em, join 'em.") Kids like Jason who are angry, unhappy, and unsupervised engage in orgies of beer-consumption, regularly drinking themselves into a stupor while trying to prove their manliness. (Teenage girls drink beer, too, but they are less likely to do so in order to show off.) In warm weather, they sneak off into the woods; in cold weather, they find a house with no adults at home, or if there is a college nearby, a dormitory. They have "continuous keg parties"— opening the spigot of a keg of beer and guzzling nonstop until the barrel is empty. Jason used to go to a college dormitory and sit around drinking beer and watching television with a group of alienated undergraduates, playing "Beer of Fortune": watching

Vanna White turn letters while the spinning wheel determined who was the next person to have to chug down a quart of beer. Another variation, popular among some of the high school kids I have talked to, is "Love Boot" (meaning barf). The kids watch reruns of the "The Love Boat," and each one is assigned a character. Every time that character appears on screen, the kid has to chug down a beer. The object is to be the last one to barf. Cute, huh?

Despite well-publicized antidrug campaigns ("Just Say No"), drugs still retain their appeal as a means of flaunting convention and authority. Even though kids are more aware of the dangers of drugs, they still think of themselves as somehow magically immune from harm. Taking drugs is wonderfully *counterphobic*—a way to deny one's own fears by engaging in risky business. (Many parents who experimented with drugs in the '60s don't realize the increased danger of drug-taking today. The active ingredient in some forms of marijuana is ten times more powerful than it was twenty years ago. Furthermore, many people don't realize that in addition to its relaxing properties, marijuana is a mild hallucinogen which impairs the user's ability to focus attention. The resulting impact on attention and motivation may last for several days. Heavy use may lead to a persistent, burned-out mental state; apathy; and withdrawal. The dangers of cocaine are today more well-known, but are still commonly underestimated.)[1]

Psychedelics, which fell out of favor in the '70s, are once again becoming popular. Kids use psychedelics because, if you stop to think about it, inducing visual hallucinations with drugs comes rather naturally to a group weaned on television and conditioned to the bright lights and electronic bleating of video arcades. They take trips. Why "trips"? Because they are a means of transcending time and space, escaping rules and pressure. Some of this pressure is external (academic and social competition), some of it is internal (self-doubt, questioning of authority, identity confusion, and the great soul-searching of adolescence).

Healthy families set realistic limits, assert their values, and recognize the limits of their authority. Adolescents *will* experiment, they *will* act out. Parents can't stop it, but they can make it worse. Often one parent supports the child's acting out, perhaps for vicarious thrills, or to fill a void in the parent's life, or as an insidious way to strike out against the spouse. The biggest mistake many parents make is transforming their teenagers' experimentation into a struggle against the family.

THE TERRIBLE TEENS

When we think of teenagers as defiant, we make two mistakes: We confuse autonomous strivings with stubbornness, and we overlook the dialectics of the child's interaction with parents. Most teenagers are strong-willed, not oppositional. They struggle to achieve a certain independence and self-determination—and they struggle however hard it takes. How far they carry that struggle, how extreme their behavior gets, is determined largely by how tenaciously parents resist in an effort to retain control. A boy who cannot win control over how to arrange his bedroom may seek to express himself by wearing an earring or perhaps by spiking his hair. If he cannot win that battle, he may escalate the confrontation further (refusing to come home at night or physically fighting with his parents) or may resort to sneaky defiance (secret drinking, shoplifting, drug-taking).

Unfortunately, many parents don't see both sides of this interaction. They see only the teenager's "unreasonable" behavior; what *they* themselves do is perfectly reasonable. This myopia starts early.

The young child's achievement of a certain capacity for volitional action leads directly to a new kind of relationship with adults. Infants can do no more than cry when they feel distressed; toddlers can choose to touch that shiny object that happens to be Mommy's crystal bowl, and they can run away when Daddy says, "Come here." It's a wonderful game! The child wants to exercise autonomy; adults feel obliged to exercise constraint and teach rules of conduct. Thus begins a complicated and close connection between the development of internal processes of autonomy, on the one hand, and the child's relations with adult authority, on the other.

In the first real flush of autonomy, at about two years, when the child has acquired a certain degree of muscular development (and therefore a greater range of volitional activity and control), adults may begin to describe the child as "willful," "stubborn," or "difficult." This is a one-sided description—the product of adult prejudice. The two-year-old is not contesting the adult's authority. The child simply wants to do what he or she wants to do.

A little girl going through "the terrible twos" is quite willing to do what she's "supposed" to do, if she happens to want to do it. But this pliancy is not due to "goodness" or "cooperation," but to coincidence. What her parents want happens to coincide with what she wants.

Since a small child's actions are still quite spontaneous, with little deliberation or planning, the parents' rules have only a concrete and short-term significance. The child has to be told again and again. Even so, she may still persist in doing what she wants. This is not negativism; it is merely determination.

Wise parents accept and honor the boundary between themselves and their children. The boundary puts the parents in charge, but also leaves the children free to explore and determine what they will do within their own sphere of responsibility.

As the child grows, volitional control is gradually extended. This extension of autonomy occurs to a greater or lesser extent under the auspices of parental authority. If the parents are sensitive to the child's own rights, will, and capacity, this shift can take place smoothly and without special difficulties. But this developmental interaction presents various possibilities for interference with the child's exercise of autonomy.

The problem need not be blamed on parental stubbornness and stupidity. Rather, the problem of willfulness and control can be understood in the context of family dynamics. As a result of enmeshment, parent-child relations become an arena for a contest of wills. When the parents exert—or attempt to exert—coercive authority, the result may be anxious obedience, a readiness to submit or surrender, or a reflexive and angry resistance to authority.

This confusion of autonomy and defiance, played out across a blurred boundary between parent and child, may seem cute during the "terrible twos." It's not so cute during adolescence. The two-year-old girl who puts her pudgy hands on her hips and says "No!" is more endearing than the fifteen-year-old who defies her mother by coming home drunk. The dynamics, however, are the same.

Normally, by around age three, children are less willful—more "agreeable," more "reasonable." It's not primarily that they have been subdued, but that their relation to adult authority changes. Between two and three, the child sees and admires the adult's competency and authority. Children want to acquire that competency, so they imitate admired adults and want to be like them. This desire is expressed most plainly when little children dress up in Daddy and Mommy's clothes. The child is eager to learn, and the adult world is eager to teach. Identification nullifies—or at least diminishes—the conflict.

In adolescence the dialectics of the relationship with adult authority reach a new stage. The potentialities of a child's reliance on his or her parents have largely been achieved. Teenagers don't want to be like Mommy and Daddy anymore, they want to be themselves. The earlier relationship, based on unilateral respect, is largely repudiated. The child is no longer a child, and as a near adult is developing respect for his or her own authority. Inevitably they will contest the remaining constraints of adult authority. The tighter the restraint, the more violent the contest.

Actually, of course, this struggle is not dyadic—parents versus child—but triadic. The relationship between parents and child is a function of two triangles. One parent's enmeshment with the child is a function of that parent's disengagement with the other parent. Likewise, a parent who is disengaged from the child is almost certainly married to a partner who is enmeshed with the child.

Adolescents don't really want to defy anybody; they want to be in charge of their own lives. They want privacy and an independent domain. Above all, they want *the right to exercise personal authority*.

Parents who are secure in themselves and respectful of their children learn to let go; they accept the child's growing autonomy and hope that values instilled earlier will win out against all the child's perplexing and disturbing experimentation. Parents who try to hang on—parents who need their children too much to let go—exert an intrusive force that is impossible to ignore. Their children have great difficulty discovering who they are or what they want. They are so overwhelmed by their parents' attempts to control them that they have only two choices: submit or rebel.

This brings us back to the Simpsons—Heather's submission and Jason's rebellion.

15

THE SIMPSONS' FAMILY THERAPY

W_e

can now return to the story of the Simpsons' family therapy with a much broader perspective. Unlike members of the family, locked in the illusion of unilateral influence, we have seen how the problems of one person reflect the workings of the entire system. The Simpsons' attempts to resolve their difficulties are limited by their individualistic and linear perspective. In Sharon's view, the problem is Jason: He's defiant and self-destructive. Jason's view is equally clear: His meddlesome mother doesn't know how to mind her own business. But we have seen that mother and son's behavior are *reciprocal*—Sharon's control and Jason's rebellion are part of a mutually reinforcing cycle. Furthermore, like all family problems, the pattern is triangular: Sharon and Jason's escalating struggle for control is a product of *enmeshment* (they fight so much because they are stuck in a ruthless intimacy), which is, in turn, a product of Stewart's *disengagement*. Jason stays focused on his mother because he has so little to do with his father; Sharon clings to maternal control of her no-longer-little boy because her marriage offers so little compensating satisfaction.

We know that the family is a complex organism, with rules and patterns of interaction that shape the lives of its members. We know, too, that the family is not a static entity. It is a living thing that grows and changes over the years, evolving new structures to accommodate to changing circumstances, but unfortunately getting stuck at certain key points of transition. The Simpsons are stuck now, stuck like Br'er Rabbit to the tar baby.

In the first family session, we heard Sharon complain about Jason's rudeness, his defiance, and his "addiction" to pornography. We saw that when Stewart agreed, but implied that Jason's behavior was not as bad as Sharon thought, she turned her fury against him. Considering the harshness of her attacks and the rigidity of her point of view, we might be tempted to consider Sharon a bitch—a mean-spirited, domineering personality. No, Sharon is not a bitch—or a shrew, or any of those unkind epithets we unthinkingly apply to mothers trapped in a pattern of disengagement from their husbands and enmeshment with their children.

We have seen what happened to this trusting and vulnerable young woman over the years. I hope we have seen it in a way that does not shift the blame from one person to another. For all his faults, Stewart did the best he could. That doesn't mean he was blameless, or that he could not change; it means only that his behavior, like Sharon's, is understandable.

We have seen Sharon and Stewart's marriage become more and more impoverished and devitalized. Now it seems dead, or almost dead. Sharon feels so thoroughly cheated of Stewart's support that tears come to her eyes when she allows herself to think about how things were. Stewart, too, has been hurt, not least by his own inability to stand up to his wife's anger—enough to fulfill his role in the family, and enough to see through Sharon's anger to the hurt behind it. Too bad. He could relate to the hurt, it would draw him closer. The anger drives him away. Sadly, these two people, once so much in love, had become increasingly separated by their private griefs, many of them inflicted on each other.

Of course, I didn't know all this about the Simpson family

at the time of my second session with them. I knew only what I saw in the first session, and I had some idea of what to expect, based on my experience with other families in similar circumstances.

I did know that they were hurting, and that they were uncomfortable about participating in family therapy. In this, they were no different from most families. Husbands are afraid their wives will demand more of them; teenagers are afraid their parents will find a way to lock away their freedom; mothers are afraid the therapist will expose their failures; small children are afraid the doctor will hurt them; and they are all afraid it isn't worth the effort.

Knowing this, I resolved to go slowly, to let the Simpsons know I understood their anxieties, and to avoid premature confrontations. Therapy, when it works, is a balancing act. The therapist offers empathy and understanding, accepting individual family members' points of view and accommodating to the way the family is structured. Salvador Minuchin calls this "joining," and it is essential to win the leverage necessary for the later confrontations designed to destabilize and then restructure the family. Later, I would challenge the Simpsons' frozen conception of what has to be and limited conception of what can be. I would say, in effect, "What you're telling me is not true; it's too narrow." I would expand their definitions of self in order to expand the possibilities of how the family works. Later.

The second family session turned out to be much different from the first. The family pulled back from the open conflict of the first session. Sharon and Stewart had struck a wordless bargain to avoid a repetition of their previous confrontation. Such *conflict-avoidance* (as family therapists call it) was a measure of the intensity of their anger *and* their skepticism about whether it could be resolved. Sharon asked Stewart's opinion less, and he voiced no further disagreement with her complaints about Jason. Even Jason seemed to realize that it wasn't safe to be so antagonistic. (At home, family members can avoid conflict altogether or walk off when arguments heat up. In therapy the door is closed, at least for an hour.)

The second session confirmed the structural patterns I had seen in the first. Jason and his mother were enmeshed, and his father was disengaged. It was easy to see.

SHARON | STEWART
. . . . |
JASON |

Unfortunately, the easier a family's structure is to see, the harder it is to change. Relatively functional families are more flexible and therefore somewhat harder to compartmentalize. With the Simpsons, I had already tried some of the usual moves to test their flexibility; I activated but did not dent their structural rigidities. This was a family suffering from an advanced stage of interpersonal arthritis—all the more reason I would have to use my structural map as a guide to help me plan therapy.

My plan was to separate Jason and his mother—to reinforce the boundary between them.

SHARON
— — — — — — —
JASON

But I would not be able to accomplish this in a vacuum. I would have to move Stewart closer to Jason and closer to Sharon.

SHARON   STEWART   SHARON ← STEWART
— — — — — ✓   — — — — — —
JASON   JASON

Heather was so quiet I wasn't exactly sure how she fit it, but she seemed to be enmeshed with her mother.

I entered the third session resolved to block Sharon and Jason from their unproductive quarreling as much as possible and to look for a pretext to encourage conversations between husband and wife, and father and son. I had my plan; they had theirs.

I could tell something was up as soon as they walked in. Jason was the first one into the room. He walked with none of his usual swagger and sat dejectedly in the chair nearest my desk. He avoided looking at his mother, but she glowered at him with such intensity that even when he was looking away, he was clearly preoccupied with her stare. Stewart, too, seemed upset. He sat next to his wife and tried to take her hand. She jerked it away without bothering to look at him. Heather was the only one who showed no emotion. As usual, she was reading.

As soon as I shut the door and sat down, Sharon turned to Jason. "Well, do you want to tell the doctor what you've done now?"

Jason didn't answer. He just looked down at his feet.

Sharon shifted around to face me. "After we left here the first time, I made him promise to get those filthy magazines out of the house—*and keep them out*. He assured me he would. I *thought* I could trust him. But yesterday afternoon I happened to be cleaning out his closet and I found a whole box full of that smut. Now I don't know what to think. This boy is sick. And he's turning into a pathological liar. Would you allow a son of yours to bring that kind of filth into *your* house?"

When I said nothing, she insisted, "Well, *would* you?"

"I don't know," I answered lamely.

"Well, *I* don't intend to tolerate it!" Then she turned back to confront Jason. "And that's not all. I told him that if he was going to live by his own rules he could just get out. I can't stand living with all this stress. If he can't behave, he can go find somewhere else to live. Do you know what he did? He started yelling at me. He told me to stop picking on him, and he said that if I didn't shut my big mouth, I'd be sorry. This boy has no control over his temper. You have no idea what he's like.

"I went down to the kitchen, and he followed me, screaming at me, totally out of control. Just then his father walked in. When he saw what was going on, he told Jason to quiet down and apologize. Jason told him to go to hell, and Stewart went crazy. He punched Jason right in the face and then the two of them started rolling around the floor, wrestling. I couldn't believe it. We are living in a mad house."

I tried to interrupt, but she wasn't about to be interrupted. Instead, she started in on Jason again. "You have *absolutely no respect* for me or your father. If you don't straighten out, and soon, you're going to find yourself out on the street."

Jason, his tough act beginning to wear thin, tried to ignore her. He gave me a look of exasperation and then swiveled around to face the window. Stewart was visibly pained, but he didn't seem to know what to do. Heather edged her chair closer to the corner and pretended to keep reading.

Here, played out in front of me, was the story of this family: the father's lack of participation, the daughter's equally passive but less apparent withdrawal, the son's relatively normal experimentation, and the mother's fury. My immediate impulse was to take this woman on, to fight back, to tell her not to be so hard on her son. But why was I feeling the pressure to do that?

Whenever I feel the urge to assume some active function in a family—discipline the children, sympathize with a neglected spouse, or counteract one parent's harshness—I ask myself, who *should* be doing that? Why is this function missing in the family, and who should I be prodding to assume it? In this case, the answer was obvious: Stewart Simpson was unwilling to protect his son from his wife's attack because he didn't want the conflict to shift to him—he couldn't (wouldn't) risk the hot emotion necessary to close the distance between them.

Since I already knew he would have trouble facing down his wife's furious attack, I decided to calm things down a bit. (Calming down a family crisis is simple—uncomplicated, not easy. Just give the emotionally distraught family members a sympathetic ear, and block the others from interrupting. Someone has to understand, not argue. What keeps the usual noisy conflict going is an escalating spiral of people repeating their own point of view, without bothering to listen to and acknowledge the others'.) After they calmed down, I could get them to speak to each other. I would play a role in the family (mediator) but only temporarily.

I spent the next few minutes talking to Sharon, drawing her out and empathizing with her distress. It wasn't hard to do. The minute she was free of Jason's defiance and her sense of her husband's lack of sympathy, her anger began to melt. "He always" and "he never" changed to "I worry so much about him" and "I don't want anything to happen to him." The change was remarkable.

Now it was time to press Stewart to talk with his wife. He did not share her harsh point of view about Jason's behavior, but as a result of refusing to contest her opinion, he left the field to her. The main point was not really, however, to get them to agree, but to close the distance between them—to break down the rigid boundary separating them, so they could become a team of parents and begin to rebuild their relationship as a couple.

"Your wife is very worried about your son, and I don't think she feels she has your support." This, I knew, was a weak-kneed invitation to dance, and I would have to use more pressure to activate this reluctant partner. "As for you, I think you have a slightly different opinion about Jason's behavior, but you are afraid to express it. Like a lot of intellectuals [zing!], you seem to want to avoid argument at any cost. In this case, I'm afraid the cost is leaving a son without a father and leaving a wife without a husband. Unless you get more involved, I don't see anything changing in this family. In fact, I see things getting worse."

That did it. Stewart turned to his wife and began to tell her that she had always worried too much about the children. "Jason's not really a bad boy. Why can't you give him a little more room to breathe? Leave the boy alone."

Sharon was stung by her husband's remarks, but her anger was tinged with sadness. She responded by saying, "If I worry too much about the children, whose fault is that? Who has never really been a parent, never really been a husband? I've had to do it all alone."

Back and forth they went, each one terribly vulnerable, each one showing it in a different way. Sharon was afraid of a deep-seated feeling of helplessness and covered it with anger; Stewart was afraid of his anger and controlled it by pulling back. But now the pressure of my attention kept them at it. They talked about Jason, they talked about their relationship, and as they talked, the hurt came pouring out. He spoke of how much her criticism hurt him—if she wanted him to be more involved with the family, why was she always finding fault with him? She spoke of her frustration at trying to get him involved. "For years, I begged you to pay a little more attention to me, to give me some of your precious time. But no, you had to read this and write that. I think you spend so much time at work just to avoid me. I don't think you ever faced up to the fact that you're married."

I didn't want this to go too far in front of the children, but there is always the question of when to interrupt. To intervene immediately after Sharon had said Stewart was a lousy husband would punctuate the interaction on a negative note. I didn't want it to end that way.

So, I asked Sharon if she thought her husband heard her. "He heard," she said. "He's heard it before."

"I don't think so," I said. "I think he can't hear you when you come on that way. I think he clenches his ears the way some people clench their fists. I don't think he hears the hurt and loneliness—because I think you're afraid to let it show."

Sharon began to weep, softly at first, then harder. She didn't say anything. She didn't have to. Stewart sat there, looking helpless, touched but not knowing what to do. "It's sad the way you two have grown apart," I said. "I think she needs you." This time when Stewart took Sharon's hand she didn't pull away. It was time to stop.

For the next three sessions, I met with Sharon and Stewart alone. I asked them about the history of their relationship. "What did you think when you first laid eyes on each other?" "When did you know you were in love?" "What did you hope marriage would be like?" These bittersweet questions opened up a lot of buried feelings.

They told me about their courtship, and the wedding; about the babies and the unbelievable strain; about how the babies grew into children, and how hard it was to keep up with them. They told me how their differences grew. Hopes and frustrations, disappointments—one damn thing after another. And the affair. The distance eating away at their relationship, until they sometimes wondered if there was anything left. And now Jason.

They'd heard all this before, of course. Heard it? They lived it. But I was offering them something different from reviewing the facts, something different even from "talking things over." I was offering them the chance to listen—and the chance to be heard. Instead of having them talk together, I had them talk to me. So, in place of a defensive listener waiting to break in to argue, "to set the record straight," they each had a disinterested and therefore sympathetic listener. I listened to what had happened; I listened to their feelings. Instead of contention, I offered empathy and understanding.

Therapists of all persuasions have tricks of teaching understanding, from behavioral training in "communication skills" to oh-so-clever analytic interpretations. But the nag factor in all this teaching and preaching often outweighs the message. The best way to teach understanding is to show understanding.

For Sharon and Stewart, sitting still and listening while I talked to the other one was like overhearing the conversation of a stranger; the common element lay in being relieved of the obligation to respond. The warmth of my empathy melted their emotional reserve and they each brought up a heartful of hurts and disappointments, feelings stored up over years of misunderstanding and neglect. Because they were talking to me, not each other, these ancient griefs came out like appeals for understanding, not like attacks. This time they heard each other's side, perhaps a little more clearly now, and they began to see some of the reciprocity of their actions.

Sharon and Stewart were moving closer together, but I did not want to do what so many therapists are tempted to do: uncover marital problems in a family with a difficult child, decide that the marriage is the *real* problem, and then devote all the time to the adults, assuming that the child's problems will automatically benefit from improvements in the parents' relationship. Besides, who wants to spend time with an unruly, hostile teenager?

Sharon and Stewart's problem wasn't just them as a couple. They managed being a couple reasonably well. Oh, they had problems, all right, but they might well have worked these out if they hadn't gotten sidetracked by a couple of little things—Jason and Heather. They never really worked out a system of being parents together. That switch from being a family of two to a family of three trips up a lot of people. No, the problem wasn't just the marriage; it was more than that. It was the marriage, and the parenting, and it was Jason.

My sessions alone with Sharon and Stewart woke up a lot of feeling, some of it anger, some of it longing. Meeting with them helped draw some of the heat away from mother and son, and put it back between husband and wife, where it belonged. With some of the heat off, Jason cooled down, some.

I knew I wanted to meet with Jason, but before that I played a gambit designed to put some distance between Sharon and Jason by moving Stewart into the space between them. I said that I thought Sharon had done more than her share of parenting (no argument), and that I thought she was tired. In fact, in my professional opinion (I love to say that), she was clinically depressed. I paused to let the authoritative-sounding diagnosis sink in. It did. Sharon nodded; Stewart looked concerned.

"Jason *has* gotten out of control," I said (no need to lie about that), "but right now, I think Sharon needs a rest. Stewart, you need to assume responsibility for the boy's discipline, and for that reason I want to meet with you and Jason for a couple of sessions to help you work it out."

They agreed, and I did spend a couple of sessions with father and son. Some of what we talked about was Jason's need to improve his behavior, and some of it was just about the two of them, father and son, spending more time together. It's easier to work on a dormant relationship than an overheated one, and these two guys made quick progress toward getting closer.

It was fun seeing the two of them together, but I knew that I should not do so for long. You can't pry an overinvolved mother away from her son without hooking her up somewhere else. Otherwise, she'll spring back like a steel coil. I reconvened the whole family for a progress review, and was careful to downplay the improvement in Jason's behavior. One message I did not want to give was that Stewart was doing a better job than Sharon. Then I said I wanted to have a series of sessions with Jason, "who is old enough to start taking some responsibility for his own actions."

I wanted to talk to Jason about the pornography—I assumed it was a harmless teenage thing, but I didn't know—and about drugs, about school, about girls, about a lot of things. By talking with him privately, I was hoping to create and reinforce a boundary between him and his mother. Adolescent sex is a private experience, one that children should not be expected to share with their parents.

But first of all I had to get him to talk. You don't just sit down with a teenager who thinks he's a badass and say, "Okay, tell me about all your problems."

I started out deliberately being as agreeable as possible. At first Jason was stubbornly unresponsive. He showed up on time and suffered through the hour, but said little. I was, after all, an extension of his parents' authority (*he* certainly wasn't paying my fee), and he did not want to expose himself. To show me his feelings would leave him open, and he didn't want to make himself any more vulnerable than he already felt he was. So I just waited, asking enough questions to keep him talking, not enough to turn our meetings into question-and-answer sessions.

It wasn't long, though, before Jason was won over. He was,

after all, a talkative kid, one in need of a listener. Jason tested me by degrees, moving slowly from safe topics to less safe ones. He told me about school and some of the pressures there. He told me how he and his friends sneaked off to drink beer, and about the late nights when they got blasted. As he told me about "The Beer of Fortune" and "The Love Boot," he watched my eyes for signs of disapproval.

I did disapprove. I'm too old to think that kids drinking themselves into a stupor on a regular basis is harmless fun. But I tried not to show it. Instead of directly opposing his excessive indulgence—which would immediately cast me in the role of the controlling, and therefore ignored, parent—I asked him more about his own experience, hoping to help him discover for himself the unhealthy consequences of his behavior. The closest I came to expressing my disapproval was asking him if some of his friends were still young enough to think that drinking a lot made them hot stuff. It was a clumsy ploy, but I was lucky. Jason said, "Yeah, a lot of them do. Stupid isn't it? I only drink to help me relax."

After a while, we got around to sex. We didn't exactly "get around" to sex, I brought it up. Jason would not have. My asking signaled a shift in my stance, from purely receptive to probing tough issues. The easiest way to be a therapist is just to be nice—to accept everything and always sympathize. This is a popular version of therapy: therapist as friend. It's an expensive friendship.

Jason told me that he had been sexually active for a long time. Recently he'd been seeing Kim, a girl ideally suited to aggravate his mother. Kim had been expelled from school for selling cocaine, and now she lived with aged grandparents who were unable to provide much supervision. Sharon had forbidden Jason from seeing Kim, and so the young lovers carried on in secret. Once or twice a week, Jason waited until his parents had gone to sleep and then climbed out his bedroom window, crawled across the roof, and dropped down to the ground. There he got on his bicycle and pedaled the two miles to Kim's house, where he repeated the same procedure in reverse, climbing up to the roof, through the window, and into Kim's bed. The clandestine nature of these meetings added the element of danger to the thrill of sex.

Tired of his everyday routine and full of hopeful expectations for pleasure and excitement, Jason planned a special weekend with Kim. Actually, it was Kim who suggested it. She was, despite her sex and being younger, by far the more daring of the two. She said, "Let's go away somewhere for the weekend and take a couple of hits of LSD." "Sure," Jason said; though he had a number of reservations, he kept them to himself.

Once he accepted the idea, it gave him a splendid chance to engage his imagination in a carefully devised plot to outwit his mother. First they'd need a place. That was easy; they could go to the old barn on his parents' property in the country. The old utility barn wasn't heated, but it was spacious, and more important, it was private. A week before Christmas, Jason mentioned casually to his mother that he might be going over to Kevin's house for the weekend after Christmas vacation. His original idea was to spend twenty-four hours with Kevin—just in case his mother should someday mention to Kevin's father that the boys had been together. Unfortunately, that plan fell through when it turned out that Kevin would be away that weekend. As an alternative, Jason considered deliberately provoking a fight with his mother, knowing that she would ask him to leave, as she had many times before, and then he could be gone for a day or so without his parents bothering him. They would assume that he'd be at Kevin's or his coach's, and—at least he thought—they wouldn't care. Finally he decided that lying to them about going to Kevin's was the best alternative.

When the eagerly awaited day finally came, Jason said, "Mom, I'm going over to Kevin's for the weekend, remember?" "Yes. Do you have any homework?" "Just a little chemistry, and Kevin and I are going to work on that before we go to the movies." "Have a good time."

Jason walked over to his friend Travis's house and together they drove over to meet Kim. Travis took them out to the country place and dropped Jason and Kim off behind the tenant's house, not far from the barn. It was a short walk, but because they had to wade through knee-high snow carrying armloads of food and blankets, it took several minutes. Once he had unlocked the barn and they were inside, Jason felt a growing excitement. And a little scared.

They decided to eat first and then get high. So, they ate a lunch of peanut butter and jelly sandwiches and Twinkies that Kim had brought, and then, while she smoked a joint, Jason ate half of one of the marijuana cookies his cousin had brought back from college. One thing he vowed he would never do was put smoke in his lungs—or put a needle in his arm, for that matter.

Being high was wonderful. He just lay back and thought about why people take drugs. It was simple, really: to feel happy and to escape from worry. What's wrong with that?

Then each of them took a tab of LSD. Jason had tried it once before at a party; that time he had been leery and had taken only half a tab. This time the effect was stronger. The kerosene lamp looked like a flickering tube of colored balloons, and the snow outside took on a kaleidoscopic array of shifting colors: blue-white, pink-white—the whole fucking world was gorgeous!

Then Jason began to think of himself as "Mad Max," the Mel Gibson character who fought off the bad guys of the future. He told Kim what he was thinking and she said, "Ooh, I love Mel Gibson," and started kissing him. Well, after that, the sex was terrific. The rest of the weekend was like a wet dream.

Jason was an imaginative liar. Previously I'd had no reason to doubt his honesty. Now his stories were an undecipherable mix of truth and fiction. The hours on the phone talking to girls, and his mother's nagging about it—that I believed. His trouble finding the nerve to ask "nice" girls to go out with him—that I believed, too. But the number and extent of his conquests, and his minimizing his involvement with pornography, seemed, shall I say, unlikely.

When I asked him directly if he still hid erotic magazines in his room, he denied it emphatically.

His self-righteous indignation gave him away. People lie with adamant denials. The truth is seldom invested with such heat. His lie, for surely that's what it was, put me in a spot. To challenge him directly would only provoke a stonger denial; what's more, it would set us at odds. He was quick to assign adults the role of jailor, and I didn't want the job. On the other hand, to act as though I wholeheartedly believed him would make me seem a fool, and it would begin an erosion of honesty between us. So I said, "Really? that's amazing," trying to walk a thin line between skepticism and distrust.

Jason responded to my almost imperceptible challenge by moving away from the subject of sex. He changed topics, but in the process he came as close as he could to telling me that his sexual exploits were fantasy.

He told me all about his fascination with science fiction. He spent hours reading fantastic and utopian visions of how things could be, losing himself in futuristic dreams. It was a good subject for us, because I knew nothing about science fiction. He taught me. He also taught me a little about rock 'n' roll, explaining the difference between "heavy metal" and "power pop/hard rock." Metal was like a sledgehammer, driving home sped-up blues guitar solos and basic three-chord onslaughts. Hard rock and power pop had more melodic diversity, the musicians avoided the almost cartoonish displays of macho strutting found in bands such as Mötley Crüe, Bon Jovi, and Whitesnake. Jason's taste in music ran toward adverturesome, passionate hard rockers such as Hüsker Dü and the Replacements. He even liked some of what he considered the "older generation" musicians—the Grateful Dead and Jimi Hendrix. What mattered to Jason was that they were real.

Now that we'd reached this level of mutual respect, I decided to explain to Jason the connection between his fights with his mother and his father's lack of involvement. I had mixed motives for teaching Jason about the family triangle. I wanted him to understand the hidden dynamic behind his struggle with his mother, but I would settle for his simply dropping the struggle as futile. If nothing else, I wanted to keep the peace in the family long enough for Jason to graduate from high school.

I explained how his mother fought with him as a stand-in for his father, who stayed in the background. I explained how his mother would continue every fight until she made him wrong and herself right. And I made him understand that by propitiating her, he would get more control and more freedom. Sometimes this meant avoiding her; but since that wasn't always possible, it also meant learning to say, "Yes, Mom, you're right."

Jason seemed to grasp the idea of the triangle. He liked it; it made him feel less of an outcast. It made us coconspirators; together, we plotted to outwit his enemy. And yet he could not seem to stop fighting with his mother. He would play it cool for a couple of days, and then he'd blow. His mother would tell him to get off the phone and he'd start yelling at her, calling her names, and refusing to back down. Stupid, stupid, stupid. I couldn't believe he was doing this. And then I thought, maybe he has to.

Why should anyone behave in a way so clearly calculated to antagonize his parents? Some of Jason's behavior seemed stupid, but surely it was purposeful, related somehow to achieving competence and enhancing his self-esteem. But how?

I did not feel I could confront the irrationality of what he was doing. For some reason, the need to court antagonism fulfilled his expectations. His mother nagged at him and he yelled at her, provoking the inevitable blow-up. It was pitifully predictable, like moths who fly at a bright light no matter how many of their fellows get burned in the process.

Jason was opposing me, too, although it took me a while to see it. He'd "forget" what we discussed and somehow "not get around" to apologizing. Things got worse at home, and I got mad.

He was doing with me what he did with everyone else— arousing antagonism—so he could play the only game he knew how to play. (Of course, I didn't deserve this. I was just trying to help—only manipulating him for his own good. Honest!)

Yes, I was angry, but I held my feelings in check. Instead of reacting reflexively to him, I tried to maintain my cool long enough to understand what he was feeling. He was responding to me not as I understood myself, but as he assumed I must be— someone who would only try to control him and make him angry.

I pointed out that what he called "forgetting" must accomplish something indirectly that he could not do openly. I was thinking that he would not let go of his fights with his mother, but his response surprised me. He said he was angry with me. "You're making *me* do everything. You're on her side!" His forgetting to apologize to his mother was a refusal to submit to my will and manipulations. Without words, he was saying to me, just as he said to his mother, *I will be manly toward you—the way I learned from my father*.

This was a turning point in my work with Jason. Here was his struggle for autonomy, not retold by his mother or even by himself, but right here between us.

Therapists love to attribute this kind of resistance to "transference," a wonderful concept that attributes the present conflict to unresolved feelings about past relationships—and modestly gives full credit to the patient. Jason was resisting me as though I were his mother. (Silly boy, I'm not your mother. I'm just acting like her.)

———◆———

Parents struggle with their teenagers to protect the children from making mistakes and to preserve the parents' rights. Teenagers fight back to win the freedom to do what they want and what they think is right. The theme of this struggle is autonomy—which is not the same thing as freedom. Autonomy means thinking for yourself, not acting without restraint. Autonomy is the product of a clear boundary between self and others, a boundary which allows one to become a *differentiated* self.

A differentiated self is an independent person with a separate identity—a solid sense of self. He or she says, in effect, *This is who I am, and this is what I believe.* Neither these beliefs nor the person's actions are products of blind conformity—or counterconformity—to other people. By contrast, the undifferentiated person is a pseudoself, with a marked discrepancy between what the person says, even believes, and what the person does under pressure from a relationship.

Differentiation is an intrapsychic (within the person) and an interpersonal (between persons) concept. Within the person, it means the ability to separate thinking from feeling, to not be overwhelmed by anxiety into acting on instinct. Between persons, it means being able to think and act independently, taking other people's wishes and expectations into account, but not being propelled into knee-jerk action by them.

In the matter of wanting his freedom, the deeper truth is Jason was divided against himself. He was at once attracted and frightened. He advanced on the world, he shrank from the world; he desired his liberty, he feared his liberty. It is a conflict within us all, and it is never resolved.

But Jason fought out the conflict with his parents, especially his mother. To her he assigned the role of speaking for his inhibitions and fears, and she readily took the part. It was a closed system. The mother must fight the son, and the son must fight not only his own fearful self, but the mother as well. No wonder they were on the ropes, those two, locked in pain and rage.

My sessions with Jason were cooling things off, draining some of his fury and providing him with an ally. But I was beginning to worry about seeing him alone. Working with a child alone can be a restructuring technique, solidifying the boundary between parents and child, and encouraging the child's exploration of the world outside the family. Or it can freeze the scapegoating process in place. Seeing the child alone suggests that the child is bad, and that there is no need for the parents to change. Treating the child under these circumstances is like breaking a wild pony.

I was afraid the struggle for control was clouding the issue of differentiation. Differentiation—individuality—does not mean letting the child run wild, it means clarifying the separate identities of family members. I didn't want to help Jason win total freedom from his family any more than I wanted him to develop a false independence like his father. Stewart's apparent independence was a product of emotional distance. He could only think and act rationally when he was cut off from emotional contact. Up close, he became as fused as Jason. They *acted* in opposite ways—Stewart disengaged, Jason enmeshed—but underneath they had equal trouble thinking for themselves under the pressure of anxiety.

It was time to see the whole family again. I had two goals in mind: differentiation and boundary-making. The most important crucible for forging an independent identity is in your relationship to your parents. I wanted Jason to discover who he was and what he thought, in contrast to automatically opposing what his parents wanted him to do and who they wanted him to be. I also wanted to help Sharon and Stewart learn to set limits without undermining Jason's fragile sense of self. Parents should not be afraid to take a stand, to tell teenagers, "This is what we believe and this is what we want from you." Teenagers will accept and reject their parents' values selectively. The most important thing is for parents to announce their values, and label them as such. Words alone don't mean everything, but notice the difference between: "Everybody knows . . ." or "You should . . ., and "I believe . . ." or "In my opinion. . . ."

I had made some progress toward realigning the boundaries in the Simpson family, meeting with the parents to bring them closer together, and meeting privately with Jason to help him break the cycle of provocation and retaliation that glued him to his mother. There is always the question of whether to see a troubled young person individually—after all, that's what we want to foster isn't it, individuality?—or to see the whole family together. I had seen them separately to initiate change, but now I felt I had to reconvene the whole family to solidify these changes and to get at some unresolved issues.

But before I return to describe the rest of the Simpsons' family therapy, I want to spell out some of the dynamics involved in families with adolescent children.

SHIFTING BOUNDARIES

Adolescence is such a difficult time for the whole family, no wonder parents ask so many questions. "My daughter is moody all the time. What should I do?" "How can I tell if my teenager is using drugs?" "My sixteen-year-old daughter is going steady. Should I take her to Planned Parenthood?" "Should I wait until my son earns the money to pay for car insurance, or is a car so vital to his social life that we should help him out?"

The questions are endless, and none of the answers are easy. They depend on personal values and preferences, and the right answer varies with the circumstances. Do you let your teenage daughter drive your new car? How responsible has she shown herself to be? Does she do her chores and keep up with her schoolwork?

Although each situation calls for a unique response, there is one large and fundamental principle that, once understood, clarifies many of the specific questions parents ask about raising teenagers.

Adolescence calls for a shift in the structural dynamics of the family. The boundary between parents and their adolescent children must be clear enough to allow the children freedom to experiment and room to grow toward independence. Adolescents should be allowed to move slightly away from the sibling unit and given increased autonomy and responsibility appropriate to their age. The underlying structure that supports the transition from parent-child to parent-young adult is a clear boundary.

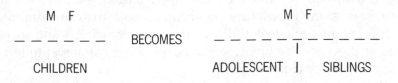

One or both parents may resist the change in relationship with the adolescent child, because *this change is not made in isolation*. It requires a shift in the relationship between the parents. A parent like Sharon, whose spouse is distant, may have great trouble letting a teenage child grow up. And as we have seen, the distant parent may join in tacit coalition against the enmeshed parent.

Divorced couples have a particularly difficult time. Tempers flare—so many opportunities for disagreement. The custodial parent may be more aware of the child's growing autonomy and need to experiment; the noncustodial parent may argue for stricter discipline because that's what always worked in the past—which is just where the noncustodial parent may be living. If the parents have remarried, the opinions of stepparents add to both the complexity and intensity of conflicts.

Just as the enmeshed parent's struggle to let go is tied to his or her ability to take hold elsewhere, so too is the adolescent's boundary struggle really two struggles. Achieving more autonomy inside the family is directly related to making more contact outside the family. These two developmental achievements are directly tied together. Parents, let your children go.

The boundary between the generations must be clear enough to allow teenagers room to grow, but still permeable enough to maintain the dialogue between parent and child. Parents need to relax their control but not ignore their teenagers. Teenagers are still children, and they need to be confirmed and supported. They need parents to listen to their troubles, their hopes and ambitions, and even some of their farfetched plans. Teenagers come up with a lot of wild ideas in the process of trying on different identities. The child may express certain preferences not so much because of profound interest, but more as a way of probing whether the parents will tolerate any deviation from existing family values. If permission to deviate is given, the child's interest in any particular choice may be short-lived.

Some parents, unfortunately, go too far in erecting a boundary between themselves and their teenage children. At this time in their lives, many parents are preoccupied with their own midlife worries. Some begin to withdraw into their own careers and social lives at precisely the time their children are most susceptible to drugs and other temptations.

Parents who have—or take—too little time to supervise rely on "communication" with their children to keep them informed. Some children learn that as long as you tell your parents what they want to hear, you can do anything you want. If their parents aren't available, the lucky teens will turn to teachers, coaches, aunts and uncles, or other accessible adults to confide in. The unlucky ones restrict their confidences to peers.

————◆————

It's hard to say exactly what a clear boundary is and how it differs from too little or too much distance. The general idea is to allow teenagers more freedom and distance, but to keep in contact. Let your children have more room to explore, and be available when they move toward you. One very important question is, What was the family pattern like before your child reached adolescence? If you were enmeshed, err in the direction of letting go. If you were disengaged, try to keep in touch. Unfortunately, unless they give these questions some hard thought, most parents are likely to continue with more of the same.

Respect teenagers' prerogatives on matters of style; retain a position of expertise on matters of substance. By the time they get to be teenagers, kids have a very strong need to win some of their battles with their parents.

In the heat of conflict with their children, parents are usually so preoccupied with the issue at hand that they lose sight of the process, the underlying theme of these discussions. What teenagers want, and need, is increased respect. Unfortunately, as long as parents insist upon winning all the arguments, the kids don't get no respect. In response, they either escalate the struggle, like Jason; go underground; or give up, like Heather.

Here is another one of those ironies of family life. We wish our teenagers to display more adult behavior, but if we order them to do so, we are defining them as children. We want them to be competent, yet go about it by criticizing their mistakes. Yelling at a kid, "Why can't you act more grown-up!" makes about as much sense as teaching a small child to tie his shoes by doing it for him. When they're little we do things for them, depriving them of the incentive to be competent; when they get older we criticize their way of doing things, depriving them of respect—the parental double whammy.

Respect your children's opinions and take their viewpoints seriously. Help them to develop their ideas and opinions within a context of connectedness. Don't force your children to isolate themselves from adults in order to find respect for their opinions.

Allow them to stay in contact by accepting that they may have something to say.

Some parents are afraid to say "You're right." They are afraid that letting their children be right makes them wrong, and afraid that letting the children win means the parents will lose. In fact, just the opposite is true.

Setting up a rigid, arbitrary rule can turn the curfew into an easy target for rebellion. Be flexible. Tailor the curfew to the night's events. If there's a dance and the kids want to get something to eat afterwards, 1:00 A.M. might be reasonable. But if there's nothing planned, there is no reason a child should be hanging out after 10:00 P.M. Negotiate limits with your children. Start by asking them, "What do you think is reasonable?" Often, children ask for less than you expect. They may want to come home at eleven instead of ten on Friday night, but they probably don't expect to be out until the wee hours. Most children will go along as long as they feel it's fair. One of the biggest complaints teenagers have is, "They don't listen to me; they don't explain. My parents don't think of me as a person." When setting limits, it helps to remember that it will only be a short time until you have no say at all. So, start practicing.

Regardless of how liberal some parents think they are, most of them have difficulty with the notion that their children will make mistakes. We want to protect them from making mistakes— unfortunately, in the process, we risk crippling their initiative. We want to bring them around to our way of thinking, but if we insist on winning all the arguments, then they will always lose. Hyper-control breeds rebellion and helplessness. Learn to lose, and lose gracefully.

HOW WORRIED SHOULD I BE ABOUT MY TEENAGER?

Adolescence is a tumultuous time during which approximately one out of every two teenagers suffer temporary adjustment reactions.[1] These reactions may show up as moodiness, irritability, rebellion, or withdrawal. Interest in school may abruptly decline, as may enthusiasm for having fun. On the way to becoming independent of their parents, even healthy teenagers may experiment with a wide range of harmful behaviors, situations, and companions.

The time to worry is when psychological impairment becomes

persistent, predictable, and pervasive. Transient adjustment reactions rarely last more than three months. Usually the distress is obvious. There is decreased pleasure in all areas, antagonistic relationships with parents, poor grades in school, loneliness, and isolation. A child is in trouble if he or she does not have at least one close friend outside the family. Another ominous sign is the child who no longer has any plans or dreams for the future. Physical symptoms—such as persistent headaches, stomachaches, or trouble sleeping—are cause for alarm if they become relatively constant. Sometimes things look fine on the outside, but the child's inner experience is bleak. These children can't seem to get relief from persistent stress, or they may rely on external means of feeling better. Abuse of food, alcohol, tobacco, drugs, and caffeine becomes a necessary crutch.

A parent's instincts are a pretty good guide, though some of us worry too much, while others may be too preoccupied with their own lives to notice their kids' problems. Remember, there is no substitute for spending time with your children. If you are uncertain as to whether or not a problem exists, talk to your children, talk to your spouse, and talk to your friends who have had teenagers. If you're still worried, talk to a professional.

Unfortunately, too many people wait until things have gotten out of hand before starting to take action. One of the most frustrating things about my practice is how often people come to me with what began as a simple problem, which because of one of two parental mistakes—either taking action where none is necessary (Sharon's trying to cure Jason of his interest in pornography) or failing to take action when action is needed (for example, not doing anything about a child's progressively deteriorating school performance)—has become tenaciously resistant to solution.

◆

Mrs. Seguin brought her son, age fifteen, to see me after he had been put on probation by the county's family court judge. Rick had been brought to court by the school for chronic truancy. This problem falls in the general category of misbehavior and can usually be resolved by monitoring and enforcing the child's school attendance. (Failure to do so is usually a sign of disengagement.) The first place to look for problems is—at the triangular level—the parents' relationship with the school; just as two parents must work together to effectively enforce discipline, so must the parents coordinate their efforts with the school, in the case of school problems, or with any other agency that may be involved with the children. The second place to look for trouble is in the boundary between parents and child. If the boundary is too rigid, the parents may not know what their child is doing; if the boundary is too diffuse, the parents may not be strict enough to enforce the rules.

Mrs. Seguin was too busy to be in touch with the school. That was easy to remedy. She was also too busy and too permissive to supervise and discipline her son. In principle, that too is easy to remedy, but I was appalled to learn how long Rick had been doing whatever he pleased.

It wasn't hard to discover the reasons for Mrs. Seguin's excessive distance and inadequate discipline. Her marriage lasted until Rick was three, and then her husband moved out. After that she started drinking heavily. The drinking got so bad that she ended up in an alcoholic rehabilitation center. Once she got her drinking under control, Mrs. Seguin went to work and Rick went to nursery school. He was a good boy, independent and so eager to please that he needed little discipline—so that's what he got. Mrs. Seguin got into the habit of letting Rick look after himself. This worked fine until he became old enough to make decisions contrary to adult expectations. In Rick's case, this started early.

When he moved to the middle school in seventh grade, Rick had trouble adjusting to the changes, especially the additional homework. About the same time, Mrs. Seguin's husband stopped making child-support payments and she became depressed. Just as her son was starting to skip classes and stay out late, she was too distressed and distracted to respond effectively.

Then the pattern of Rick's defiance started getting out of hand. He stayed out until all hours and skipped school more and more frequently. He failed one grade and then another. Finally, the school principal decided that Rick was in trouble and he decided to take action. By this time, unfortunately, the problems had become so entrenched that it was very difficult to make a change. How do you help an overworked and depressed mother start taking effective control of a fifteen-year-old boy who has been doing things his own way for three years?

The simplest solution—setting and enforcing rules—had by

now become almost impossible. Recapturing control once you have lost it requires enormous power. If the child you have lost control over is a teenager, regaining control may be impossible without the intercession of outside agencies, including the police and courts. Even then it isn't easy. Mrs. Seguin never really succeeded in taking charge of Rick. Eventually, he dropped out of school and took a job. She maintained their relationship by recognizing that she couldn't stop him from quitting school, and so when he told her his plans, she accepted them. Her hope was that someday he might return to school. Under the circumstances it was probably the best she could do. Still, it was a shame that she hadn't taken action earlier.

Don't be afraid to establish rules for your teenagers and expect them to obey. When you establish a rule, state it explicitly and give a reason: "Please have the car back by ten-thirty because I worry about you out driving later than that, and I want to get to sleep." Expect obedience, but tolerate grumbling. Obedience means accepting the family hierarchy that puts parents in charge; grumbling is just a way of expressing feelings. Don't overreact. Let our children have their feelings; settle for obedience.

If a rule is broken, consistently apply swift, brief penalties. For example, for every half hour past his curfew your son comes home, he misses one night going out.

"Suppose things have gotten out of hand with my teenager, how do I regain some control?"

First, recognize the boundaries of what you can control. You can make and enforce rules about what the child does in the house, including when to come home at night, but you cannot enforce rules about what goes on outside the house. So don't try. Setting rules that you cannot enforce only erodes what little authority you have left. Forbidding a sixteen-year-old boy from going to X-rated movies only puts him in a position to start lying to you if he decides to find out what all the fuss is about. The same is true with experimenting with drugs, sex, and alcohol.

Second, remember that teenagers have the right to negotiate the rules. Discipline should now be explained and guidelines worked out between you. When kids are six, the parent is the unquestioned boss; at ten, it's time to start explaining your decisions; at thirteen, negotiate the rules, but retain the parent's prerogative to have the last word. At eighteen, be available to discuss rules and problems, but recognize that now the child has the last word about his or her behavior. Be as flexible as you can.

◆

Be available to talk to your teenagers. Contrary to what you've heard about the generation gap, three out of four adolescents look to their families in times of stress. Mothers and fathers are the front line of mental health support. Remember to keep your feelings from overwhelming your objectivity and compassion. Threatening, nagging, or giving unasked-for advice only drives your children away. Be available to talk to them *when they want*. Listen to how they feel. Try to understand. Then, ask them if they would like your advice. Give it only if they ask.

If you're available, your teenagers will ask you many questions. Be frank, but not nosy. Offer fewer opinions and ask, "What do you think?"

Try to remember what you were like at that age. That will help you appreciate them, but don't forget to listen openly to their experience. Listen attentively to their thoughts and their feelings, but don't pry. Some doors are closed. Respect that.

All of this may sound like a pious call to be perfect parents: open, unconflicted, nonjudgmental, firm but understanding, to-tally empathic. The truth is, of course, that (except for you and me) parents are not always paragons of loving acceptance. Parents are threatened, they get cranky; they become competitive and controlling on some days, worn out and distant on others. We can't help reacting this way from time to time. We can't be perfect. What we can do is catch ourselves in the process (or shortly after the fact) of acting badly. We can check on what we are doing, reassess whether or not it is working, and if necessary alter our habitual mode of response.

◆

The most important thing is to recognize the nature of your family's structure and the need to readjust boundaries as your children enter adolescence. The principle is simple; the hard part is applying it to your own family. Hard for two reasons: we don't know ourselves, and parents usually come in unmatched pairs.

You probably have a better sense of whether your spouse is enmeshed or disengaged than you do an objective idea of your own position.

Remember, don't confuse strictness with disengagement or permissiveness with enmeshment. If your spouse tends to ignore the kids, thinks they can take care of themselves, that it isn't necessary to worry about them, and is generally uninterested in talking about them, chances are he or she is disengaged. If on the other hand, your partner worries about the children a great deal of the time, spends a lot of time with them, interacts with them somewhat more like a peer than a parent (playing together and arguing), then he or she is probably enmeshed. You are probably the complement. In fact, you probably have wanted to change your spouse's position. But, just as likely, you have tried. You can't change your spouse, but—pay attention, this is a crucial difference—you can make it possible for him or her to change.

If your spouse is disengaged, you can make it more attractive and necessary for him to become more involved. What *doesn't work* is nagging the disengaged partner to get involved, or giving up and ignoring him. Berating your spouse ("You never . . .!" "You always . . .!") usually creates, at best, pseudocompliance. As soon as possible, the disengaged person withdraws again.

Take Stewart, for example. He had turned into the sort of father who pretended to agree with Sharon, but only did so to avoid argument. He listened to her complaints and shook his head in a show of shared disapproval, then waited for his chance to get away. As soon as he dared, he would leave the room, hoping to escape the prosecutory list of Jason's latest crimes.

You can make it attractive for a disengaged partner to move closer by asking him or her to join you and the kids, doing things that the disengaged person likes to do. Instead of asking your husband (or wife, or the children's stepmother, or whoever) to participate in the things he usually doesn't (shopping in the malls, going to after-school programs) invent family activities that will appeal to that person (outdoor sports, going to the movies, or whatever it takes to capture the disengaged person's imagination). The scientific principle here is: You catch more flies with honey.

The way to make it more necessary for a disengaged person to participate is to emphasize your own and the children's needs, problems, shortcomings, or deficiencies, and your spouse's strengths, competencies, and skills. A disengaged parent (or stepparent) is more likely to respond to:

> "Gina needs to have a woman to talk to. Can you figure out some way for the two of you to spend some time together?" or
>
> "John needs to pick out some clothes for college. You have good taste; would you please take him shopping?" or
>
> "If Julie is going to have a chance to make the high school soccer team, she's going to have to improve a lot over the summer. I know how busy you are, but is there any way you could find time to practice with her?"

than to:

> "How come you never spend any time with Gina? All you ever do is criticize her," or
>
> "I wish you'd stop trying to discipline John. It just makes him angry, and reminds him how different you are from his real father," or
>
> "Why do I always have to be the one to take Julie places? I drive her to baby-sit, I take her to the movies, I take her to her friends' houses; you don't do anything!"

If your spouse is enmeshed, you can make it possible for him or her to step back by becoming more involved yourself, with your mate and with the kids. A husband who is jealous of all the time his wife spends with the kids can create space for her to want to be with him by spending more time with the kids himself. This strategy works much better than complaining about her neglect. Likewise, a parent who worries about a partner's overly intense relationship with the children will have a greater impact by becoming involved with the kids himself or herself than by criticizing the other one's overinvolvement. In families, what we say doesn't count for much; it's what we do that matters.

Stewart Simpson was as aware of Sharon's preoccupation with the children as she was of his lack of involvement. Unfortunately, her criticisms yielded only occasional, grudging participation on his part, and his disapproval didn't have much effect since he was unwilling to become more involved himself.

Although he had tenure, Stewart continued to worry about his career. He felt that if he didn't continue to publish, he'd become deadwood. None of his colleagues would have guessed how badly he needed continued successes to shore up his self-esteem, but Sharon certainly should have known. Although he didn't express much interest in Sharon's day or in the children's activities, he still expected a certain amount of attention when he came home at night.

One Thursday, two days before our Saturday session, Stewart had a particularly tough day at the office. One of his weakest students was defending her doctoral dissertation, and Stewart had to endure the embarrassment of championing something he knew wasn't very good at a meeting with his colleagues, the chairman, and the dean. He did his best, but it was a trying ordeal. The student passed, and Stewart tried to concentrate on her success rather than on his own feeling of having to defend mediocrity in front of the dean. After it was all over, Stewart looked forward to going home.

What did he find when he got home? On the stove there was no dinner, just a note on the counter informing him that Heather was having dinner at Sherri's house and Sharon was at a town council meeting. And Jason? Jason was sprawled out on the couch watching MTV, the remains of a TV dinner lying on the rug at his feet. He hadn't fed the cat, emptied the garbage, or started on his homework. Stewart just stood there for a moment, surveying the room, too tired to protest.

Jason could feel his father's eyes on him. He didn't turn around. Jason would like to have talked to his dad, but he didn't want to hear a lot of nagging about the mess in the room. Stewart wondered what was going on in Jason's life. But the father didn't ask and the son didn't answer. Stewart just stood there, nursing his private burden of grief—another moment of self-pity to add to his collection.

ALL TOGETHER AGAIN, AND OUT

The Simpsons still had a lot of unresolved problems and I was tempted to drift into an extended and indefinite therapeutic alliance with them. Sharon was emotionally hungry? I would feed her. Stewart was isolated from the family? I would help him stand up to Sharon's criticism, and I would help him see past her complaints to her loneliness. I would lend him strength and help the two of them stay in contact. I would promote clear and open communication between the couple. Heather was shy and depressed? I would reassure and encourage her. Jason prolonged the fight with his mother to avoid growing into young manhood? I would support him to develop his own interests and competence. Unlike Stewart, I would be available to him. Unlike Sharon, I would let him come to me when he wanted to talk. I would be their hero, offering them a magically protective relationship. They could adopt me; that way I'd always be around to help resolve differences, soothe hurt feelings, and make everything okay. (If you're going to argue against a particular position, you might as well make it ridiculous, right?)

Despite my broad portrayal of the therapist as Pygmalion, nevertheless therapy often becomes just that. With a therapist around to translate between the generations, calm things down, settle arguments, and handle each crisis as it arises, who needs to change?

Although there was much that could be done in the Simpson family, I felt that my job was to help them get past the point at which they were stuck. No, not just to help them resolve the immediate crisis, but to help them readjust the rigid boundaries that had led to the problems with Jason. However, once I'd helped them achieve a more functional family structure, and taught them a little about the need for altering boundaries so that the family could grow with the children, I would gently shift the responsibility back where it belonged—to the family. I would get out, so they could get on with it.

I would like to say that I had already transformed the Simpson family's structure. But I think a more honest assessment is that they had begun to see that they were not simply a family with an out-of-control adolescent. They were a mother and son locked in combat, which was partly a result of displaced animosity between husband and wife. Stewart chose not to contest his wife's harsh judgment of their son because he did not wish to feel the heat of her wrath on him. As a result, not only was the conflict between the couple preserved, like a fossil in ice, but Jason's defiant behavior was becoming increasingly self-destructive. In joint sessions, I had begun to separate the boy and his problems from the parents and their problems. In my sessions with Jason, I had helped him see how his fight with his mother was getting nowhere and, moreover, that he was acting as a stand-in for his father. My appeal to him was: Stop fighting with your mother, stop being so preoccupied with her, don't go out of your way to antagonize her, so that you will have more room to work out your own issues with school, girls, friends, and your future.

In the language of family dynamics, I had begun the process of boundary-making that would demarcate the parents from the son, putting their emotional energy back between the two of them and freeing the boy to grow up. What remained was to solidify these changes and tie up a few loose ends.

One of the things I hoped to accomplish before I terminated with the Simpsons was getting Heather to open up. She seemed to brighten up after my sessions with her parents, but I still wasn't sure whether she was depressed or just shy. It might seem reasonable for me to see her alone for a few sessions to get to know her better and to assess whether or not her moodiness was a sign of serious depression. Although I had seen Jason separately, to emphasize his independent status in the family and to separate him from his mother, I did not wish to pull Heather out of the family. I wanted to see how her parents related to her, how they dealt with the idea that their good (quiet) girl might be unhappy and need them more, and I wanted to see if I could bring the siblings closer together.

Heather did not want to be dragged in as part of the problem. She was biding her time until she could get out of this family, with all its messy conflict. If she could become more of an ally to Jason, their bond might give her more strength in the adolescent world, at the same time it might help Jason let go of the fight with his mother. I didn't try to force them into an alliance—it's hard to force anyone over twelve into anything—but I did try to get them to talk together.

The hardest thing for Heather was telling her brother how angry she was at him for causing such trouble. But I thought she had to get that off her chest before she could get in touch with any sympathetic feelings. When she denied that she was angry at him, I said, "That's impossible; I don't believe it." I was leaving her with two difficult alternatives. Own up to her angry feelings at her brother and risk an argument, or stand up to me. She chose a middle course, saying "Well, it's true," but without force or conviction.

It was then that I suggested to her parents that she was depressed, offering the evidence of her moodiness, her constant reading, and her refusal to engage in normal arguments. I was trying to put the ball in their court. They tried to throw it back. They were incredulous. "What do you mean? She's doing well in school" (Stewart). "She seems happy . . . she never complains" (Sharon).

"Well, I don't know," I said. "Why don't you talk to her."

Not surprisingly, Sharon began. "What is this, honey? You heard what the doctor said. Are you unhappy?"

Heather, mortified by self-consciousness, mumbled something that sounded like "I'm okay, leave me alone."

Before Sharon went any further, I took advantage of the moment to try a strategic ploy. "I know that you two (indicating Sharon and Heather) are pretty close and that she can talk to you. What worries me is that she is too depressed to talk openly to anyone else—her father, for example. When a kid gets depressed, she can fool her mother, but she probably can't express herself openly to anyone else."

All three of them set out to prove me wrong. Stewart pressed his daughter to talk about what was going on in her life, Heather tried hard to put her feelings into words, and Sharon kept out of it.

Father and daughter talked back and forth for almost fifteen minutes, proving that it's easier to open up a dormant relationship than to calm down a stormy one. In the process of their conversation, I learned—we all learned—a lot about what was going on inside this quiet child.

Heather talked about how she hated her parents always fighting with Jason. She talked about how no one at school liked her, and she didn't blame them. And she went on to describe a rather obsessive dissatisfaction with herself. Nothing was right—not her looks, or her personality; she was no good at sports; and she wasn't even true to her principles. As to why she ate so little, she said eating was disgusting. They slaughtered plants and animals just so people like her could eat. When she walked she squashed insects. She tried not to swat mosquitoes that lit on her skin in the summer, but sometimes she did anyway. She was weak, otherwise she wouldn't do these things.

I listened very carefully. This was a little morbid, but not abnormal. I was relieved to conclude that although she was certainly unhappy, she was not clinically depressed. She was moody alright, and definitely spent too much time alone with her thoughts. But she didn't show the warning signs of depression: chronic depressed mood, distorted negative thinking, *anhedonia* (*nothing* gives any pleasure), and slowed mental and physical functioning. Heather was an unhappy, brooding child, but she hadn't lost her ability to concentrate, and did not show the classic red flags of depression: hopelessness and desperation. There being no need for me to take over, I watched to see how her parents would respond.

Sharon and Stewart jumped in like two tag-team wrestlers, taking turns trying to bolster Heather's feelings. At least they were together on this one. They told her they loved her, and they pointed out all her good qualities. To Heather, this only sounded like "Cheer up, you have no reason to be unhappy." For once, though, she told them what was on her mind. She told them that they didn't really care about her, all they thought about was Jason. Good for her, she was finally standing up for herself, even if it was only for her right to be unhappy.

Time to go. I was very pleased with this session. Things were headed in the right direction. On impulse I decided to push Stewart a little closer to Heather by giving him a homework assignment. It seemed to me that this extremely private man might make more changes at home, outside of his wife's presence, than in our sessions with everyone together.

I said it was too bad that Heather was growing up without really getting to know her father, who was, after all, the primary man in a young woman's life. "I wonder," I said, hoping to pique his interest, "if you'd be willing to try a little experiment" (*The Devil's Pact*: first get the commitment, then explain the details.)

"Sure, why not. I'm game."

I said he should spend some time during the week sharpening his writer's understanding of adolescent girls. He should get together to talk further with Heather about what she liked about her life and what she wished were different. Then, I wanted him to write a short story about a shy teenage girl, based loosely on

Heather. ("Loosely" because I wanted Stewart to engage his empathy for what a girl like Heather might be going through, and I felt that if I encouraged him to fictionalize the story, he would feel less compelled to gloss over the girl's unhappiness.) "Use Heather as the model, but don't feel you have to stick too closely to the facts."

When the family arrived for their session the following Saturday morning, Stewart said nothing about his story. In fact, he had talked with Heather on several occasions during the week, and had indeed written a short story about a teenage girl—a shy girl, something like Heather. He hadn't said anything because he was a little embarrassed. "Would you read it?" I asked him. He did.

Stewart's story, "Sketches of Theresa," was remarkable, much of it obviously about Heather, some of it embellished but still probably pretty close to the mark. Theresa was a shy girl, so quiet on the outside that no one realized how sensitive she was. Her mind was vigorous, straightforward, and brave. Her spirit longed for emotional adventure. Her body was on the verge of deep feeling. But she was afraid.

Like most girls, Theresa was closer to her mother than to her father. She shared a lot with her mother, but there was much that she felt she could not share. (At this, Heather flushed.) When she became a woman (Stewart's pretty way of describing menarche), she became increasingly self-absorbed. At first this was reflected in a growing preoccupation with her appearance. Theresa inspected her body, feature by feature, spending hour after hour in front of a full-length mirror, trying on everything in her closet. (Heather's face turned bright red.) She had lots of clothes, but none of them were just right. If only she had something new, something special, maybe that would give her the panache she wanted. Sometimes she even practiced smiling. The mirror smiled back, but it wasn't quite right. Gradually, she began to lose interest in her looks, and started wondering instead, *Who am I? What am I going to do?*

Theresa wanted more than anything to be popular. She saw other girls flirting, obviously working at it, but she was embarrassed to follow their example. So she inhibited herself, holding back the one thing that might have made her popular, her natural friendly self. She cultivated an interesting persona but kept to herself. Her mother tried to help, taking Theresa shopping for new clothes, giving her tips on being friendly—how to let a boy know you're interested in him. But a mother doesn't have the power to make her children popular (Sharon shot Stewart a look but she didn't say anything).

Alone in her room, clouds of longing descended on Theresa, just as when a plane escapes the noisy lower world into the pure cloudbank of the silent altitudes. (Jason made a face at this flowery bit. I liked it.) Theresa wished for so much, especially the unattainable: flawless skin, to grow up overnight, to have more friends. Above all, she longed to be loved. Her longing for love was personified by a series of passing fancies: movie stars— "Yeah," Jason chimed in, "E.T. and the Aliens." "Shut up!" Heather answered. Stewart went on. Passing fancies: movie stars, older boys, sometimes even young teachers who seemed kind.

That was all. The story ended inconclusively.

When Stewart finished reading, no one spoke a word. After a long silence, I asked, "How does it turn out for Theresa?"

"I don't know," Stewart said, his eyes full of tears.

Heather started to speak and then changed her mind. Instead, she walked over to her father and put her arms around him. "Daddy, I love you." He held her for a long minute.

Before anyone could break the spell, I announced that the session was over. But as they were leaving, I said one more thing. "Sharon, you've done a good job. Stewart is finally learning what it means to be a loving parent."

Next session, Sharon was back to business as usual with Jason. She'd gotten an unusually high phone bill, and when she checked into it, she found that someone had placed three calls to one of those dial-a-porn numbers. "I didn't recognize the number— somewhere in California—so I called. It was disgusting! I got a recorded message of some woman talking about all the filthy things she wanted to do to me. Those idiots don't even bother to check to see who's calling."

Fine. I wanted one more chance to strengthen the boundary between Jason and his mother, while at the same time breaking down the one that kept Stewart on the periphery. I would have liked an easier issue, but they didn't give me the chance. As far as Sharon was concerned, this business about the pornography was still serious, and still unfinished.

"This sounds serious," I said. "What do you two plan to do about it?"

Sharon turned to Jason. "Why do you do this to me? Why do you hate me so much?"

To my surprise, Stewart answered her. "Sharon, this is something most boys Jason's age go through. I did. When I was his age, I used to sneak looks at the underwear ads in the Sears catalogue. Jason's going through the great sexual awakening. When you're that age, all you think about is sex."

If these two had been more equally matched, I'd have stayed out of it; but they weren't, and I didn't. "I think you're both right. The problem *is* serious (Sharon relaxed noticeably). But the problem isn't just pornography. Jason is at an age when *all* kids think about sex. It's not just their hormones, sex is all around them. Jason's problem is that he doesn't have enough of a social life to begin to channel these sexual feelings the way he'd like to.

"Stewart, can you say a little about how you felt about dating when you were Jason's age, and what your parents did that was helpful, and what they could have done to be more helpful."

Stewart described his shyness at Jason's age, his great wish to ask girls out, and his fear of getting turned down. I added that I thought Jason's problem with pornography was circular. He was ashamed of himself after he looked at that stuff, but he soothed his shame by doing it more. "I think this boy needs you two. He needs you to help him feel better about himself and he needs you to support his socializing any way you can."

This was a little too much for Sharon. "Why should I have to praise him? Nobody pats me on the head for taking care of this family."

I explained how I thought the family was trapped in an unhappy pattern. Acting badly gets noticed, acting positively (here, I looked right at Heather) gets ignored. Finally, I said (pushing my luck), "If you are hurt and angry because nobody shows any appreciation for all that you do, wouldn't it be better to say that to Stewart rather than passing on the same treatment to the kids?"

That I was able to be so direct with them was a sign that they had all become much more flexible. In the few sessions that remained, I said less and less, pleased that the family was now handling their own problems with minimal input from me. Stewart and Sharon talked increasingly together about how to respond to the kids, and although Stewart generally went along with Sharon, he'd occasionally disagree. I helped them work out a little gimmick for renegotiating family rules to accommodate to the children's increasing need for independence. I suggested that they let the kids write down what they thought the rule for a particular situation should be, and then discuss the policy between themselves before getting back to the kids. It turned out that the kids were (usually) remarkably reasonable in their requests, and the structured talking-it-over sessions helped insure Stewart's participation. My job was to undercut parental overreaction without undermining parental authority.

The most remarkable changes occurred in Heather. I'll take the credit for being such a fine therapist; the fact that she was growing up was just a coincidence.

Sharon took the lead, using her bond with Heather to encourage Heather to get out of the house. The first thing she did was enroll the two of them in an aerobic dancing class. Then she concentrated on helping Heather get out of the house on the weekend. At first, much of the impetus for this change came from Sharon, but after a while Heather became a self-starter, going to movies, basketball games, and shopping with her friends.

Heather's first open arguments with her mother came over what to wear to school. Miniskirts were coming back in style and Heather wanted to wear them to school. "Not in this house, young lady! You're not going off to school looking like a little tramp as long as I'm your mother." I expected Heather to wilt, but she didn't. She spoke right up. "Oh, Mom, don't be such a drip, all the other kids wear them." Heather's fear of breaking the adolescent dress code was apparently stronger than her fear of standing up to her mother. Eventually, they compromised. Heather was allowed to wear the most conservative of her minis to school; the others were to be reserved for parties.

———◆———

Things were going along nicely. How would I know when my job was finished? Most therapists look for certain changes to let them know their work is done. I work for the changes, but take my cue from the family. When things are going reasonably well at home, therapy sessions become somewhat boring. There isn't much to talk about. In short, families outgrow their need for a therapist. That's what happened with the Simpsons. After three

weeks in a row of desultory discussions of who was doing what—
more like progress reports than problems—I suggested that maybe
they had better things to do with their Saturday mornings and
didn't need me any more.

Nobody said anything for a minute. I think they had gotten to
depend on these sessions, each one of them for different reasons.
Then Sharon said, "Well, if that's what you think."

I asked her what she thought. She thought things were going
better, but then added, "I suppose we can always call if things get
worse." I said that I didn't think things would get worse, that
Jason had outgrown his need to provoke his parents, that Stewart
would continue to be more involved, and that Heather would
continue venturing more and more outside the family. I couldn't
help adding, "Maybe that will be hard for you, Sharon, letting
Heather grow up. Maybe you'll find some way to try to keep her
young, so that you still have a child to take care of."

Sharon didn't think so. That was that.

16

LETTING GO

*I*t
was 7:30 on a Thursday morning. I like to get to the office early on Thursdays, drink a cup of coffee, and read over my case notes before the clinic staff meeting. This morning, however, was three weeks before Christmas and I was looking through my address book, trying to decide who to send cards to. Most of the names in my address book are friends and colleagues, but when I got to the S's I came across *Sharon and Stewart Simpson*, put there in case of emergency. *God, it's been three years*, I thought. *I wonder how they're doing.*

Being a therapist is a funny business. People drop into your life and you get to know them about as well as one person ever can know another one; then one day they outgrow their need for you and drop out of sight. Some therapists become friendly with their patients who finish treatment, but I prefer to maintain a certain professional distance, because you never can tell when a patient might need you again. So, for me, no news is good news. Still, it's sad to lose sight of so many people over the years.

I decided to send the Simpsons a Christmas card—better make that Season's Greetings. On impulse I added a postscript, asking them to give me a call to let me know how they were doing.

A week later, Sharon Simpson called. Everybody was fine. Jason was now a sophomore in college and he would be home for the holidays in two weeks. Heather was in her senior year of high school, about to be inducted into the National Honor Society. Stewart's book on F. Scott Fitzgerald was out and he was already working on another book. Sharon thought it was about Philip Roth. "And me? I'm fine. I still have my job at the university, and I spend a lot of time with my friends."

I was very glad to hear that Jason had gotten into college. Everything else sounded good, too, but I was really curious to learn more, so I asked Sharon if they would like to come in for a follow-up session. "It would just be a progress report," I said, "as much for my benefit as yours." There would be no charge. "Sure," she said, "we'd be glad to come in." We made an appointment for Saturday morning during the week between Christmas and New Year's. I gave them my last appointment so that there would be extra time in case we needed it.

Sharon and Stewart showed up alone. Neither of the kids had wanted to come, and their parents decided to respect their wishes. I was disappointed to miss seeing Jason and Heather, but I figured this way might give the grown-ups more of a chance to speak openly.

We chatted for a few minutes about the snow and the parking and the holidays. Then Sharon told me that she'd taken over Jason's bedroom for a sewing room. "When he came home from college, he was shocked to find that I'd repainted his bedroom and packed away most of his old toys and sports equipment into cardboard boxes and put them in the attic. Where his stereo used to be, now sits my sewing machine. When he saw it, Jason said, 'What's that!' I said, 'It must not be a bear; if it was a bear it would bite you.' He didn't think that was funny. Same old Jason."

Same old Jason, but this seemed like a different Sharon—calmer, more independent. Not only had she cleaned up The Shrine of Disorder, she'd even replaced some of the sacred relics. It seemed like a pretty clear sign that she was getting on with her life.

I wondered how they'd gotten from that turbulent time in their lives, when I'd seen them, to this more peaceful, apparently stable plateau. "What happened after I stopped seeing you? Jason was still in his junior year of high school, right?"

Jason had settled down quite a bit after the family therapy sessions. He no longer seemed to go out of his way to defy his parents. "That's good," I said. "You two must have been doing something right."

"I don't know," Sharon answered. "I think the change was mostly Jason. He was growing up, starting to realize that we weren't the enemy, and he started thinking more about his future. I don't think we did much different; the change was really his doing. In fact, I had kind of given up on him. If he wanted to make a mess of his life, let him. But he surprised me by starting to straighten out."

"I think Sharon's right," Stewart said. "Things got better at home, but it wasn't anything special we did. One thing, though, was that I tried to spend a little more time at home that spring. So I was more aware of Jason's comings and goings, and I tried to be more involved in checking up on him."

"Yes, he did," Sharon agreed. "That is one thing; Stewart was around a little more, and when Jason did try to fight us over something, it was as likely to be with Stewart as with me."

So, I thought, this sounded like a significant shift—Sharon let go and Stewart became more involved—but they did not think of the improvements in Jason's behavior as particularly their doing. It was him. It was Jason who had caused the problems in the first place, and it was Jason who was responsible for the improvement. So much for insight.

———————◆———————

The summer between his junior and senior years, Jason got a job pumping gas at a filling station. He grew up a lot that summer. Although he had never in his life been very responsible, somehow he managed to get to his job every day. Sometimes he'd stay out pretty late, but he always got himself to work. "I could hardly believe he was the same kid," Sharon said. "One weekend toward the end of the summer, Jason had agreed to mow the lawn. I reminded him on Sunday morning, and he said to stop bugging him, he'd do it. But that weekend came and went and so did the next one; he still hadn't touched the lawn. I remember being really annoyed and I said, 'How come you're so conscientious at your job and yet you can't be responsible in your own house?' He said, 'Aw Ma, that's different. Mr. Wintle's my adult boss, you're my child boss. It's different.' "

When he went back to school in the fall, Jason became very

concerned about grades. He decided he wanted to go to college, and he knew that he'd have to bring his average up to get in. Before that, Jason just seemed to be in school to hang around with other kids. That year he seemed like a different person.

At the same time that Jason started straightening out, Heather became a little less agreeable. There were moments when Sharon thought, *Oh no, am I going to have to go through the same crap all over again with this one?* But Heather's rebellion—if you can call it that— was very different.

Jason used to attack his parents personally, berating them about something they did, telling them they were wasteful, stupid, wrong. Most of the time, his comments were too rude and too annoying to pay attention to. Heather was different. Her anger was quiet, cynical, less direct. She was like a silent, disapproving witness. For example, Heather would watch as her mother burned the milk in the clam chowder, making Sharon feel stupid, disorganized. Or she'd glance wordlessly at her father hurrying to have a drink before dinner. She read her parents' intentions and their weaknesses with uncanny and troubling accuracy. Her disparaging looks made them feel self-conscious—it was another kind of punishment teenagers inflict on their parents. Sharon and Stewart began to feel as though they were living with Ralph Nader.

This was around the time when people were becoming very concerned about the environment. Toxic waste convinced sensitive teenagers of the stupid cynicism of their elders, just as Viet Nam had done for an earlier generation. Heather was full of stories about cancerous solvents leaking from storage tanks, arsenic drifting up from smokestacks into the pure blue sky, and radioactive sewage pouring into the rivers and streams. The whole planet was being poisoned, and all her parents could think about was Jason. She never said this in so many words, but that was the way she made them feel.

It was an interesting paradox. It seemed that Jason was letting go of the angry struggle that glued him to his mother, while his sister was apparently generating antagonism as a necessary prelude to propelling herself out of the nest. Jason's job had been to distract his parents from their conflict with each other. It was a job he never really volunteered for; nevertheless, he filled the bill nicely. The three of them had been locked in an emotional triangle for years; now one leg of the triangle was going off to college. It seemed for a while that Heather might be taking over Jason's role.

With Jason and Sharon fighting less, there was less of a buffer between Heather and her mother. Heather started getting nasty like her brother, but her anger took the form of social consciousness, and her relationship with her parents never really got bad.

◆

I knew that the first child's leaving home can be a momentous time for families, and I wondered how Sharon and Stewart handled Jason's leaving. "How did you feel when Jason went off to college?" I asked.

They both answered at once: "Fine." "Awful." This was a surprise; Sharon felt "fine," Stewart felt "awful."

It's a large moment when you move out of your parents' house, leave the town you grew up in, and sail away from your childhood. It's a large moment, but it doesn't necessarily sink in. Jason was standing on the steps of his dormitory—on the brink of his future—but as far as his parents could tell, he lacked the sentimental turn of mind to think of it that way. To Sharon and Stewart, he seemed to be thinking neither of the past, all that he was leaving behind, nor even of the present, this moment of leave-taking. He was thinking only about the immediate future: Would his roommate smoke cigarettes? How hard was college, really? Would it be difficult to meet girls? This large moment meant little to him. To his parents, it was enormous.

Sharon had spent eighteen years heavily invested in her children, but she had been so overburdened that Jason's leaving was a relief. She had anticipated the loss and prepared for it. Helping him fill out applications and then driving him around to look at colleges, she had thought about Jason's growing up and growing away, and thus dealt with the loss by degrees. She still had Heather to take care of, but that seemed more like a pleasure than a burden. Now she was ready for a new chapter in her life. She was tired of being a mother.

Stewart had worried with Sharon about whether or not Jason would get his act together and get into college, but he hadn't thought much about Jason's leaving as a loss. After they'd installed Jason in his room at the dormitory, Stewart had wanted to stay for a while, maybe see some of the campus. But Jason seemed anxious for them to leave. He didn't want his parents hanging around. He was eager to say good-bye to his family, and in a rush to meet his new life. Stewart and Sharon took the hint.

Driving home, Stewart was flooded with unexpected feeling. He remembered his small son toddling in to take him by the hand to supper: "It's foody-time, Dad." Was anything ever as dear to him as those baby-talk expressions? Stewart assumed that Sharon must also be feeling sad. "Our baby is all grown up, isn't he?" Her answer surprised him: "Yes, thank God. I never thought this day would come."

Stewart told Sharon how let down and empty it made him feel that Jason was leaving home. Various alien emotions were washing through him and, uncharacteristically, he wanted to talk to Sharon about it. Sharon was amazed at this outpouring of feeling. *Why now?* she wondered.

After a while they lapsed into silence. It's hard to talk when you're not on the same wavelength. Stewart turned on the radio and fiddled with the dial until he found a station that played quiet jazz. Billie Holiday came on and he turned up the volume. Listening to the sweet suffering in the singer's voice was like putting a hot cloth over a sunburn—the heat of the cloth drew the heat out of the flesh. They played "God Bless the Child," "Lady Sings the Blues," and "The Man I Love." That voice—that rough, throaty croon. It went right through him, all steely soft, warm and sad all at once. When the lady sang, "I'll be seeing you, in all those old familiar places. . . ." Stewart was very much moved. In the darkness, his face burned and his eyes filled with tears. The tears just hung there, but he felt better. A few minutes later, Sharon fell asleep and Stewart turned down the radio. Alone with his thoughts again, Stewart resolved to get closer to Jason and to take advantage of his remaining time at home with Heather.

◆

With Jason away at college, the house seemed suddenly empty. Heather was still around, of course, but she always seemed to blend in. One of the forms that Sharon's urge to reclaim her space took was fixing up the place. She enlisted Stewart's help to rearrange Jason's room, and as she went around the house looking for ways to make it more livable, she gave him a series of other jobs to do.

When Stewart was straightening up the den, he moved a

bookcase away from the wall and found a plastic safety stopper in the electrical outlet. Suddenly he remembered the chubby, pink little babies crawling around on the floor. He would love to hold one of those babies again. Too bad he hadn't taken more advantage of his opportunities when he had them. Just then he heard a knock at the door.

"Dad?" It was Heather.

"Oh, hi, come on in."

"Dad, can I borrow the car? Mom gave me some money to buy clothes, but she said I'd have to ask you if I could take your car to the mall."

"Sure, honey, but sit down for a minute." Heather walked over to the stuffed chair in the corner and perched tentatively on the armrest. "How's it going?" Stewart asked.

"Fine, Dad . . . but really, I've got to go."

"Okay, sweetheart. Have a nice time." He watched her walk away, and then for some reason he could not have explained, he went to the window and stood looking out until the car pulled out of the driveway and disappeared up the street.

◆

Later that fall, when Jason's college sent home a notice about Parents' Weekend, Stewart surprised Sharon by saying that he wanted to go. She hadn't expected that; he'd always been so negative about what he called "structured occasions." As it turned out, they couldn't go. Sharon's father had a heart attack, and Sharon and Stewart went down to see him in the hospital. There were a few anxious days, but Mr. Nathan proved to have strong recuperative powers and the crisis passed.

To make up for missing Parents' Weekend, Stewart decided that he would go by himself to visit Jason, during the week, so he could see what was going on. It would be a chance to see the school, and a chance to get to know his son.

When the day for Stewart's visit approached, he felt a boyish eagerness to return to college and to see Jason. It was the same kind of feeling he had once had on those rare occasions when he went fishing with his own father. Now Stewart felt the same sort of anxiousness about how to please his son as he'd felt about pleasing his father. Would Jason like to go into town for a fancy lunch? Would he mind if Stewart went to some classes with him?

Jason seemed happy to see his father. He showed Stewart around the dormitory and then around campus. They chatted about school. Jason told Stewart how terrible the food was, how he had too much work and had to stay up all night to study for exams and write term papers—the usual freshman complaints. Stewart had heard the same gripes from his own students for years, but it felt good to be talking this openly to Jason. Jason seemed happy to be with his dad and to have his attention, but he did not seem eager to introduce his father to his friends. It was as though he didn't want the two worlds to mix.

When Stewart suggested that they go into town to have a drink before dinner, Jason readily agreed. It was a recognition of his adult status that he was happy to accept. They went to the hotel where Stewart had planned to spend the night, and after making reservations for dinner in the dining room, father and son went into the bar—man to man.

Jason chatted idly and superficially about what he was doing and then switched subjects to talk about the school's football team. They were having a good season and, Jason said, they had a chance to win the conference title. Stewart felt put off. He wanted to hear more about what Jason was doing. He wanted to know about his social life, what courses he liked, what plans he had for the future. He also hoped that Jason would want to know what was going on in Stewart's life. No such luck.

Each time Stewart tried to turn the conversation to more personal subjects, Jason grew restless and unresponsive. Stewart made a few jokes—his most comfortable approach to affection—but that didn't seem to make much difference. Finally, Stewart said that he was proud of Jason and that he hoped the two of them could become friends. Jason said, "Sure, I'd like that too," but his eyes seemed to say, *It's too late, Dad.*

Stewart gave up trying to have a deep conversation and accepted Jason's wish to keep things light. Stewart knew that staying overnight at the hotel would be a mistake, so he told Jason that he should be getting back home. He drove Jason back to his dorm and said good-night. He would have liked to hug his son, but he guessed that would only make Jason uncomfortable. So he contented himself with a handshake and set off for home.

The visit hadn't lived up to his expectations, but then, Stewart realized, maybe he was expecting too much. I was glad to hear that he hadn't gotten bitter.

———◆———

Jason's first two years at college followed a familiar form. The fall semester of his freshman year, everything was terrible: too much work, lousy food, no social life. In November, Jason called home and said, "This place is weird. Maybe I'll transfer." By the second semester, though, he stopped talking about transferring. He joined the ski club, made some friends, and seemed to get used to studying. In his sophomore year, he moved out of the dormitory and shared a house with three other kids. By then he seemed much happier. He no longer called home as often, and when he did, he was as likely to be pleased about something as complaining.

The rest of the family changed too. The first semester Jason was away, Sharon and Stewart worried about his welfare. Would he be able to handle the studying? Would he make friends? Would he behave himself? Would he eat right? Gradually, though, they worried less. Jason seemed to be able to manage on his own.

Sharon commented that Stewart had more trouble adjusting to Jason's leaving than she did. "You were so melodramatic that night driving home after we first took him to school. Then, do you remember in the second year when we helped him move into that old house? The place was a mess. There was a bathtub sitting right in the middle of the living room floor and an old blanket stuffed into the refrigerator. You thought it was such a big deal. Everything worked out okay, though, didn't it?"

"I guess it did," Stewart agreed.

———◆———

I agreed too. Things had worked out. This wasn't exactly a fairy-tale ending, but maybe real life is more like living *reasonably* happily ever after.

Fathers and mothers may have trouble letting their children grow up—although as we've seen, the reasons have as much to do with the resistance of systems to change as with the private conflicts of individuals. Mothers don't necessarily suffer when the nest is emptied; in fact, many find it a positive and liberating experience. Today, when the children leave home, it is often fathers who feel the keenest loss. When they see their children leaving, many fathers realize how much they missed. It's a poignant discovery, because it's too late to do much about it. Parents who do become depressed after their children leave home are not necessarily dependent or inadequate. From a systems perspective, the empty-nest syndrome—if it occurs—is a signal that the whole family needs to readjust from being a family of three or four to being a family of two or three. The family is transformed, and the parents must learn once again how to be alone with each other.

Leaving home can be thought of as a personal accomplishment—a developmental milestone—but it's also a transition for the whole family. Two of the family's subsystems— parent-child and husband-wife—are radically altered when the children leave home. Unless family members accommodate to the changes, the children may not make the successful transition to independent status.

"IT'S THE END OF OUR FAMILY"

When Jason went off to college, Stewart told Sharon he was sad that they would soon no longer be parents. She wisely answered that they would still be parents. Parenting isn't over when the children move out; it's different. When children leave home it may feel like the end of the family, but it isn't.

Leaving home is a reciprocal process: letting go of family ties and taking hold of life beyond childhood. Ordinarily, a young person forms intimate relationships outside the family that in time become more important than relationships within the family. To move out of childhood and into adulthood, the young person must establish a social base outside the family and must strive for success in work or school. Inside the family, boundaries must shift; new alliances are formed and old ones strengthened.

Some children have trouble leaving the nest. When this happens, we usually think of the child as somehow insecure and dependent. In certain instances this is true: Some people are willing to leave home but have a far more difficult time with the renunciation of childhood. There are kids who arrange trouble— they can't face their wish to stay, but if they get mad instead of sad, they can avoid the pain of separation. These abrupt and angry departures are often followed by failure and a return home. Many of these kids have more growing up to do. Some never will grow up.

Away from home, unsupported by their families, many college kids falter and fail. When I worked at a college counseling center, I treated many students whose main problem seemed to be that they couldn't stand the pain of leaving home. Their symptoms varied widely; eating binges, drug abuse, and depression were common. Perhaps the most common symptom was "test anxiety." These students seemed to do well in school but somehow got too nervous to pass their final examinations. The standard treatment for this problem is to help the student learn to relax enough to survive exams—an ordeal nobody likes. However, a significant number of students with "test anxiety" turned out not to *want* to pass their tests. The real problem was that they didn't want to be in school.

Some of the more confused students I treated assuaged their loneliness for family by entering religious cults. I remember one very disturbed young woman in particular. She couldn't stand being away from home, but couldn't admit this to herself. For a while she felt better as a member of "The Way Ministry." They conducted groups with titles like "Power for Abundant Living"— promising "the euphoric life." But this organization didn't really give her enough of the family feeling she wanted, so she responded to the voice of a mythical goddess who told her to smash her head against the radiator—to drive out the devil (loneliness). She did so repeatedly and was admitted to the hospital. After she was treated medically and then stabilized on medication, she was sent home—where she still is today.

Another young woman used to come into the infirmary at least twice a month. She would fall down, break a leg, or somehow manage to get bruised enough to earn a bandage—the child's badge of hurt. Finally, she wound up in the counseling center. Not long afterward, she realized that she did not want to be in college—she wanted to go home.

The most fascinating of these unhappy students was a young man whose first question upon meeting me was, "Do you believe in astral projection?" I said I didn't know much about it but was willing to learn. He taught me. For three weeks, he explained various theories about how people can transport themselves through time and space. In the fourth week, he told me how he came by all this interesting information. He himself was a frequent flyer. Two or three times a week he transported himself through time and space. Where did he go? Home, of course. At this point, I felt a nervous excitement, like being about to land a big fish. Unfortunately, I made the mistake of questioning him too closely instead of continuing a little longer to just listen. I asked him if he imagined seeing the ground as he traveled, or did he just end up with a vision of his family? He answered politely—of course he saw the ground, he actually was traveling—but I never saw him again.

Such cases, in which the attachment to family is so strong that a person is unable to leave home at all or is unable to stay away, are exceptional. A more common occurrence is leaving in anger with many relationship issues unresolved. This is what family therapist Murray Bowen calls an *emotional cutoff*. The more intense the person's cutoff with the past, the more likely the person will recreate problems in his or her own marriage, and the more likely the next generation of children will also be cut off. The person who runs away is often as emotionally dependent as the one who never leaves. Healthy separation involves transformation of parent-child relationships into something less intense—less needy and conflicted.

The hallmark of maturity is being able to leave home well, without undue anxiety or precipitous flight. Ideally, this takes place when young adults have managed to transform their relationships with their parents from parent-child to adult-adult (and vise versa). In practice, this means being independent—able to think for themselves, able to disagree without becoming emotionally reactive, and able to agree without fear of losing their identity. This ideal is seldom fully realized, of course, and many children have to deal with either continuing enmeshment or with emotional cutoff.

Less-than-ideal separations are a product of the young person's anxieties about leaving and the family's difficulty letting go. Many children who are worried and uncertain about their futures project their internal struggles onto their parents, and thus a war within themselves becomes a war between themselves and their parents. It helps if you can see this happening. Some children (like Heather) seem to manufacture a certain amount of antagonism to push themselves out of the nest. The trick is not to respond in kind—if you can help it. Meeting nasty with nasty may escalate the problem. The rift yawns wider and the child leaves in anger. These abrupt departures may propel the child out into the world but leave him or her with a lifelong anxiety about separating, which typically takes one of two forms—either an excessive dependence, with a reluctance to leave anyone or anything, or an inability to develop roots and repeated leaving in an illusory search for an ideal situation.

When the family needs a young person to remain involved at home, they prevent or undercut intimate relationships. The family boundary becomes impermeable—in Lyman Wynne's apt phrase, a *rubber fence*, which stretches but not very far. Try to prevent this by expressing your confidence in your children—"I trust your judgment." And try not to interfere too much. Be available to talk with your children about their plans, but try to leave the initiative with them. It's okay to bring up the subject of the future—"So what are you thinking about for next fall?"—but listen to what they want to do; don't expect them to do what you want.

When discussing their plans for the future or what they want from their parents, some kids have trouble telling their parents directly. Listen for clues in their stories about other children and their parents. The daughter of one of my friends told him that some of her friends' parents who came to visit them at college stayed two whole days—"Can you imagine?" He got the hint.

One of the surest ways to cheat yourself out of intimacy with your children is to press them for more than they want.

To many parents it feels like the success of launching the children depends on what has already gone before. This is partly true. If you have achieved a decent relationship with your children, if they know you love them but can also get along without them, they generally make the transition out of childhood without undue complications. However, there are a few specific things families can do to make this transition go smoother.

Families do have a history, but they can keep writing it and keep making it.

THE LONG GOOD-BYE

Departures resonate with the core of one's being. There is a psychological task, to face and feel your feelings, and an interpersonal one, to say what needs to be said, to tell each other the truth about your feelings.

When your children leave home, recognize that you will have complex feelings—a mixture of pain and promise. Let the feelings come up, spend time with your memories. Accept that you cannot control all the reactions you will have; they well up from your earliest separations in life. Arrange some time alone with your child to tell him or her what you feel. It should be just the two of you, and it should be as relaxed as possible. Say, as honestly as you can, what you feel.

Several parents I talked with about their children's leaving home commented that saying good-bye doesn't happen only once. You have to say good-bye many times, in many different ways. One father told me, "We had faced many small good-byes— when he boarded the bus for the first day of school, when he got on the plane to Grandmother's house, and when he went off to summer camp. But all of these good-byes were temporary. This one is permanent. Oh, we'll see him, of course, but never again as our little boy."

Saying good-bye is a big step. Anticipate it. It is much more difficult for many parents than they imagine. Thinking about it ahead of time—and talking with each other—allows the loss to be absorbed in small doses. Psychoanalysts say that the ego deals best with potentially traumatic events by having time to prepare for them, so that defenses are in place. Family therapists say that the trauma of a child's leaving is an interpersonal event; share it. Appreciate your children while you still have them. Say what you need to say. A good time to deal with the coming separation is when discussing the children's future plans or driving them around to visit colleges. Use the anticipation of leave-taking to transform and strengthen the relationship.

Let go. Don't pursue your child, but be available. Don't demand that your child tell you what he or she is feeling—this is beyond most young people—and don't demand frequent phone calls or letters. A good policy is to tell your children that you'd like to hear from them, but that you will leave the calling to them. That doesn't mean that you can't call your children to find out how they are doing (or just because you miss them), but it does mean not pressuring them. Giving your child space accomplishes two things: It gives the child room to form new attachments *and* it allows the child to *choose* to be in touch with the family.

When I left for college, each of my parents gave me one piece of parting advice. I remember what they said because neither of them was much given to making pronouncements. My mother, who is a very shy person, told me to be sure to make friends. My father, a workaholic, told me to remember that all work and no play is a good way to get ahead. I think I would rather have heard what they were feeling.

Some parents unknowingly prolong their children's dependency by being "helpful"—buying them things they have not worked to earn or bailing them out of crises they have created. How much money parents have and how they choose to spend it is, of course, their business. Moreover, relatively few young couples today can make a down-payment on a house without some assistance from their parents. There is, however, no free lunch. Financial dependency prolongs an outmoded relationship. Young adults cannot be truly independent until they have resolved their financial dependence on their parents. Adult children who remain financially connected to their families often feel guilty, which may inferfere with their willingness to spend time with their families—or to not spend time with them.

When a young adult becomes relatively independent, the relationship between the generations can be less charged and less chaotic. Such an individual will be busy taking responsibility for his or her own development (emotionally, functionally, and financially), leaving the parents little room to question whether their assistance is required.

The young adults who maintain contact with the family are better equipped for continuing development than those who break off contact. Where contact is not maintained, expectations are not modified. Ideally, each generation maintains an awareness of its own needs and the other's needs, while learning to accept—and insist upon—diminished involvement and control. The young person learns to do for himself or herself, to expect less, and to get over longing for what could have been or what might be, someday. Young adult children benefit from a clear acknowledgment of their autonomy, and when this is evident they may feel free to seek out parental counsel.

If only one generation becomes anxious and attempts to reestablish greater dependency on the other, little regression will actually occur, because the responding generation will protect the developing separation. It is, of course, easier for parents to take pleasure in their growing children's developmental autonomy if their own lives are full. A reciprocal rearrangement of boundaries is necessary: In order for the parents to be comfortable allowing their children greater distance, the parents must move closer to each other and to their interests outside the family. This boundary-making puts a certain amount of pressure on the marriage.

Relating to each other through parenting stabilizes a couple's relationship. Even in a good marriage, the spouses will feel a renewed strain and pressure when their children leave them alone together. Unresolved marital tensions are reactivated and must be resolved. This is a time of increased self-examination and an opportunity for redefining the marital relationship. Veteran spouses may be better able to say what they want from each other than they were so many years ago when they were young and in love and afraid.

Post-childrearing couples have the luxury of time—time to become more intimate, time to appreciate and enjoy being together. But often unfinished business stands in the way. Where there are old angers and old hurts, apply forgiveness. The past is over; try to arrange to live in the present.

Although it is possible to become closer and more intimate with one's mate after the children leave, not all couples want this or can manage it. The functioning of the spouses during the time when they lived together without children reflects the stability of the marital dyad. Be realistic.

Talk with each other concerning your feelings about launching the children and moving on. You may be surprised to discover that you want pretty much the same thing. On the other hand, you must also be prepared to accept the possibility of different feelings—about the children's leaving (remember Stewart's sadness and Sharon's relief?) and about what you want from each other now. A whole new period of accommodation is required, but this time you know each other better—and you are older and wiser. Push past your imagined barriers. Test the possibility of becoming more open and honest with each other.

BOOMERANG KIDS

Parents want their kids to grow up and be happy. In time, most of us learn that what our children do is less important than how they feel. A friend of mine, for example, had his heart set on his son's going to the same prestigious university that he had gone to, and maybe following his father's footsteps into medicine. When the boy dropped out of college midway through his first year and moved home, his father said, "Fine, take a year off, if that's what you want. Then go back." One year turned into two, and then three. Living at home didn't work out at all. The parents weren't sure what to expect of their nearly adult son, and there were constant arguments about chores, contributing to the rent, and which friends were allowed to visit the house (and whether or not they could stay overnight).

Instead of going back to college, the boy took a job as an auto mechanic and moved into an apartment on the seedy side of town with his girlfriend. My friend told me that he had gotten over wanting to live vicariously through his children; he wanted his son to do whatever made him happy. He wasn't very convincing, though. It's hard for most parents to get over the idea that their children are their report cards.

If children are their parents' report cards, more and more parents are getting incompletes. According to the U.S. Census Bureau, 22 million young adults are now living in the same households as their parents, almost a 50 percent increase since 1970. And in 1984, over half (54 percent, to be exact) of all young men aged twenty to twenty-four were living at home.[1]

There are a variety of reasons for this increasing return to the nest. The sexual revolution and consequent rising age of marriage means that for many adult children the most common rite of passage out of the family is postponed until their mid-twenties. Not only are marriages starting later, they are ending sooner. Divorce leaves many young adults emotionally battered and financially devastated. Where do you go when you are lonely and broke? For many young people, the answer is home. The economy has also contributed to the numbers of children who return to live with their parents. For some families, the expense of an out-of-town college education is too high, and so the children live at home while attending local schools. Even after they graduate, many young adults find the cost of housing so high that they choose to live at home in order to save money.

These are the generally accepted reasons for young adult children returning home. There may also be less tangible and less attractive reasons. One of these reasons is that many young people are spoiled. When the hippie generation gave way to the yuppie generation, we became a zealously child-centered culture. We gave our children every advantage we could think of— progressive schools with flexible curricula, a plethora of after-school activities, and a wealth of material possessions. Unfortunately, however, in the process some families did not prepare their children for the adult world by teaching them responsibility and how to deal with failure. When the kids had problems, their parents took over and rescued them. The result was a generation of children who became increasingly—and resentfully—dependent on their parents. Many of these young people, reared in affluence, cannot accept the idea of not living as well as their parents—downward mobility. Writing in *The Privileged Ones*, psychiatrist Robert Coles calls this phenomenon *narcissistic entitlement.*[2]

I certainly do not mean to say that all adult children who return to live at home are emotional weaklings, spoiled by their parents. However, I have noticed that many of these young people who "cannot afford" to live on their own nevertheless drive expensive cars, buy elegant clothes, and have plenty of money to spend on entertainment.

A second insidious motive for adult children returning home has to do with the dynamics of the family. Some families need children, and cannot function without them.

Some parents are secretly relieved when they have children to worry about again. It keeps them from facing the emptiness in their own lives. Parents who don't know what to do with themselves, or who aren't ready to be alone together, may welcome—even subtly support—the return of their children.

◆

One woman I know raised two daughters who were only marginally successful. They passed their courses in school, but just barely; they had friends, but not many. They left home, but always seemed to need to borrow money or be driven somewhere. Both girls held a series of jobs, but none of them for very long. Their mother became depressed. She was, she felt, a failure as a mother. How could she be happy as long as her girls weren't succeeding and as long as they kept pestering her?

Then one of the daughters took a turn for the worse. She lost her latest job, broke up with her boyfriend, and was evicted from her apartment owing three months' rent. Her mother was unhappy, then angry. She felt sorry for her daughter's problems, but did not sympathize with her irresponsibility. Still, the girl needed a place to stay, so she moved back home. The mother's complaints didn't let up, but her depression did. Apparently, the daughter's failure and return home was necessary to stabilize the family.

In the midst of writing these cautionary remarks about boomerang kids, I suddenly remembered something about a friend of mine that I'd completely forgotten. My friend, a successful business executive and family man whom I have always looked up to and admired, returned to live with his parents for a few months when he was in his mid-twenties. So, have I been too smug and too critical? Perhaps, but I remember that my friend returned home for a specific reason (he was changing jobs and going through a period with no income), for a specified period of time, and with a clear understanding between him and his parents about what was expected. I think the point is this: You can go home again—but you cannot return to childhood.

"UNDER CERTAIN CONDITIONS"

When adult children ask if they can move back home, parents would be well-advised to say, "Yes—under certain conditions." As children get older, it becomes increasingly difficult to maintain the clear hierarchy of authority that makes for an effective family structure. The ambiguity over who's in charge of what that occurs when the children reach adolescence is likely to be even greater when adult children return home. For this reason, it is very important to negotiate agreements about what is expected, and to make these agreements as clear as possible.

First, parents have to decide for themselves what they expect. Single parents need only consult their own ideas and wishes; married parents may have to work out compromises between themselves. Remember that the best way to minimize intergenerational conflict is to have a united parental front. Among the expectations that parents may want to spell out—before the child returns home—are: how much rent to expect, when and how it should be paid, what services will be expected of the child, and how transportation will be arranged. Perhaps the most important subject to discuss is how long the boomerang kid expects to stay. It isn't possible or even necessary to say exactly, but raising the issue makes it clear that the arrangement is limited.

One of the things that makes it difficult to set and enforce businesslike agreements is that returning children are often wounded and fragile. They seem more in need of understanding than ultimatums.

Most kids feel disappointed in themselves for having to return home. Having stumbled, they are worried about themselves and apt to be acutely sensitive to any form of criticism, advice, or regulation. Above all, they need empathy. Children who return home are likely to have shattered illusions about the world and their place in it. They are often confused, disillusioned, embarrassed, floundering, and ashamed. Some parents feel the same way. If the child is a failure, then the parents too must be failures. (Children are the parents' report cards, aren't they?) Often this is not true. Leaving home is not necessarily accomplished in one single step, at age eighteen. One-year-olds learning to walk stumble; two-year-olds learning to talk mispronounce words; young adults may accomplish their independence after one or two false starts.

So what am I saying? First I advise being tough—setting clear limits and enforcing regulations. Then I talk about being understanding and showing support. These two seemingly contradictory guidelines are the twin tasks of parenthood: nurturance and control. Finding the right balance is what makes being a parent so damned difficult. Nothing makes it easy, but thinking about the need for a clear boundary between the generations—neither too rigid nor too porous—may at least clarify some of the issues.

The older the children get, the clearer the boundary needed between them and their parents. Normally, this boundary-making is facilitated when children move out and set up their own lives. When they return home, it becomes important to make sure the boundary stays clear. Living at home induces passivity. Mother must change the children's image of her as the nurturer whose job it is to attend to all their needs. Until she figures this out, she may revert to the old parental role. Adult children do not become youngsters again just because they return home. You can no longer control their lives, and they can no longer live at home unconditionally. They can, of course, but it's not a good idea, for you or for them.

Adult children who return home are more like roommates— you can be friendly, but each of you needs to take care of yourself. For example, it's a good idea to ask the child to pay for room and board. If he or she is temporarily broke, you should work out some exchange of specific services. Remember, it's your house. You should feel perfectly free to insist on no smoking, no loud music, and no anything else that you don't want in your house. This might include no overnight guests of the opposite gender. It's up to you.

The other side of the clear boundary is their side. If you want them to respect you, you must respect them. It's now up to them what they eat, where they go, how they dress, how much or how little sleep they get, and who they spend time with. The same goes for jobs and money. It's their right to work where they want and to spend as much money as they please. Don't ask them where they are going, unless it directly affects you. If they come home at three o'clock in the morning and it keeps you up or wakes you up, then it becomes your concern.

Respecting the boundary between the generations means more than staying out of their business, though. By coming home, they have to some extent made their business your business. Encourage them to take initiative—inside and outside the home. Don't, for example, do for them what they can do for themselves. Don't do their laundry, and cook all their meals, or clean their rooms. The more helpful you are, the more helpless they become.

Most kids who return to live at home do so under unhappy circumstances. They may be depressed or they may be confused. Some of them may be constantly getting into trouble. It's hard, but you should avoid becoming overinvolved. Accept their discouragement. Be sympathetic, but offer advice only if it's asked for. Unasked-for advice is about as useful as being told to be careful after you've dropped something.

One woman I know somehow managed to avoid getting embroiled in her adult children's problems—she listened but didn't become panicked or give unwanted advice. When I asked her how she managed this neat trick, she said, "Easy—I just pretend they're my friend's kids; that way I can be sympathetic without trying to control them."

Guilt is one of the things that makes it hard for some parents to refuse to pay the bills and clean up after their grown children. Parents are forever worrying that they didn't do enough. Perhaps if they'd been better parents, spent more time, given more, given less, the children would have become self-sufficient—would have turned out all right. Nuts! Few parents are perfect, but most of them do the best they can. Besides, suppose you weren't a perfect parent, will overindulging a twenty-three-year-old adolescent make up for that now?

───◆───

When children return to the family after a false start into the world, we tend to think they were unable to take hold. Maybe they weren't ready to let go. Maybe they still need something from their parents.

In the chapter on in-laws, I described how most of us continue wanting something—something almost ineffable—from our parents well into our thirties or forties. We may be grown up, but we go on wanting something from them: attention, a demonstration of affection, or a declaration of respect. I also said that part of becoming mature is facing the fact that if your parents haven't given you everything you wanted, they probably aren't going to—so let go of those wishes and get on with your life.

When our own children return to live at home, the shoe is on the other foot. *We* are the parents and *they* want something from us. It isn't always apparent—it may seem that all they want are material things: a place to stay, a car to borrow, someone to cook their meals, and so on. (Sometimes it seems like these wants are endless.) But one of the most powerful reasons children are unable to let go of their parents is that they haven't gotten what they wanted emotionally, and they still hope, somehow, to get it. What they want may not even be conscious. Their actions, however, give it away.

A middle-aged patient of mine, a very wise woman who taught me a lot about being a parent under difficult circumstances, recently told the following story. Her daughter was a trial. Have you ever seen the test tracks made up of ruts and bumps and water holes that they use to find out if cars and trucks can really take it? "Torture tests," they're called. This girl was a torture test for her parents. As a teenager she got into almost every kind of trouble you can think of: drugs, promiscuous sex, stealing, vandalism, assault—you get the idea. She left home and returned several times between ages seventeen and twenty. When she got to be twenty, her parents felt that it was time they put their foot (feet?) down and they insisted that she leave.

They installed her in an apartment and slowly weaned her from depending upon them for money and for bailing her out when she got into trouble—which was often. At times it seemed like the daughter would never grow up and straighten out, but when she became twenty-two she began to be relatively independent. She got and held her first job that lasted more than a month, she called home less often, and when she did call it wasn't always to present her parents with some crisis or other. Things seemed to be going along pretty well.

About six months into this stable period, the daughter called to tell her mother that she'd been fired from her job as a waitress in a pizza parlor for telling her boss to go to hell. It was in the middle of the winter and she'd been planning for a long time to go to Florida for two weeks with her boyfriend. Should she find a new job and forget about the trip? Should she start a job and then tell them she was taking a vacation? Or should she just go, and then look for a job when she came back? Her mother said, "Honey, I can't tell you what to do. [That's what most people say before they get to the advice.] You have to make these decisions for yourself. But it sounds like you really want to go. You've looked forward to this trip and you've worked hard for it. So, if you go, you can get a job when you come back."

The daughter was thrilled. It was just what she wanted to hear.

It's what she had always wanted to hear: Have fun, you deserve it.

We parents are usually so busy telling our kids what they should do that they rarely hear from us what they so badly yearn to hear: that we love them, that we're proud of them, and that they should be good to themselves. If you can arrange to tell your children what they want to hear, that will help complete the relationship. "Complete" meaning make whole or consummate, not end it. It releases them from the frustrated longing that keeps them tied to you. Of course, some children make it hard for us to say these things to them. They screw up so often and create such headaches for us that it seems impossible to tell them that we love them and they're terrific, and they should do what they want. It is precisely the ones who screw up so much who probably need to hear this most.

———◆———

Now, in dealing with one of the last anomalies of parenthood, we return to two of the keys to successful family living: circular causality and the need for clear boundaries between family subsystems. Difficult children and children who return home (not always the same) seem to do things that make trouble for their parents. Seem to? They do. But whether we are aware of it or not, each of us is always participating in circular loops of interaction. All of our relationships are maintained by these recurrent cycles. What makes life so frustrating for us is that by failing to see the circular loops in which we participate, we are continually surprised and disappointed by the failure of our efforts to yield more positive results.

When other people make life difficult for us, we wish to God they'd change. If only they'd change, we could relax and be nicer. If our children would straighten out and be responsible, then we could praise them. If our spouses would be a little more considerate, then we'd be appreciative—and probably reciprocate. Stop waiting. Reach out to your family. Acting lovingly creates love.

NOTES

CHAPTER 2. FAMILY THERAPY.

1. Don Jackson, "Suicide," in *Scientific American*, 1954, *191*, 88–96.
2. Lyman Wynne et al., "Pseudo-Mutuality in the Family Relationships of Schizophrenics," in *Psychiatry*, 1958, *21*, 205–220.
3. Frank MacShane, ed., *Selected Letters of Raymond Chandler*. New York: Dell, 1981.
4. Gregory Bateson, Don Jackson, Jay Haley, and John Weakland, "Toward a Theory of Schizophrenia," in *Behavioral Science*, 1956, *1*, 251–264.
5. Don Jackson, "Family Rules: Marital Quid Pro Quo," in *Archives of General Psychiatry*, 1965, *12*, 589–594.
6. Jay Haley, *Strategies of Psychotherapy*. New York: Grune & Stratton, 1963.
7. Paul Watzlawick et al., *Pragmatics of Human Communication*. New York: Norton, 1967.
8. Murray Bowen, *Family Therapy in Clinical Practice*. New York: Jason Aronson, 1978.
9. Monica McGoldrick and Randy Gerson, *Genograms in Family Assessment*. New York: Norton, 1985.
10. Minuchin's pioneering work at the Wiltwyck School is described in Salvador Minuchin et al., *Families of the Slums*. New York: Basic Books, 1967.
11. Salvador Minuchin, *Families and Family Therapy*. Cambridge, Mass.: Harvard University Press, 1974.
    Salvador Minuchin and Charles Fishman, *Family Therapy Techniques*. Cambridge, Mass.: Harvard University Press, 1981.
12. Michael Nichols, *Family Therapy: Concepts & Methods*. New York: Gardner Press, 1984.

CHAPTER 3. THE MAKING OF A FAMILY THERAPIST.

1. Michael Nichols, *Family Therapy: Concepts & Methods*.

CHAPTER 5. POSTMARITAL DISILLUSIONMENT.

1. Sigmund Freud, "Observations on Transference Love (Further Recommendations on the Technique of Psychoanalysis III)," in *Standard Edition, 12,* 157–172. London: Hogarth Press, 1958.
2. Heinz Kohut, *The Analysis of the Self*. New York: International Universities Press, 1971.
    Heinz Kohut, *The Restoration of the Self*. New York: International Universities Press, 1977.

CHAPTER 7. THE DEPRESSED YOUNG MOTHER.

1. Eugene Paykel et al., "Life Events and Social Support in Puerperal Depression," in *British Journal of Psychiatry*, 1980, *136*, 339–346.
2. Ramona Mercer, *First-Time Motherhood: Experiences from Teens to Forties*. New York: Springer, 1986.
3. Alexander Thomas and Stella Chess, *Temperament and Development*. New York: Brunner/Mazel, 1977.
4. Jerome Kagan, *The Nature of the Child*. New York: Basic Books, 1984.
5. Carolyn Cutrona and Beth Troutman, "Social Support, Infant Temperament, and Parenting Self-Efficacy: A Mediational Model of Postpartum Depression," in *Child Development*, 1986, *57*, 1507–1518.
6. Berry Brazelton, *Infants and Mothers: Differences in Development*. New York: Dell, 1983.
7. Daniel Levinson, *The Seasons of a Man's Life*. New York: Ballantine Books, 1978.
   Gail Sheehy, *Passages: Predictable Crises of Adult Life*. New York: E.P. Dutton, 1976.
   Roger Gould, *Transformations: Growth and Change in Adult Life*. New York: Simon & Schuster, 1978.
8. Philip Guerin et al., *The Evaluation and Treatment of Marital Conflict: A Four-Stage Approach*. New York: Basic Books, 1987.

CHAPTER 8. WHY CAN'T JASON BEHAVE?

1. Don Jackson, "Family Rules: Marital Quid Pro Quo," in *Archives of General Psychiatry*, 1965, *12*, 589–594.
2. Salvadore Minuchin, *Families and Family Therapy*. Cambridge, Mass.: Harvard University Press, 1974.
3. Margaret Mahler et al., *The Psychological Birth of the Human Infant*. New York: Basic Books, 1975.

CHAPTER 9. THE TWO-PAYCHECK FAMILY.

1. Betty Friedan, *The Feminine Mystique*. New York: Norton, 1963.
2. Victor Fuchs, *How We Live*. Cambridge, Mass.: Harvard University Press, 1983.
3. Michael Nichols, *Turning Forty in the Eighties*. New York: Norton, 1986.
4. UNESCO study cited in Caroline Bird, *The Two-Paycheck Marriage*. New York: Rawson Wade, 1979.
5. Caroline Bird, *The Two-Paycheck Marriage*.

CHAPTER 10. THE OVERINVOLVED MOTHER AND PERIPHERAL FATHER.

1. Robin Norwood, *Women Who Love Too Much*. New York: St. Martin's Press, 1985.

CHAPTER 11. FAMILY FEUD.

1. Adele Faber and Elaine Mazlish, *Siblings Without Rivalry*. New York: Norton, 1987.

CHAPTER 12. LOSS OF INNOCENCE.
1. Shere Hite, *Women and Love*. New York: Knopf, 1987, p. 409.
2. Frank Pittman, *Turning Points: Treating Families in Transition and Crisis*. New York: Norton, 1987.
3. Anthony Thompson, "Extramarital Sex: A Review of the Research Literature," in *Journal of Sex Research*, 1983, *19*, 1–22. (Shere Hite's estimate that 70 percent of married women have affairs has been widely discredited.)
4. Hite, *Women and Love*, p. 409.
5. Hite, *Women and Love*, p. 409.

CHAPTER 13. DIVORCE, REMARRIAGE, AND STEPPARENTING.
1. Constance Ahrons, "The Binuclear Family: Two Households, One Family," in *Alternate Lifestyles*, 1979, *2*, 499–515.
2. Mavis Hetherington, "Divorce: A Child's Perspective," in *American Psychologist*, 1979, *34*, 851–858.
   Judith Wallerstein and Joan Kelly, *Surviving the Breakup: How Children and Parents Cope with Divorce*. New York: Basic Books, 1980.
3. Constance Ahrons, "The Binuclear Family: Two Households, One Family," in *Alternate Lifestyles*, 1979, *2*, 499–515.
   Judith Greif, "Fathers, Children and Joint Custody," in *American Journal of Orthopsychiatry*, 1979, *49*, 311–319.
   Harry Keshet and Kristine Rosenthal, "Fathering After Marital Separation," in *Social Work*, 1978, *23*, 11–18.
   Helen Mendes, "Single Fatherhood," in *Social Work*, 1976, *21*, 308–313.
4. Ruth Brandwein et al., "Women and Children Last: The Social Situation of Divorced Mothers and Their Families," in *Journal of Marriage and the Family*, 1974, *36*, 498–514.
   Mavis Hetherington et al., "Stress and Coping in Divorce: Focus on Women," in Jeanne Gullahorn (ed.), *Psychology and Women in Transition*. New York: B. H. Winston and Sons, 1979.
5. Gary Becker et al., "An Economic Analysis of Marital Instability," in *Journal of Political Economy*, 1977, *85*, 1141–1187.
6. Catherine Bitterman, "The Multi-Marriage Family," in *Social Casework*, 1968, *49*, 218–221.
   Charles Bowerman and Donald Irish, "Some Relationships of Stepchildren to Their Parents," in *Marriage and Family Living*, 1962, 24, 113–121.
   Irene Fast and Albert Cain, "The Stepparent Role: Potential for Disturbances in Family Functioning," in *American Journal of Orthopsychiatry*, 1966, *36*, 485–491.

CHAPTER 14. SEX, DRUGS, AND ROCK 'N' ROLL.
1. William McKim, *Drugs and Behavior: An Introduction of Behavioral Pharmacology*. Englewood Cliffs, N.J.: Prentice-Hall, 1986.

CHAPTER 15. THE SIMPSONS' FAMILY THERAPY.
1. One of two adolescents suffers from temporary adjustment problems;

one of ten succumbs to more serious disturbance. The figures for emotional disturbance among adolescents vary from about 5 percent to as high as 20 percent, depending on the population studied and the criteria used to define mental disturbance. For an authoritative overview see Michael Rutter, *Changing Youth in a Changing Society: Patterns of Adolescent Disorder*. Cambridge, Mass.: Harvard University Press, 1980.

CHAPTER 16. LETTING GO.

1. Jean Okimoto and Phyllis Stegall, *Boomerang Kids: How to Live with Adult Children Who Return Home*. Boston: Little, Brown, 1987.
2. Robert Coles, *Children of Crisis*, vol. 5: *Privileged Ones: The Well-Off & Rich in America*. Boston: Little, Brown, 1978.

RECOMMENDED READINGS

General Principles of Family Therapy

Murray Bowen, *Family Therapy in Clinical Practice*. New York: Jason Aronson, 1978.

  This collection of Murray Bowen's papers is addressed to a professional audience. The writing is a bit ponderous at times, but well worth the effort. Bowen's ideas are among the most profound and useful in family therapy, and this is the best source for them. One particularly excellent chapter, "Toward the Differentiation of a Self in One's Own Family," describes Bowen's long-term efforts to develop an independent but loving bond with his own family.

Elizabeth Carter and Monica McGoldrick (eds.), *The Changing Family Life Cycle: A Framework for Family Therapy* (Second Edition). New York: Gardner Press, 1988.

  A revised edition of one of the most widely read and influential books in family therapy. Chapters covering every phase of family life, as well as excellent chapters on the nature of the life cycle (Carter and McGoldrick) and the process of discontinuous change (Lynn Hoffman). Among the best of the other sections are chapters on women in the family (McGoldrick), rites of passage (Edwin Friedman), and families in later life (Froma Walsh).

Salvador Minuchin, *Families and Family Therapy*. Cambridge, Mass.: Harvard University Press, 1974.

  By far the largest-selling professional book on family therapy, and for good reason. Minuchin's structural family therapy (boundaries and sybsystems) is easily grasped and yet enormously enlightening. Regardless of what other techniques they employ, few family therapists fail to incorporate structural family guidelines into their work. Minuchin has a very accessible style, and in this classic he brings the principles of structural family therapy to life, using actual transcripts of family therapy sessions.

Michael Nichols, *Family Therapy: Concepts & Methods*. New York: Gardner Press, 1984.

  A comprehensive overview of family therapy, beginning with a history of the field and its basic theoretical underpinnings, followed by an explanation of eight different schools of family therapy. The final chapter is an analysis and comparison of the different approaches to family therapy. This substantial volume (609 pages) is most useful as a reference work, providing an introduction to all the basic theories and practical techniques of family therapy.

Thomas Paolino and Barbara McCrady (eds.), *Marriage and Marital Therapy*. New York: Brunner/Mazel, 1978.

This book, written for professionals, is both technical and somewhat dense. While it is probably not useful for readers in search of self-improvement, it does offer a comprehensive and thoughtful introduction to theories of marital and family therapy, including psychoanalytic, behavioral, and communications theory.

Paul Watzlawick, John Beavin, and Don Jackson, *Pragmatics of Human Communication*. New York: Norton, 1967.

The most accessible book based upon the work of Gregory Bateson. Key aspects of communication are explained and related to cybernetic and general systems concepts. A readable and informative introduction to the role of multilayered communication in family life.

Marriage

William Lederer and Don Jackson, *Mirages of Marriage*. New York: Norton, 1968.

A popular and practical application of the ideas of communications theory to marriage. Explores prevalent myths about marriage and describes attributes of a good marriage—tolerance, respect, honesty, and the desire to stay together, usually between two people of similar backgrounds, interests, and values. For those not lucky enough to have one of these marriages made in heaven, the authors offer numerous suggestions for making marriage work. Also contains a series of self-help exercises which encourage husbands and wives to confront each other with their innermost feelings. Couples who can successfully do these exercises need a pretty solid relationship to begin with. For those readers with less-than-ideal marriages, I would advise caution about actually carrying out these exercises.

Harriet Lerner, *The Dance of Anger: A Woman's Guide to Changing Patterns of Intimate Relationships*. New York: Harper & Row, 1985.

This book is not specifically about marriage (nor is its usefulness limited to women); it is valuable for understanding all phases of family life, especially relationships between couples. Lerner translates key concepts of Murray Bowen's family systems theory into crystal-clear and highly practical form, using anger as an organizing concept. Explains how to establish a differentiated self—balancing individuality and togetherness—and how to disentangle oneself from relationship triangles. In addressing the difficulties women (and men) have, not only getting angry but also using their anger to form more satisfying relationships and a stronger sense of self, Lerner has written one of the most useful books based on family systems concepts.

William Masters and Virginia Johnson, *Human Sexual Inadequacy*. Boston: Little, Brown, 1970.

Presents the famous Masters and Johnson research and treatment program. Written for professionals, but uses clear language and easy-to-follow concepts. Shows how anxiety enters into and erodes a couple's sex life, and outlines a step-by-step program for resolving sexual problems. Excellent and practical descriptions of "the squeeze technique" (for delaying premature ejaculation) and "sensate focus" (for giving and receiving pleasure in a way that slowly builds sexual arousal while minimizing anxiety). Not intended as a self-help book, but you *can* use these techniques at home.

Maggie Scarf, *Intimate Partners: Patterns in Love and Marriage*. New York: Random House, 1987.

Deservedly a best-seller. Uses a series of interviews with unhappily married couples to illustrate the principles of family therapy (especially the Bowenian model). Emphasizes connections between a couple's present relationship and the individual family history of each of the partners. Extremely useful explanations of: forces of attraction, genograms, collusive arrangements in marriage, triangles, levels of conflict, and idealization. Concludes with especially fine sections on "the child-launching years" and "the postparenting phase."

In-Laws and the Extended Family

Philip Guerin, *Family Therapy: Theory and Practice*. New York: Gardner Press, 1976.

This collection of papers written for family therapists contains some very useful information. Particularly good are chapters by: Guerin and Eileen Pendagast (on genograms and the extended family); Elizabeth Carter and Monica Orfanidis (on improving relationships with one's parents); Thomas Fogarty (two chapters, one on differentiating the self and one on marital crisis); and Bowen (on coming to terms with the death of a family member).

Monica McGoldrick and Randy Gerson, *Genograms in Family Assessment*. New York: Norton, 1985.

This highly readable book provides a rationale and specific procedures for constructing and interpreting genograms—those enormously useful diagrams of the family tree. Two special values of this book are detailed practical instructions for exploring your own family, and fascinating examples of patterned relationships in the families of such notables as John F. Kennedy, Sigmund Freud, Virginia Woolf, and Jane Fonda.

Caring for Babies and Young Children

Berry Brazelton, *Infants and Mothers: Differences in Development* (Revised Edition). New York: Dell, 1983.
    One of the most authoritative and useful guides to raising an infant. An invaluable resource for parents.

Adele Faber and Elaine Mazlish, *Liberated Parents, Liberated Children*. New York: Grosset & Dunlap, 1974.
    This book, inspired by the teachings of Haim Ginott, contains a wealth of practical suggestions for dealing with children. The emphasis is on balancing acceptance with discipline, and the book is filled with dialogues between parents and children illustrating effective communication. Contains particularly useful ideas for fostering autonomy and self-reliance; using praise effectively; dealing with the whiny child; and putting parents in charge, using a blend of compassion and firmness.

Haim Ginott, *Between Parent and Child*. New York: Macmillan, 1969.
    A classic on how to talk to your children, by one of the great child psychologists. Ginott's approach is based on accepting feelings but setting a limit on actions. Simple and direct; an invaluable resource. Explains the deleterious effect of judgment and evaluation, and how to avoid them; rich in practical suggestions.

Gerald Patterson, *Families: Applications of Social Learning to Family Life*. Champaign, Ill.: Research Press, 1975.
    An extremely simple and practical guide to applying behavioral principles to family problems. Written from the early behavioristic point of view, with little attention to family dynamics (triangles, boundaries, etc.), but a good resource for parents. Contracting and time out are particularly clear and well-illustrated with examples.

Raising Older Children

Stephen Bank and Michael Kahn, *The Sibling Bond*. New York: Basic Books, 1982.
    A comprehensive examination of sibling relationships, not written with a general audience in mind but quite informative. In exploring various aspects of how siblings relate to and affect one another, the authors draw heavily on psychoanalytic theory, especially Kohut's psychology of the self. Among the most interesting topics addressed are: "frozen misunderstandings," patterns of identification (from hero worship to polarized rejection), sexuality between brothers and sisters, aggression and rivalry, why one sibling becomes a "parental child" and assumes primary responsibility for brothers and sisters, and psychotherapy with siblings.

Peter Blos, *The Adolescent Passage: Developmental Issues*. New York: International Universities Press, 1979.

This collection of papers is only for those interested in a serious study of psychoanalytic concepts of adolescence. Readers interested in a depth analysis of theoretical and developmental issues will find excellent papers on: prolonged male adolescence, the generation gap, character formation in adolescence, the overappreciated child, acting-out, and when and how adolescence ends.

Edward Brecher, *Licit and Illicit Drugs*. Boston: Little, Brown, 1972.

Parents who are ill-informed about drugs risk failing to recognize warning signs of their own children's abuse as well as disqualifying themselves as sources of information whom children can turn to for understanding and advice. This volume, produced by the editors of *Consumer Reports*, is both fascinating and highly informative. From it we learn the dangers of the major licit drugs—caffeine, nicotine, and alcohol—as well as much pertinent information about illicit drugs. Contains such interesting historical facts as the story of "French Wine Coca—Ideal Nerve and Tonic Stimulant," a red wine elixer containing caffeine and cocaine which was the forerunner of Coca-Cola. In addition to extremely valuable explanations of the uses and abuses of drugs, also contains provocative analyses of the effects of drug laws and policies. One drawback is that the sections on marijuana and cocaine are somewhat outdated. (For a more up-to-date review, especially with regard to marijuana, see Schlaadt and Shannon, *Drugs of Choice*.)

Elizabeth Fishel, *Sisters: Love and Rivalry Inside the Family and Beyond*. New York: Quill/William Morrow, 1979.

A moving and informative book on sisterhood, based on a sampling of the experiences of 150 women. Among the topics explored are: importance of birth order, influence of roles in the family, rivalry between sisters, how longing for a sister leads many women to search for sisters outside the family, how sisters model and pattern their lives on each other, and adult sibling relationships. The far-reaching effects that sisters can have on each other's lives is documented by interviews with sisters both famous (Carly Simon, Gloria Steinem, Kate Millett, Margaret Mead) and obscure.

Adele Faber and Elaine Mazlish, *Siblings Without Rivalry*. New York: Norton, 1987.

This best-seller was written by two women who conduct workshops for parents on Long Island. Their ideas are derived from child therapist Haim Ginott's methods—reflecting children's feelings and setting limits (You're very angry at your brother. But children are not for hitting")—and augmented by their own experience as parents. The book offers dozens of practical guidelines and real-life examples for fostering wholesome, cooperative sibling relationships and for straightening out those already twisted into intense rivalries.

Richard Schlaadt and Peter Shannon, *Drugs of Choice* (Second Edition). Englewood Cliffs, N.J. Prentice-Hall, 1986.

This informative and readable book provides an objective and balanced survey of commonly used drugs. The sections on cocaine and marijuana are particularly good—thorough and containing the latest up-to-date information. There are also useful chapters on commonly used over-the-counter drugs (such as cough relievers, antihistamines, laxatives, and diet pills) and prescription drugs (including antibiotics, Valium, antidepressants, and oral contraceptives). In addition to providing careful information on the physiological and behavioral effects of drugs, Schlaadt and Shannon also take into account the context of drug-taking and so offer excellent chapters on why people use drugs, the drug scene, and alternatives to drug-taking.

Divorce, Remarriage, and Stepparenting

Constance Ahrons and Roy Rodgers, *Divorced Families: A Multidisciplinary Developmental View*. New York: Norton, 1987.

The format of this book is somewhat academic, but it contains a wealth of information. Places divorce in demographic, historical, and cultural context, making the case that it is part of an understandable transformation of families. Excellent summary of several theories of family therapy (especially of Minuchin and Bowen) and how they are relevant to understanding divorce. Particularly useful in clarifying the "separation transition" and "divorce transition." Describes four patterns of relationship among divorced spouses: "perfect pals," "cooperative colleagues," "angry associates," and "fiery foes."

Richard Gardner, *The Boys and Girls Book About Divorce*. New York: Bantam Books, 1971.

Written at about a third-grade level, although younger children can understand if parents read. Excellent descriptions and accounts of feelings that a child may expect. Answers many questions and offers a host of useful suggestions.

Richard Stuart and Barbara Jacobson, *Second Marriage: Make It Happy! Make It Last!* New York: Norton, 1985.

Written by two experts in family therapy, this book focuses on making relationships work. Excellent sections on coming to terms with unfinished business from first marriages (emphasizing ways to understand one's own contribution), how to make a better choice the second time around, developing clear communication, the role of extramarital sex in breaking up first marriages and how to prevent them from destroying second marriages, and ways to maximize intimacy in relationships.

Diane Vaughan, *Uncoupling: Turning Points in Intimate Relationships*. New York: Oxford University Press, 1986.

This is a very personal but highly informative exploration of the experience of going through a separation. It is particularly helpful in describing the stages of separation—from discontent to decision-making to separation and, finally, to the healing of wounds. One couple (who were planning to separate) that I gave this book to said they found it somewhat depressing in that it made them feel that once separation was begun, there was no turning back. (They decided to stay together.)

Emily Visher and John Visher, *How to Win as a Stepfamily*. New York: Dembner Books, 1982.

This is a translation of the Vishers' earlier book, *Stepfamilies: A Guide to Working with Stepparents and Stepchildren* (Brunner/Mazel, 1979), for a popular audience. Among family therapists, the Vishers are the acknowledged experts on stepfamilies, and they are credited with pioneering the idea that stepfamilies, though they have unique problems, are a normal development in the history of the family. Particularly useful guidelines for dealing with former spouses, grandparents, legal issues, and helping children adjust.

Ciji Ware, *Sharing Parenthood After Divorce*. New York: Viking, 1982.

An extremely practical guide to coping with the many problems of sharing parenthood after divorce. It begins with a persuasive brief for shared custody (and mediated rather than litigated settlements) and then goes into great detail about how children of various ages respond to divorce and how to help them adjust. There are numerous self-adminstered questionnaires, covering such topics as: how involved a father is, how much a mother wants to control her children herself, and ways in which divorced parents may be adding to the emotional pressure on their children. There are also many useful tips on working out effective schedules for visitation or joint custody, and even sample shared custody and property settlement agreements.

Richard Weiss, *Marital Separation*. New York: Basic Books, 1975.

Describes and illustrates the process of separation and divorce, using many accounts of those going through the process. Useful analyses of: why separation takes place, the emotional impact of separation, relationships between separating spouses and friends and relatives, difficulties with children, and establishing a new life.

Leaving Home and the Post-Childrearing Years

Daniel Levinson, *The Seasons of a Man's Life*. New York: Ballantine Books, 1978.

This extremely interesting and informative book is a description and analysis of typical patterns of adult development. Levinson divides adulthood into early, middle, and late periods, and describes the transition points between these stages as crucial turning points in the life cycle—sources of renewal or stagnation, depending upon how well and how wisely they are handled. Although the book is based on an in-depth study of only men, and therefore does not address some of the special problems of women in our culture, it is nevertheless one of the finest books ever written on adult development.

Michael Nichols, *Turning Forty in the Eighties*. New York: Fireside/Simon & Schuster, 1987.

An exploration of the transition from young to middle adulthood, which brings both psychoanalytic and family systems concepts to bear. Using the midlife crisis as a focal point, the book describes why so many adults go through a period of self-doubt—almost like a second identity crisis—somewhere between thirty and forty-five. A number of topics important to family life are explored, including: accommodation, boundaries, triangles, affairs, and divorce. Many readers have found the section on how to improve relationships with parents particularly helpful.

Gail Sheehy, *Passages: Predictable Crises of Adult Life*. New York: E.P. Dutton, 1976.

This extraordinarily popular book translates Daniel Levinson's ideas about adult development into popular form, using many brief personal stories to illustrate the stages of adult development.

Judith Viorst, *Necessary Losses*. New York: Simon & Schuster, 1986.

This best-selling book about development through the life cycle is beautifully and immediately written; people find it very helpful. Viorst writes from a psychoanalytic perspective, and thus does an excellent job of illuminating the inner experience of the phenomena of letting go. Viorst talks about early fears of separation and then explains how these fears are played out through the rest of our lives. She speaks of the bliss of connectedness as a condition known to lovers, saints, and infants—and, I might add, sought by enmeshed parents. Two particularly fine chapters are one on sibling rivalry, "When Are You Taking That New Kid Back to the Hospital?" and one on adolescence, "Childhood's End."

GLOSSARY

accommodation Elements of a system automatically adjust to coordinate their functioning. When the system is a family and the "elements" are human beings, this mutual adjustment often takes hard and deliberate effort—as Sharon and Stewart found out when they married.

aversive control The use of punishment and criticism to eliminate undesirable behavior is understandable but ineffective. Most criticism does more to create anger and resentment than it does to constructively alter behavior. When Sharon felt neglected by Stewart, she held her feelings in until finally they came pouring out in a flood of angry criticism. The criticism—aversive control—only made Stewart feel attacked and pull further away.

boundary Boundaries are emotional barriers that regulate the distance and amount of interaction between people. Clear boundaries serve to protect and enhance the integrity and autonomy of the family as a whole, subsystems of the family, and individual family members.

circular causality The idea that events are related through a series of interacting loops or repeating cycles. Most people, unfortunately, continue to think linearly and thus, like Sharon and Stewart, believe that someone else's behavior causes their reactions—and that the only way to improve matters is for the other person to change. Once you begin to think of human relationships as circular—repetitive cycles of interaction—then you can break the cycle at any point.

complementary Complementary relationships (in contrast to symmetrical ones) are based on differences that fit together. One person is competent in areas where the other is not. In traditional—complementary—marriages, husbands had careers, wives had babies. Today, although both spouses may be working, the outmoded, complementary model persists in the minds of husbands who expect their wives to do all the housekeeping—and in the minds of many wives who feel guilty asking their husbands to share the load.

cross-complaining Instead of responding directly to a complaint, many people become defensive and made a countercomplaint. When Stewart

449

complained that Sharon was too lenient with young Jason, she complained that Stewart left all the responsibility to her. Cross-complaining makes it difficult to settle an argument; as long as the parties feel free to change the subject, they may never agree on anything.

differentiation Psychological separation of intellect from feeling, and independence of self from others; the opposite of fusion. The differentiated—autonomous—person is able to be close to others without becoming emotionally reactive or losing his or her separate identity. Lack of differentiation takes two forms: togetherness-oriented people like Sharon and emotionally cut-off people like Stewart. The truly differentiated person never asserts more than he or she knows or less than he or she believes.

disengagement Psychological isolation that results from overly rigid boundaries around individuals or subsystems in a family. Disengaged—detached—persons, like Stewart, are able to function autonomously, but find it difficult to function interdependently, or to give or request support when needed.

double bind A conflict created when a person receives contradictory messages on different levels of abstraction in an important relationship, and cannot leave or comment. Stewart's conspiratorial smile at Jason's adolescent acting-out contradicted his expressed disapproval, leaving Jason in the peculiar position of sensing without really knowing that there was no way to satisfy his father.

emotional cutoff Flight from unresolved emotional overreactivity. We see emotional cutoff in action when Stewart becomes upset at Sharon and, instead of working it out, leaves the room. The results of emotional cutoff sometimes look like independence, but the difference is that the independent person can tolerate intimacy, while the emotionally cutoff person cannot.

empathy The ability to understand what someone else is feeling may be the single most important ingredient in successful relationships. Immature and emotionally upset people are usually too preoccupied with their own feelings to have any real appreciation of what others are feeling. Enmeshed and poorly differentiated people sometimes confuse sympathy (feeling upset about a family member's predicament) with empathy (understanding what the other person is feeling).

enmeshment Overinvolvement and loss of autonomy from a blurring of psychological boundaries. Enmeshed relationships like Sharon and Jason's foster closeness, affection, and support. This works fine for a mother and young child. However, when the child grows older and begins to seek independence, enmeshment interferes with autonomy.

expressive role In traditional families, the wife's role was to serve social and emotional functions. Men and women like Sharon and Stewart who grew up in the 1950s expected that a wife would take on the "expressive role" to complement her husband's "instrumental role." When the women's movement and changes in the economy resulted in a breakdown of these rigid stereotypes, young couples grew up freer to be whole people; older couples were often caught in a crunch between old expectations and new realities.

extended family In contrast to the nuclear family (husband and wife and their children), the extended family includes all of one's kin—parents, siblings, aunts and uncles, cousins, and grandparents. The extended family is a rich resource, one which is, unfortunately, too often cut off and neglected by many mobile, middle-class adults.

family life cycle The stages of a family's life begin with young adults separating from their parents, then marriage, bearing and raising children, growing older, retirement, and finally death. As we have seen in the case of the Simpson family, the stages of a family's life are more than the separate development of individuals; the family itself grows and changes shape, adding and subtracting members, and forming and readjusting interpersonal boundaries.

first-order change Superficial changes in a system which itself remains unchanged often fail to resolve family problems. Sharon's attempts to become stricter with Jason when he was a teenager were largely counterproductive. Rebellion was Jason's attempt to break out of an overly close relationship with his mother. As long as the underlying family structure did not change—as long as Sharon remained enmeshed with Jason and disengaged from Stewart—it was difficult for Jason and his mother to stop their conflict and get on with other things.

fusion The opposite of differentiation: a blurring of psychological boundaries between self and others, and a tendency for thinking to be overwhelmed by emotion.

general systems theory General systems theory was formulated by Ludwig von Bertalanffy in 1945 as a general scientific theory of living systems as whole entities. Each subsystem has a boundary and degrees of autonomy, but it is interactive with and depends upon the general control of the suprasystem of which it is a part. Living systems—like the Simpson family—are made up of subsystems (spouses, siblings), and in turn they themselves make up larger systems (extended family, community, nation).

genogram Genograms are schematic diagrams of the family system. They are drawn using squares to represent men, circles to represent women, horizontal lines to indicate marriages, and vertical lines for children. Dates of marriage may be indicated on horizontal lines, and the ages of individuals may be entered in the circles or squares. Divorce is indicated by an "X" on the horizontal marriage line; death is shown by an "'X'"over the circle or square. Other important events may be listed, and geographical locations often reveal striking patterns of enmeshment (most of the family lives in one area) or disengagement (the family is widely dispersed).

hierarchical structure Most organizations work best when someone is in charge. One of the hallmarks of successful families is a clear generational boundary, where the parents maintain control and authority, and the children are supported and cared for.

homeostasis   Systems tend to maintain a balanced steady state of equilibrium. In families, interactions maintain a relative constancy or balance of relationships. This is one of the reasons they resist change. When, for example, Sharon went back to work, the family system tried to maintain itself unchanged—Stewart and the children continued to expect Sharon to run the house, and she had to make a concerted and persistent effort to cause the system to shift to a new level of homeostasis.

idealization   The intensity of idealization—exaggerating the virtues of someone special, someone to rely on—is a reflection of doubt in one's own self-reliance. The stronger and more secure one is, the less the need to idealize others. Idealization is inevitably part of the process of falling in love. When idealized fantasies are disillusioned, the important thing—which only took Stewart and Sharon twenty years to figure out—is not to dwell on bitterness or try to change the other person, but to let go of the fantasies and learn to appreciate the real person you married.

instrumental role   Decision-making and task functions. In traditional families, this was the husband's role, the counterpart of the "feminine" expressive role.

introject   A mental image about persons and relationships, formed at an early age—and therefore not easily altered. Stewart and Sharon grew up with introjected models of family life, each based on their very different experience. If these images were conscious—and Stewart and Sharon were more aware of the need to compromise—they would have found it much easier to accommodate to each other. Instead, however, since introjects are deeply ingrained, they often seem, as they did to Stewart and Sharon, "the way things should be."

linear causality   The traditional way of thinking about cause and effect: one event, *A*, causes another, *B*. In relationships, linear thinking creates problems because it perpetuates the idea that what we do is caused by what someone else did first. Thus, Jason saw his rebellion as caused by his mother's overcontrol; Sharon saw her control as caused by Jason's wild behavior; and neither one was free to break the cycle.

metacommunication   A message about a message. Every message has two levels; the content, and qualifying comment conveying the sender's attitude about the message and about the relationship between sender and receiver. Messages are usually qualified by posture, tone of voice, and inflection.

mirroring   Admiring acceptance of another person's feelings. This may be the most important psychological need of young children, for it is the basis of forming a secure sense of self.

nuclear family   A husband and a wife and their children.

polarization   This is an important process that takes place in marriages, whereby one spouse's behavior and attitudes tend to push the other spouse into a complementary, or opposing, position. Its most important manifestation is in childrearing: parents almost automatically polarize each other's positions. The more permissive Sharon was with young

Jason, the more Stewart wanted to be strict—and vice versa. It is interesting to note that two opposite relationship pressures operate in family systems—accommodation (compromise) and polarization (contraposition). Polarization occurs when there is anxiety or ill will between a twosome, and, to an even greater degree, with most couples, parenting, which creates triangulation.

process/content This is the distinction between what members of a family or group say (content) and how they relate (process). The process, or pattern of interaction, is often more significant—though usually less apparent—than the content.

pseudomutuality Lyman Wynne's term for the facade of family harmony that masks differences and conflicts. Schizophrenic families often manifest extreme pseudomutuality; most normal families practice this suppression of honest conflict to a lesser extent.

pursuer-distancer A mutually reinforcing relationship pattern in which the more one party strives to get closer, the more the other moves away— as though they were joined in the middle by a wooden rod. In the early years of their marriage, Sharon pursued Stewart emotionally and he distanced himself from her. By contrast, when it came to sex, Stewart pursued, Sharon distanced.

reciprocal reinforcement One of the reasons that parents persist in habits of poor discipline is that when they give in to their children—reinforcing the children's behavior—the parents' permissive behavior is also reinforced by an immediate cessation of the children's complaints. When Jason threw temper tantrums and Sharon eventually gave him what he wanted, his tantrums were reinforced; unfortunately, so was Sharon's capitulation.

reciprocity Reciprocity—the mutual influence between individuals and subsystems—is, in part, an automatic consequence of systems functioning. For example, in Stewart and Sharon's relationship, like in any marital subsystem, one partner's behavior automatically influenced the other's. When Stewart distanced himself from Sharon's emotional pursuing, he was unintentionally giving her more reason to pursue him. If he had figured out the pattern—pursuer-distancer—he could have acted to give himself more freedom and independence by deliberating spending more time with Sharon and being closer with her; that would have satisfied some of her need and allowed her to back off.

Subsystems too are reciprocal. The more a mother is enmeshed with her child, the more likely the child will be disengaged from other relationships. If the mother wants the child to spend more time with friends, it may be more effective for her to spend less time with and focus less emotional energy on the child than it would be to coax and cajole the child to socialize.

reinforcement Any event, behavior, or object that increases the rate of a particular response. If a response (say, Stewart's sulking) is followed by a positive outcome (after a while, Sharon gives in and makes up), that response will likely be repeated. To break habits, no reinforcement—

"extinction"—is often more effective than punishment. The problem with punishment is twofold: it has a deleterious effect on self-esteem, and many punishments carry some inadvertent reward, even if it's only attention or making up afterward.

roles   Roles are a familiar and important example of the way context influences behavior. Roles that are defined by position—father, son, supervisor—bring out certain behaviors that are appropriate to the role. Families also assign roles to children that have a profound influence on behavior and self-image. Roles are part description and part prescription—a projection of parents' wishes. A daughter like Sharon who is labeled a "good girl" may spend much of her life taking care of other people and trying to live up to their expectations.

rubber fence   Lyman Wynne's term for the rigid boundary around some families; it stretches to allow necessary contact outside the family, but springs back to prevent family members from straying too far from the family and its traditions.

rules   Rules describe how a system works. In families, rules consist of norms and expectations that govern family life. What makes rules particularly interesting is that they often exert a powerful controlling influence although they may not be conscious. Moreover, when rules are not specified—as, for example, when a husband adheres to a rule that does not permit him to refuse his wife's requests for help around the house but does permit him to procrastinate indefinitely—it is difficult to discuss or change them. (If you want to test whether or not a particular rule exists in your family, try breaking it and see what happens.)

second-order change   Basic change in the structure or functioning of a system. Jason's birth was a second-order change that had an automatic impact on the Simpson family's system. Sharon's hard-come-by decision to back away from trying to control Jason—and thus become less enmeshed with him—was a deliberate second-order change, one that had ramifications for the entire system.

selfobject   Heinz Kohut's term for a person who is related to not really as a separate individual, but as an extension of the self. Infants relate to their mothers as selfobjects, experiencing Mommy's good moods as though they themselves were good, and feeling that they themselves are bad when Mommy is angry. Even adults relate to some people more as reflections of their own worth than as individuals in their own right.

shaping   Reinforcing changes in small steps. When Sharon went back to work, she alternated between expecting Stewart to take over a large share of housekeeping and giving up on him altogether. Shaping—encouraging and reinforcing—steady steps in the direction of his doing more might have produced better results.

structure   Recurrent patterns of interaction define and stabilize the shape of relationships. Although structure may not be visible, it has a powerful effect on what happens in families. A man like Stewart who is disengaged from his wife and children may try all he wants to influence his wife to be less overprotective and controlling, but unless he alters his part in the enmeshed/disengaged structure, his words will have little effect.

subsystem   Systems are differentiated into smaller subsystems that serve a variety of functions. In families, subsystems are determined by generation (the parents), sex, interest, and functions. Subsystems are differentiated by boundaries.

symmetrical   Relationships based on equality and sameness are, unfortunately, often less stable than complementary relationships. Traditional marriages were generally complementary, which may be one reason they were more stable.

system, closed   A functionally related group of elements that form a collective entity that does not interact with the surrounding environment. A president and his advisors may form a closed system if the advisors are so interested in supporting and currying favor with their leader that they tell him only what he wants to hear. One result of such a closed system was an escalation and prolongation of the Vietnam War.

system, open   A functionally related group of elements that form a collective entity that exchanges energy and information from the surrounding environment. Among the important inputs and outputs of a healthy family are: income and satisfaction from careers; friendships; relationships with extended family members; knowledge of how other parents cope with various stages of childhood; news of the community and contributions to its welfare.

triadic model   Explanations based on the interactions among three people. To say, for example, that Jason misbehaved because Sharon was a lax disciplinarian would be incomplete and ineffective. Coaching her in the ways of setting and enforcing rules would have had only limited success, because the intervention would not have taken into account that her permissiveness was partly a function of her enmeshment, which in turn was a function of her disengagement from Stewart.

triangle   A three-person relationship system. Some triangles are as familiar and obvious as the one between Sharon and Stewart and Angela, the woman Stewart had an affair with. However, even when it is not apparent, all relationships involve at least three poles. Even in the early years of their marriage, it would have been inaccurate and misleading to describe Stewart and Sharon's marriage without taking into account his relationship with his career or her relationship with her parents. All relationships are like this—what goes on between two people also includes what goes on between them and third persons (or other involvements).

triangulation   The process of detouring conflict between two people by involving a third person stabilizes the relationship between the original pair but freezes conflict in place. When the Simpsons were first married, Sharon's frequent phone calls to her mother helped ease the tension between her and Stewart, but by complaining to her mother about Stewart, Sharon lost some of the incentive to work things out with him.

INDEX

acceptance, forgiveness vs., 93
accommodation, 101–4, 111, 112–15, 124–31, 429
Ackerman, Nathan, 48
adolescents, 358–75
  assertiveness of, 365, 367, 368–69, 373, 375
  boundary changes for, 201, 393–395, 400
  discipline of, 396, 399–400, 411
  harmful activities of, 371–73, 386, 396–97
  parental reactions to, 368–70, 372–75, 393–400
  sexual experimentation by, 30–31, 370, 371, 385, 410
  social life of, 370–71
affection, control and, 204–5
After Baby's Arrival, 155
Ahrons, Constance, 347
alienation, 176
ambition, 81
anhedonia, 407
anomie, defined, 344
anorexia, 37
appraisal support, 155
arguments:
  of children, 282–84, 292–93, 295
  conversations and, 333
  in first interviews, 19
  marital, 92–94, 327
  reconciliation of, 93
  see also conflict
Auerswald, E. H., 49
authority, parental:
  autonomy development and, 373–375
  democratic principles and, 185–86
  divorce and, 259, 350–51, 355–56
  hierarchical distinctions and, 187, 197–99, 431
  therapist as extension of, 385

autonomy:
  clear boundaries and, 198, 394
  development of, 190–91, 373–75, 390–91, 393–94
  intimacy vs., 105–6, 107–8
  isolation vs., 254
  oppostion as, 30
aversive control, 266

Bateson, Gregory, 39–41, 42, 44
bedtime procedures, 185, 202–3
beer, 371–72
behavior, interrelatedness of, 174
behavioral boundaries, 105
behavior therapy, 66
Big Sleep, The (Chandler), 40
binuclear family, 347
Bird, Caroline, 237
blame, 173–74, 251
blended families, 353–57
boomerang kids, 429–36
boundaries, 104–9
  for adolescents, 201, 393–95, 400
  adult children and, 428, 432–33
  children and, 280–88, 291, 294, 393–95
  clear, 196–98, 394, 395, 436
  common misconceptions about, 192–93
  diagrams of, 205–6, 230–31
  in divorce, 337–38, 357, 394
  emotional vs. behavioral, 105
  in family therapy, 392
  friendship and, 172
  for grandparents, 171
  infidelity and, 320–22
  in-laws and, 124–31
  of men vs. women, 251
  reciprocity of, 194
  of sibling subsystem, 280–86
  social systems concepts vs. psychoanalytic theory on, 193–94

individual boundaries and, 198
sex differences and, 108–9
threat of, 136
togetherness vs., 265
introjects, defined, 120
isolation vs. autonomy, 254
isomorphic interactions, 189

Jackson, Don, 35–36, 39, 40, 41–42, 184
jealousy, 163, 167, 275
joining, defined, 378
joint custody, 347–48
jokes, 75

Kagan, Jerome, 152
Kohut, Heinz, 98

labor, sexual division of, 225–28, 239–40
La Leche League, 154
lawyers, matrimonial, 343–44
Levinson, Daniel, 156
lies, 388
life cycle, 156–58, 160–61, 199
linear causality, 25–26, 264
love:
  conditional, 277
  dependency vs., 128
  friendship vs., 80
  idealization and, 95–98
  obsessive, 263
  of projected images, 81
  revitalization of, 164–65
  romantic, 316
  symbiotic, 191–92
loyalties:
  divorce and, 336, 337, 351, 355
  of enmeshment, 193
  to spouse vs. parents, 124–25, 126, 128, 131–34
LSD, 387, 388
Lyman, Frankie, 79

marriage(s):
  accommodation in, 101–4, 111, 112–15
  arguments in, 92–94, 327
  career as refuge from, 221–22
  children's departure and, 428–429
  commitment of, 321–22

complementary vs. symmetrical, 42, 225–30
extended family and, 120–21
family background and, 88–91, 94, 135–41
in family therapy, 25, 382–84
fantasies about, 77, 100
feelings hidden in, 235–36
first vs. second, 353
friendships and, 171
idealization in, 95–100, 109
motivations for, 79–81, 95–96, 120
new parents and, 161–65
parental model of, 259–60
personal boundaries in, 104–9
personal growth and, 86–87
psychotherapy and, 332, 343
pursuer-distancer pattern in, 252–255, 266–70
revitalization of, 163–65
rising age of, 429
successful attitudes for, 109–15
variety of, 195–96
of working parents, 218–20
  see also infidelity, marital; in-laws
masochism, female, 265
maternal depression, 153
maturity, 424, 434
Mazlish, Elaine, 284
Mead, Margaret, 42
mealtime, discipline at, 207
men:
  closeness/distance patterns of, 108–9, 232, 243–44, 251
  marital expectations of, 111
  men's attitudes toward women, 31, 265
  see also fathers; husbands
Mencken, H. L., 306
Menninger Clinic, 44
Mercer, Ramona, 149
metacommunication, 39–40
Minuchin, Salvador, 47, 48–49, 56, 105, 188–89, 190, 193, 378
mirroring, 98, 99
mirrors, one-way, 57–60
Montalvo, Braulio, 49
Mother Care, 155
mothers:
  closeness maintained by, 232
  infant care and, 148–56